# THE MEANINGS OF SOCIAL LIFE

# THE MEANINGS OF SOCIAL LIFE
## A Cultural Sociology

JEFFREY C. ALEXANDER

OXFORD
UNIVERSITY PRESS
2003

# OXFORD
UNIVERSITY PRESS

Oxford   New York
Auckland   Bangkok   Buenos Aires   Cape Town   Chennai
Dar es Salaam   Delhi   Hong Kong   Istanbul   Karachi   Kolkata
Kuala Lumpur   Madrid   Melbourne   Mexico City   Mumbai   Nairobi
São Paulo   Shanghai   Taipei   Tokyo   Toronto

Copyright © 2003 by Oxford University Press, Inc.

Published by Oxford University Press, Inc.,
198 Madison Avenue, New York, New York 10016

www.oup.com

Library of Congress Cataloging-in-Publication Data
Alexander, Jeffrey C.
The meanings of social life : a cultural sociology / by Jeffrey C.
Alexander.
p. cm.
Includes bibliographical references and index.
ISBN 0-19-516084-3
1. Sociology. 2. Prejudices. 3. Culture. 4. Violence. I. Title.
HM585 .A5 2003
301—dc21      2002155273

29.95

1 2 3 4 5 6 7 8 9
Printed in the United States of America
on acid-free paper

*To the members of the*
**CULTURE CLUB**
*Past, Present, and Future*

# ACKNOWLEDGMENTS

I am grateful to the following for giving me permission to republish essays that first appeared in their pages. Most of these essays have been revised for this book.

"Cultural Sociology or Sociology of Culture: Towards a Strong Program for Sociology's Second Wind," with Philip Smith, in *Sociologie et Societes* 30 (1) 1998.

"Modern, Ante, Post and Neo: How Intellectuals Have Tried to Understand the 'Crisis of our Time,'" in *Zeitschrift fur Soziologie* 23 (3) 1994.

"The Discourse of American Civil Society: A New Proposal for Cultural Studies," with Philip Smith, in *Theory and Society* 22 (2) 1993.

"The Promise of a Cultural Sociology: Technological Discourse and the Sacred and Profane Information Machine," N. Smelser and K. Munch, eds., in *Theory of Culture*, University of California Press, 1993.

"Towards a Sociology of Evil: Getting Beyond Modernist Common Sense about the Alternative to the Good," in M. P. Lara, ed., *Rethinking Evil: Contemporary Perspectives*. Berkeley and Los Angeles, University of California Press, 2001.

# PREFACE

The perspective I have developed in this book grew from a seed planted by Robert Bellah during my graduate work at the University of California, Berkeley, in the early 1970s. Years before the cultural turn, Bellah's concept of "symbolic realism" pointed the way. The essays that form the chapters of this book grew from that seed, but only after a transformation in my sociological understanding that began in the mid 1980s and extended until I left Los Angeles, in 2001, after teaching for twenty-five years at UCLA.

This period is neatly bound by two periods of intense and uninterrupted study, the first at the Institute for Advanced Studies in Princeton in 1985–86, the Second at the Center for Advanced Studies (CADIS) in the Behavioral Sciences in Palo Alto in 1998–99. I would like to record my gratitude to my hosts on these occasions, Michael Walzer at Princeton and Neil Smelser in Palo Alto, both of whom, by their intellectual examples and their exemplary persons, have had profound effects on my intellectual life. This delimited period was intersected by a sabbatical year in Paris in 1993–94, where I was the guest of the Ecole des Hautes Etudes des Sciences Sociales. I would like to thank Alain Touraine, Michel Wiewiorka, and Francois Dubet, and the other members of CADIS, for their friendship and support during that deeply stimulating year. During the 1990s I benefited as well from two extended stays in Uppsala, Sweden, as a fellow at the Swedish Center for Advanced Study in the Social Sciences, (SCASSS), headed by my friend and colleague, Bjorn Wittrock.

My thinking and development during this period was critically marked by my close relationship with an extraordinary series of graduate students at UCLA. In 1984, to explore the possibilities of a newly cultural kind of sociology, I formed a discussion group with graduate students who would take this intellectual trip with me. We met once a month for the next decade and a half, sometimes at their apartments, sometimes in my home. We read one another's papers critically but supportively and engaged in free wheeling argument about what might be necessary to create a sociological version of the cultural turn. The membership of what came to be called the "Culture Club" changed gradually over the years, but its intellectual ethos remained steady, as did the brilliant level of its student participants. Many of the ideas expressed in the following chapters emerged during the course of these ritualized occasions. Many alumnae of the "Culture Club" are now professors, and some are even colleagues. Their successors are members of Culture Club II, which continues on the East Coast of the United States, where I now reside.

During this same period of time, I developed a close network of personal relationships that also nourished the ideas presented here. With Roger Friedland, Nicholas Entrikin, Steven Seidman, Kenneth Thompson, Bernhard Giesen, and Ron Eyerman I have shared not only the deepest friendship but an ongoing conversation about the meanings of social life and the social life of meanings. They have given me confidence and criticism, and at different times and places each has pushed me to critical recognitions I could never have reached on my own.

My development over this period was nourished by three intimate relationships. I would like to record my gratitude to Ruth Bloch and Maria Pia Lara for their intellectual stimulation and their faith in my person and my work.

I would like to declare my gratitude to my wife, Morel Morton—for everything. Her loving kindness buoyed me in the last years of this work, and I know that there is a great deal more to come.

# CONTENTS

# THE MEANINGS OF SOCIAL LIFE

THE MEANING OF SOCIAL LIFE

# INTRODUCTION

## THE MEANINGS OF (SOCIAL) LIFE

### On the Origins of a Cultural Sociology

Modern men and women go about their lives without really knowing why. Why do we work for such a long time every day? Why do we finish one war only to fight another? Why are we so obsessed with technology? Why do we live in an age of scandal? Why do we feel compelled to honor those, like the victims of the Holocaust, who have been murdered for an unjust cause?

If we had to explain these things, we would say "it just makes sense" or "it's necessary" or "it's what good people do." But there is nothing natural about any of this. People don't naturally do any of these things. We are compelled to be this way.

We are not anywhere as reasonable or rational or sensible as we would like to think. We still lead lives dictated more by unconscious than conscious reason. We are still compelled by feelings of the heart and the fearful instincts of the gut.

America and its allies are waging today a war against terrorism. This is said to be necessary and rational, a means to attain the end of safety. Is the war against terrorism only this, or even primarily this? No, for it rests on fantasy as much as on fact. The effort to protect the people of the United States and Europe is shrouded in the rhetoric of good and evil, of friends and enemies, of honor, conscience, loyalty, of God and country, of civilization and primeval chaos. These are not just ideas. They are feelings, massive ones. Our leaders evoke these rhetorics in solemn tones, and we honor the victims of terrorism in the most rhetorical of benedictions.

These rhetorics are cultural structures. They are deeply constraining but also enabling at the same time. The problem is that we don't understand them. This is the task of a cultural sociology. It is to bring the unconscious cultural structures that regulate society into the light of the mind. Understanding may change but not dissipate them, for without such structures society cannot survive. We need myths if we are to transcend the banality of material life. We need narratives if we are to make progress and experience tragedy. We need to divide the sacred from profane if we are to pursue the good and protect ourselves from evil.

Of course, social science has always assumed that men and women act without full understanding. Sociologists have attributed this to the force of social structures that are "larger" and more "powerful" than mere individual human beings. They have pointed, in other words, to the compulsory aspects of social life.

But what fascinates and frightens me are those collective forces that are not compulsory, the social forces to which we enthusiastically and voluntarily respond. If we give our assent to these, without knowing why, it is because of meaning. Materialism is not forced on us. It is also a romance about the sacrality of things. Technology is not only a means. It is also an end, a desire, a lust, a salvationary belief. People are not evil, but they are made to be. Scandals are not born from the facts but constructed out of them, so that we can purify ourselves. We do not mourn mass murder unless we have already identified with the victims, and this only happens once in a while, when the symbols are aligned in the right way.

The secret to the compulsive power of social structures is that they have an inside. They are not only external to actors but internal to them. They are meaningful. These meanings are structured and socially produced, even if they are invisible. We must learn how to make them visible. For Freud, the goal of psychoanalysis was to replace the unconscious with the conscious: "Where Id was, Ego shall be." Cultural sociology is a kind of social psychoanalysis. Its goal is to bring the social unconscious up for view. To reveal to men and women the myths that think them so that they can make new myths in turn.

In the middle 1980s, in the lunch line at the UCLA Faculty Center, I was engaging three sociology colleagues in a heated debate. An assistant professor was struggling for tenure, and the faculty were lining up pro and con. Those skeptical of the appointment objected that the candidate's work could not even be called sociology. Why not, I asked? He was not sociological, they answered: He paid more attention to the subjective framing and interpreting of social structures than to the nature of those social structures themselves. Because he had abandoned social-structural causality, he had given up on explanation, and thus on sociology itself. I countered: While his work was indeed different, it remained distinctly sociological. I suggested that it might possibly be seen as a kind of "cultural" sociology.

This remark did not succeed in its intended effect. Instead it generated a kind of incredulity—at first mild snickers, then guffaws, and then real belly laughs. *Cultural* sociology? my colleagues scoffed. This idea struck them not only as deeply offensive to their disciplinary sense but intellectually absurd. The very phrase "cultural sociology" seemed an oxymoron. Culture and sociology could not be combined as adjective and noun. If there were a sociological approach to culture, it should be a sociology *of* culture. There certainly could not be a *cultural* approach to sociology.

My colleagues were right about the present and the past of our discipline, but events did not prove them prescient about its future. In the last fifteen years, a new and specifically cultural approach to sociology has come into existence. It never existed before—not in the discipline's first hundred and fifty years. Nor has such a cultural approach been present in the other social sciences that have concerned themselves with modern or contemporary life.

In the history of the social sciences there has always been a sociology *of* culture. Whether it had been called the sociology of knowledge, the sociology of art, the sociology of religion, or the sociology of ideology, many sociologists paid respect to the significant *effects* of collective meanings. However, these sociologists of culture did not concern themselves primarily with interpreting collective meanings, much less with tracing the moral textures and delicate emotional pathways by which individuals and groups come to be influenced by them. Instead, the sociology-of approach sought to explain what *created* meanings; it aimed to expose how the ideal structures of culture are formed by *other structures*—of a more material, less ephemeral kind.

By the mid-1980s, an increasing if still small number of social scientists had come to reject this sociology-of approach. As an enthusiastic participant in this rejection, I, too, accused sociology of basic misunderstanding, one that continues to hobble much of the sociological investigation into culture today. To recognize the immense impact of ideals, beliefs, and emotions is not to surrender to an (unsociological) voluntarism. It is not to believe that people are free to do as they will. It is not to lapse into the idealism against which sociology should indeed define itself, nor the wish-fulfilling moralism to which it is a welcome antidote. Cultural sociology can be as hardheaded and critical as materialistic sociology. Cultural sociology makes collective emotions and ideas central to its methods and theories precisely because it is such subjective and internal feelings that so often seem to rule the world. Socially constructed subjectivity forms the will of collectivities; shapes the rules of organizations; defines the moral substance of law; and provides the meaning and motivation for technologies, economies, and military machines.

But if idealism must be avoided, the facts of collective idealization must not be. In our postmodern world, factual statements and fictional narratives are densely interwoven. The binaries of symbolic codes and true/false statements are implanted one on the other. Fantasy and reality are so hopelessly intertwined that we can separate them only in a posthoc way. It was the same in modern society. In this respect, little has changed since traditional life. Classical and modern sociologists did not believe this to be true. They saw the break from the "irrationalities" of traditional society as radical and dichotomous. One needs to develop an alternative, more cultural sociology because reality is not nearly as transparent and rational as our sociological forefathers believed.

My sensitivity to this reality, and my ability to understand it, has been mediated by a series of critical intellectual events: the linguistic turn in philosophy, the rediscovery of hermeneutics, the structuralist revolution in the human sciences, the symbolic revolution in anthropology, and the cultural turn in American historiography. Behind all these contemporary developments has been the continuing vitality of psychoanalytic thinking in both intellectual and everyday life. It has been in response to these significant movements in our intellectual environment that the slow, uneven, but nevertheless steadily growing strand of a genuinely cultural sociology has developed.

These essays do not aim at building a new model of culture. They do not engage in generalizing and deductive theory. In this respect they are postfoundational. I see them, rather, to borrow from Merleau-Ponty, as adventures in the dialectics of cultural thought. They move back and forth between theorizing and researching, between interpretations and explanations, between cultural logics and cultural pragmatics. They enter into interpretive disputes with some of the exemplars of classical, modern, and postmodern thinking.

Even when they offer models and manifest generalizing ambitions—aiming toward science, in the hermeneutic sense—these essays are also rooted in pragmatic, broadly normative interests. As a chastened but still hopeful post–sixties radical, I was mesmerized by the Watergate crisis that began to shake American society in 1972. It showed me that democracy still lived and that critical thought was still possible, even in an often corrupted, postmodern, and still capitalist age. More fascinating still was how this critical promise revealed itself through a ritualized display of myth and democratic grandeur, a paradox I try to explain in chapter 6.

In the decade that followed this early political investigation, my interest turned to the newly revived concept of civil society. Over the same period, as my understanding of the mythical foundations of democracy became elaborated more semiotically, I discovered that a deep, and deeply ambiguous, structure underlies the struggles for justice in democratic societies. When Philip Smith and I discuss the binary discourse of American civil society, in chapter 5, we show that combining Durkheim with Saussure demonstrates how the good of modern societies is linked to the evils, how democratic liberation has so often been tied to democratic repression. As I suggest in chapter 4, these considerations point us to a sociology of evil. Like every other effort to realize normative ideals, modernity has had a strong vision of social and cultural pollution and has been motivated to destroy it.

In chapter 2, I try to come to grips with the event that has been defined as the greatest evil of our time, the Holocaust. This evil is a constructed one, for it is not a fact that reflects modern reality but a collective representation that has constituted it. Transforming the mass murder of the Jews into an "engorged" evil has been fundamental to the expansion of moral universalism that marks the hopeful potential of our times, and it is paradigmatic of the way cultural traumas shape collective identities, for better and for worse.

Indeed, the very notion of "our times" can itself be construed as the creation of an ever-shifting narrative frame. It is with this in mind that in chapter 8 I offer a cultural-sociological approach to the venerable topic of intellectual ideology. Comparing intellectuals to priests and prophets, I bracket the reality claims that each of these groups of postwar intellectuals has made.

A similar commitment to relativizing the reality claims of intellectual-cum-political authority inspired chapter 7. When he first came to power, President Ronald Reagan embarked on the hapless quest to create an impregnable missile defense shield for the United States. Tens of billions of dollars were spent on this pursuit, which formed a backdrop to Soviet President Michael Gorbachev's suit to end the Cold War. While personally resistant to President Reagan's claims, sociologically I was fascinated by them. To understand their mythical roots, I have tried to reconstruct technology in a fundamentally cultural-sociological way.

But more than pragmatic-political and scientific-empirical interests have guided me in approaching the topics in this book. My aim has always also been theoretical. By applying the cultural-sociological method to a widely dispersed range of topics, I wish to demonstrate that culture is not a thing but a dimension, not an object to be studied as a dependent variable but a thread that runs through, one that can be teased out of, every conceivable social form. These essays enter into thick description. They tease out overarching grand narratives. They build maps of complex symbolic codes. They show how the fates of individuals, groups, and nations are often determined by these invisible but often gigantically powerful and patterned ideational rays.

Yet, at the same time, these investigations also pay careful attention to the "material factor"—that terrible misnomer—in its various forms: to the interests of racial, national, class, religious, and party-political groups; to capitalist economic demands; to the deracinating pressures of demography, the centralizing forces of bureaucracy, and the geopolitical constrictions of states. Such "hard" structural factors are never ignored; they are, rather, put into their appropriate place. Once again: To engage in cultural sociology is not to believe that good things happen or that idealistic motives rule the world. To the contrary, only if cultural structures are understood in their full complexity and nuance can the true power and persistence of violence, domination, exclusion, and degradation be realistically understood.

With the exception of the programmatic first chapter, written also with Philip Smith, I have tried not to overload these essays with theoretical disquisition. Some orienting abstraction there certainly must be. Yet in selecting the essays to be included in this book, and in editing them, my goal has been to make the theoretical ideas that inspire cultural sociology live through the empirical discussions, the social narratives, the case studies. In fact, from several of these chapters I have expunged large chunks of theoretical discussion that accompanied them in their originally published forms. Much of my academic life has been devoted to writing "pure theory." This book is different. Its purpose is to lay out a research program for a cultural sociology and to show how this program can be concretely applied to some of the principal concerns of contemporary life.

A great aporia marks the birth of sociology—a great, mysterious, and unexplained rupture. It concerns the relation between religion and rationality, tradition and modernity. The extraordinary German founder of sociology, Max Weber, devoted a large part of his maturity to the historical-comparative study of world religions. He showed that the human desire for salvation became patterned in different ways, that each difference contained a practical ethic, and that these ethics, carried on the wings of salvation, had enormous impact on the social organization of practical life. With the other part of his energetic maturity, however, Weber devoted himself to laying out the concepts of a much more materialistic economic and political sociology, one that emphasized instrumental motives and domination, not ideas about salvation and moral ethics. Weber never explained how these two parts of his work could be reconciled. Instead he finessed the issue by suggesting, via his rationalization thesis, that faith was relevant only to the creation of modernity, not to the project of its ongoing institutionalization.

We must go beyond this disconnect, which has merely been replicated by more contemporary theories of social life. If we are to understand how the insights of Weber's *religion-soziologie* can be applied to the nonreligious domains of secular society, we need a cultural sociology. Only by understanding the nature of social narrative can we see how practical meanings continue to be structured by the search for salvation. How to be saved—how to jump to the present from the past and into the future—is still of urgent social and existential concern. This urgency generates fantasies and myths and inspires giant efforts at practical transformation. We must respectfully disagree with Weber's contention that modernity has forced charisma to become routinized in a fateful and permanent way.

It is striking that the French founder of modern sociology, Emile Durkheim, suffered from a similar theoretical affliction. There is a great divide between Durkheim's early and middle studies of social structure on the one hand and the symbolic and ritual studies that occupied his later work on the other. Durkheim called this later work his "religious sociology," and he promised that his study of Aboriginal societies, *The Elementary Forms of Religious Life*, would be the beginning, not the end, of exploration of society's symbolic dimensions. Was it Durkheim's premature death or some more fundamental ideological or theoretical inhibition that prevented him from fulfilling this promise, from demonstrating the continuity between the religion of early societies and the cultural life of later, more complex ones? If the love of the sacred, the fear of pollution, and the need for purification have continued to mark modern as much as traditional life, we can find out how and why only by following a cultural-sociological path.

In the history of social science, the "friends of culture" have tended to be conservative. They have betrayed a nostalgia for the organicism and the solidity of traditional life. The idea of a cultural sociology has foundered on this yearning, on the idea that only in simple, religiously ordered, undemocratic, or old-fashioned societies do myths and narratives and codes play a fundamental role. These essays demonstrate the opposite. Reflection and criticism are imbedded in myths that human beings cannot be entirely reflective and critical about. If we understand this, we can separate knowledge from power and not become only a servant to it.

# THE STRONG PROGRAM IN CULTURAL SOCIOLOGY

Elements of a Structural Hermeneutics
(with Philip Smith)

Throughout the world, culture has been doggedly pushing its way onto the center stage of debates not only in sociological theory and research but also throughout the human sciences. As with any profound intellectual shift, this has been a process characterized by leads and lags. In Britain, for example, culture has been making headway since the early 1970s. In the United States, the tide began to turn unmistakably only in the mid-1980s. In continental Europe, it is possible to argue that culture never really went away. Despite this ongoing revival of interest, however, there is anything but consensus among sociologists specializing in the area about just what the concept means and how it relates to the discipline as traditionally understood. These differences of opinion can be usefully explained only partly as empirical reflections of geographical, sociopolitical, or national traditions. More important, they are manifestations of deeper contradictions relating to axiomatic and foundational logics in the theory of culture. Pivotal to all these disputes is the issue of "cultural autonomy" (Alexander, 1990a; Smith, 1998a). In this chapter, we employ the concept of cultural autonomy to explore and evaluate the competing understandings of culture currently available to social theory. We suggest that fundamental flaws characterize most of these models, and we argue for an alternative approach that can be broadly understood as a kind of structural hermeneutics.

Lévi-Strauss (1974) famously wrote that the study of culture should be like the study of geology. According to this dictum, analysis should account for surface variation in terms of deeper generative principles, just as geomorphology explains the distribution of plants, the shape of hills, and the drainage patterns followed by rivers in terms of underlying geology. In this chapter, we intend to apply this principle to the enterprise of contemporary cultural sociology in a way that is both reflexive and diagnostic. Our aim is not so much to review the field and document its diversity, although we will indeed conduct such a review, as to engage in a seismographic enterprise that will trace a fault line running right through it. Understanding this fault line and its theoretical implications allows us not only to reduce complexity but also to transcend the kind of purely taxonomic mode of discourse that so often plagues essays of this programmatic kind. This seismographic principle will provide a powerful tool for getting to the heart of current controversies and understanding the slippages and instabilities that undermine so much of the territory of cultural inquiry. Contra Lévi-Strauss, however, we do not see our structural enquiry as a disinterested scientific exercise. Our discourse here is openly polemical, our language slightly colored. Rather than affecting neutrality, we are going to propose one particular style of theory as offering the best way forward for cultural sociology.

## THE FAULT LINE AND ITS CONSEQUENCES

The fault line at the heart of current debates lies between "cultural sociology" and the "sociology of culture."[1] To believe in the possibility of a cultural sociology is to subscribe to the idea that every action, no matter how instrumental, reflexive, or coerced vis-à-vis its external environments (Alexander, 1988), is embedded to some extent in a horizon of affect and meaning. This internal environment is one toward which the actor can never be fully instrumental or reflexive. It is, rather, an ideal resource that partially enables and partially constrains action, providing for both routine and creativity and allowing for the reproduction and transformation of structure (Sewell, 1992). Similarly, a belief in the possibility of a cultural sociology implies that institutions, no matter how impersonal or technocratic, have an ideal foundation that fundamentally shapes their organization and goals and provides the structured context for debates over their legitimation.[2] When described in the folk idiom of positivism, one could say that the more traditional sociology of culture approach treats culture as a dependent variable, whereas in cultural sociology it is an "independent variable" that possesses a relative autonomy in shaping actions and institutions, providing inputs every bit as vital as more material or instrumental forces.

Viewed from a distance, the sociology of culture offers the same kind of landscape as cultural sociology. There is a common conceptual repertoire of terms like values, codes, and discourses. Both traditions argue that culture is something important in society, something that repays careful sociological study. Both speak of the recent "cultural turn" as a pivotal moment in social theory. But these resemblances are only superficial. At the structural level we find deep antinomies. To speak of the sociology of culture is to suggest that culture is something to be explained, by something else entirely separated from the domain of meaning itself. To speak of the sociology of culture is to suggest that explanatory power lies in the study of the "hard" variables of social structure, such that structured sets of meanings become superstructures and ideologies driven by these more "real" and tangible social forces. In this approach, culture becomes defined as a "soft," not really independent variable: it is more or less confined to participating in the reproduction of social relations.

A notion that has emerged from the extraordinary new field of science studies is the sociologically inspired idea of the "strong program" (e.g., Bloor, 1976; Latour & Woolgar, 1986). The argument here is that scientific ideas are cultural and linguistic conventions as much as they are simply the results of other, more "objective" actions and procedures. Rather than only "findings" that hold up a mirror to nature (Rorty, 1979), science is understood as a collective representation, a language game that reflects a prior pattern of sense-making activity. In the context of the sociology of science, the concept of the strong program, in other words, suggests a radical uncoupling of cognitive content from natural determination. We would like to suggest that a strong program also might be emerging in the sociological study of culture. Such an initiative argues for a sharp analytical uncoupling of culture from social structure, which is what we mean by cultural autonomy (Alexander, 1988; Kane, 1992). As compared to the sociology of culture, cultural sociology depends on establishing this autonomy, and it is only via such a strong program that sociologists can illuminate the powerful role that culture plays in shaping social life. By contrast, the sociology of culture offers a "weak program" in which culture is a feeble and ambivalent variable. Borrowing from Basil Bernstein (1971), we might say that the strong program is powered by an elaborated theoretical code, whereas the weak program is limited by a restricted code that reflects the inhibitions and habitus of traditional, institutionally oriented social science.

Commitment to a cultural-sociological theory that recognizes cultural autonomy is the single most important quality of a strong program. There are, however, two other defining characteristics that must drive any such approach, characteristics that can be described as methodological. One is the commitment to hermeneutically reconstructing social texts in a rich and persuasive way. What is needed here is a Geertzian "thick description" of the codes, narratives, and symbols that create the textured webs of social meaning. The contrast here is to the "thin description" that typically characterizes studies inspired by the weak program, in which meaning is either simply read off from social structure or reduced to abstracted descriptions of reified values, norms, ideology, or fetishism. The weak program fails to fill these empty vessels with the rich wine of symbolic significance. The philosophical principles for this hermeneutic position were articulated by Dilthey (1962), and it seems to us that his powerful methodological injunction to look at the "inner meaning" of social structures has never been surpassed. Rather than inventing a new approach, the deservedly influential cultural analyses of Clifford Geertz can be seen as providing the most powerful contemporary application of Dilthey's ideas.[3]

In methodological terms, the achievement of thick description requires the bracketing-out of wider, nonsymbolic social relations. This bracketing-out, analogous to Husserl's phenomenological reduction, allows the reconstruction of the pure cultural text, the theoretical and philosophical rationale for which Ricoeur (1971) supplied in his important argument for the necessary linkage between hermeneutics and semiotics. This reconstruction can be thought of as creating, or mapping out, the culture structures (Rambo & Chan, 1990) that form one dimension of social life. It is the notion of the culture structure as a social text that allows the well-developed conceptual resources of literary studies—from Aristotle to such contemporary figures as Frye (1971, [1957]) and Brooks (1984)—to be brought into social science. Only after the analytical bracketing demanded by hermeneutics has been completed, after the internal pattern of meaning has been reconstructed, should social science move from analytic to concrete autonomy (Kane, 1992). Only after having created the analytically autonomous culture object does it become possible to discover in what ways culture intersects with other social forces, such as power and instrumental reason in the concrete social world.

This brings us to the third characteristic of a strong program. Far from being ambiguous or shy about specifying just how culture makes a difference, far from speaking in terms of abstract systemic logics as causal processes (à la Lévi-Strauss), we suggest that a strong program tries to anchor causality in proximate actors and agencies, specifying in detail just how culture interferes with and directs what really happens. By contrast, as Thompson (1978) demonstrated, weak programs typically hedge and stutter on this issue. They tend to develop elaborate and abstract terminological (de)fenses that provide the illusion of specifying concrete mechanisms, as well as the illusion of having solved intractable dilemmas of freedom and determination. As they say in the fashion business, however, the quality is in the detail. We would argue that it is only by resolving issues of detail—who says what, why, and to what effect—that cultural analysis can become plausible according to the criteria of a social science. We do not believe, in other words, that hardheaded and skeptical demands for causal clarity should be confined to empiricists or to those who are obsessively concerned with power and social structure.[4] These criteria also apply to a cultural sociology.

The idea of a strong *program* carries with it the suggestions of an agenda. In what follows we discuss this agenda. We look first at the history of social theory, showing how this agenda failed to emerge until the 1960s. We go on to explore several contemporary traditions in the social scientific analysis of culture. We suggest that, despite appearances, each comprises a weak program, failing to meet in one way or another the defining criteria we have set forth here. We conclude by pointing to an emerging tradition of cultural sociology, most of it American, that in our view establishes the parameters of a strong program.

## CULTURE IN SOCIAL THEORY FROM THE CLASSICS TO THE 1960S

For most of its history, sociology, both as theory and method, has suffered from a numbness toward meaning. Culturally unmusical scholars have depicted human action as insipidly or brutally instrumental, as if it were constructed without reference to the internal environments of actions that are established by the moral structures of sacred–good and profane–evil (Brooks, 1984) and by the narrative teleologies that create chronology (White, 1987) and define dramatic meaning (Frye, 1971, [1957]). Caught up in the ongoing crises of modernity, the classical founders of the discipline believed that epochal historical transformations had emptied the world of meaning. Capitalism, industrialization, secularization, rationalization, anomie, and egoism, these core processes were held to create confused and dominated individuals, to shatter the possibilities of a meaningful telos, to eliminate the ordering power of the sacred and profane. Only occasionally does a glimmer of a strong program come through in this classical period. Weber's (1958) religious sociology, and most particularly his essay "Religious Rejections of the World and Their Directions" (see Alexander, 1988) suggested that the quest for salvation was a universal cultural need whose various solutions had forcefully shaped organizational and motivational dynamics in world civilizations. Durkheim's later sociology, as articulated in critical passages from *The Elementary Forms of Religious Life* (1968) and in posthumously recovered courses of lectures (Alexander, 1982), suggested that even contemporary social life had an ineluctable spiritual-cum-symbolic component. While plagued by the weak program symptom of causal ambivalence, the young Marx's (1963b) writings on species-being also forcefully pointed to the way nonmaterial forces tied humans together in common projects and destinies. This early suggestion that alienation is not only the reflection of material relationships adumbrated the critical chapter in *Capital*, "The Fetishism of Commodities and the Secret Thereof," (Marx, 1963a [1867], 71–83) which has so often served as an unstable bridge from structural to cultural Marxism in the present day.

The communist and fascist revolutionary upheavals that marked the first half of this century were premised on the same kind of widespread fear that modernity had eroded the possibility of meaningful sociality. Communist and fascist thinkers attempted to alchemize what they saw as the barren codes of bourgeois civil society into new, resacralized forms that could accommodate technology and reason within wider, encompassing spheres of meaning (Smith, 1998C). In the calm that descended on the postwar period, Talcott Parsons and his colleagues, motivated by entirely different ideological ambitions, also began to think that modernity did not have to be understood in such a corrosive way. Beginning from an analytical rather than eschatological premise, Parsons theorized that "values" had to be central to actions and institutions if a society was to be able to function as a coherent enterprise. The result was a theory that seemed to many of Parsons's modern contemporaries to exhibit an idealizing culturalist bias (Lockwood, 1992). We ourselves would suggest an opposite reading.

From a strong program viewpoint, Parsonian functionalism can be taken as insufficiently cultural, as denuded of musicality. In the absence of a musical moment where the social text is reconstructed in its pure form, Parsons's work lacks a powerful hermeneutic dimension. While Parsons theorized that values were important, he did not explain the nature of values themselves. Instead of engaging in the social imaginary, diving into the febrile codes and narratives that make up a social text, he and his functionalist colleagues observed action from the outside and induced the existence of guiding valuations using categorical frameworks supposedly generated by functional necessity. Without a counterweight of thick description, we are left with a position in which culture has autonomy only in an abstract and analytic sense. When we turn to the empirical world, we find that functionalist logic ties up cultural form with social function and institutional dynamics to such an extent that it is difficult to imagine where culture's autonomy might lie in any concrete setting. The result was an ingenious systems theory that remains too hermeneutically feeble, too distant on the issue of autonomy to offer much to a strong program.

Flawed as the functionalist project was, the alternatives were far worse. The world in the 1960s was a place of conflict and turmoil. When the Cold War turned hot, macrosocial theory shifted toward the analysis of power from a one-sided and anticultural stance. Thinkers with an interest in macrohistorical process approached meaning through its contexts, treating it as a product of some supposedly more "real" social force, when they spoke of it at all. For scholars like Barrington Moore and C. Wright Mills and later followers such as Charles Tilly, Randall Collins, and Michael Mann, culture must be thought of in terms of self-interested ideologies, group process, and networks rather than in terms of texts. Meanwhile, during the same period, microsociology emphasized the radical reflexivity of actors. For such writers as Blumer, Goffman, and Garfinkel, culture forms an external environment in relation to which actors formulate lines of action that are "accountable" or give off a good "impression." We find precious little indication in this tradition of the power of the symbolic to shape interactions from within, as normative precepts or narratives that carry an internalized moral force.

Yet during the same period of the 1960s, at the very moment when the halfway cultural approach of functionalism was disappearing from American sociology, theories that spoke forcefully of a social text began to have enormous influence in France. Through creative misreadings of the structural linguistics of Saussure and Jacobson, and bearing a (carefully hidden) influence from the late Durkheim and Marcel Mauss, thinkers like Lévi-Strauss, Roland Barthes, and the early Michel Foucault created a revolution in the human sciences by insisting on the textuality of institutions and the discursive nature of human action.

When viewed from a contemporary strong program perspective, such approaches remain too abstracted; they also typically fail to specify agency and causal dynamics. In these failings they resemble Parsons' functionalism. Nevertheless, in providing hermeneutic and theoretical resources to establish the autonomy of culture, they constituted a turning point for the construction of a strong program. In the next section we discuss how this project has been derailed by a succession of weak programs that continue to dominate research on culture and society today.

## WEAK PROGRAMS IN CONTEMPORARY CULTURAL THEORY

One of the first research traditions to apply French *nouvelle vague* theorizing outside of the hothouse Parisian environment was the Centre for Contemporary Cultural Studies, widely known as the Birmingham School. The masterstroke of the school was to meld ideas about cultural texts onto the neo-Marxist understanding that Gramsci established about the role played by cultural hegemony in maintaining social relations. This allowed exciting new ideas about how culture worked to be applied in a flexible way to a variety of settings, all the while without letting go of comforting old ideas about class domination. The result was a "sociology of culture" analysis, which tied cultural forms to social structure as manifestations of "hegemony" (if the analyst did not like what they saw) or "resistance" (if they did). At its best, this mode of sociology could be brilliantly illuminating. Paul Willis's (1977) ethnographic study of working-class school kids was outstanding in its reconstruction of the zeitgeist of the "lads." Hall, Critcher, Jefferson, Clarke, and Roberts's (1978) classic study of the moral panic over mugging in 1970s Britain, *Policing the Crisis,* managed in its early pages to decode the discourse of urban decay and racism that underpinned an authoritarian crackdown. In these ways, Birmingham work approached a "strong program" in its ability to recreate social texts and lived meanings. Where it fails, however, is in the area of cultural autonomy (Sherwood, Smith, & Alexander, 1993). Notwithstanding attempts to move beyond the classical Marxist position, neo-Gramscian theorizing exhibits the telltale weak program ambiguities over the role of culture that plague the luminous *Prison Notebooks* (Gramsci, 1971) themselves. Terms like "articulation" and "anchoring" suggest contingency in the play of culture. But this contingency is often reduced to instrumental reason (in the case of elites articulating a discourse for hegemony purposes) or to some kind of ambiguous systemic or structural causation (in the case of discourses being anchored in relations of power).

Failure to grasp the nettle of cultural autonomy and quit the sociology of culture–driven project of "Western Marxism" (Anderson, 1979) contributed to a fateful ambiguity over the mechanisms through which culture links with social structure and action. There is no clearer example of this latter process than in *Policing the Crisis* (Hall, Jefferson, Clarke, & Roberts, 1978) itself. After building up a detailed picture of the mugging panic and its symbolic resonances, the book lurches into a sequence of insistent claims that the moral panic is linked to the economic logic of capitalism and its proximate demise; that it functions to legitimate law-and-order politics on streets that harbor latent revolutionary tendencies. Yet the concrete mechanisms through which the incipient crisis of capitalism (has it arrived yet?) are translated into the concrete decisions of judges, parliamentarians, newspaper editors, and police officers on the beat are never spelled out. The result is a theory that despite a critical edge and superior hermeneutic capabilities to classical functionalism curiously resembles Parsons in its tendency to invoke abstracted influences and processes as adequate explanation for empirical social actions.

In this respect, in contrast to the Birmingham School, the work of Pierre Bourdieu has real merits. While many Birmingham-style analyses seem to lack any clear application of method, Bourdieu's oeuvre is resolutely grounded in middle-range empirical research projects of both a qualitative and quantitative nature. His inferences and claims are more modest and less manifestly tendentious. In his best work, moreover, such as the description of a Kabyle house or a French peasant dance (Bourdieu, 1962, 1977), Bourdieu's thick description abilities show that he has the musicality to recognize and decode cultural texts that is at least equal to that of the Birmingham ethnographers. Despite these qualities, Bourdieu's research also can best be described as a weak program dedicated to the sociology of culture rather than cultural sociology. Once they have penetrated the thickets of terminological ambiguity that always mark out a weak program, commentators agree that in Bourdieu's framework culture has a role in ensuring the reproduction of inequality rather than permitting innovation (Alexander, 1995a; Honneth,1986; Sewell, 1992). As a result, culture, working through habitus, operates more as a dependent than an independent variable. It is a gearbox, not an engine. When it comes to specifying exactly how the process of reproduction takes place, Bourdieu is vague. Habitus produces a sense of style, ease, and taste. Yet to know just how these influence stratification, something more would be needed: a detailed study of concrete social settings where decisions are made and social reproduction ensured (see Lamont, 1992). We need to know more about the thinking of gatekeepers in job interviews and publishing houses, the impact of classroom dynamics on learning, or the logic of the citation process. Without this "missing link" we are left with a theory that points to circumstantial homologies but cannot produce a smoking gun.

Bourdieu's understanding of the links of culture to power also falls short of demanding strong program ideals. For Bourdieu, stratification systems make use of status cultures in competition with each other in various fields. The semantic content of these cultures has little to do with how society is organized. Meaning has no wider impact. While Weber, for example, argued that forms of eschatology have determinate outputs on the way that social life is patterned, for

Bourdieu cultural content is arbitrary and without import. In his formulation there always will be systems of stratification defined by class, and all that is important for dominant groups is to have their cultural codes embraced as legitimate. In the final analysis, what we have here is a Veblenesque vision in which culture provides a strategic resource for actors, an external environment of action, rather than a Text that shapes the world in an immanent fashion. People use culture, but they do not seem to really care about it.

Michel Foucault's works, and the poststructural and postmodern theoretical program they have initiated, provides the third weak program we discuss here. Despite its brilliance, what we find here, yet again, is a body of work wrought with the tortured contradictions that indicate a failure to grasp the nettle of a strong program. On the one hand, Foucault's (1970, 1972) major theoretical texts, *The Archaeology of Knowledge* and *The Order of Things,* provide important groundwork for a strong program with their assertion that discourses operate in arbitrary ways to classify the world and shape knowledge formation. His empirical applications of this theory also should be praised for assembling rich historical data in a way that approximates the reconstruction of a social text. So far so good. Unfortunately, there is another hand at work. The crux of the issue is Foucault's genealogical method; his insistence that power and knowledge are fused in power/knowledge. The result is a reductionist line of reasoning akin to functionalism (Brenner, 1994), where discourses are homologous with institutions, flows of power, and technologies. Contingency is specified at the level of "history," at the level of untheorizable collisions and ruptures, not at the level of the dispositif. There is little room for a synchronically arranged contingency that might encompass disjunctures between culture and institutions, between power and its symbolic or textual foundations, between texts and actors interpretations of those texts. This binding of discourse to social structure, in other words, leaves no room for understanding how an autonomous cultural realm hinders or assists actors in judgment, in critique, or in the provision of transcendental goals that texture social life. Foucault's world is one where Nietzsche's prison house of language finds its material expression with such force that no room is left for cultural autonomy or, by implication, the autonomy of action. Responding to this sort of criticism, Foucault attempted to theorize self and resistance in his later work. But he did so in an ad hoc way, seeing acts of resistance as random dysfunctions (Brenner, 1994: 698) or unexplained self-assertions. These late texts do not work through the ways that cultural frames might permit "outsiders" to produce and sustain opposition to power.

In the currently most influential stream of work to come out of the Foucauldian stable, we can see that the latent tension between the Foucault (1972) of the *Archaeology* and Foucault's genealogical avatar has been resolved decisively in favor of an anticultural mode of theory. The proliferating body of work on "governmentality" centers on the control of populations (Miller & Rose, 1990; Rose, 1993) but does so through an elaboration of the role of administrative techniques and expert systems. To be sure, there is acknowledgment that "language" is important, that government has a "discursive character." This sounds promising, but on closer inspection we find that "language" and "discourse" boil down to dry modes of technical communication (graphs, statistics, reports, etc.) that operate as technologies to allow "evaluation, calculation, intervention" at a distance by institutions and bureaucracies (Miller & Rose, 1990: 7). There is little work here to recapture the more textual nature of political and administrative discourses. No effort is made to go beyond a "thin description" and identify the broader symbolic patterns, the hot, affective criteria through which policies of control and coordination are appraised by citizens and elites alike. Here the project of governmentality falls short of the standards set by Hall et al. (1978), which at least managed to conjure up the emotive spirit of populism in Heath-era Britain.

Research on the "production and reception of culture" marks the fourth weak program we will identify. Unlike those we have just discussed, it is one that lacks theoretical bravura and charismatic leadership. For the most part it is characterized by the unsung virtues of intellectual modesty, diligence, clarity, and a studious attention to questions of method. Its numerous proponents make sensible, middle-range empirical studies of the circumstances in which "culture" is produced and consumed (for an overview see Crane, 1992). For this reason it has become particularly powerful in the United States, where these kinds of properties assimilate best to professional norms within sociology. The great strength of this approach is that it offers explicit causal links between culture and social structure, thus avoiding the pitfalls of indeterminacy and obfuscation that have plagued more theoretically ambitious understandings. Unfortunately, this intellectual honesty usually serves only to broadcast a reductionist impulse that remains latent in the other approaches we have examined. The insistent aim of study after study (e.g., Blau, 1989; Peterson, 1985) seems to be to explain away culture as the product of sponsoring institutions, elites, or interests. The quest for profit, power, prestige, or ideological control sits at the core of cultural production. Reception, meanwhile, is relentlessly determined by social location. Audience ethnographies, for example, are undertaken to document the decisive impact of class, race, and gender on the ways that television programs are understood. Here we find the sociology of culture writ large. The aim of analysis is not so much to uncover the impact of meaning on social life and identity formation but rather to see how social life and identities constrain potential meanings.

While the sociological credentials of such an undertaking are to be applauded, something more is needed if the autonomy of culture is to be recognized, namely a robust understanding of the codes that are at play in the cultural objects under consideration. Only when these are taken into account can cultural products be seen to have internal cultural inputs and constraints. However, in the production of culture approach, such efforts at hermeneutic understanding are rare. All too often meaning remains a sort of black box, with analytical attention centered on the circumstances of cultural production and reception. When meanings and discourses are explored, it is usually in order to talk through some kind of fit between cultural content and the social needs and actions of specific producing and receiving groups. Wendy Griswold (1983), for example, shows how the trickster figure was transformed with the emergence of Restoration drama. In the medieval morality play, the figure of "vice" was evil. He was later to morph into the attractive, quick-thinking "gallant." The new character was one that could appeal to an audience of young, disinherited men who had migrated to the city and had to depend on their wits for social advancement. Similarly, Robert Wuthnow (1989) argues that the ideologies of the Reformation germinated and took root as an appropriate response to a particular set of social circumstances. He persuasively demonstrates that new binary oppositions emerged in theological discourse, for example, those between a corrupt Catholicism and a pure Protestantism. These refracted the politics and social dislocations underlying religious and secular struggles in sixteenth-century Europe.

We have some concerns about singling such work out for criticism, for they are among the best of the genre and approximate the sort of thick description we advocate. There can be little doubt that Griswold and Wuthnow correctly understand a need to study meaning in cultural analysis. However, they fail to systematically connect its exploration with the problematic of cultural autonomy. For all their attention to cultural messages and historical continuities, they do little to reduce our fear that there is an underlying reductionism in such analysis. The overall effect is to understand meanings as infinitely malleable in response to social settings. A more satisfying approach to Griswold's data, for example, would recognize the dramatic narratives as inevitably structured by constraining, cultural codes relating to plot and character, for it is the combinations between these that make any kind of drama a possibility. Similarly, Wuthnow should have been much more sensitive to the understanding of binary opposition advocated by Saussure: it is a precondition of discourse rather than merely a description of its historically specific form.[5] And so to our reading, such efforts as Griswold's and Wuthnow's represent narrowly lost opportunities for a decisive demonstration cultural autonomy as a product of culture-structure. In the final section of this chapter, we look for signs of a structuralist hermeneutics that can perhaps better accomplish this theoretical goal.

## STEPS TOWARD A STRONG PROGRAM

All things considered, the sociological investigation of culture remains dominated by weak programs characterized by some combination of hermeneutic inadequacy, ambivalence over cultural autonomy, and poorly specified, abstract mechanisms for grounding culture in concrete social process. In this final section we discuss recent trends in cultural sociology where there are signs that a bona fide strong program might finally be emerging.

A first step in the construction of a strong program is the hermeneutic project of "thick description" itself, which we have already invoked in a positive way. Drawing on Paul Ricoeur and Kenneth Burke, Clifford Geertz (1973, [1964]) has worked harder than any other person to show that culture is a rich and complex text, with a subtle patterning influence on social life. The result is a compelling vision of culture as webs of significance that guide action. Yet while superior to the other approaches we have considered, this position too has its flaws. Nobody could accuse Geertz of hermeneutic inadequacy or of neglecting cultural autonomy, yet on close inspection his enormously influential concept of thick description seems rather elusive. The precise mechanisms through which webs of meaning influence action on the ground are rarely specified with any clarity. Culture seems to take on the qualities of a transcendental actor (Alexander, 1987). So in terms of the third criterion of a strong program that we have specified—causal specificity—the program initiated by Geertz runs into trouble. One reason is the later Geertz's reluctance to connect his interpretive analyses to any kind of general theory. There is a relentless emphasis on the way that the local explains the local. He insists that societies, like texts, contain their own explanation. Writing the local, as a consequence, comes into play as a substitute for theory construction. The focus here is on a novelistic recapitulation of details, with the aim of analysis being to accumulate these and fashion a model of the cultural text within a particular setting. Such a rhetorical turn has made it difficult to draw a line between anthropology and literature, or even travel writing. This in turn has made Geertz's project vulnerable to takeover bids. Most notably, during the 1980s the idea that society could be read like a text was taken over by poststructural writers who argued that culture was little more than contending texts or "representations" (Clifford, 1988) and that ethnography was either allegory, fantasy, or biography. The aim of analysis now shifted to the exposition of professional representations and the techniques and power relations behind them. The resulting program has been one that has told us a good deal about academic writing, ethnographic museum displays, and so on. It helps us to understand the discursive conditions of cultural production but has almost given up on the task of explaining ordinary social life or the possibility of a general understanding. Not surprisingly, Geertz enthusiastically devoted himself to the new cause, writing an eloquent text on the tropes through which anthropologists construct their ethnographic authority (Geertz, 1988). As the text replaces the tribe as the object of analysis, cultural theory begins to look more and more like critical narcissism and less and less like the explanatory discipline that Dilthey so vividly imagined.

Inadequate as it may be, the work of Geertz provides a springboard for a strong program in cultural analysis. It indicates the need for the explication of meaning to be at the center of the intellectual agenda and offers a vigorous affirmation of cultural autonomy. What is missing, however, is a theory of culture that has autonomy built into the very fabric of meaning as well as a more robust understanding of social structure and institutional dynamics. We suggest, following Saussure, that a more structural approach toward culture helps with the first point. In addition, it initiates the movement toward general theory that Geertz avoids. In short, it can recognize the autonomy and the centrality of meaning but does not develop a hermeneutics of the particular at the expense of a hermeneutics of the universal.

As the 1980s turned into the 1990s, we saw the revival of "culture" in American sociology and the declining prestige of anticultural forms of macro- and micro-thought. This strand of work, with its developing strong program characteristics, offers the best hope for a truly cultural sociology finally to emerge as a major research tradition. To be sure, a number of weak programs organized around the sociology of culture remain powerful, perhaps dominant, in the U.S. context. One thinks in particular of studies of the production, consumption, and distribution of culture that (as we have shown) focus on organizational and institutional contexts rather than content and meanings (e.g., Blau, 1989; Peterson, 1985). One also thinks of work inspired by the Western Marxist tradition that attempts to link cultural change to the workings of capital, especially in the context of urban form (e.g., Davis, 1992; Gottdeiner, 1995). The neoinstitutionalists (see DiMaggio & Powell, 1991) see culture as significant but only as a legitimating constraint, only as an external environment of action, not as a lived text, as Geertz might (see Friedland & Alford, 1991). Of course, there are numerous United States–based apostles of British cultural studies (e.g., Fiske, 1987; Grossberg, Nelson, & Treichler, 1991), who combine virtuoso hermeneutic readings with thin, stratification-oriented forms of quasimaterialist reduction. Yet it is equally important to recognize that there has emerged a current of work that gives to meaningful and autonomous texts a much more central place (for a sample, see Smith, 1998b). These contemporary sociologists are the "children" of an earlier generation of culturalist thinkers, Geertz, Bellah (1970; see Alexander & Sherwood, 2002), Turner (1974), and Sahlins (1976) foremost among them, who wrote against the grain of 1960s and 1970s reductionism and attempted to demonstrate the textuality of social life and the necessary autonomy of cultural forms. In contemporary scholarship, we are seeing efforts to align these two axioms of a strong program with the third imperative of identifying concrete mechanisms through which culture does its work.

Responses to the question of transmission mechanisms have been decisively shaped, in a positive direction, by the American pragmatist and empiricist traditions. The influence of structural linguistics on European scholarship sanctioned a kind of cultural theory that paid little attention to the relationship between culture and action (unless tempered by the dangerously "humanist" discourses of existentialism or phenomenology). Simultaneously, the philosophical formation of writers like Althusser and Foucault permitted a dense and tortured kind of writing, where issues of causality and autonomy could be circled around in endless, elusive spirals of words. By contrast, American pragmatism has provided the seedbed for a discourse where clarity is rewarded; where it is believed that complex language games can be reduced to simpler statements; where it is argued that actors have to play some role in translating cultural structures into concrete actions and institutions. While the influence of pragmatism has reached American cultural sociologists in a diffuse way, its most direct inheritance can be seen in the work of Swidler (1986), Sewell (1992), Emirbayer and his collaborators (e.g., Emirbayer & Goodwin, 1996; Emirbayer & Mische, 1998), and Fine (1987), where efforts are made to relate culture to action without recourse to the materialistic reductionism of Bourdieu's praxis theory.

Other forces also have played a role in shaping the emerging strong program in American cultural sociology. Because these are more closely related than the pragmatists to our argument that a structuralist hermeneutics is the best way forward, we will expand on them here. Pivotal to all such work is an effort to understand culture not just as a text (à la Geertz) but rather as a text that is underpinned by signs and symbols that are in patterned relationships to each other. Writing in the first decades of the twentieth century, Durkheim and his students such as Hertz and Mauss understood that culture was a classification system consisting of binary oppositions. At the same time Saussure was developing his structural linguistics, arguing that meanings were generated by means of patterned relationships between concepts and sounds. A few decades later, Lévi-Strauss was to pull these linguistic and sociological approaches to classification together in his pioneering studies of myth, kinship, and totemism. The great virtue of this synthesis was that it provided a powerful way for understanding the autonomy of culture. Because meanings are arbitrary and are generated from within the sign system, they enjoy a certain autonomy from social determination, just as the language of a country cannot be predicted from the knowledge that it is capitalist or socialist, industrial or agrarian. Culture now becomes a structure as objective as any more material social fact.

With the thematics of the "autonomy of culture" taking center stage in the 1980s, there was a vigorous appreciation of the work of the late Durkheim, with his insistence on the cultural as well as functional origins of solidarity (for a review of this literature, see Emirbayer, 1996; Smith & Alexander, 1996). The felicitous but not altogether accidental congruence between Durkheim's opposition of the sacred and the profane and structuralist theories of sign-systems enabled insights from French theory to be translated into a distinctively sociological discourse and tradition, much of it concerned with the impact of cultural codes and codings. Numerous studies of boundary maintenance, for example, reflect this trend (for a sample, see Lamont & Fournier, 1993), and it is instructive to contrast them with more reductionist weak program alternatives about processes of "othering." Emerging from this tradition has been a focus on the binary opposition as a key tool for asserting the autonomy of cultural forms (see Alexander & Smith, 1993; Edles, 1998; Magnuson, 1997; Smith, 1991).

Further inspirations for structural hermeneutics within a strong program for cultural theory have come from anthropology. The new breed of symbolic anthropologists, in addition to Geertz, most notably Mary Douglas (1966), Victor Turner (1974), and Marshall Sahlins (1976, 1981), took on board the message of structuralism but tried to move it in new directions. Postmodernisms and poststructuralisms also have played their role but in an optimistic guise. The knot between power and knowledge that has stunted European weak programs has been loosened by American postmodern theorists like Steven Seidman (1988). For postmodern pragmatistic philosophers like Richard Rorty (e.g., 1989), language tends to be seen as a creative force for the social imaginary rather than as Nietzsche's prison house. As a result, discourses and actors are provided with greater autonomy from power in the construction of identities.

These trends are well known, but there also is an interdisciplinary dark horse to which we wish to draw attention. In philosophy and literary studies, there has been growing interest in narrative and genre theory. Cultural sociologists such as Robin Wagner-Pacifici (1986, 1994, 2000; Wagner-Pacifici & Schwartz, 1991), Margaret Somers (1995), Wendy Griswold (1983), Ronald Jacobs (1996, 2000), Agnes Ku (1999), William Gibson (1994), and the authors of this chapter are now reading literary theorists like Northrup Frye, Peter Brooks, and Fredric Jameson, historians like Hayden White, and Aristotelian philosophers like Ricoeur and MacIntyre (see Lara, 1998). The appeal of such theory lies partially in its affinity for a textual understanding of social life. The emphasis on teleology carries with it some of the interpretive power of the classical hermeneutic model. This impulse toward reading culture as a text is complemented, in such narrative work, by an interest in developing formal models that can be applied across different comparative and historical cases. In other words, narrative forms such as the morality play or melodrama, tragedy, and comedy can be understood as "types" that carry with them particular implications for social life. The morality play, for example, does not seem to be conducive to compromise (Wagner-Pacifici, 1986, 1994). Tragedy can give rise to fatalism (Jacobs, 1996) and withdrawal from civic engagement, but it also can promote moral responsibility (Alexander, 1995b; Eyerman, 2001). Comedy and romance, by contrast, generate optimism and social inclusion (Jacobs & Smith, 1997; Smith, 1994). Irony provides a potent tool for the critique of authority and reflexivity about dominant cultural codes, opening space for difference and cultural innovation (Jacobs & Smith, 1997; Smith, 1996).

A further bonus for this narrative approach is that cultural autonomy is assured (e.g., in the analytic sense, see Kane, 1992). If one takes a structuralist approach to narrative (Barthes, 1977), textual forms are seen as interwoven repertoires of characters, plot lines, and moral evaluations whose relationships can be specified in terms of formal models. Narrative theory, like semiotics, thus operates as a bridge between the kind of hermeneutic inquiry advocated by Geertz and the impulse toward general cultural theory. As Northrop Frye recognized, when approached in a structural way narrative allows for the construction of models that can be applied across cases and contexts but at the same time provides a tool for interrogating particularities.

It is important to emphasize that while meaningful texts are central in this American strand of a strong program, wider social contexts are not by any means necessarily ignored. In fact, the objective structures and visceral struggles that characterize the real social world are every bit as important as in work from the weak programs. Notable contributions have been made to areas such as censorship and exclusion (Beisel, 1993), race (Jacobs, 1996), sexuality (Seidman, 1988), violence (Gibson, 1994; Smith, 1991, 1996; Wagner-Pacifici, 1994), and failed sociohistorical projects for radical transformation (Alexander, 1995b). These contexts are treated, however, not as forces unto themselves that ultimately determine the content and significance of cultural texts; rather, they are seen as institutions and processes that refract cultural texts in a meaningful way. They are arenas in which cultural forces combine or clash with material conditions and rational interests to produce particular outcomes (Ku, 1999; Smith, 1996). Beyond this they are seen as cultural metatexts themselves, as concrete embodiments of wider ideal currents.

## CONCLUSIONS

We have suggested here that structuralism and hermeneutics can be made into fine bedfellows. The former offers possibilities for general theory construction, prediction, and assertions of the autonomy of culture. The latter allows analysis to capture the texture and temper of social life. When complemented by attention to institutions and actors as causal intermediaries, we have the foundations of a robust cultural sociology. The argument we have made here for an emerging strong program has been somewhat polemical in tone. This does not mean we disparage efforts to look at culture in other ways. If sociology is to remain healthy as a discipline, it should be able to support a theoretical pluralism and lively debate. There are important research questions, in fields from demography to stratification to economic and political life, to which weak programs can be expected to make significant contributions. But it is equally important to make room for a genuinely cultural sociology. A first step toward this end is to speak out against false idols, to avoid the mistake of confusing reductionist sociology of culture approaches with a genuine strong program. Only in this way can the full promise of a cultural sociology be realized during the coming century.

# ON THE SOCIAL CONSTRUCTION
# OF MORAL UNIVERSALS

## The "Holocaust" from War Crime to Trauma Drama

If we bear this suffering, and if there are still Jews left, when it is over, then Jews, instead of being doomed, will be held up as an example. Who knows, it might even be our religion from which the world and all peoples learn good, and for that reason and for that alone do we have to suffer now.

—Anne Frank, 1944

"Holocaust" has become so universal a reference point that even contemporary Chinese writers, who live thousands of miles from the place of Nazi brutality and possess only scanty knowledge of the details of the Holocaust, came to call their horrendous experiences during the Cultural Revolution "the ten-year holocaust."

—Sheng Mei Ma, 1987

The term history unites the objective and the subjective side, and denotes . . . not less what happened than the narration of what happened. This union of the two meanings we must regard as of a higher order than mere outward accident; we must suppose historical narrations to have appeared contemporaneously with historical deeds and events.

—G. W. F. Hegel, *The Philosophy of History*

How did a specific and situated historical event, an event marked by ethnic and racial hatred, violence, and war, become transformed into a generalized symbol of human suffering and moral evil, a universalized symbol whose very existence has created historically unprecedented opportunities for ethnic, racial, and religious justice, for mutual recognition, and for global conflicts becoming regulated in a more civil way?[1] This cultural transformation has been achieved because the originating historical event, traumatic in the extreme for a delimited particular group, has come over the last fifty years to be redefined as a traumatic event for all of humankind.[2] Now free-floating rather than situated—universal rather than particular—this traumatic event vividly "lives" in the memories of contemporaries whose parents and grandparents never felt themselves even remotely related to it.

In what follows, I explore the social creation of a cultural fact and the effects of this cultural fact on social and moral life.

_____ In the beginning, in April 1945, the Holocaust was not the "Holocaust." In the torrent of newspaper, radio, and magazine stories reporting the discovery by American infantrymen of the Nazi concentration camps, the empirical remains of what had transpired were typified as "atrocities." Their obvious awfulness, and indeed their strangeness, placed them for contemporary observers at the borderline of the category of behavior known as "man's inhumanity to man." Nonetheless, qua atrocity, the discoveries were placed side by side—metonymically and semantically—with a whole series of other brutalities that were considered to be the natural results of the ill wind of this second, very unnatural, and most inhuman world war.

The first American reports on "atrocities" during that second world war had not, in fact, even referred to actions by German Nazis, let alone to their Jewish victims, but to the Japanese army's brutal treatment of American and other allied prisoners of war after the loss of Corregidor in 1943. On January 27, 1944, the United States released sworn statements by military officers who had escaped the so-called Bataan Death March. In the words of contemporary journals and magazines, these officers had related "atrocity stories" revealing "the inhuman treatment and murder of American and Filipino soldiers who were taken prisoner when Bataan and Corregidor fell." In response to these accounts, the U.S. State Department had lodged protests to the Japanese government about its failure to live up to the provisions of the Geneva Prisoners of War Convention (*Current History*, March 1944: 249). Atrocities, in other words, were a signifier specifically connected to war. They referred to war-generated events that transgressed the rules circumscribing how national killing could normally be carried out.[3] Responding to the same incident, *Newsweek*, in a section entitled "The Enemy" and under the headline "Nation Replies in Grim Fury to Jap Brutality to Prisoners," reported that "with the first impact of the news, people had shuddered at the story of savage *atrocity* upon Allied prisoners of war by the Japanese" (February 7, 1944: 19, italics added).[4]

It is hardly surprising, then, that it was this nationally specific and particular war-related term that was employed to represent the grisly Jewish mass murders discovered by American GIs when they liberated the Nazi camps.[5] Through April 1945, as one camp after another was discovered, this collective representation was applied time after time.[6] When, toward the end of that month, a well-known Protestant minister explored the moral implications of the discoveries, he declared that, no matter how horrifying and repulsive, "it is important that the full truth be made known so that a clear indication may be had of the nature of the enemy we have been dealing with, as well of as a realization *of the sheer brutalities that have become the accompaniment of war.*" The *New York Times* reported this sermon under the headline "Bonnell Denounces German Atrocities" (April 23, 1945: 23, italics added). When alarmed American Congressmen visited Buchenwald, the *Times* headlined that they had witnessed firsthand the "*War Camp Horror*" (April 26, 1945: 12, italics added). When a few days later the U.S. army released a report on the extent of the killings in Buchenwald, the *Times* headlined it an "Atrocity Report" (April 29, 1945: 20). A few days after that, under the headline "Enemy Atrocities in France Bared," the *Times* wrote that a just-released report had shown that "in France, German brutality was not limited to the French underground or even to the thousands of hostages whom the Germans killed for disorders they had nothing to do with, but was practiced almost systematically against entirely innocent French people" (May 4, 1945: 6).

The Nazis' anti-Jewish mass murders had once been only putative atrocities. From the late thirties on, reports about them had been greeted with widespread public doubt about their authenticity. Analogizing to the allegations about German atrocities during World War I that later had been thoroughly discredited, they were dismissed as a kind of Jewish moral panic. Only three months before the GI's "discovery" of the camps, in introducing a firsthand report on Nazi mass murder from a Soviet-liberated camp in Poland, *Collier's* magazine acknowledged: "A lot of Americans simply do not believe the stories of Nazi mass executions of Jews and anti-Nazi Gentiles in eastern Europe by means of gas chambers, freight cars partly loaded with lime and other horrifying devices. These stories are so foreign to most Americans' experience of life in this country that they seem incredible. Then, too some of the atrocity stories of World War I were later proved false" (January 6, 1945: 62).[7] From April 3, 1945, however, the date when the GIs first liberated the concentration camps, all such earlier reports were retrospectively accepted as facts, as the realistic signifiers of Peirce rather than the "arbitrary" symbols of Saussure. That systematic efforts at Jewish mass murder had occurred, and that the numerous victims and the few survivors had been severely traumatized, the American and worldwide audience now had little doubt.[8] Their particular and unique fate, however, even while it was widely recognized as representing the grossest of injustices, did not itself become a traumatic experience for the audience to which the mass media's collective representations were transmitted, that is, for those looking on, either from near or from far. Why this was not so defines my initial explanatory effort here.

For an audience to be traumatized by an experience that they themselves do not directly share, symbolic extension and psychological identification are required. This did not occur. For the American infantrymen who first made contact, for the general officers who supervised the rehabilitation, for the reporters who broadcast the descriptions, for the commissions of Congressmen and influentials who quickly traveled to Germany to conduct on-site investigations, the starving, depleted, often weird-looking and sometimes weird-acting Jewish camp survivors seemed like a foreign race. They could just as well have been from Mars, or from hell. The identities and characters of these Jewish survivors rarely were personalized through interviews or individualized through biographical sketches; rather, they were presented as a mass, and often as a mess, a petrified, degrading, and smelly one, not only by newspaper reporters but by some of the most powerful general officers in the Allied high command. This depersonalization made it more difficult for the survivors' trauma to generate compelling identification.

Possibilities for universalizing the trauma were blocked not only by the depersonalization of its victims but by their historical and sociological specification. As I have indicated, the mass murders semantically were immediately linked to other "horrors" in the bloody history of the century's second great war and to the historically specific national and ethnic conflicts that underlay it. Above all, it was never forgotten that these victims were Jews. In retrospect, it is bitterly ironic, but it is also sociologically understandable, that the American audience's sympathy and feelings of identity flowed much more easily to the non-Jewish survivors, whether German or Polish, who had been kept in better conditions and looked more normal, more composed, more human. Jewish survivors were kept for weeks and sometimes even for months in the worst areas and under the worst conditions of what had become, temporarily, displaced persons camps. American and British administrators felt impatient with many Jewish survivors, even personal repugnance for them, sometimes resorting to threats and even to punishing them.[9] The depth of this initial failure of identification can be seen in the fact that when American citizens and their leaders expressed opinions and made decisions about national quotas for emergency postwar immigration, displaced German citizens ranked first, Jewish survivors last.

How could this have happened? Was it not obvious to any human observer that this mass murder was fundamentally different from the other traumatic and bloody events in a modern history already dripping in blood, that it represented not simply evil but "radical evil," in Kant's remarkable phrase (Kant, 1960),[10] that it was unique? To understand why none of this was obvious, to understand how and why each these initial understandings and behaviors were radically changed, and how this transformation had vast repercussions for establishing not only new moral standards for social and political behavior but unprecedented, if still embryonic, regulatory controls, it is important to see the inadequacy of common-sense understandings of traumatic events.

There are two kinds of common-sense thinking about trauma, forms of thinking that comprise what I call "lay trauma theory."[11] These commonsensical forms of reasoning have deeply informed thinking about the effects of the Holocaust. They are expressed in the following strikingly different conceptualizations of what happened after the revelations of the mass killings of Jews.

*The Enlightenment version.* The "horror" of onlookers provoked the postwar end of anti-Semitism in the United States. The common-sense assumption here is that because people have a fundamentally "moral" nature—as a result of their rootedness in Enlightenment and religious traditions—they will perceive atrocities for what they are and react to them by attacking the belief systems that provided legitimation.

*The psychoanalytic version.* When faced with the horror, Jews and non-Jews alike reacted not with criticism and decisive action but with silence and bewilderment. Only after two or even three decades of repression and denial were people finally able to begin talking about what happened and to take actions in response to this knowledge.

Enlightenment and psychoanalytic forms of lay trauma thinking have permeated academic efforts at understanding what happened after the death camp revelations. One or the other version has informed not only every major discussion of the Holocaust but virtually every contemporary effort to investigate trauma more generally, efforts that are, in fact, largely inspired by Holocaust debates.[12]

What is wrong with this lay trauma theory is that it is "naturalistic," either in the naively moral or the naively psychological sense. Lay trauma theory fails to see that there is an interpretive grid through which all "facts" about trauma are mediated, emotionally, cognitively, and morally. This grid has a supraindividual, cultural status; it is symbolically structured and sociologically determined. No trauma interprets itself: Before trauma can be experienced at the collective (not individual) level, there are essential questions that must be answered, and answers to these questions change over time.

## THE CULTURAL CONSTRUCTION OF TRAUMA

### Coding, Weighting, Narrating

Elie Wiesel, in a moving and influential statement in the late 1970s, asserted that the Holocaust represents an "ontological evil." From a sociological perspective, however, evil is epistemological, not ontological. For a traumatic event to have the status of evil is a matter of its *becoming* evil. It is a matter of how the trauma is known, how it is coded.[13] "At first glance it may appear a paradox," Diner has noted—and certainly it does—but, considered only in and of itself, "Auschwitz *has* no appropriate narrative, only a set of statistics" (Diner, 2000: 178). Becoming evil is a matter, first and foremost, of representation. Depending on the nature of representation, a traumatic event may be regarded as ontologically evil, or its badness, its "evilness," may be conceived as contingent and relative, as something that can be ameliorated and overcome. This distinction is theoretical, but it is also practical. In fact, decisions about the ontological versus contingent status of the Holocaust were of overriding importance in its changing representation.

If we can deconstruct this ontological assertion even further, I would like to suggest that the very existence of the category "evil" must be seen not as something that naturally exists but as an arbitrary construction, the product of cultural and sociological work. This contrived binary, which simplifies empirical complexity to two antagonistic forms and reduces every shade of gray between, has been an essential feature of all human societies but especially important in those Eisenstadt (1982) has called the Axial Age civilizations. This rigid opposition between the sacred and profane, which in Western philosophy has typically been constructed as a conflict between normativity and instrumentality, not only defines what people care about but establishes vital safeguards around the shared normative "good." At the same time it places powerful, often aggressive barriers against anything that is construed as threatening the good, forces defined not merely as things to be avoided but as sources of horror and pollution that must be contained at all costs.

### The Material "Base": Controlling the Means of Symbolic Production

Yet if this grid is a kind of functional necessity, how it is applied very much depends on who is telling the story, and how. This is first of all a matter of cultural power in the most mundane, materialist sense: Who controls the means of symbolic production?[14] It was certainly not incidental to the public understanding of the Nazis' policies of mass murder, for example, that for an extended period of time it was the Nazis themselves who were in control of the physical and cultural terrain of their enactment. This fact of brute power made it much more difficult to frame the mass killings in a distinctive way. Nor is it incidental that, once the extermination of the Jews was physically interrupted by Allied armies in 1945, it was America's "imperial republic"—the perspective of the triumphant, forward-looking, militantly and militarily democratic new world warrior—that directed the organizational and cultural responses to the mass murders and their survivors. The contingency of this knowledge is so powerful that it might well be said that, if the Allies had not won the war, the "Holocaust" would never have been discovered.[15] Moreover, if it had been the Soviets and not the Allies who "liberated" most of the camps, and not just those in the Eastern sector, what was discovered in those camps might never have been portrayed in a remotely similar way.[16] It was, in other words, precisely and only because the means of symbolic production were not controlled by a victorious postwar Nazi regime, or even by a triumphant communist one, that the mass killings could be called the Holocaust and coded as evil.

### Creating the Culture Structure

Still, even when the means of symbolic production came to be controlled by "our side," even when the association between evil and what would become known as the Holocaust trauma was assured, this was only the beginning, not the end. After a phenomenon is coded as evil, the question that immediately follows is: How evil is it? In theorizing evil, this refers to the problem not of coding but of weighting. For there are degrees of evil, and these degrees have great implications in terms of responsibility, punishment, remedial action, and future behavior. Normal evil and radical evil cannot be the same.

Finally, alongside these problems of coding and weighting, the meaning of a trauma cannot be defined unless we determine exactly what the "it" is. This is a question of narrative: What were the evil and traumatizing actions in question? Who was responsible? Who were the victims? What were the immediate and long-term results of the traumatizing actions? What can be done by way of remediation or prevention?

What these theoretical considerations suggest is that even after the physical force of the Allied triumph and the physical discovery of the Nazi concentration camps, the nature of what was seen and discovered had to be coded, weighted, and narrated. This complex cultural construction, moreover, had to be achieved immediately. History does not wait; it demands that representations be made, and they will be. Whether or not some newly reported event is startling, strange, terrible, or inexpressibly weird, it must be "typified," in the sense of Husserl and Schutz, that is, it must be explained as a typical and even anticipated example of some thing or category that was known about before.[17] Even the vastly unfamiliar must somehow be made familiar. To the cultural process of coding, weighting, and narrating, in other words, what comes before is all-important. Historical background is critical, both for the first "view" of the traumatic event and, as "history" changes, for later views as well. Once again, these shifting cultural constructions are fatefully affected by the power and identity of the agents in charge, by the competition for symbolic control, and the structures of power and distribution of resources that condition it.

## BACKGROUND CONSTRUCTIONS

### Nazism as the Representation of Absolute Evil

What was the historical structure of "good and evil" within which, on April 3, 1945, the "news" of the Nazi concentration camps was first confirmed to the

American audience? To answer this question, it is first necessary to describe what came before. In what follows I will venture some observations, which can hardly be considered definitive, about how social evil was coded, weighted, and narrated during the interwar period in Europe and the United States.

In the deeply disturbing wake of World War I, there was a pervasive sense of disillusionment and cynicism among mass and elite members of the Western "audience," a distancing from protagonists and antagonists that, as Paul Fussell has shown, made irony the master trope of that first postwar era.[18] This trope transformed "demonology"—the very act of coding and weighting evil—into what many intellectuals and lay persons alike considered to be an act of bad faith. Once the coding and weighting of evil were delegitimated, however, good and evil became less distinct from one another and relativism became the dominant motif of the time. In such conditions, coherent narration of contemporary events becomes difficult if not impossible. Thus it was that, not only for many intellectuals and artists of this period but for many ordinary people as well, the startling upheavals of these interwar years could not easily be sorted out in a conclusive and satisfying way.

In this context of the breakdown of representation, racism and revolution, whether fascist or communist, emerged as compelling frames, not only in Europe but also in the United States. Against a revolutionary narrative of dogmatic and authoritarian modernism on the Left, there arose the narrative of reactionary modernism, equally revolutionary but fervently opposed to rationality and cosmopolitanism.[19] In this context, many democrats in western Europe and the United States withdrew from the field of representation itself, becoming confused and equivocating advocates of disarmament, nonviolence, and peace "at any price." This formed the cultural frame for isolationist political policy in both Britain and the United States.

Eventually the aggressive military ambition of Nazism made such equivocation impossible to sustain. While racialism, relativism, and narrative confusion continued in the United States and Britain until the very beginning of World War II, and even continued well into it, these constructions were countered by increasingly forceful and confident representations of good and evil that coded liberal democracy and universalism as unalloyed goods and Nazism, racism, and prejudice as deeply corrosive representations of the polluting and profane.

From the late 1930s on, there emerged a strong, and eventually dominant, antifascist narrative in Western societies. Nazism was coded, weighted, and narrated in apocalyptic, Old Testament terms as "the dominant evil of our time." Because this radical evil aligned itself with violence and massive death, it not merely justified but compelled the risking of life in opposing it, a compulsion that motivated and justified massive human sacrifice in what came later to be known as the last "good war."[20] That Nazism was an absolute, unmitigated evil, a radical evil that threatened the very future of human civilization, formed the presupposition of America's four-year prosecution of the world war.[21]

The representation of Nazism as an absolute evil emphasized not only its association with sustained coercion and violence but also, and perhaps even especially, the way Nazism linked violence with ethnic, racial, and religious hatred. In this way, the most conspicuous example of the practice of Nazi evil—its policy of systematic discrimination, coercion, and, eventually, mass violence against the Jews—was initially interpreted as "simply" another horrifying example of the subhumanism of Nazi action.

### Interpreting *Kristallnacht*: Nazi Evil as Anti-Semitism

The American public's reaction to *Kristallnacht* demonstrates how important the Nazis' anti-Jewish activities were in crystallizing the polluted status of Nazism in American eyes. It also provides a prototypical example of how such representations of the evils of anti-semitism were folded into the broader and more encompassing symbolism of Nazism. *Kristallnacht* refers, of course, to the rhetorically virulent and physically violent expansion of the Nazi repression of Jews that unfolded throughout German towns and cities on November 9 and 10, 1938. These activities were widely recorded. "The morning editions of most American newspapers reported the *Kristallnacht* in banner headlines," according to one historian of that fateful event, "and the broadcasts of H. V. Kaltenborn and Raymond Gram Swing kept the radio public informed of Germany's latest adventure" (Diamond, 1969: 198). Exactly why these events assumed such critical importance in the American public's continuing effort to understand "what Hitlerism stood for" (201) goes beyond the simple fact that violent and repressive activities were, perhaps for the first time, openly, even brazenly, displayed in direct view of the world public sphere. Equally important was the altered cultural framework within which these activities were observed. For *Kristallnacht* occurred just six weeks after the now infamous Munich agreements, acts of appeasement to Hitler's expansion that at that time were understood, not only by isolationists but by many opponents of Nazism, indeed by the vast majority of the American people, as possibly reasonable accessions to a possibly reasonable man (197). What occurred, in other words, was a process of understanding fueled by symbolic contrast, not simply observation.

What was interpretively constructed was the cultural difference between Germany's previously apparent cooperativeness and reasonableness—representations of the good in the discourse of American civil society—and its subsequent demonstration of violence and irrationality, which were taken to be representations of anticivic evil. Central to the ability to draw this contrast was the ethnic and religious hatred Germans demonstrated in their violence against Jews. If one examines the American public's reactions, it clearly is this anti-Jewish violence that is taken to represent the evil of Nazism. Thus it was with references to this violence that the news stories of the *New York Times* employed the rhetoric of pollution to further code and weight Nazi evil: "No foreign propagandist bent upon blackening the name of Germany before the world could outdo the tale of beating, of blackguardly assaults upon defenseless and innocent people, which degraded that country yesterday" (quoted in Diamond, 1969: 198). The *Times'* controversial columnist, Anne O'Hare McCormick, wrote that "the suffering [the Germans] inflict on others, now that they are on top, passes all understanding and mocks all sympathy," and she went on to label *Kristallnacht* "the darkest day Germany experienced in the whole post-war period" (quoted in Diamond, 1969: 199). The *Washington Post* identified the Nazi activities as "one of the worst setbacks for mankind since the Massacre of St. Bartholomew" (quoted in Diamond, 1969: 198–9).

This broadening identification of Nazism with evil, simultaneously triggered and reinforced by the anti-Jewish violence of *Kristallnacht*, stimulated influential political figures to make more definitive judgments about the antipathy between American democracy and German Nazism than they had up until that point. Speaking on NBC radio, Al Smith, the former New York governor and democratic presidential candidate, observed that the events confirmed that the German people were "incapable of living under a democratic government" (quoted in Diamond, 1969: 200). Following Smith on the same program, Thomas E. Dewey, soon to be New York governor and a future presidential candidate, expressed the opinion that "the civilized world stands revolted by the bloody pogrom against a defenseless people . . . by a nation run by madmen" (quoted in Diamond, 1969: 201). Having initially underplayed America's official reaction to the events, four days later President Franklin Roosevelt took advantage of the public outrage by emphasizing the purity of the American nation and its distance from this emerging representation of violence and ethnic hatred: "The news of the past few days from Germany deeply shocked public opinion in the United States. . . . I myself could scarcely believe that such things could occur in a twentieth century civilization" (quoted in Diamond, 1969: 205).

Judging from these reactions to the Nazi violence of *Kristallnacht,* it seems only logical that, as one historian has put it, "most American newspapers or journals" could "no longer . . . view Hitler as a pliable and reasonable man, but as an aggressive and contemptible dictator [who] would have to be restrained" (quoted in Diamond, 1969: 207). What is equally striking, however, is that in almost none of the American public's statements of horror is there explicit reference to the identity of the victims of *Kristallnacht* as Jews. Instead they are referred to as a "defenseless and innocent people," as "others," and as a "defenseless people" (quoted in Diamond, 1969: 198, 199, 201). In fact, in the public statement just quoted, President Roosevelt goes well out of his way to separate his moral outrage from any link to a specific concern for the fate of the Jews. "Such news from *any part* of the world," the President insists, "would inevitably produce similar profound reaction among Americans in *any part* of the nation" (Diamond, 1969: 205, italics added). In other words, despite the centrality of the Nazis' anti-Jewish violence to the emerging American symbolization of Nazism as evil, there existed—at that point in historical and cultural time—a reluctance for non-Jewish Americans to identify with Jewish people as such. Jews were highlighted as vital representations of the evils of Nazism: their fate would be understood only in relation to the German horror that threatened democratic civilization in America and Europe. This failure of identification would be reflected seven years later in the distantiation of the American soldiers and domestic audience from the traumatized Jewish camp survivors and their even less fortunate Jewish compatriots whom the Nazis had killed.

### Anti-Anti-Semitism: Fighting Nazi Evil by Fighting for the Jews

It was also during the 1930s, in the context of the Nazi persecution of German Jews, that a historically unprecedented attack on anti-Semitism emerged in the United States. It was not that Christians suddenly felt genuine affection for, or identification with, those whom they had villified for countless centuries as the killers of Christ.[22] It was that the logic of symbolic association had dramatically and fatefully changed. Nazism was increasingly viewed as the vile enemy of universalism, and the most hated enemies of Nazism were the Jews. The laws of symbolic antinomy and association thus were applied. If Nazism singled out the Jews, then the Jews must be singled out by democrats and anti-Nazis. Anti-Semitism, tolerated and condoned for centuries in every Western nation, and for the preceding fifty years embraced fervently by proponents of American "nativism," suddenly became distinctly unpopular in progressive circles throughout the United States (Gleason, 1981; Higham, 1984).[23]

What I will call "anti-anti-Semitism"[24] became particularly intense after the United States declared war on Nazi Germany. The nature of this concern is framed in a particularly clear manner by one leading historian of American Jewry: "The war saw the merging of Jewish and American fates. Nazi Germany was the greatest enemy of both Jewry and the United States" (Shapiro, 1992: 16). For the first time, overly positive representations of Jewish people proliferated in popular and high culture alike. It was during this period that the phrase "Judeo-Christian tradition" was born. It appeared as Americans tried to fend off the Nazi enemy that threatened to destroy the sacred foundations of Western democratic life (Silk, 1986).

## MASS MURDER UNDER THE PROGRESSIVE NARRATIVE

Nazism marked a traumatic epoch in modern history. Yet, while coded as evil and weighted in the most fundamental, *weltgeschichte* (world-historical) terms, it was narrated inside a framework that offered the promise of salvation and triggered actions that generated confidence and hope.[25] What I will call the "progressive narrative" proclaimed that the trauma created by social evil would be overcome, that Nazism would be defeated and eliminated from the world, that it would eventually be relegated to a traumatic past whose darkness would be obliterated by a new and powerful social light. The progressivity of this narrative depended on keeping Nazism situated and historical, which prevented this representation of absolute evil from being universalized and its cultural power from being equated, in any way, shape, or form with the power possessed by the good. In narrative terms, this asymmetry, this insistence on Nazism's anomalous historical status, assured its ultimate defeat. In the popular consciousness and in the dramas created by cultural specialists, the origins of Nazism were linked to specific events in the interwar period and to particular organizations and actors within it, to a political party, to a crazy and inhuman leader, to an anomalous nation that had demonstrated militaristic and violent tendencies over the previous one hundred years.

Yes, Nazism had initiated a trauma in modern history, but it was a liminal trauma presenting "time out of time," in Victor Turner's sense.[26] The trauma was dark and threatening, but it was, at the same time, anomalous and, in principle at least, temporary. As such the trauma could and would be removed, via a just war and a wise and forgiving peace.[27] The vast human sacrifices demanded by the winds of war were measured and judged in terms of this progressive narrative and the salvation it promised. The blood spilled in the war sanctified the future peace and obliterated the past. The sacrifice of millions could be redeemed, the social salvation of their sacred souls achieved, not by dwelling in a lachrymose manner on their deaths but by eliminating Nazism, the force that had caused their deaths, and by planning the future that would establish a world in which there could never be Nazism again.

## Framing Revelations about the Jewish Mass Murder

While initially received with surprise, and always conceived with loathing, the gradual and halting but eventually definitive revelations of Nazi plans for displacing, and quite possibly murdering, the entirety of European Jewry actually confirmed the categorizing of evil already in place: the coding, weighting, and narrating of Nazism as an inhuman, absolutely evil force. What had been experienced as an extraordinary trauma by the Jewish victims, was experienced by the audience of others as a kind of categorical vindication.[28] In this way, and for this reason, the democratic audience for the reports on the mass murders experienced distance from, rather than identification with, the trauma's victims. The revelations had the effect, in some perverse sense, of normalizing the abnormal.

The empirical existence of Nazi plans for the "Final Solution," as well as extensive documentation of their ongoing extermination activities, had been publicly documented by June 1942 (Dawidowicz, 1982; Laqueur, 1980; Norich, 1998–99). In July of that year more than twenty thousand persons rallied in

Madison Square Garden to protest the Nazis' war against the Jews. Though he did not attend in person, President Franklin Roosevelt sent a special message that what he called "these crimes" would be redeemed by the "final accounting" following the Allied victory over Nazism. In March 1943 the American Jewish Congress announced that two million Jews had already been massacred and that millions more were slated for death. Its detailed descriptions of the "extermination" were widely reported in the American press.[29] By March 1944, when the Germans occupied Hungary and their intention to liquidate its entire Jewish population became known, Dawidowicz shows that "Auschwitz was no longer an unfamiliar name" (Dawidowicz, 1982).

Yet it was this very familiarity that seemed to undermine the sense of astonishment that might have stimulated immediate action. For Auschwitz was typified in terms of the progressive narrative of war, a narrative that made it impossible to denormalize the mass killings, to make the Holocaust into the "Holocaust." As I indicated in my earlier reconstruction of the discourse about atrocity, what eventually came to be called the Holocaust was reported to contemporaries as a war story, nothing less but nothing more. In private conferences with the American president, Jewish leaders demanded that Allied forces make special efforts to target and destroy the death camps. In describing these failed efforts to trigger intervention, a leading historian explains that the leaders "couldn't convince a preoccupied American President and the American public of the significance of Auschwitz for their time in history" (Feingold, 1974: 250). In other words, while Auschwitz was coded as evil, it simply was not weighted in a sufficiently dire way.

In these symbolically mediated confrontations, attention was not focused on the mass killings in and of themselves. What was definitely not illuminated or asserted was the discovery of an evil unique in human history. The evil of that time had already been discovered, and it was Nazism, not the massive killing of European Jews. The trauma that this evil had created was a second world war. The trauma that the Jews experienced in the midst of their liquidation was represented as one among a series of effects of Nazi evil. When the *London Times* reported Adolph Hitler's death, on May 2, 1945—in the month following the death camp revelations—its obituary described the German dictator as "the incarnation of absolute evil" and only briefly mentioned Hitler's "fanatical aversion to Jews" (quoted in Benn, 1995: 102). As one historian has put it, "the processed mass murders became merely another atrocity in a particularly cruel war" (quoted in Benn, 1995: 102).[30] The mass murders were explained, and they would be redeemed, within the framework of the progressive struggle against Nazism.

To fully understand the initial, frame-establishing encounter between Americans and the Jewish mass murder, it is vital to remember that narratives, no matter how progressive and future oriented, are composed of both antagonists and protagonists. The antagonists and their crimes were well established: the

German Nazis had murdered the Jews in a gigantic, heinous atrocity of war. The protagonists were the American GIs, and their entrance into the concentration camps was portrayed not only as a discovery of such horrendous atrocities but as another, culminating stage in a long and equally well-known sequence of "liberation," with all the ameliorating expectations that utopian term implies. "When the press entered the camps of the western front," the cultural historian Barbie Zelizer writes, "it found that the most effective way to tell the atrocity story was as a chronicle of liberation" (Zelizer, 1998: 63). In fact, Zelizer entitles her own detailed reconstruction of these journalist encounters "Chronicles of Liberation" (63–85). When readers of the *New York Times* and *Los Angeles Times* were confronted, on April 16, with the photo from Buchenwald of bunk beds stuffed to overflowing with haunted, pathetically undernourished male prisoners, they were informed that they were looking at "freed slave laborers" (183). On May 5, the *Picture Post* published a six-page spread of atrocity photos. Framing the heartwrenching visual images, the theme of forward progress was palpable. One collective caption read: "These Were Inmates of Prison Camps Set Free in the Allied Advance: For Many We Came Too Late" (129). Photos of dead or tattered and starving victims were often juxtaposed with pictures of well-dressed, well-fed German citizens from the surrounding towns, pointedly linking the crime to the particular nature of the German people themselves. In a sidebar story entitled "The Problem That Makes All Europe Wonder," the *Picture Post* described "the horror that took place within the sight and sound of hundreds of thousands of seemingly normal, decent German people. How was it possible? What has happened to the minds of a whole nation that such things should have been tolerated for a day?" (quoted in Zelizer, 1998: 128). The same photos often included a representative GI standing guard, passing judgment looking on the scene. The text alongside another widely circulated photo in the *Picture Post* made the progressive answer to such questions perfectly plain. "It is not enough to be mad with rage. It is no help to shout about 'exterminating' Germany. Only one thing helps: the attempt to understand how men have sunk so far, and the firm resolve to face the trouble, the inconvenience and cost of seeing no nation gets the chance to befoul the world like this again" (quoted in Zelizer, 1998: 129).

It was within this highly particularized progressive narrative that the first steps toward universalization actually took place. Because the Jewish mass killings came at the chronological conclusion of the war and because they without doubt represented the most gruesome illustration of Nazi atrocities, they came very quickly to be viewed not merely as symptoms but as emblems and iconic representations of the evil that the progressive narrative promised to leave behind. As the novelist and war correspondent Meyer Levin wrote of his visit to Ohrdruf, the first camp American soldiers liberated, "it was as though we had penetrated at last to the center of the black heart, to the very crawling inside of the vicious heart" (quoted in Abzug, 1985: 19). On the one hand, the trauma was localized and particularized—it occurred in this war, in this place, with these persons. On the other hand, the mass murder was universalized. Within months of the initial revelations, indeed, the murders frequently were framed by a new term, "genocide," a crime defined as the effort to destroy an entire people, which, while introduced earlier, during the war period itself, came to be publicly available and widely employed only after the discovery of the Nazi atrocities.[31]

In response to this new representation, the scope of the Nuremberg War Crimes Tribunal was enlarged. Conceived as a principal vehicle for linking the postwar Allied cause to progressive redemption, the trials were now to go beyond prosecuting the Nazi leaders for crimes of war to considering their role in the mass murder against the Jewish people. Justice Robert Jackson, the chief American prosecutor, promised that the trial would not only prosecute those responsible for the war but would present "undeniable proofs of incredible events"—the Nazi crimes (quoted in Benn, 1995: 102). The first three counts of the twenty-thousand-word indictment against the twenty-three high-ranking Nazi officials concerned the prosecution of the war itself. They charged conspiracy, conducting a war of aggression, and violating the rules of war. The fourth count, added only in the months immediately preceding the October trial in Nuremberg, accused the Nazi leaders of something new, namely of "crimes against humanity." This was the first step toward universalizing the public representation of the Jewish mass murder. From the perspective of the present day, however, it appears as a relatively limited one, for it functioned to confirm the innocent virtue and national ambitions of one particular side. In its first report on the indictments, for example, the *New York Times* linked the Jewish mass murder directly to the war itself and placed its punishment within the effort to prevent any future "war of aggression." Under the headline "The Coming War Trials," the paper noted that "the authority of this tribunal to inflict punishment is directly from victory in war" and that its goal was "to establish the principle that no nation shall ever again go to war, except when directly attacked or under the sanction of a world organization" (October 9, 1945: 20). The Nuremberg trials were not, in other words, perceived as preventing genocide or crimes against humanity as such. At that time the commission of such crimes could not be conceived apart from the Nazis and the recently concluded aggressive war.

The force of the progressive narrative meant that, while the 1945 revelations confirmed the Jewish mass murder, they did not create a trauma for the postwar audience. Victory and the Nuremburg war trials would put an end to Nazism and alleviate its evil effects. Postwar redemption depended on putting mass murder "behind us," moving on, and getting on with the construction of the new world.

From the end of the war until the early 1960s, a "can-do," optimistic spirit per-
vaded America. Those who had returned from the war were concerned with
building a family and a career, not with dwelling on the horrors of the past.
. . . It did not seem to be an appropriate time to focus on a painful past, particularly a past which seemed to be of no direct concern to this country. This
event had transpired on another continent. It had been committed by another
country against "an-other" people. What relevance did it have for Americans?
(Lipstadt, 1996: 195–214)

[As for] the terms in which Americans of the mid-1950s were prepared to confront the Holocaust: a terrible event, yes, but ultimately not tragic or depressing; an experience shadowed by the specter of a cruel death, but at the same
time not without the ability to inspire, console, uplift. . . . Throughout the
late 1940s and well into the 50s, a prevalent attitude was to put all of "that" behind one and get on with life. (Rosenfeld, 1995: 37–8)

After the War, American Jewry turned – with great energy and generosity – to
liquidating the legacy of the Holocaust by caring for the survivors [who] were
urged to put the ghastly past behind them, to build new lives in their adopted
homes. . . . When a proposal for a Holocaust memorial in New York City
came before representatives of the leading Jewish organizations in the late
1940s, they unanimously rejected the idea: it would, they said, give currency to
the image of Jews as "helpless victims," an idea they wished to repudiate.
(Novick, 1994: 160)

It was neither emotional repression nor good moral sense that created the
early responses to the mass murder of the Jews. It was, rather, a system of collective representations that focused its beam of narrative light on the triumphant
expulsion of evil. Most Americans did not identify with the victims of the Jewish trauma. Far from being implicated in it, Americans had defeated those responsible for the mass murders and righteously engaged in restructuring the social and political arrangements that had facilitated them. This did not mean
that the mass murder of Jews was viewed with relativism or equanimity. According to the progressive narrative, it was America's solemn task to redeem the
sacrifice of this largest of all categories of Nazi victims. In postwar America, the
public redeemed the sacrifices of war by demanding the thorough de-Nazifica-
tion not only of German but of American society. As Sumner Welles eloquently
framed the issue a month after the GIs had entered the Nazi death camps,

the crimes committed by the Nazis and by their accomplices against the Jewish
people are indelible stains upon the whole of our modern civilization. . . .
They are stains which will shame our generation in the eyes of generations still
unborn. For we and our governments, to which we have entrusted power during

these years between the Great Wars, cannot shake off the responsibility for having permitted the growth of world conditions which made such horrors possible. The democracies cannot lightly attempt to shirk their responsibility. No recompense can be offered the dead. . . . But such measure of recompense as can be offered surely constitutes the moral obligation of the free peoples of the earth as soon as their victory is won. (Welles, 1945: 511)

## Purifying America and Redeeming
## the Murder of the Jews

Propelled by the logic of this progressive understanding of redemption, in America's immediate postwar years the public legitimation of anti-Semitism was repeatedly attacked and some of its central institutional manifestations destroyed. The longstanding anti-anti-Semitism framing the progressive narrative, and crystallized during the interwar years by leading figures in the American intellectual and cultural elite, culminated in the immediate postwar period in a massive shift of American public opinion on the Jewish question (Stember, 1966). Only days after the hostilities ceased, in response to an appeal from the National Council of Christians and Jews, the three candidates for mayor of New York City pledged to "refrain from appeals to racial and religious divisiveness during the campaign." One of them made explicit the connection of this public anti-anti-Semitism to the effort to remain connected to, and enlarge on, the meaning of America's triumph in the anti-Nazi war.

This election will be the first held in the City of New York since our victory over nazism and Japanese fascism. It will therefore be an occasion for a practical demonstration of democracy in action – a democracy in which all are equal citizens, in which there is not and never must be a second class citizenship and in which . . . the religion of a candidate must play no part in the campaign. (New York Times, October 1, 1945: 32)

In an influential article, Leonard Dinnerstein has documented the vastly heightened political activism of Jewish groups in the immediate postwar period from 1945 to 1948 (Dinnerstein, 1981–82). He records how these newly surfaced and often newly formed groups held conferences, wrote editorials, and issued specific proposals for legal and institutional changes. By 1950, these activities had successfully exposed and often defeated anti-Jewish quotas and, more generally, created an extraordinary shift in the practical and cultural position of American Jews. During the same month that New York's mayoral candidates announced their anti-anti-Semitism, the American Mercury published an article, "Discrimination in Medical Colleges," replete with graphs and copious documentation, detailing the existence of anti-Jewish quotas in some of America's most prestigious professional institutions. While the specific focus was anti-Jewish discrimination, these facts were narrated in terms of the over-arching promise of America and democracy. The story began with a vignette about "Leo, a bright and personable American lad" who "dreamed of becoming a great physician."

> [He] made an excellent scholastic record [but] upon graduation . . . his first application for admission to a medical school . . . was mysteriously turned down. He filed another and another—at eighty-seven schools—always with the same heartbreaking result . . . not one of the schools had the courage to inform Leo frankly that he was being excluded because he was a Jew. . . . The excuse for imposing a quota system usually advanced is that there ought to be some correlation between the number of physicians of any racial or religious strain and the proportion of that race or religion in the general population [but] the surface logic of this arithmetic collapses as soon as one subjects it to *democratic or sheerly human*, let alone scientific, tests. [It is] spurious and *un-American* arithmetic. (October, 1945: 391–9, italics added)[32]

Earlier that year, an "Independent Citizens Committee" had asked three hundred educators to speak out against restricting Jewish enrollment in the nation's schools. Ernest Hopkins, the president of Dartmouth College, refused, openly defending Dartmouth's Jewish quota on the grounds that German Nazism had been spurred because a large proportion of the German professions had become Jewish. A storm of public opprobrium followed Hopkins's remarks. The *New York Post* headlined, "Dartmouth Bars Jews 'To End Anti-Semitism,' Says Prexy." The next day, the rival tabloid, *PM,* placed Hopkins's picture side by side with the Nazi ideologue Alfred Rosenberg and accused the Dartmouth president of "spouting the Hitler-Rosenberg line" (quoted in "Sense or Nonsense?" *Time,* August 20, 1945: 92, italics added). In an article entitled "Anti-Semitism at Dartmouth," the *New Republic* brought a progressive perspective to the controversy by suggesting that it could bring "us a step nearer to amelioration of one of the outstanding blots on American civilization *today.*" Anti-semitism belonged to the outmoded past that had been shattered by the anti-Nazi war: "We can *no longer* afford the luxury of these *obsolete* myths of racial differentiation, Mr. Hopkins; if you don't believe it, ask Hitler" (August 20, 1945: 208–9, italics added).

In the years that followed, the fight against quotas continued to be informed by similar themes. In 1946, an educational sociologist wrote in the *American Scholar* that such restrictions were "in contradistinction to the *growing* realization which has come as a result of the war." Quotas must be abolished if postwar progress were to be made.

*Today,* our society as a whole sees the relationship between social welfare and prejudices which thwart the development of the capacities of individuals. This threat to the basic concepts of democracy is so plain that almost all of us, except the vested interests, have seen it. The question is whether or not the colleges and universities have seen it and are willing to bring their practices into line with *present day* insights, even though some of their most precious traditions be jeopardized. (Dodson, 1946: 268, italics added)

Similar connections between the anti-Nazi war, antiquotas, and the progress of anti-anti-Semitism informed another popular magazine article the following year: "It is extremely regrettable that *in 1946*, the children of [parents] who are returning from all parts of the world where they have been engaged in mortal combat to preserve democracy, are confronted with the same closed doors that greeted their 'alien' fathers" (Hart, 1947: 61). In 1949, *Collier's* published an article describing the "scores of college men to whom fraternities" for "'full-blooded Aryans' are a little nauseating *in this day.*" Quoting the finding of an Amherst College alumni committee that exclusive fraternities gave young men "a false and undemocratic sense of superiority," the article claimed that "the anti-discrimination movement is hopping from campus to campus" (Whitman, 1949: 34–5).

While Jewish voluntary organizations had begun to organize in 1943–45, they entered the American public sphere as aggressive political advocates only after 1945, an intervention that marked the first time Jews had forcefully entered the civil sphere as advocates for their own rather than others' causes. In the prewar period, and even less in earlier times, such an explicit and aggressively Jewish public intervention would certainly have been repelled; in fact, it would only have made anti-Semitism worse. In the postwar period, however, despite their failure to identify with the Jewish victims of Nazism, the American non-Jewish audience was determined to redeem them. If, as Dinnerstein writes, Jewish groups intended to "mobilize public opinion against intolerance, and [thus to] utilize the courts and legislative bodies" (Dinnerstein, 1981–1982: 137) in their anti-semitic fight, they were able to carry on these political activities only because postwar public opinion had already been defined as committed to "tolerance."

Progress toward establishing civil relations between religious and ethnic groups was woven into the patriotic postwar narratives of the nation's mass circulation magazines. *Better Homes and Gardens* ran such stories as "Do You Want Your Children to Be Tolerant?" "The old indifference and local absorption cannot continue. If we relapse into our *before-the-war* attitudes and limitations, war will burst upon us as suddenly and as unexpectedly as the atomic bomb fell upon the people of Hiroshima—and we shall be as helpless." (Buck, 1947: 135, italics added).

In another piece in *Better Homes and Gardens* the same year, "How to Stop the Hate Mongers in Your Home Town," a writer observed: "I suspect that many a decent German burgher, hearing tales of Nazi gangs, likewise shrugged off the implications of uncurbed racial and religious persecution" (Carter, 1947: 180). The following year, the *Saturday Evening Post* profiled "the story of the Jewish family of Jacob Golomb." The lengthy article concluded with the by now widely expected forward-looking line.

> As a family, the Golombs are more than just nice folks who lead busy, fruitful, decent lives; a family whose sons have sprung, in time of national emergency, with promptness to the defense of their country. As members of a race with a long history of persecution, they have kept the faith, since Abraham Golomb's time, that the United States really was, or *would soon be*, the land of the genuinely free. They are still convinced. (Perry, 1948: 96, italics added)

Four years later, America's most popular photo magazine published "*Life* Goes to a Bar Mitzvah: A Boy Becomes a Man" (October 13, 1952: 170–6).

The anti-anti-Semitism theme also entered popular culture through the movies. In the 1945 box office hit *Pride of the Marines*, the Jewish protagonist Larry Diamond chided a friend for pessimism about the possibility of eliminating prejudice in the postwar years. He did so by connecting their present situation to the progressive ideals that had sustained their anti-Nazi war: "Ah, come on, climb out of your foxholes, what's a matter you guys, don't you think anybody learned anything since 1930? Think everybody's had their eyes shut and brains in cold storage?" (Short, 1981: 161). Diamond goes on to remark that, if and when prejudice and repression dare to show their ugly heads in the postwar United States, he will fight to defeat them, just as he has learned to fight in the war: "I fought for me, for the right to live in the USA. And when I get back into civilian life, if I don't like the way things are going, O.K. it's my country; I'll stand on my own two legs and holler! If there's enough of us hollering we'll go places—Check?" (Short, 1981: 161). The narrative of progress is forcefully extended from the anti-Nazi war into the post-Nazi peace. Diamond had been "the pride of the marines," and the war's progressive narrative is fundamentally tied to assertions about the utopian telos of the United States. As the movie's closing music turns into "America the Beautiful," Diamond wraps it up this way: "One happy afternoon when God was feeling good, he sat down and thought of a rich beautiful country and he named it the USA. All of it, Al, the hills, the rivers, the lands, the whole works. Don't tell me we can't make it work in peace like we do in war. Don't tell me we can't pull together. Don't you see it guys, can't you see it?" (Short, 1981: 161–2).

Two years later, a movie promoting anti-anti-Semitism, *Gentleman's Agreement*, won the Academy Award for best motion picture, and another, *Crossfire*, had been nominated as well. Both are conspicuously progressive, forward-looking narratives. In the final dialogue of *Gentlemen's Agreement*, the film's future-oriented, utopian theme could not be more clear. "Wouldn't it be wonderful," Mrs. Green asks Phil, "if it turned out to be everybody's century, when people all over the world, free people, found a way to live together? I'd like to be around to see some of that, even a beginning" (quoted in Short, 1981: 180).[33]

As they had immediately before and during the war, "Jews" held symbolic pride of place in these popular culture narratives because their persecution had been preeminently associated with the Nazi evil. In fact it was not tolerance as such that the progressive narrative demanded but tolerance of the Jews.[34] Thus, despite their feelings of solidarity with their foreign coreligionists, Jewish leaders carefully refrained from publicly endorsing the wholesale lifting of antiimmigration quotas after 1945. They realized that the idea of immigration remained so polluted by association with stigmatized others that it might have the power to counteract the ongoing purification of Jewishness. In the preceding half century, antiimmigration and anti-Semitism had been closely linked, and Jews did not want to pollute "Jewishness" with this identity again. While demonstrating their support in private, Jewish leaders resolutely refused to make any public pronouncements against lifting the immigration quotas (Dinnerstein, 1981–82: 140).

What Dinnerstein has called the "turnabout in anti-Semitic feelings" represented the triumph over Nazism, not recognition of the Holocaust trauma. News about the mass murder, and any ruminations about it, disappeared from newspapers and magazines rather quickly after the initial reports about the camps' liberation, and the Nazis' Jewish victims came to be represented as displaced persons, potential immigrants, and potential settlers in Palestine, where a majority of Americans wanted to see a new, and redemptive, Jewish state. This interpretation suggests that it was by no means simply realpolitik that led President Truman to champion, against his former French and British allies, the postwar creation of Israel, the new Jewish state. The progressive narrative demanded a future-oriented renewal. Zionists argued that the Jewish trauma could be redeemed, that Jews could both sanctify the victims and put the trauma behind them, only if they returned to Jerusalem. According to the Zionist worldview, if Israel were allowed to exist, it would create a new race of confident and powerful Jewish farmer-warriors who would redeem the anti-Jewish atrocities by developing such an imposing military power that the massive murdering of the Jews would never, anywhere in the world, be allowed to happen again. In important respects, it was this convergence of progressive narratives in relation to the war and the Jewish mass killings that led the postwar paths of the United States and the state of Israel to become so fundamentally intertwined. Israel would have to prosper and survive for the redemptive telos of America's progressive narrative to be maintained.

These cultural-sociological considerations do not suggest that the postwar American fight against anti-Semitism was in any way morally inauthentic. It was triggered by grassroots feelings as deep as those that had motivated the earlier anti-Nazi fight. When one looks at these powerful new arguments against anti-Semitism, it is only retrospectively surprising to realize that the "atrocities" revealed in 1945—the events and experiences that defined the trauma for European Jews—figure hardly at all. This absence is explained by the powerful symbolic logic of the progressive narrative, which already had been established in the prewar period. With the victory in 1945, the United States got down to the work of establishing the new world order. In creating a Nazi-free future, Jewishness came for the first time to be analogically connected with core American symbols of "democracy" and "nation."

In the course of this postwar transformation, American Jews also became identified with democracy in a more primordial and less universalistic way, namely as newly minted, patriotic representations of the nation. "After 1945," a leading historian of that period remarks, "other Americans no longer viewed the Jews as merely another of the many exotic groups within America's ethnic and religious mosaic. Instead, they were now seen as comprising one of the country's three major religions" (Shapiro, 1992: 28). This patriotic-national definition was expressed by the Jewish theologian Will Herberg's insistence on the "Judeo-Christian" rather than "Christian" identity of the religious heritage of the United States (53).[35] As I have indicated, what motivated this intense identification of anti-anti-Semitism with the American nation was neither simple emotional revulsion for the horrors of the Jewish mass killings nor common-sense morality. It was, rather, the progressive narrative frame. To end anti-Semitism, in President Truman's words, was to place America alongside "the moral forces of the world" (quoted in Shapiro, 1992: 143). It was to redeem those who had sacrificed themselves for the American nation, and, according to the teleology of the progressive narrative, this emphatically included the masses of murdered European Jews.

The critical point is this: What was a trauma for the victims was not a trauma for the audience.[36] In documenting this for the American case, I have examined the principal carrier group for the progressive narrative, the nation that in the immediate postwar world most conspicuously took the lead in "building the new world upon the ashes of the old." I have shown that the social agents, both Jewish and non-Jewish Americans, who took the lead in reconstructing a new moral order, dedicated themselves to redeeming those who had been sacrificed to the anti-Nazi struggle, and most especially to the Jewish victims, by putting an end to anti-Semitism in the United States. The goal was focused not on the Holocaust but on the need to purge postwar society of Nazi-like pollution.

## JEWISH MASS MURDER UNDER THE TRAGIC NARRATIVE

I will now show how a different kind of narrative developed in relation to the Nazis' mass murder of the Jews, one that gave the evil it represented significantly greater symbolic weight. I will treat this new culture structure both as cause and effect. After reconstructing its internal contours, I will examine the kind of "symbolic action" it caused and how these new meanings compelled the trauma of the mass murders to be seen in a radically different way, with significant consequences for social and political action that continue to ramify to the present day.[37] After completing this analytic reconstruction of the new cultural configuration, I will proceed to a concrete examination of how it was constructed in real historical time, looking at changes in carrier groups, moral contexts, and social structural forces. Finally, I will examine some of the long-term ramifications of the highly general, decontextualized, and universal status that the trauma of the Holocaust came to assume.

### The New Culture Structure

Ever since Dilthey defined the method specific to the *Geisteswissenschaften*— literally "sciences of the spirit" but typically translated as "human sciences"—it has been clear that what distinguishes the hermeneutic from the natural scientific method is the challenge of penetrating beyond the external form to inner meaning of actions, events, and institutions. Yet to enter into this thicket of subjectivity is not to embrace impressionism and relativism. As Dilthey emphasized, meanings are governed by structures just as surely as economic and political processes; they are just governed in different ways. Every effort at interpretive social science must begin with the reconstruction of this culture structure.[38]

#### Deepening Evil

In the formation of this new culture structure, the coding of the Jewish mass killings as evil remained, but its weighting substantially changed. It became burdened with extraordinary gravitas. The symbolization of the Jewish mass killings became generalized and reified, and in the process the evil done to the Jews became separated from the profanation of Nazism per se. Rather than seeming to "typify" Nazism, or even the nefarious machinations of any particular social movement, political formation, or historical time, the mass killings came to be seen as not being typical of anything at all. They came to be understood as a unique, historically unprecedented event, as evil on a scale that had never occurred before.[39] The mass killings entered into universal history, becoming a "world-historical" event in Hegel's original sense, an event whose emergence onto the world stage threatened, or promised, to change the fundamental course of the world.[40] In the introduction to an English collection of his essays on Nazi history and the Holocaust, the German-Israeli historian Dan Diner observes that "well into the 1970s, wide-ranging portraits of the epoch would grant the Holocaust a modest (if any) mention."[41] By contrast, "it now tends to fill the entire picture. . . . The growing centrality of the Holocaust has altered the entire warp and woof of our sense of the passing century. . . . The incriminated event has thus become the epoch's marker, its final and inescapable wellspring" (Diner, 2000: 1).

The Jewish mass killings became what we might identify, in Durkheimian terms, as a sacred-evil, an evil that recalled a trauma of such enormity and horror that it had to be radically set apart from the world and all of its other traumatizing events. It became inexplicable in ordinary, rational terms. As part of the Nazi scheme of world domination, the Jewish mass killing was heinous, but at least it had been understandable. As a sacred-evil, set apart from ordinary evil things, it had become mysterious and inexplicable. One of the first to comment on, and thus to characterize, this postprogressive inexplicability was the Marxist historian Isaac Deutscher. This great biographer of Trotsky, who had already faced the consequences of Stalinism for the myth of communist progress, was no doubt already conditioned to see the tragic dimensions of the Holocaust. In 1968, in "The Jewish Tragedy and the Historian," Deutscher suggested that comprehending the Holocaust "will not be just a matter of time." He meant that there would not be progress in this regard.

> I doubt whether even in a thousand years people will understand Hitler, Auschwitz, Majdanek, and Treblinka better than we do now. Will they have a better historical perspective? On the contrary, posterity may even understand it all even less than we do. Who can analyze the motives and the interests behind the enormities of Auschwitz. . . . We are confronted here by a huge and ominous mystery of the generation of the human character that will forever baffle and terrify mankind. (Deutscher, 1968: 163)

For Deutscher, such a huge and mysterious evil, so resistant to the normal progress of human rationality, suggested tragedy and art, not scientific fact-gathering. "Perhaps a modern Aeschylus and Sophocles could cope with this theme," he suggested, "but they would do so on a level different from that of historical interpretation and explanation" (Deutscher, 1968: 164). Geoffrey Hartman, the literary theorist who has directed Yale University's Video Archive for the Holocaust since 1981 and has been a major participant in postsixties discussions of the trauma, points to the enigma that, while no historical event has ever "been so thoroughly documented and studied," social and moral "understanding comes and goes; it has not been progressive." By way of explaining this lack of progress, Hartman acknowledges that

> The scholars most deeply involved often admit an "excess" that remains dark and frightful. . . . Something in the . . . Shoah remains dark at the heart of the event. . . . A comparison with the French Revolution is useful. The sequence *French Revolution: Enlightenment* cannot be matched by *Holocaust: Enlightenment*. What should be placed after the colon? "Eclipse of Enlightenment" or "Eclipse of God"? (Hartman, 1996: 3–4)

To this day the Holocaust is almost never referred to without asserting its inexplicability. In the spring of 1999, a *New York Times* theater reviewer began his remarks on *The Gathering*, a newly opened drama, by asserting that "the profound, agonizing mystery of the Holocaust echoes through the generations and across international borders," presenting "an awesome human and theological enigma as an old century prepares to give way to a new millennium" (van Gelder, 1999: 1).

This separateness of sacred-evil demanded that the trauma be renamed, for the concept of "mass murder" and even the notion of "genocide" now appeared unacceptably to normalize the trauma, to place it too closely in proximity to the banal and mundane. In contrast, despite the fact that the word "Holocaust" did have a formally established English meaning—according to the *Oxford English Dictionary*, "something wholly burnt up" (Garber & Zuckerman, 1989: 199)—it no longer performed this sign function in everyday speech. Rather the term entered into ordinary English usage, in the early 1960s, as a proper rather than a common noun.[42] Only several years after the Nazis' mass murder did Israelis begin to employ the Hebrew word *shoah*, the term by which the Torah evoked the kind of extraordinary sufferings God had periodically consigned to the Jews. In the official English translation of the phrase "Nazi *shoah*" in the preamble to the 1948 Israeli Declaration of Independence, one can already find the reference to "Nazi holocaust"(Novick, 1999: 132). With the decline of the progressive narrative, in other words, as "Holocaust" became the dominant representation for the trauma, it implied the sacral mystery, the "awe-fullness," of the transcendental tradition. "Holocaust" became part of contemporary language as an English symbol that stood for that thing that could not be named.[43] As David Roskies once wrote, "it was precisely the nonreferential quality of 'Holocaust' that made it so appealing" (quoted in Garber & Zuckerman, 1989: 201).

This new linguistic identity allowed the mass killings of the Jews to become what might be called a bridge metaphor: it provided the symbolic extension so necessary if the trauma of the Jewish people were to become a trauma for all humankind. The other necessary ingredient, psychological identification, was not far behind. It depended on configuring this newly weighted symbolization of evil in a different narrative frame.

### Suffering, Catharsis, and Identification

The darkness of this new postwar symbolization of evil cast a shadow over the progressive story that had thus far narrated its course. The story of redeeming Nazism's victims by creating a progressive and democratic world order could be called an ascending narrative, for it pointed to the future and suggested confidence that things would be better over time. Insofar as the mass killings were defined as a Holocaust, and insofar as it was the very emergence of this sacred-evil, not its eventual defeat, that threatened to become emblematic of "our time,"[44] the progressive narrative was blocked, and in some manner overwhelmed, by a sense of historical descent, by a falling away from the good. Recent Holocaust commentators have drawn this conclusion time and again. According to the progressive narrative, the Nazis' mass murder of the Jews would provide a lesson for all humankind, a decisive learning process on the way to a better world. Reflecting on the continuing fact of genocidal mass murders in the post-Holocaust world, Hartman revealingly suggests that "these developments raise questions about our species, our preconceptions that we are the human, the 'family of man.' Or less dramatically, we wonder about the veneer of progress, culture, and educability."

In dramaturgical terms, the issue concerns the position occupied by evil in the historical narrative. When Aristotle first defined tragedy in the *Poetics,* he linked what I have here called the weight of the representation of suffering to temporal location of an event in plot:

> Tragedy is the representation of a complete, i.e., whole action *which has some magnitude* (for there can be a whole action without magnitude). A whole is that which has a beginning, a middle and a conclusion. A beginning is that which itself does not of necessity follow something else, but after which there naturally is, or comes into being, something else. A conclusion, conversely, is that which itself naturally follows something else, either of necessity or for the most part, but has nothing else after it. A middle is that which itself naturally follows something else, and has something else after it. Well-constructed plots, then, should neither begin from a random point nor conclude at a random point, but should use the elements we have mentioned [i.e., beginning, middle and conclusion]. (Aristotle, 1987: 3.2.1, italics added)

In the progressive narrative frame, the Jewish mass killings were not an end but a beginning. They were part of the massive trauma of World War II, but in the postwar period they and related incidents of Nazi horror were regarded as a birth trauma, a crossroads in a chronology that would eventually be set right. By contrast, the newly emerging world-historical status of the mass murders suggested that they represented an end point, not a new beginning, a death trauma rather than a trauma of birth, a cause for despair, not the beginning of hope. In place of the progressive story, then, there began to emerge the narrative of tragedy. The end point of a narrative defines its telos. In the new tragic understanding of the Jewish mass murder, suffering, not progress, became the telos toward which the narrative was aimed.

In this tragic narrative of sacred-evil, the Jewish mass killings become not an event in history but an archetype, an event out-of-time. As archetype, the evil evoked an experience of trauma greater than anything that could be defined by religion, race, class, region—indeed, by any conceivable sociological configuration or historical conjuncture. This transcendental status, this separation from the specifics of any particular time or space, provided the basis for psychological identification on an unprecedented scale. The contemporary audience cares little about the second and third installments of Sophocles' archetypal story of Oedipus, the tragic hero. What we are obsessed with is Oedipus's awful, unrecognized, and irredeemable mistake, how he finally comes to recognize his responsibility for it, and how he blinds himself from guilt when he understands its full meaning. Tragic narratives focus attention not on some future effort at reversal or amelioration—"progress," in the terms I have employed here—but on the nature of the crime, its immediate aftermath, and on the motives and relationships that led up to it.

A tragic narrative offers no redemption in the traditionally religious, Judeo-Christian sense.[45] There is no happy ending, no sense that something else could have been done, and no belief that the future could, or can, necessarily be changed. Indeed, protagonists are tragic precisely because they have failed to exert control over events. They are in the grip of forces larger than themselves—impersonal, even inhuman forces that often are not only beyond control but, during the tragic action itself, beyond comprehension. This sense of being overwhelmed by unjust force or fate explains the abjection and helplessness that permeates the genre of tragedy and the experience of pity it arouses.

Instead of redemption through progress, the tragic narrative offers what Nietzsche called the drama of the eternal return. As it now came to be understood, there was no "getting beyond" the story of the Holocaust. There was only the possibility of returning to it: not transcendence but catharsis. Hartman resists "the call for closure" on just these grounds. "Wherever we look, the events of 1933–1945 cannot be relegated to the past. They are not over; anyone who comes in contact with them is gripped, and finds detachment difficult." Quoting from Lawrence Langer's book *Admitting the Holocaust*, Hartman suggests that "those who study it must 'reverse history and progress and find a way of restoring to the imagination of coming generations the depth of the catastrophe'" (Hartman, 1996: 2, 5).

As Aristotle explained, catharsis clarifies feeling and emotion. It does so not by allowing the audience to separate itself from the story's characters, a separation, according to Frye, that defines the very essence of comedy (Frye, 1971 [1957]). Rather, catharsis clarifies feeling and emotion by forcing the audience to identify with the story's characters, compelling them to experience their suffering with them and to learn, as often they did not, the true causes of their death. That we survive and they do not, that we can get up and leave the theater while they remain forever prostrate—this allows the possibility of catharsis, that strange combination of cleansing and relief, that humbling feeling of having been exposed to the dark and sinister forces that lie just beneath the surface of human life and of having survived.[46] We seek catharsis because our identification with the tragic narrative compels us to experience dark and sinister forces that are also inside of ourselves, not only inside others. We "redeem" tragedy by experiencing it, but, despite this redemption, we do not get over it. Rather, to achieve redemption we are compelled to dramatize and redramatize, experience and reexperience the archetypal trauma. We pity the victims of the trauma, identifying and sympathizing with their horrible fate. Aristotle argued that the tragic genre could be utilized only for the "sorts of occurrence [that] arouse dread, or compassion in us" (Aristotle, 1987: 4.1.2). The blackness of tragedy can be achieved only if, "first and foremost, the [suffering] characters should be good," for "the plot should be constructed in such a way that, even without seeing it, someone who hears about the incidents will shudder and feel pity at the outcome, as someone may feel upon hearing the plot of the Oedipus" (Aristotle, 1987: 4.2.1, 4.1.1.3). It is not only the fact of identification, however, but its complexity that makes the experience of trauma as tragedy so central to the assumption of moral responsibility, for we identify not only with the victims but with the perpetrators as well. The creation of this cultural form allows the psychological activity of internalization rather than projection, acceptance rather than displacement.[47]

### The Trauma Drama of Eternal Return

In the tragic narration of the Holocaust, the primal event became a "trauma drama" that the "audience" returned to time and time again. This became, paradoxically, the only way to ensure that such an event would happen "never again." This quality of compulsively returning to the trauma drama gave the story of the Holocaust a mythical status that transformed it into the archetypical sacred-evil of our time. Insofar as it achieved this status as a dominant myth, the tragedy of the Holocaust challenged the ethical self-identification, the self-esteem, of modernity—indeed, the very self-confidence that such a thing as "modern progress" could continue to exist. For to return to the trauma drama of the Holocaust, to identify over and over again with the suffering and helplessness of its victims, was in some sense to give that confidence-shattering event a continuing existence in contemporary life. It was, in effect, to acknowledge that it *could* happen again.

In this way, the tragic framing of the Holocaust fundamentally contributed to postmodern relativism and disquiet. Because the tragic replaced the progressive narrative of the Nazi mass murder, the ethical standards protecting good from evil seemed not nearly as powerful as modernity's confident pronouncements had promised they would be. When the progressive narrative had organized understanding, the Nazi crimes had been temporalized as "medieval," in order to contrast them with the supposedly civilizing standards of modernity. With the emergence of the more tragic perspective, the barbarism was lodged within the essential nature of modernity itself.[48] Rather than maintaining and perfecting modernity, as the postwar progressive narrative would have it, the path to a more just and peaceful society seemed now to lead to postmodern life (Bauman, 1989).[49]

It would be wrong, however, to imagine that because a trauma drama lies at the center of the Holocaust's tragic narration, with all the ambition of exciting pity and emotional catharsis that this implies, that this lachrymose narrative and symbol actually became disconnected from the ethical and the good.[50] While it is undeniable that the Jewish mass killings came to assume a dramaturgical form, their significance hardly became aestheticized, that is, turned into a free-floating, amoral symbol whose function was to entertain rather than to instruct.[51] The events of the Holocaust were not dramatized for the sake of drama itself but rather to provide what Martha Nussbaum once described as "the social benefits of pity" (Nussbaum, 1992).[52] The project of renaming, dramatizing, reifying, and ritualizing the Holocaust contributed to a moral remaking of the (post)modern (Western) world. The Holocaust story has been told and retold in response not only to an emotional need but a moral ambition. Its characters, its plot, and its pitiable denouement have been transformed into a less nationally bound, less temporally specific, and more universal drama. This dramatic universalization has deepened contemporary sensitivity to social evil. The trauma drama's message, like that of every tragedy, is that evil is inside all of us, and in every society. If we are all the victims, and all the perpetrators, then there is no audience that can legitimately distance itself from collective suffering, either from its victims or its perpetrators.

This psychological identification with the Jewish mass killings and the symbolic extension of its moral implications beyond the immediate parties involved has stimulated an unprecedented universalization of political and moral responsibility. To have created this symbol of sacred-evil in contemporary time, then, is to have so enlarged the human imagination that it is capable, for the first time in human history, of identifying, understanding, and judging the kinds of genocidal mass killings in which national, ethnic, and ideological groupings continue to engage today.[53] This enlargement has made it possible to comprehend that heinous prejudice with the intent to commit mass murder is not something from an earlier, more "primitive" time or a different, "foreign" place, committed by people with values we do not share. The implication of the tragic narrative is not that progress has become impossible. It has had the salutary effect, rather, of demonstrating that progress is much more difficult to achieve than moderns once believed. If progress is to be made, morality must be universalized beyond any particular time and place.[54]

The New Social Processes

Most Western people today would readily agree with the proposition that the Holocaust was a tragic, devastating event in human history. Surely it was, and is. One implication of my discussion thus far, however, is that this perception of its moral status is not a natural reflection of the event itself. The Jewish mass killings first had to be dramatized—as a tragedy. Some of the most eloquent and influential Holocaust survivors and interpreters have disagreed sharply, and moralistically, with this perspective, insisting on that fictional representations must not be allowed to influence the perception of historical reality. In 1978, Elie Wiesel excoriated NBC for producing the *Holocaust* miniseries, complaining that "it transforms an ontological event into soap-opera" and that "it is all make-believe." Because "the Holocaust transcends history," Wiesel argued, "it cannot be explained nor can it be visualized" (Wiesel, 1978: 1). In response to *Schindler's List*, Claude Lanzman said much the same thing. Writing that the Holocaust "is above all unique in that it erects a ring of fire around itself," he claimed that "fiction is a transgression" and that "there are some things that cannot and should not be represented" (quoted in Hartman, 1996: 84).[55]

I am obviously taking a very different perspective here. Thus far I have reconstructed the internal patterning of the culture structure that allowed the new, tragic dramatization to take place. I would like now to turn to the historically specific social processes, both symbolic and social structural, that made this new patterning attractive and, eventually, compelling. While my reference here is primarily to the United States, I believe some version of this analysis also applies to those other Western societies that attempted to reconstruct liberal democracies after World War II.[56]

I have earlier shown how the struggle against anti-Semitism became one of the primary vehicles by which the progressive narrative redeemed those who had been sacrificed in the war against Nazi evil. Fighting anti-Semitism was not the only path to redemption, of course; for America and its victorious allies, there was a whole new world to make. At the same time, the struggle against anti-Semitism had a special importance. The understanding of Nazism as an absolute evil stemmed not only from its general commitment to anticivil domination but also from its effort to legitimate such violence according to the principles of prejudice and primordiality. Because the Jewish people were by far the most conspicuous primordial target, symbolic logic dictated that to be anti-Nazi was to be anti-anti-Semitic.[57]

As I have suggested earlier, the rhetorics and policies of this anti-anti-Semitism did not require that non-Jewish Americans positively identify with Jews, any more than the role that the Holocaust played in the postwar progressive narrative depended on a sense of identification with the weary and bedraggled survivors in the concentration camps themselves. To narrate the Holocaust in a tragic manner, however, did depend on just such an identification being made. This identification was a long time in coming, and it depended on a number of factors unrelated to public opinion and cultural change.[58] Nonetheless, it certainly depended, in addition to such social structural factors, on the fact that the cultural idiom and the organizational apparatus of anti-Semitism had, indeed, been attacked and destroyed in the early "progressive" postwar years, and that, for the first time in American history, Jews seemed, to a majority of Christian Americans, not that much different from anybody else.

As this tragic narrative crystallized, the Holocaust drama became, for an increasing number of Americans, and for significant proportions of Europeans as well, the most widely understood and emotionally compelling trauma of the twentieth century. These bathetic events, once experienced as traumatic only by Jewish victims, became generalized and universalized. Their representation no longer referred to events that took place at a particular time and place but to a trauma that had became emblematic, and iconic, of human suffering as such. The horrific trauma of the Jews became the trauma of all humankind.[59]

## The Production of New Social Dramas

How was this more generalized and universalized status achieved? Social narratives are not composed by some hidden hand of history. Nor do they appear all at once. The new trauma drama emerged in bits and pieces. It was a matter of this story and that, this scene and that scene from this movie and that book, this television episode and that theater performance, this photographic capturing of a moment of torture and suffering. Each of these glimpses into what Meyer Levin had called, in April 1945, "the very crawling inside of the vicious heart" contributed some element to the construction of this new sensibility, which highlighted suffering, helplessness, and dark inevitability and which, taken together and over time, reformulated the mass killing of the Jews as the most tragic event in Western history. It is not the purpose of this discussion to provide anything approaching a thick description of this process of symbolic reconstruction but only to identify the signposts along this new route and the changing "countryside" that surrounded it.

### Personalizing the Trauma and Its Victims

In the course of constructing and broadcasting the tragic narrative of the Holocaust, there were a handful of actual dramatizations—in books, movies, plays, and television shows—that played critically important roles. Initially formulated for an American audience, they were distributed worldwide, seen by tens and possibly hundreds of millions of persons, and talked incessantly about by high-, middle-, and lowbrow audiences alike. In the present context, what seems most important about these dramas is that they achieved their effect by personalizing the trauma and its characters. This personalization brought the trauma drama "back home." Rather than depicting the events on a vast historical scale, rather than focusing on larger-than-life leaders, mass movements, organizations, crowds, and ideologies, these dramas portrayed the events in terms of small groups, families and friends, parents and children, brothers and sisters. In this way, the victims of trauma became everyman and everywoman, every child and every parent.

The prototype of this personalizing genre was Anne Frank's famous *Diary*. First published in Holland in 1947,[60] the edited journals appeared in English in 1952. They became the basis for a Pulitzer Prize–winning Broadway play in 1955 and in 1959 a highly acclaimed and equally popular but immensely more widely influential Hollywood movie. This collective representation began in Europe as the journal recorded by a young Dutch girl in hiding from the Nazis and evolved, via a phase of Americanization, into a universal symbol of suffering and transcendence. This transmogrification was possible, in the first place, precisely because Anne's daily jottings focused less on the external events of war and Holocaust—from which she was very much shut off—than on her inner psychological turmoil and the human relationships of those who shared her confinement. Anne's father, Otto Frank, the only family member surviving the camps, supervised the publications and dramatizations of his daughter's journals, and he perceived very clearly the relation between Anne's personal focus and the *Diary*'s potentially universalizing appeal. Writing to Meyer Shapiro, a potential dramatist who insisted, by contrast, on the specifically Jewish quality of the reminiscence, Otto Frank replied that "as to the Jewish side you are right that I do not feel the same you do. . . . I always said, that Anne's book is not a war book. War is the background. It is not a Jewish book either, though [a] Jewish sphere, sentiment and surrounding is the background. . . . It is read and understood more by gentiles than in Jewish circles. So do not make a Jewish play out of it" (quoted in Doneson, 1987: 152).[61] When dramatists for the *Diary* were finally chosen—Francis Goodrich and Albert Hackett—Frank criticized their initial drafts on similar grounds.

> Having read thousands of reviews and hundreds of personal letters about Anne's book from different countries in the world, I know what creates the impression of it on people and their impressions ought to be conveyed by the play to the public. Young people identify themselves very frequently with Anne in their struggle during puberty and the problems of the relations [between] mother-daughter are existing all over the world. These and the love affair with Peter attract young people, whereas parents, teachers, and psychologists learn about the inner feelings of the young generation. When I talked to Mrs. [Eleanor] Roosevelt about the book, she urged me to give permission for [the] play and film as only then we could reach the masses and influence them by the mission of the book which she saw in Anne's wish to work for mankind, to achieve something valuable still after her death, her horror against war and discrimination. (quoted in Doneson, 1987: 153)

This impulse to facilitate identification and moral extension prompted the dramatists to translate into English the *Diary*'s pivotal Hanukkah song, which was sung, and printed, in the original Hebrew in the earlier book version. They explained their reasoning in a letter to Frank. To have left the song in its original Hebrew, they wrote, would set the characters in the play apart from the people watching them . . . for the majority of our audience is not Jewish. And the thing that we have striven for, toiled for, fought for throughout the whole play is to make the audience understand and identify themselves . . . to make them one with them . . . that will make them feel "that, but for the grace of God, might have been I." (quoted in Doneson, 1987: 154)

Frank agreed, affirming that it "was my point of view to try to bring Anne's message to as many people as possible even if there are some who think it a sacrilege" from a religious point of view (quoted in Doneson, 1987: 154). Years later, after the unprecedented success of both the theatre and screen plays, the dramatists continued to justify their decision to abandon Hebrew in the dramaturgic terms of facilitating psychological identification and symbolic extension.

What we all of us hoped, and prayed for, and what we are devoutly thankful to have achieved, is an identification of the audience with the people in hiding. They are seen, not as some strange people, but persons like themselves, thrown into this horrible situation. With them they suffer the deprivations, the terrors, the moments of tenderness, of exaltation and courage beyond belief. (quoted in Doneson, 1987: 155)

In the course of the 1960s, Anne Frank's tragic story laid the basis for psychological identification and symbolic extension on a mass scale. In 1995, the director of Jewish Studies at Indiana University reported that

The Diary of a Young Girl is . . . widely read in American schools, and American youngsters regularly see the stage and film versions as well. Their teachers encourage them to identify with Anne Frank and to write stories, essays, and poems about her. Some even see her as a kind of saint and pray to her. During their early adolescent years, many American girls view her story as their story, her fate as somehow bound up with their fate. (Rosenfeld, 1995: 37)

The symbolic transformation effected by Anne Frank's Diary established the dramatic parameters and the stage for the rush of books, television shows, and movies that in the decades following crystallized the mass murder of the Jews as the central episode in a tragic rather than progressive social narrative. As this new genre became institutionalized, representation of Nazism and World War II focused less and less on the historical actors who had once been considered central. In 1953 the acclaimed Billy Wilder movie Stalag 17 had portrayed the grueling plight of U.S. soldiers in a German prisoner-of-war camp. It never mentioned the Jews (Shapiro, 1992: 4). In the early 1960s, a widely popular evening television show, *Hogan's Heroes* also portrayed American soldiers in a Nazi prison. It didn't mention "Jews" either. Indeed, the prison camp functioned as a site for comedy, lampooning the misadventures arising from the casual intermixing of Americans with Nazi camp guards and often portraying the latter as bemusing, well-intended buffoons. By the late 1960s, neither comedy nor romance were genres that audiences felt comfortable applying to that earlier historical time. Nor was it possible to leave out of any dramatization what by then were acknowledged to be the period's central historical actor, the concentration camp Jews.[62]

This transition was solidified in Western popular culture by the miniseries *Holocaust*, the stark family drama that unfolded over successive evening nights to a massive American audience in April 1978. This four-part, nine-and-a-half-hour drama, watched by nearly one hundred million Americans, personalized the grisly and famous landmarks of the Third Reich, following ten years in the lives of two fictional families, one assimilated Jews, the other that of a high-ranking SS official.

This extraordinary public attention was repeated, to even greater cathartic effect, when the bathetic drama was later broadcast to recordbreaking television audiences in Germany.[63] German critics, commentators, and large sections of the pubic at large were transfixed by what German commentators described as "the most controversial series of all times" and as "the series that moved the world." During and after this German broadcast, which was preceded by careful public preparation and accompanied by extensive private and public discussion, German social scientists conducted polls and interviews to trace its remarkable effects. They discovered that the resulting shift in public opinion had put a stop to a burgeoning "Hitler revival" and quelled longstanding partisan demands for "balance" in the presentation of the Jewish mass murder. In the wake of the drama, neutralizing terms like "the Final Solution" gave way in German popular and academic discussion to the English term *Holocaust*, and the German Reichstag removed the statute of limitations on Nazis who had participated in what were now defined not as war crimes but as crimes against humanity. The trauma drama thus continued to work its universalizing effects.[64]

### *Enlarging the Circle of Perpetrators*

Corresponding to the personalization that expanded identification with the victims of the tragedy, a new understanding developed of the perpetrators of the Holocaust that removed them from their historically specific particularities and made them into universal figures with whom members of widely diverse groups felt capable not of sympathizing but of identifying. The critical event initiating this reconsideration was undoubtedly the 1961 trial of Adolph Eichmann in Jerusalem. Here was a personal and singular representation of the Nazis' murders brought back into the present from the abstract mists of historical time, compelled to "face the music" after being captured by Israeli security forces in a daring extralegal mission right out of a spy novel or science fiction book. The trial received extraordinary press coverage in the United States. That summer, Gallup conducted a series of in-depth interviews with five hundred randomly selected residents of Oakland, California, and found that 84 percent of those sampled met the minimum criterion for awareness of this faraway event, a striking statistic, given American indifference to foreign affairs (Lipstadt, 1996: 212, n. 54). At least seven books were published about Eichmann and his trial in the following year (196).

The first legal confrontation with the Holocaust since Nuremburg, the trial was staged by Israel not to generalize away from the originating events but to get back to them. As Prime Minister Ben-Gurion put it, the trial would give "the generation that was born and educated after the Holocaust in Israel . . . an opportunity to get acquainted with the details of this tragedy about which they knew so little" (Braun, 1994: 183). The lessons were to be drawn from, and directed to, particular places and particular peoples, to Germany, the Nazis, Israel, and the Jews—in Ben-Gurion's words, to "the dimensions of the tragedy which *our people* experienced" (Lipstadt, 1996: 213, italics added). By the time it was over, however, the Eichmann trial paradoxically had initiated a massive universalization of Nazi evil, best captured by Hannah Arendt's enormously controversial insistence that the trial compelled recognition of the "banality of evil." This framing of Nazi guilt became highly influential, even as it was sharply and bitterly disputed by Jews and non-Jews alike. For as a banally evil person, Eichmann could be "everyman." Arendt herself had always wanted to make just such a point. In her earliest reaction to the Nazi murders, the philosopher had expressed horror and astonishment at the Nazis' absolute inhumanity. For this she was rebuked by her mentor and friend Karl Jaspers, who cautioned against making the Nazis into "monsters" and "supermen." To do so, Jaspers warned, would merely confirm the Nazis in their grandiose Nietzchean fantasies and relieve others of responsibility as well.[65] Because of Arendt's singular influence, the antagonists in the trauma began to seem not so different from anybody else.[66] The trial and its aftermath eventually became framed in a manner that narrowed the once great distance between postwar democratic audience and evil Nazis, connecting them rather than isolating them from one another. This connection between audience and antagonist intensified the trauma's tragic dramaturgy.

During this same period, other forces also had the effect of widening the circle of "perpetrators." Most spectacularly, there was Stanley Milgram's experiment demonstrating that ordinary, well-educated college students would "just follow the orders" of professional authority, even to the point of gravely endangering the lives of innocent people. These findings raised profoundly troubling questions about the "good nature" of all human beings and the democratic capacity of any human society. Milgram appeared on the cover of *Time* magazine, and "the Milgram experiment" became part of the folklore of the 1960s. It generalized the capacity for radical evil, first demonstrated by the Nazis, to the American population at large, synergistically interacting with the symbolic reconstruction of perpetrators that Arendt on Eichman had begun. In one interview Milgram conducted with a volunteer after he had revealed to him the true nature of the experiment, the volunteer remarked: "As my wife said: 'You can call yourself Eichmann'" (quoted in Novick, 1999: 137).[67]

In the decades that followed, other powerful cultural reconstructions of the perpetrators followed in this wake. In 1992, Christopher Browning published a widely discussed historical ethnography called *Ordinary Men: Reserve Police Battalion 101 and the Final Solution in Poland* (Browning, 1992), which focused on the everyday actions and motives of Germans who were neither members of the professional military nor particularly ideological but who nonetheless carried out systematic and murderous cleansings of the Jews. When four years later Daniel Goldhagen published *Hitler's Willing Executioners: Ordinary Germans and the Holocaust* (Goldhagen, 1996), his aim was to shift blame back to what he described as the unprecedented and particular kind of anti-Semitism, what he called "eliminationist," of the Germans themselves. Browning's critical response to Goldhagen was based on historical evidence, but it also decried the moral particularity that Goldhagen's argument seemed to entail. Indeed, Browning connected his empirical findings about the "ordinariness" of perpetrators to the necessity for universalizing the moral implications of Nazi crimes, and in doing so he pointed all the way back to Milgram's earlier findings.

> What allowed the Nazis to mobilize and harness the rest of society to the mass murder of European Jewry? Here I think that we historians need to turn to the insights of social psychology—the study of pyschological reactions to social situations. . . . We must ask, what really is a human being? We must give up the comforting and distancing notions that the perpetrators of the Holocaust were fundamentally a different kind of people because they were products of a radically different culture. (Browning, 1996: A72)[68]

In the realm of popular culture, Steven Spielberg's blockbuster movie *Schindler's List* must also be considered in this light. In a subtle but unmistakable manner, the movie departicularizes the perpetrators by showing the possibilities that "even Germans" could be good.[69]

### Losing Control of the Means of Symbolic Production

It was in this context of tragic transformation—as personalization of the drama increased identification beyond the Jewish victims themselves, and as the sense of moral culpability became fundamentally widened beyond the Nazis themselves—that the United States government, and the nation's authoritative interlocutors, lost control over the telling of the Holocaust story. When the American government and its allies defeated Nazi Germany in 1945 and seized control over strategic evidence from the death camps, they had taken control of the representation process away from the Nazis and assured that the Jewish mass murder would be presented an anti-Nazi way. In this telling of this story, naturally enough, the former Allies—America most powerfully but Britain and France as well—presented themselves as the moral protagonists, purifying themselves as heroic carriers of the good. As the 1960s unfolded, the Western democracies were forced to concede this dominant narrative position. This time around, however, control over the means of symbolic production changed hands as much for cultural reasons as by the force of arms.[70]

In the "critical years" from the mid-1960s to the end of the 1970s, the United States experienced a sharp decline in its political, military, and moral prestige. It was during this period that, in the eyes of tens of millions of Americans and others, the domestic and international opposition to America's prosecution of the Vietnam War transformed the nation, and especially its government and armed forces, into a symbol not of salvationary good but of apocalyptic evil. This transformation was intensified by other outcroppings of "the sixties," particularly the revolutionary impulses that emerged out of the student and black power movements inside the United States and guerilla movements outside it. These "real-world" problems caused the United States to be identified in terms that had, up until that time, been reserved exclusively for the Nazi perpetrators of the Holocaust. According to the progressive narrative, it could only be the Allies' World War II enemy who represented radical evil. As America became "Amerika," however, napalm bombs were analogized with gas pellets and the flaming jungles of Vietnam with the gas chambers. The powerful American army that claimed to be prosecuting a "good war" against Vietnamese communists—in analogy with the lessons that Western democracies had learned in their earlier struggle against Nazism—came to be identified, by influential intellectuals and a wide swath of the educated Western public, as perpetrating genocide against the helpless and pathetic inhabts of Vietnam. Bertrand Russell and Jean-Paul Sartre established a kind of counter–"War Crimes Tribunal" to apply the logic of Nuremberg to the United States. Indefensible incidents of civilian killings, like the My Lai massacre of 1968, were represented, not as anomalous incidents, but as typifications of this new American-made tragedy.[71]

This process of material deconstruction and symbolic inversion further contributed to the universalization of the Holocaust: It allowed the moral criteria generated by its earlier interpretation to be applied in a less nationally specific and thus less particularistic way. This inversion undermined still further the progressive narrative under which the mass killings of the Jews had early been framed. For the ability to leave the trauma drama behind, and to press ahead toward the future, depended on the material and symbolic existence of an unsullied protagonist who could provide salvation for survivors by leading them into the promised land. "Vietnam" and "the sixties" undercut the main agent of this progressive narrative. The result was a dramatic decline in the confidence that a new world order could be constructed in opposition to violence and coercion; if the United States itself committed war crimes, what chance could there be for modern and democratic societies ever to leave mass murder safely behind?

As a result of these material and symbolic events, the contemporary representatives of the historic enemies of Nazism lost control over the means of symbolic production. The power to present itself as the purified protagonist in the worldwide struggle against evil slipped out of the hands of the American government and patriotic representatives more generally, even as the framing of the drama's triggering trauma shifted from progress to tragedy. The ability to cast and produce the trauma drama, to compel identification and channel catharsis, spread to other nations and to antigovernment groups, and even to historic enemies of the Jewish people. The archetypical trauma drama of the twentieth century became ever more generalized and more accessible, and the criteria for moral responsibility in social relations, once closely tied to American perspectives and interests, came to be defined in a more evenhanded, more egalitarian, more self-critical, in short a more universalistic, way.

Perhaps the most visible and paradoxical effect of this loss of the American government's control over the means of symbolic production control was that the morality of American leadership in World War II came to be questioned in a manner that established polluting analogies with Nazism.[72] One issue that now became "troubling," for example, was the justification for the Allied firebombings of Dresden and Tokyo. The growing climate of relativism and reconfiguration threatened to undermine the coding, weighting, and narrating that once had provided a compelling rationale for those earlier events that were in themselves so massively destructive of civilian life. In a similar manner, but with much more significant repercussions, the symbolic implications of the atomic bombings of Hiroshima and Nagasaki began to be fundamentally reconfigured. From being conceived as stages in the unfolding of the progressive narrative, influential groups of Westerners came to understand the atomic bombings as vast human tragedies. Younger generations of Americans, in fact, were increasingly responsive to the view of these events that had once been promoted exclusively by Japan, the fascist Axis power against which their elders had waged war. The interpretation of the suffering caused by the atomic bombings became separated from the historical specifics of time and place. With this generalization, the very events that had once appeared as high points of the progressive narrative came to constructed as unjustifiable, as human tragedies, as slaughters of hundreds of thousands of innocent and pathetic human beings—in short, as typifications of the "Holocaust."[73]

Perhaps the most pointed example of what could happen after America lost control over the Holocaust story was the way in which its redemptive role in the narrative was challenged. Rather than being portrayed as the chief prosecutor of Nazi perpetrators—as chief prosecutor, the narrative's protagonist along with the victims themselves—the American and the British wartime governments were accused of having at least indirect responsibility for allowing the Nazis to carry out their brutal work. A steady stream of revisionist historical scholarship emerged, beginning in the 1970s, suggesting that the anti-Semitism of Roosevelt and Churchill and of American and British citizens had prevented them from acting to block the mass killings; for they had received authenticated information about German plans and activities as early as June 1942.[74]

This analogical linkage between the Allies and the perpetrators quickly became widely accepted as historical fact. On September 27, 1979, when the President's Commission on the Victims of the Holocaust issued a report recommending the American establishment of a Holocaust Museum, it listed as one of its primary justifications that such a public construction would give the American nation an opportunity to compensate for its early, "disastrous" indifference to the plight of the Jews (quoted in Linenthal, 1995: 37). When the museum itself was eventually constructed, it enshrined this inversion of the progressive narrative in the exhibitions themselves. The third floor of the museum is filled with powerfully negative images of the death camps, and is attached by an internal bridge to a tower whose rooms display actual artifacts from the camps. As visitors approach this bridge, in the midst of the iconic representations of evil, they confront a photomural of an U.S. Air Force intelligence photograph of Auschwitz-Birkenau, taken on May 31, 1944. The text attached to the mural informs visitors: "Two freight trains with Hungarian Jews arrived in Birkenau that day; the large-scale gassing of these Jews was beginning. The four Birkenau crematoria are visible at the top of the photograph" (quoted in Linenthal, 1995: 217). Placed next to the photomural is what the principal ethnographer of the museum project, Edward Linenthal, has called "an artifactual indictment of American indifference." It is a letter, dated August 14, 1944, from John J. McCloy, assistant secretary of war. According to the text, McCoy "rejected a request by the World Jewish Congress to bomb the Auschwitz concentration camp." This rejection is framed in the context not of physical impossibility, or in terms of the vicissitudes of a world war, but as the result of moral diminution. Visitors are informed that the U.S. Air Force "could have bombed Auschwitz as early as May 1944," since U.S. bombers had "struck Buna, a synthetic-rubber works relying on slave labor, located less than five miles east of Auschwitz-Birkenau." But despite this physical possibility, the text goes on to note, the death camp "remained untouched." The effective alignment of Allied armies with Nazi perpetrators is more than implicit: "Although bombing Auschwitz would have killed many prisoners, it would also have halted the operation of the gas chambers and, ultimately, saved the lives of many more" (quoted in Linenthal, 1995: 217–8). This authoritative reconstruction, it is important to emphasize, is not a brute empirical fact, any more than the framework that had earlier previous sway. In fact, within the discipline of American history, the issue of Allied indifference remains subject to intensive debate (quoted in Linenthal, 1995:

219–24).[75] At every point in the construction of a public discourse, however, factual chronicles must be encased in symbolically coded and narrated frames.

Eventually, this revision of the progressive narrative about exclusively Nazi perpetrators extended, with perhaps even more profound consequences, to other Allied powers and to the neutrals in that earlier conflict as well. As the charismatic symbol of French resistance to German occupation, Charles de Gaulle had woven a narrative, during and after the war, that purified his nation by describing his nation as first the victim and later the courageous opponent of Nazi domination and the "foreign" collaborators in Vichy.[76] By the late 1970s and 1980s, however, a younger generation of French and non-French historians challenged this definition, seriously polluting the earlier Republican government, and even some of its postwar socialist successors, by documenting massive French collaboration with the antidemocratic, anti-Semitic regime.[77]

In the wake of these reversals, it seemed only a matter of time until the nations who had been "neutral" during the earlier conflict would also be forced to relinquish symbolic control over how the telling of their own stories, at least in the theatre of Western opinion if not on their own national stage. Austria, for example, had long depicted itself as a helpless victim of Nazi Germany. When Kurt Waldheim ascended to the position of secretary-general of the United Nations, however, his hidden association with the Hitler regime was revealed, and the symbolic status of the Austrian nation, which rallied behind their ex-president, began to be publicly polluted as a result.[78] Less than a decade later, Switzerland became subject to similar inversion of its symbolic fortunes. The tiny republic had prided itself on its long history of decentralized canton democracy and the benevolent, universalizing neutrality of its Red Cross. In the midnineties, journalists and historians documented that the wartime Swiss government had laundered, for example, "purified," Nazi gold. In return for gold that had been plundered from the bodies of condemned and already dead Jews, Swiss bankers gave to Nazi authorities acceptable, unmarked currency that could much more readily be used to finance the war.

This discussion of how the non-Jewish agents of the progressive narrative were undercut by "real-world" developments would be incomplete without some mention of how the Israeli government, which represented the other principal agent of the early, progressive Holocaust story, also came to be threatened with symbolic reconfiguration. The rise of Palestinian liberation movements inverted the Jewish nation's progressive myth of origin, for it suggested, at least to more liberally inclined groups, an equation between Nazi and Israeli treatment of subordinate ethnic and religious groups. The battle for cultural position was not, of course, given up without a fight. When Helmut Schmidt, chancellor of West Germany, spoke of Palestinian rights, Menachem Begin, prime minister of Israel, retorted that Schmidt, a Wehrmacht officer in World War II, had "remained faithful to Hitler until the last moment," insisting that the Palestine Liberation Organization was a "neo-Nazi organization" (quoted in Novick,

1994: 161). This symbolic inversion vis-à-vis the newly generalized and reconfigured Holocaust symbol was deepened by the not-unrelated complicity of Israel in the massacres that followed the Lebanon invasion and by the documented reports of Palestinian torture and occasional death in Israeli prisons.

## THE HOLOCAUST AS BRIDGING METAPHOR

Each of the cultural transformations and social processes I have described has had the effect of universalizing the moral questions provoked by the mass killings of the Jews, of detaching the issues surrounding the systematic exercise of violence against ethnic groups from any particular ethnicity, religion, nationality, time, or place. These processes of detachment and deepening emotional identification are thoroughly intertwined. If the Holocaust were not conceived as a tragedy, it would not attract such continuous, even obsessive attention; this attention would not be rewarded, in turn, if the Holocaust were not understood in a detached and universalizing way. Symbolic extension and emotional identification both are necessary if the audience for a trauma, and its social relevance, are to be dramatically enlarged. I will call the effects of this enlargement the "engorgement of evil."

Norms provide standards for moral judgment. What is defined as evil in any historical period provides the most transcendental content for such judgments. What Kant called radical evil, and what I have called here, drawing on Durkheim, sacred-evil, refers to something considered absolutely essential to defining the good "in our time." Insofar as the "Holocaust" came to define inhumanity in our time, then, it served a fundamental moral function. "Post-Holocaust morality"[79] could perform this role, however, only in a sociological way: it became a bridging metaphor that social groups of uneven power and legitimacy applied to parse ongoing events as good and evil in real historical time. What the "Holocaust" named as the most fundamental evil was the intentional, systematic and organized employment of violence against members of a stigmatized collective group, whether defined in a primordial or an ideological way. Not only did this representation identify as radical evil the perpetrators and their actions but it polluted as evil nonactors as well. According to the standards of post-Holocaust morality, one became normatively required to make an effort to intervene against any Holocaust, regardless of personal consequences and cost. For as a crime against humanity, a "Holocaust" is taken to be a threat to the continuing existence of humanity itself. It is impossible, in this sense, to imagine a sacrifice that would be too great when humanity itself is at stake.[80]

Despite the moral content of the Holocaust symbol, then, the primary, first-order effects of this sacred-evil do not work in a ratiocinative way. Radical evil is a philosophical term, and it suggests that evil's moral content can be defined and discussed rationally. Sacred-evil, by contrast, is a sociological term, and it suggests that defining radical evil, and applying it, involves motives and relationships, and institutions, that work more like those associated with religious institutions than with ethical doctrine. In order for a prohibited social action to be powerfully moralized, the symbol of this evil must become engorged. An engorged evil overflows with badness. Evil becomes labile and liquid; it drips and seeps, ruining everything it touches. Under the sign of the tragic narrative, the Holocaust became engorged, and its seepage polluted everything with which it came into contact.

## Metonymy

This contact pollution established the basis for what might be called metonymic guilt. Under the progressive narrative, guilt for the genocidal mass killings depended on being directly and narrowly responsible in the legal sense worked out and applied at the Nuremberg trials. It wasn't simply a matter of being "associated" with mass murders. In this legal framework, any notion of collective responsibility, the guilt of the Nazi party, the German government, much less the German nation was ruled as unfair, as out of bounds. But as the Holocaust became engorged with evil, and as post-Holocaust morality developed, guilt could no longer be so narrowly confined. Guilt now came from simple propinquity, in semiotic terms from metonymic association.

To be guilty of sacred-evil did not mean, any more, that one had committed a legal crime. It was about the imputation of a moral one. One cannot defend oneself against an imputed moral crime by pointing to exculpating circumstances or lack of direct involvement. The issue is one of pollution, guilt by actual association. The solution is not the rational demonstration of innocence but ritual cleansing: purification. In the face of metonymic association with evil, one must engage in performative actions, not only in ratiocinative, cognitive arguments. As the "moral conscience of Germany," the philosopher Jürgen Habermas, put it during the now famous *Historichstreich* among German historians during the 1980s, the point is to "attempt to expel shame," not to engage in "empty phrases" (quoted in Kampe, 1987: 63). One must *do* justice and *be* righteousness. This performative purification is achieved by returning to the past, entering symbolically into the tragedy, and developing a new relation to the archetypal characters and crimes. Habermas wrote that it was "only after and through Auschwitz" that postwar Germany could once again attach itself "to the political culture of the West" (quoted in Kampe, 1987: 63). Retrospection is an effective path toward purification because it provides for catharsis, although of course it doesn't guarantee it. The evidence for having achieved catharsis is confession. If there is neither the acknowledgment of guilt nor sincere apology, punishment in the legal sense may be prevented, but the symbolic and moral taint will always remain.

Once the trauma had been dramatized as a tragic event in human history, the engorgement of evil compelled contemporaries to return to the originating trauma drama and to rejudge every individual or collective entity who was, or might have been, even remotely involved. Many individual reputations became sullied in this way. The list of once admired figures who were "outed" as apologists for, or participants in, the anti-Jewish mass murders stretched from such philosophers as Martin Heidegger to such literary figures as Paul de Man and such political leaders as Kurt Waldheim. In the defenses mounted by these tarnished figures or their supporters, the suggestion was never advanced that the Holocaust does not incarnate evil—a self-restraint that implicitly reveals the trauma's engorged, sacred quality. The only possible defense was that the accused had, in fact, never been associated with the trauma in any way.

More than two decades ago, the U.S. Justice Department established the Office of Special Investigation, the sole purpose of which was to track down and expel not only major but minor figures who had been associated in some manner with Holocaust crimes. Since then, the bitter denunciations of deportation hearings have echoed throughout virtually every Western country. In such proceedings, the emotional-cum-normative imperative is to assert the moral requirements for humanity. Media stories revolve around questions of the "normal," as in how could somebody who seems like a human being, who since World War II has been an upstanding member of the (French, American, Argentinian) community, have ever been involved in what now is universally regarded as an anti-human event? Issues of legality are often overlooked, for the issue is purification of the community through expulsion of a polluted object.[81] Frequently, those who are so polluted give up without a fight. In the spate of recent disclosures about Jewish art appropriated by Nazis and currently belonging to Western museums, directors have responded simply by asking for time to catalogue the marked holdings to make them available to be retrieved.

### Analogy

The direct, metonymic association with Nazi crimes is the most overt effect of the way evil seeps from the engorged Holocaust symbol, but it is not the cultural process most often employed. The bridging metaphor works much more typically, and profoundly, through the device of analogy.

In the 1960s and 1970s, such analogical bridging powerfully contributed to a fundamental revision in moral understandings of the historical treatment of minorities inside the United States. Critics of earlier American policy, and representatives of minority groups themselves, began to suggest analogies between various minority "victims" of white American expansion and the Jewish victims of the Holocaust. This was particularly true of Native Americans, who argued that genocide had been committed against them, an idea that gained wide currency and that eventually generated massive efforts at legal repair and monetary payments.[82] Another striking example of this domestic inversion was the dramatic reconfiguration, in the 1970s and 1980s, of the American government's internment of Japanese-American citizens during World War II. Parallels be-tween this action and Nazi prejudice and exclusion became widespread, and the internment camps became reconfigured as concentration camps. What followed from this symbolic transformation were not only formal governmental "apolo-gies" to the Japanese-American people but actual monetary "reparations."

In the 1980s, the engorged, free-floating Holocaust symbol became analogi-cally associated with the movement against nuclear power and nuclear testing and, more generally, with the ecological movements that emerged during that time. Politicians and intellectuals gained influence in their campaigns against the testing and deployment of nuclear weapons by telling stories about the "nu-clear holocaust" that would be unleashed if their own, democratic governments continued their nuclear policies. By invoking this Holocaust-inspired narrative, they were imagining a disaster that would have such generalized, supranational effects that the historical particularities of ideological rightness and wrongness, winners and losers, would no longer matter. In a similar manner, the activists' evocative depictions of the "nuclear winter" that would result from the nuclear holocaust gained striking support from the images of "Auschwitz," the iconic representations of which were rapidly becoming a universal medium for express-ing demented violence, abject human suffering, and "meaningless" death. In the environmental movement, claims were advanced that the industrial societies were committing ecological genocide against species of plant and animal life and that there was a danger that Earth itself would be exterminated.

In the 1990s, the evil that seeped from the engorged metaphor provided the most compelling analogical framework for framing the Balkan events. While there certainly was dispute over which historical signifier of violence would pro-vide the "correct" analogical reference—dictatorial purge, ethic rampage, civil war, ethnic cleansing, or genocide—it was the engorged Holocaust symbol that propelled first American diplomatic and then American-European military in-tervention against Serbian ethnic violence.[83] The part played by this symbolic analogy was demonstrated during the early U.S. Senate debate in 1992. Citing "atrocities" attributed to Serbian forces, Senator Joseph Lieberman told re-porters that "we hear echoes of conflicts in Europe little more than fifty years ago." During the same period, the Democratic presidential nominee, Bill Clin-ton, asserted that "history has shown us that you can't allow the mass extermi-nation of people and just sit by and watch it happen." The candidate promised, if elected, to "begin with air power against the Serbs to try to restore the basic conditions of humanity," employing antipathy to distance himself from the pol-luting passivity that had retrospectively been attributed to the Allies during the initial trauma drama itself (quoted in *Congressional Quarterly*, August 8, 1992: 2374). While President Bush initially proved more reluctant than candidate Clinton to put this metaphorical linkage into material form—with the result-ing deaths of tens of thousands of innocents—it was the threat of just such mil-itary deployment that eventually forced Serbia to sign the Dayton Accords and to stop what were widely represented, in the American and European media, as its genocidal activities in Bosnia and Herzogovina.

When the Serbians threatened to enter Kosovo, the allied bombing campaign was initiated and justified by evoking the same symbolic analogies and the antipathies they implied. The military attacks were represented as responding to the widely experienced horror that the trauma drama of the Holocaust was being reenacted "before our very eyes." Speaking to a veterans' group at the height of the bombing campaign, President Clinton engaged in analogical bridging to explain why the current Balkan confrontation should not be understood, and thus tolerated, as "the inevitable result . . . of centuries-old animosities." He insisted that these murderous events were unprecedented because they were a "systematic slaughter," carried out by "people with organized, political and military power," under the exclusive control of a ruthless dictator, Slobodan Milosevic. "You think the Germans would have perpetrated the Holocaust on their own without Hitler? Was there something in the history of the German race that made them do this? No. We've got to get straight about this. This is something political leaders do" (*New York Times,* May 14, 1999: A 12).

The same day in Germany, Joschka Fischer, foreign minister in the coalition "Red-Green" government, appeared before a special congress of his Green Party to defend the allied air campaign. He, too, insisted on that the uniqueness of Serbian evil made it possible to draw analogies with the Holocaust. Fischer's deputy foreign minister and party ally, Ludger Volmer, drew rousing applause when, in describing President Milosevic's systematic cleansing policy, he declared: "my friends, there is only one word for this, and that word is Fascism." A leading opponent of the military intervention tried to block the bridging process by symbolic antipathy. "We are against drawing comparisons between the murderous Milosevic regime and the Holocaust," he proclaimed, because "doing so would mean an unacceptable diminishment of the horror of Nazi Fascism and the genocide against European Jews." Arguing that the Kosovars were not the Jews and Milosevic not Hitler protected the sacred-evil of the Holocaust, but the attempted antipathy was ultimately unconvincing. About 60 percent of the Green Party delegates believed the analogies were valid and voted to support Fischer's position.[84]

Two weeks later, when the allied bombing campaign had not yet succeeded in bringing Milosevic to heel, President Clinton asked Elie Wiesel to make a three-day tour of the Kosovar Albanians' refugee camps. A spokesperson for the U.S. embassy in Macedonia explained that "people have lost focus on why we are doing what we are doing" in the bombing campaign. The proper analogy, in other words, was not being consistently made. The solution was to create direct, metonymic association. "You need a person like Wiesel," the spokesperson continued, "to keep your moral philosophy on track." In the lead sentence of its report on the tour, the *New York Times* described Wiesel as "the Holocaust survivor and Nobel Peace Prize winner." Despite Wiesel's own assertion that "I don't believe in drawing analogies," after visiting the camps analogizing was precisely the rhetoric in which he engaged. Wiesel declared that "I've learned something from my experiences as a contemporary of so many events." What he had learned was to apply the post-Holocaust morality derived from the originating trauma drama: "When evil shows its face, you don't wait, you don't let it gain strength. You must intervene" (Rolde, 1999: 1).

During that tour of a camp in Macedonia, Elie Wiesel had insisted that "the world had changed fifty years after the Holocaust" and that "Washington's response in Kosovo was far better than the ambivalence it showed during the Holocaust." When, two weeks later, the air war, and the growing threat of a ground invasion, finally succeeded in expelling the Serbian forces from Kosovo, the *New York Times* "Week in Review" section reiterated the famous survivor's confidence that the Holocaust trauma had not been in vain, that the drama erected on its ashes had fundamentally changed the world, or at least the West. The Kosovo war had demonstrated that analogies were valid and that the lessons of post-Holocaust morality could be carried out in the most utterly practical way.

> It was a signal week for the West, no doubt about it. Fifty-four years after the Holocaust revelations, America and Europe had finally said "enough," and struck a blow against a revival of genocide. Serbian ethnic cleansers were now routed; ethnic Albanians would be spared further murders and rapes. Germany was exorcising a few of its Nazi ghosts. Human rights had been elevated to a military priority and a pre-eminent Western value. (Wines, 1999: 1)

Twenty-two months later, after Western support has facilitated the electoral defeat of Milosevic and the accession to the Yugoslav presidency of the reformer Vojilslav Kostunica, the former president and accused war criminal was arrested and forcably taken to jail. While President Kostunica did not personally subscribe to the authority of the war crimes tribunal in the Hague, there was little doubt that he had authorized Milosevic's imprisonment under intensive American pressure. Though initiated by the Congress rather than the U.S. president, George W. Bush responded to the arrest by Holocaust typification. He spoke of the "chilling images of terrified women and children herded into trains, emaciated prisoners interned behind barbed wire and mass graves unearthed by United Nations investigators," all traceable to Milosevic's "brutal dicatorship" (quoted in Perlez, 2001: 6). Even among those Serbian intellectuals, like Aleksa Djilas, who criticized the Hague tribunal as essentially a political and thus particularistic court, there was recognition that the events took place within a symbolic framework that would inevitably universalize them and contribute to the possibility of a new moral order on a less particularist scale. "There will be a blessing in disguise through his trial," Djilas told a reporter on the day after Milosevic's arrest. "Some kind of new international order is being constructed, intentionally or not. . . . Something will crystallize: what kinds of nationalism are justified or not, what kinds of intrervention are justified or not, how much are great powers entitled to respond, and how. It will not be a sterile exercise" (Erlanger, 2001: 8).

In the 1940s, the mass murder of the Jews had been viewed as a typification of the Nazi war machine, an identification that had limited its moral implications. Fifty years later, the Holocaust itself had displaced its historical context. It had itself become the master symbol of evil in relation to which new instances of grievous mass injury would be typified.[85]

### Legality

As the rhetoric of this triumphant declaration indicates, the generalization of the Holocaust trauma drama has found expression in the new vocabulary of "universal human rights." In some part, this trope has simply degendered the Enlightenment commitment to "the universal rights of man" first formulated in the French Revolution. In some other part, it blurs the issue of genocide with social demands for health and basic economic subsistence. Yet from the beginning of its systematic employment in the postwar period, the phrase has also referred specifically to a new legal standard for international behavior that would simultaneously generalize and make more precise and binding what came to be regarded as the "lessons" of the Holocaust events. Representatives of various organizations, both governmental and nongovernmental, have made sporadic but persistent efforts to formulate specific, morally binding codes, and eventually international laws, to institutionalize the moral judgments triggered by metonymic and analogic association with the engorged symbol of evil. This possibility has inspired the noted legal theorist Martha Minow to suggest an unorthodox answer to the familiar question: "Will the twentieth century be most remembered for its mass atrocities?" "A century marked by human slaughter and torture, sadly, is not a unique century in human history. Perhaps more unusual than the facts of genocides and regimes of torture marking this era is the invention of new and distinctive legal forms of response" (Minow, 1998: 1).

This generalizing process began at Nuremberg in 1945, when the longplanned trial of Nazi war leaders was expanded to include the moral principle that certain heinous acts are "crimes against humanity" and must be recognized as such by everyone (Drinan, 1987: 334). In its first report on those indictments, the New York Times insisted that while "the authority of this tribunal to inflict punishment is directly derived from victory in war," it derived "indirectly from an intangible but nevertheless very real factor which might be called the dawn of a world conscience" (October 9, 1945: 20). This universalizing process continued the following year, when the United Nations General Assembly adopted Resolution 95, committing the international body to "the principles of international law recognized by the charter of the Nuremberg Tribunal and the judgment of the Tribunal" (quoted in Drinan, 1987: 334).[86] Two years later, the United Nations issued the Universal Declaration of Human Rights, whose opening preamble evoked the memory of "barbarous acts which have outraged the conscience of mankind."[87] In 1950, the International Law Commission of the United Nations adopted a statement spelling out the principles that the Declaration implied. "The core of these principles states that leaders and nations can be punished for their violations of international law and for their crimes against humanity. In addition, it is not a defense for a person to state that he or she was required to do what was done because of an order from a military or civilian superior" (quoted in Drinan, 1987: 334).

In the years since, despite President Truman's recommendation that the United States draft a code of international criminal law around these principles, despite the "human rights" foreign policy of a later Democratic president, Jimmy Carter, and despite the nineteen UN treaties and covenants condemning genocide and exalting the new mandate for human rights, new international legal codes were never drafted (Drinan, 1987: 334). Still, over the same period, an increasingly thick body of "customary law" was developed that militated *against* nonintervention in the affairs of sovereign states when they engage in systematic human rights violations.

> The long-term historical significance of the rights revolution of the last fifty years is that it has begun to erode the sanctity of state sovereignty and to justify effective political and military intervention. Would there have been American intervention in Bosnia without nearly fifty years of accumulated international opinion to the effect that there are crimes against humanity and violations of human rights which must be punished wherever they arise? Would there be a safe haven for the Kurds in northern Iraq? Would we be in Kosovo? (Ignatieff, 1999: 62)[88]

When the former Chilean dictator Augusto Pinochet was arrested in Britain and detained for more than a year in response to an extradiction request by a judge in Spain, the reach of this customary law and its possible enforcement by national police first became crystallized in the global public sphere. It was at about the same time that the first internationally sanctioned War Crimes Tribunal since Nuremberg began meeting in the Hague to prosecute those who had violated human rights on any and all sides of the decade's Balkan wars.

### The Dilemma of Uniqueness

As the engorged symbol bridging the distance between radical evil and what at some earlier point was considered normal or normally criminal behavior, the reconstructed Holocaust trauma became enmeshed in what might be called the dilemma of uniqueness. The trauma could not function as a metaphor of archetypal tragedy unless it were regarded as radically different from any other evil act in modern times. Yet it was this very status—as a unique event—that eventually compelled it to become generalized and departicularized. For as a metaphor for radical evil, the Holocaust provided a standard of evaluation for judging the evility of other threatening acts. By providing such a standard for comparative judgment, the Holocaust became a norm, initiating a succession of metonymic, analogic, and legal evaluations that deprived it of "uniqueness" by establishing its degrees of likeness or unlikeness to other possible manifestations of evility.

In this regard, it is certainly ironic that this bridging process, so central to universalizing critical moral judgment in the post-Holocaust world, has time after time been attacked as depriving the Holocaust of its very significance. Yet these very attacks have often revealed, despite themselves, the trauma drama's new centrality in ordinary thought and action. One historically oriented critic, for example, mocked the new "Holocaust consciousness" in the United States, citing the fact that the Holocaust "is invoked as reference point in discussions of everything from AIDS to abortion" (Novick, 1994: 159). A literature professor complained about the fact that "the language of 'Holocaust'" is now "regularly invoked by people who want to draw public attention to human-rights abuses, social inequalities suffered by racial and ethnic minorities and women, environmental disasters, AIDS, and a whole host of other things" (Rosenfeld, 1995: 35). Another scholar decried the fact that "any evil that befalls anyone anywhere becomes a Holocaust" (quoted in Rosenfeld, 1995: 35).[89]

While no doubt well-intentioned in a moral sense, such complaints miss the sociological complexities that underlie the kind of cultural-moral process I am exploring here. Evoking the Holocaust to measure the evil of a non-Holocaust event is nothing more, and nothing less, than to employ a powerful bridging metaphor to make sense of social life. The effort to qualify as the referent of this metaphor is bound to entail sharp social conflict, and in this sense social relativization, for successful metaphorical embodiment brings to a party legitimacy and resources. The premise of these relativizing social conflicts is that the Holocaust provides an absolute and nonrelative measure of evil. But the effects of the conflict are to relativize the application of this standard to any particular social event. The Holocaust is unique and not-unique at the same time. This insoluble dilemma marks the life history of the Holocaust, since it became a tragic archetype and a central component of moral judgment in our time.[90] Inga Clendinnen has recently described this dilemma in a particularly acute way, and her observations exemplify the metaphorical bridging process I have tried to describe here.

There have been too many recent horrors, in Rwanda, in Burundi, in one-time Yugoslavia, with victims equally innocent, killers and torturers equally devoted, to ascribe uniqueness to any one set of atrocities on the grounds of their exemplary cruelty. I find the near-random terror practiced by the Argentinean military, especially their penchant for torturing children before their parents, to be as horrible, as "unimaginable," as the horrible and unimaginable things done by Germans to their Jewish compatriots. Certainly the scale is different—but how much does scale matter to the individual perpetrator or the individual victim? Again, the willful obliteration of long-enduring communities is surely a vast offence, but for three years we watched the carpet-bombings of Cambodia, when the bombs fell on villagers who could not have had the least understanding of the nature of their offence. *When we think of innocence afflicted, we see those unforgettable children of the Holocaust staring wide-eyed into the camera of their killers, but we also see the image of the little Vietnamese girl, naked, screaming, running down a dusty road, her back aflame with American napalm.* If we grant that "holocaust," the total consumption of offerings by fire, is sinisterly appropriate for the murder of those millions who found their only graves in the air, it is equally appropriate for the victims of Hiroshima, Nagasaki and Dresden [and for] Picasso's horses and humans screaming [in *Guernica*] under attack from untouchable murderers in the sky. (Clendinnen, 1999: 14, italics added)

## FORGETTING OR REMEMBERING?

### Routinization and Institutionalizaton

As the sense that the Holocaust was a unique event in human history crystallized and its moral implications became paradoxically generalized, the tragic trauma drama became increasingly subject to memorialization. Special research centers were funded to investigate its most minute details and to sponsor debates about its wider applications. College courses were devoted to it, and everything, from university chairs to streets and parks, was named for it. Monuments were constructed to honor the tragedy's victims. Major urban centers in the United States, and many outside it as well, constructed vastly expensive, and vastly expansive, museums to make permanent its moral lessons. The U.S. military distributed instructions for conducting "Days of Remembrance," and commemorative ceremonies were held annually in the Capitol Rotunda.

Because of the dilemma of uniqueness, all of these generalizing processes were controversial; they suggested to many observers that the Holocaust was being instrumentalized and commodified, that its morality and affect were being displaced by specialists in profit-making on the one hand and specialists in merely cognitive expertise on the other. In recent years, indeed, the idea has grown that the charisma of the original trauma drama is being routinized in a regrettably, but predictably, Weberian way.[91]

The moral learning process that I have described in the preceding pages does not necessarily deny the possibility that instrumentalization develops *after* a trauma drama has been created and *after* its moral lessons have been externalized and internalized. In American history, for example, even the most sacred of the founding national traumas, the Revolution and the Civil War, have faded as objects of communal affect and collective remembering, and the dramas associated with them have become commodified as well. Still, the implications of what I have presented here suggest that such routinization, even when it takes a monetized and commodity form, does not necessarily indicate meaninglessness. Metaphorical bridging shifts symbolic significance, and audience attention, from the originating trauma to the traumas that follow in a sequence of analogical associations. But it does not, for that, inevitably erase or invert the meanings associated with the trauma that was first in the associational line. Nor does the effort to concretize the cultural meanings of the trauma in monumental forms have this effect. The American Revolution and the Civil War both remain resources for triumphant and tragic narration, in popular and high culture venues. It is only very infrequently, and very controversially, that these trauma dramas are subjected to the kind of comic framing that would invert their still sacred place in American collective identity. As I have mentioned earlier, it is not commodification, but "comedization"—a change in the cultural framing, not a change in economic status—that indicates trivialization and forgetting.

### Memorials and Museums: Crystallizing Collective Sentiment

A less Weberian, more Durkheimian understanding of routinization is needed.[92] When they are first created, sacred-good and sacred-evil are labile and liquid. Objectification can point to the sturdier embodiment of the values they have created, and even of the experiences they imply. In this period, the intensifying momentum to memorialize the Holocaust indicates a deepening institutionalization of its moral lessons and the continued recalling of its dramatic experiences rather than to their routinization and forgetting. When, after years of conflict, the German parliament approved a plan for erecting a vast memorial of two thousand stone pillars to the victims of the Holocaust at the heart of Berlin, a leading politician proclaimed: "We are not building this monument solely for the Jews. We are building it for ourselves. It will help us confront a chapter in our history" (Cohen, 1999: 3).

In the Holocaust museums that are sprouting up throughout the Western world, the design is not to distance the viewer from the object in a dry, deracinated, or "purely factual" way. To the contrary, as a recent researcher into this phenomenon has remarked, "Holocaust museums favor strategies designed to arouse strong emotions and particular immersion of the visitor into the past" (Baer, unpublished).[93] The informational brochure to the Simon Wiesenthal Museum of Tolerance in Los Angeles, which houses the West Coast's largest Holocaust exhibition, promotes itself as a "high tech, hands-on experiential museum that focuses on . . . themes through interactive exhibits" (Baer, unpublished).

From its very inception in 1979, the Holocaust Museum in Washington, D.C., was metonymically connected to the engorged symbolism of evil. According to the official Report submitted to President Jimmy Carter by the President's Commission on the Victims of the Holocaust, the purpose of the museum was to "protect against future evil" (quoted in Linenthal, 1995: 37). The goal was to create a building through which visitors would reexperience the original tragedy, to find "a means," as some central staff members had once put it, "to convey both dramatically and soberly the enormity of the human tragedy in the death camps" (quoted in Linenthal, 1995: 212).[94] Rather than instrumentalizing or commodifying, in other words, the construction was conceived as a critical means for deepening psychological identification and broadening symbolic extension. According to the ethnographer of the fifteen-year planning and construction process, the design team insisted that the museum's interior mood should be so "visceral" that, as the ethnographer of the construction put it, museum visitors "would gain no respite from the narrative."

The feel and rhythm of space and the setting of mood were important. [The designers] identified different qualities of space that helped to mediate the narrative: constructive space on the third floor, for example, where as visitors enter the world of the death camps, the space becomes tight and mean, with a feeling of heavy darkness. Indeed, walls were not painted, pipes were left exposed, and, except for fire exits and hidden elevators on the fourth and third floors for people who, for one reason or another, had to leave, there is no escape. (quoted in Linenthal, 1995: 169)

According to the Museum's head designer,

the exhibition was intended to take visitors on a journey. . . . We realized that if we followed those people under all that pressure as they moved from their normal lives into ghettos, out of ghettos onto trains, from trains to camps, within the pathways of the camps, until finally to the end. . . . If visitors could take that same journey, they would understand the story because they will have experienced the story. (quoted in Linenthal, 1995: 174)[95]

The dramatization of the tragic journey was in many respects quite literal, and this fosters identification. The visitor receives a photo passport/identity card representing a victim of the Holocaust, and the museum's permanent exhibition is divided into chronological sections. The fourth floor is "The Assault: 1933–39," the third floor "The Holocaust: 1940–44," and the second floor "Bearing Witness: 1945." At the end of each floor, visitors are asked to insert their passports to find out what happened to their identity-card "alter egos" during that particular phase of the Holocaust tragedy. By the time visitors have passed through the entire exhibit, they will know whether or not the person with whom they have been symbolically identified survived the horror or perished (Linenthal, 1995: 169).

The identification process is deepened by the dramatic technique of personalization. The key, in the words of the project director, was connecting museum visitors to "real faces of real people" (Linenthal, 1995: 181).[96]

Faces of Holocaust victims in the exhibition are shattering in their power. . . . Polish school teachers, moments before their execution, look at visitors in agony, sullen anger, and despair. . . . Two brothers, dressed alike in matching coats and caps, fear etched on their faces, gaze at the camera, into the eyes of the visitors. . . . The Faces . . . assault, challenge, accuse, and profoundly sadden visitors throughout the exhibition. (174)[97]

At every point, design decisions about dramatization were made with the narrative of tragedy firmly in mind. Exhibit designers carefully avoided displaying any of the camp prisoners' "passive resistance," for fear it would trigger progressive narratives of heroism and romance. As a historian associated with such decisions remarked, the fear was that such displays might contribute to an "epic" Holocaust narrative in which resistance would gain "equal time" with the narrative of destruction (Linenthal, 1995: 192). This dark dramatization, however, could not descend into a mere series of grossly displayed horrors, for this would undermine the identification on which the very communication of the tragic lessons of the Holocaust would depend.

The design team faced a difficult decision regarding the presentation of horror. Why put so much effort into constructing an exhibition that was so horrible that people would not visit? They worried about word-of-mouth evaluation after opening, and feared that the first visitors would tell family and friends, "Don't go, it's too horrible." . . . The museum's mission was to teach people about the Holocaust and bring about civic transformation; yet . . . the public had to desire to visit. (198, italics in original)

It seems clear that such memorializations aim to create structures that dramatize the tragedy of the Holocaust and provide opportunities for contemporaries, now so far removed from the original scene, powerfully to reexperience it. In these efforts, personalization remains an immensely important dramatic vehicle, and it continues to provide the opportunity for identification so crucial to the project of universalization. In each Holocaust museum, the fate of the Jews functions as a metaphorical bridge to the treatment of other ethnic, religious, and racial minorities.[98] The aim is manifestly not to "promote" the Holocaust as an important event in earlier historical time, but to contribute to the possibilities of pluralism and justice in the world of today.

## From Liberators to Survivors: Witness Testimonies

Routinization of charisma is certainly an inevitable fact of social life, and memorialization a much-preferred way to understand that it can institutionalize, and not only undermine, the labile collective sentiments that once circulated in a liquid form. It is important also not to view the outcome of such processes in a naturalistic, noncultural way. It is not "meaning" that is crystallized but particular meanings. In terms of Holocaust memorialization and routinization, it is the objectification of a narrative about tragedy that has been memorialized over the last decade, not a narrative about progress.

The postwar memorials to World War II were, and are, about heroism and liberation. They centered on American GIs and the victims they helped. If the Holocaust had continued to be narrated within the progressive framework of the anti-Nazi war, it would no doubt have been memorialized in much the same way. Of course, the very effect of the progressive narrative was to make the Holocaust less visible and central, with the result that, as long as the representation of contemporary history remained within the progressive framework, few efforts to memorialize the Holocaust were made. For that very reason, the few that were attempted are highly revealing. In Liberty State Park, in New Jersey, within visual sight of the proud and patriotic Statue of Liberty, there stands a statue called *Liberation*. The metal sculpture portrays two figures. The larger, a solemn American GI, walks deliberately forward, his eyes on the ground. He cradles a smaller figure, a concentration camp victim, whose skeletal chest, shredded prison garb, outstretched arms, and vacantly staring eyes exemplify his helplessness (Young, 1993: 320–32). Commissioned not only by the State of New Jersey but also by a coalition of American Legion and other veterans' organizations, the monument was dedicated only in 1985. During the ceremony, the state's governor made a speech seeking to reconnect the progressive narrative still embodied by the "last good war" to the growing centrality of the Holocaust narrative, whose symbolic and moral importance had by then already begun to far outstrip it. The defensive and patriotic tone of the speech indicates that, via this symbolic linkage, the state official sought to resist the skepticism about America's place in the world, the very critical attitude that had helped frame the Holocaust in a narrative of tragedy.

> To me, this monument is an affirmation of my American heritage. It causes me
> to feel deep pride in my American values. The monument says that we, as a collective people, stand for freedom. We, as Americans, are not oppressors, and we,
> as Americans, do not engage in military conflict for the purpose of conquest.
> Our role in the world is to preserve and promote that precious, precious thing

that we consider to be a free democracy. Today we will remember those who gave their lives for freedom. (321)

The *Liberation* monument, and the particularist and progressive sentiments it crystallized, could not be further removed from the memorial processes that have crystallized in the years since. Propelled by the tragic transformation of the Jewish mass murder, in these memorials the actions and beliefs of Americans are often implicitly analogized with those of the perpetrators, and the U.S. army's liberation of the camps plays only a minimal role, if any. In these more universalized settings, the focus is on the broader, world-historical causes and moral implications of the tragic event, on creating symbolic extension by providing opportunities for contemporaries to experience emotional identification with the suffering of the victims.

It was in the context of this transformation that there emerged a new genre of Holocaust writing and memorializing, one that focuses on a new kind of historical evidence, direct "testimony," and a new kind of historical actor, the "survivor." Defined as persons who lived through the camp experiences, survivors provide a tactile link with the tragic event. As their social and personal role was defined, they began to write books, give speeches to local and national communities, and record their memories of camp experiences on tape and video. These testimonies have become sacralized repositories of the core tragic experience, with all the moral implications that this suffering has come to entail. They have been the object of two amply funded recording enterprises. One, organized by the Yale University Video Archive of the Holocaust, was already begun in 1981. The other, the Shoah Visual History Foundation, was organized by the film director Steven Spielberg in 1994, in the wake of the worldwide effects of his movie *Schindler's List*.

Despite the publicity these enterprises have aroused and the celebrity that has accrued to the new survivor identity, what is important to see is that this new genre of memorialization has inverted the language of liberation that was so fundamental to the earlier, progressive form. It has created not heroes, but anti-heroes. Indeed, those who have created and shaped this new genre are decidedly critical of what they see as the "style of revisionism that crept into Holocaust writing after the liberation of the camps." They describe this style as a "natural but misguided impulse to romanticize staying alive and to interpret painful endurance as a form of defiance or resistance" (Langer, 2000: xiv). Arguing that survivor testimony reveals tragedy, not triumph, they suggest that it demands the rejection of any progressive frame.

No one speaks of having survived through bravery or courage. These are hard assessments for us to accept. We want to believe in a universe that rewards good character and exemplary behavior. We want to believe in the power of the human spirit to overcome adversity. It is difficult to live with the thought that human nature may not be noble or heroic and that under extreme conditions we, too, might turn brutal, selfish, "too inhuman." (Greene & Kumar, 2000: xxv–xxvi)

In reacting against the heroic, progressive frame, some of these commentators go so far as to insist on the inherent "meaninglessness" of the Holocaust, suggesting that the testimonies reveal "uncompensated and unredeemable suffering" (Langer, 2000: xv). Yet it seems clear that the very effort to create survivor testimony is an effort to maintain the vitality of the experience by objectifying and, in effect, depersonalizing it. As such, it helps to sustain the tragic trauma drama, which allows an ever-wider audience redemption through suffering. It does so by suggesting the survival not of a few scattered and particular victims but of humanity as such.

> The power of testimony is that it requires little commentary, for witnesses are the experts and they tell their own stories in their own words. The perpetrators work diligently to silence their victims by taking away their names, homes, families, friends, possessions, and lives. The intent was to deny their victims any sense of humanness, to erase their individuality and rob them of all personal voice. Testimony reestablishes the individuality of the victims who survived— and in some instances of those who were killed—and demonstrates the power of their voices. (Greene & Kumar, 2000: xxiv)

Those involved directly in this memorializing process see their own work in exactly the same way. Geoffrey Hartman, the director of the Yale Video Archive, speaks about a new "narrative that emerges through the alliance of witness and interviewer" (Hartman, 1996: 153), a narrative based on the reconstruction of a human community.

> However many times the interviewer may have heard similar accounts, they are received as though for the first time. This is possible because, while the facts are known, while historians have labored—and are still laboring—to establish every detail, each of these histories is animated by something in addition to historical knowledge: there is a quest to recover or reconstruct a recipient, an "affective community" . . . and [thus] the renewal of compassionate feelings. (153–4)

However "grim its contents," Hartman insists, testimony does not represent an "impersonal historical digest" but rather "that most natural and flexible of human communications, a story—a story, moreover, that, even if it describes a universe of death, is communicated by a living person who answers, recalls, thinks, cries, carries on" (Hartman, 1996: 154). The president of the Survivors of the Shoah Visual History Foundation, Michael Berenbaum, suggesting that the goal of the Spielberg group is "to catalogue and to disseminate the testimonies to as many remote sites as technology and budget will permit, [a]ll in the service of education," ties the contemporary moral meaning of the historical events to the opportunity for immediate emotional identification that testimonies provide: "In classrooms throughout the world, the encounter between survivors and children [has] become electrifying, the transmission of memory, a discussion of values, a warning against prejudice, antisemitism, racism, and indifference" (Berenbaum, 1999: ix).

## IS THE HOLOCAUST WESTERN?

While the rhetoric of Holocaust generalization refers to its *weltgeschichte* relevance—its world-historical relevance—throughout this essay I have tried to be careful in noting that this universalization has primarily been confined to the West. Universalization, as I have described it, depends on symbolically generated, emotionally vicarious participation in the trauma drama of the mass murder of the Jews. The degree to which this participation is differentially distributed throughout the West is itself a question that further research will have to pursue. This "remembering" is much more pronounced in western Europe and North America than in Latin America. Mexicans, preoccupied with their national traumas dating back to the European conquest, are much less attached to the "Holocaust" than their northern neighbors—against whose very mythologies Mexicans often define themselves. The result may be that Mexican political culture is informed to a significantly lesser degree by "post-Holocaust morality." On the other hand, it is also possible that Mexicans translate certain aspects of post-Holocaust morality into local terms, for example, being willing to limit claims to national sovereignty in the face of demands by indigenous groups who legitimate themselves in terms of broadly human rights.

Such variation is that much more intense when we expand our assessment to non-Western areas. What are the degrees of attachment to, vicarious participation in, and lessons drawn from the "Holocaust" trauma in non-Western civilizations? In Hindu, Buddhist, Confucian, Islamic, African, and still-communist regions and regimes, reference to the "Holocaust," when made at all, is by literary and intellectual elites with markedly atypical levels of participation in the global discourse dominated by the United States and Western Europe. Of course, non-Western regions and nations, as I indicate in chapter 3, have their own identity-defining trauma dramas. What is unclear is the degree to which the cultural work that constructs these traumas, and responds to them, reaches beyond issues of national identity and sovereignty to the universalizing, supranational ethical imperatives increasingly associated with the "lessons of post-Holocaust morality" in the West.

The authorized spokespersons for Japan, for example, have never acknowledged the empirical reality of the horrific mass murder their soldiers inflicted on native Chinese in Nanking, China, during the runup to World War II—the "Rape of Nanking." Much less have they apologized for it, or made any effort to share in the suffering of the Chinese people in a manner that would point to a universalizing ethic by which members of different Asian national and ethnic groupings could be commonly judged. Instead, the atomic bombings of Hiroshima have become an originating trauma for postwar Japanese identity. While producing an extraordinary commitment to pacificism, the dramatization of this trauma, which was inflicted on Japan by its wartime enemy, the United States, has had the effect of confirming rather than dislodging Japan in its role as narrative agent. The trauma has functioned, in other words, to steadfastly oppose any effort to widen the circle of perpetrators, which makes it less likely that the national history of Japan will be submitted to some kind of supranational standard of judgment.

Such submission is very difficult, of course, in any strongly national context, in the West as well as in the East. Nonetheless, the analysis presented in this chapter compels us to ask this question: Can countries or civilizations that do not acknowledge the Holocaust develop universalistic political moralities? Obviously, non-Western nations cannot "remember" the Holocaust, but in the context of cultural globalization they certainly have become gradually aware of its symbolic meaning and social significance. It might also be the case that non-Western nations could develop trauma dramas that are functional equivalents to the Holocaust. It has been the thesis of this essay that moral universalism rests on social processes that construct and channel cultural trauma. If this is indeed the case, then globalization will have to involve a very different kind of social process than the ones that students of this supranational development have talked about so far: East and West, North and South must learn to share the experiences of one another's traumas and to take vicarious responsibility for the other's afflictions.

Geoffrey Hartman has recently likened the pervasive status of the Holocaust in contemporary society to a barely articulated but nonetheless powerful and pervasive legend. "In Greek tragedy . . . with its moments of highly condensed dialogue, the framing legend is so well known that it does not have to be emphasized. A powerful abstraction, or simplification, takes over. In this sense, and in this sense only, the Holocaust is on the way to becoming a legendary event" (Hartman, 2000: 16).

Human beings are story-telling animals. We tell stories about our triumphs. We tell stories about tragedies. We like to believe in the verisimilitude of our accounts, but it is the moral frameworks themselves that are real and constant, not the factual material that we employ them to describe. In the history of human societies, it has often been the case that narrative accounts of the same event compete with one another, and that they eventually displace one another over historical time. In the case of the Nazis' mass murder of the Jews, what was once described as a prelude and incitement to moral and social progress has come to be reconstructed as a decisive demonstration that not even the most "modern" improvements in the condition of humanity can ensure advancement in anything other than a purely technical sense. It is paradoxical that a decided increase in moral and social justice may eventually be the unintended result.

# CULTURAL TRAUMA AND COLLECTIVE IDENTITY

Cultural trauma occurs when members of a collectivity feel they have been subjected to a horrendous event that leaves indelible marks on their group consciousness, marking their memories forever and changing their future identity in fundamental and irrevocable ways.[1]

As I develop it here, cultural trauma is first of all an empirical, scientific concept, suggesting new meaningful and causal relationships between previously unrelated events, structures, perceptions, and actions. But this new scientific concept also illuminates an emerging domain of social responsibility and political action. It is by constructing cultural traumas that social groups, national societies, and sometimes even entire civilizations not only cognitively identify the existence and source of human suffering but "take on board" some significant responsibility for it. Insofar as they identify the cause of trauma, and thereby assume such moral responsibility, members of collectivities define their solidary relationships in ways that, in principle, allow them to share the sufferings of others. Is the suffering of others also our own? In thinking that it might in fact be, societies expand the circle of the we. By the same token, social groups can, and often do, refuse to recognize the existence of others' trauma, and because of their failure they cannot achieve a moral stance. By denying the reality of other's suffering, they not only diffuse their own responsibility for other's suffering but often project the responsibility for their own suffering on these others. In other words, by refusing to participate in what I will later describe as the process of trauma creation, social groups restrict solidarity, leaving others to suffer alone.

## ORDINARY LANGUAGE AND REFLEXIVITY

One of the great advantages of this new theoretical concept is that it partakes so deeply of everyday life. Throughout the twentieth century, first in Western societies and then, soon after, throughout the rest of the world, people have spoken continually about being traumatized by an experience, by an event, by an act of violence or harrassment, or even, simply, by an abrupt and unexpected, and sometimes not even particularly malevolent, experience of social transformation and change.[2] People also have continually employed the language of trauma to explain what happens, not only to themselves but to the collectivities they belong to. We often speak of an organization being traumatized when a leader departs or dies, when a governing regime falls, when an unexpected reversal of fortune is suffered by an organizations. Actors describe themselves as traumatized when the environment of an individual or a collectivity suddenly shifts in an unforeseen and unwelcome manner.

We know from ordinary language, in other words, that we are onto something widely experienced and intuitively understood. Such rootedness in the lifeworld is the soil that nourishes every social scientific concept. The trick is to gain reflexivity, to move from the sense of something commonly experienced to the sense of strangeness that allows us to think sociologically. For trauma is not something naturally existing; it is something constructed by society.

In this task of making trauma strange, its embeddedness in everyday life and language, so important for providing an initial intuitive understanding, now presents itself as a challenge to be overcome. In fact, the scholarly approaches to trauma developed thus far actually have been distorted by the powerful, common-sense understandings of trauma that have emerged in everyday life. Indeed, it might be said that these common-sense understandings constitute a kind of "lay trauma theory" in contrast to which a more theoretically reflexive approach to trauma must be erected.

## LAY TRAUMA THEORY

According to lay theory, traumas are naturally occurring events that shatter an individual or collective actor's sense of well-being. In other words, the power to shatter—the "trauma"—is thought to emerge from events themselves. The reaction to such shattering events—"being traumatized"—is felt and thought to be an immediate and unreflexive response. According to the lay perspective, the trauma experience occurs when the traumatizing event interacts with human nature. Human beings need security, order, love, and connection. If something happens that sharply undermines these needs, it hardly seems surprising, according to the lay theory, that people will be traumatized as a result.[3]

## ENLIGHTENMENT THINKING

There are "Enlightenment" and "psychoanalytic" versions of this lay trauma theory. The Enlightenment understanding suggests that trauma is a kind of rational response to abrupt change, whether at the individual or social level. The objects or events that trigger trauma are perceived clearly by actors; their responses are lucid; and the effects of these responses are problem-solving and progressive. When bad things happen to good people, they become shocked, outraged, indignant. From an Enlightenment perspective, it seems obvious, perhaps even unremarkable, that political scandals are cause for indignation; that economic depressions are cause for despair; that lost wars create a sense of anger and aimlessness; that disasters in the physical environment lead to panic; that assaults on the human body lead to intense anxiety; that technological disasters create concerns, even phobias, about risk. The responses to such traumas will be efforts to alter the circumstances that caused them. Memories about the past guide this thinking about the future. Programs for action will be developed, individual and collective environments will be reconstructed, and eventually the feelings of trauma will subside.

This Enlightenment version of lay trauma theory has recently been exemplified by Arthur Neal in his *National Trauma and Collective Memory*. In explaining whether or not a collectivity is traumatized, Neal points to the quality of the event itself. National traumas have been created, he argues, by "individual and collective reactions to a volcano-like event that shook the foundations of the social world" (Neal, 1998: ix). An event traumatizes a collectivity because it is "an extraordinary event," an event that has such "an explosive quality" that it creates "disruption" and "radical change . . . within a short period of time" (Neal, 1998: 3, 9–10, italics added). These objective empirical qualities "command the attention of all major subgroups of the population," triggering emotional response and public attention because rational people simply cannot react in any other way (9–10). "Dismissing or ignoring the traumatic experience is not a reasonable option," nor is "holding an attitude of benign neglect" or "cynical indifference" (4, 9–10). It is precisely because actors are reasonable that traumatic events typically lead to progress: "The very fact that a disruptive event has occurred" means that "new opportunities emerge for innovation and change" (18). It is hardly surprising, in other words, that "permanent changes were introduced into the [American] nation as a result of the Civil War, the Great Depression, and the trauma of World War II" (5).

Despite what I will later call the naturalistic limitations of such an Enlightenment understanding of trauma, what remains singularly important about Neal's approach is its emphasis on the collectivity rather than the individual, an emphasis that sets it apart from the more individually oriented, psychoanalytically informed approaches discussed below. In focusing on events that create trauma for national, not individual identity, Neal follows the pathbreaking sociological model developed by Kai Erikson in his widely influential book, *Everything in Its Path*. While this heartwrenching account of the effects on a small Appalachian community of a devastating flood is likewise constrained by a naturalistic perspective, it established the groundwork for the distinctively sociological approach I follow here. Erikson's theoretical innovation was to conceptualize the difference between collective and individual trauma. Both the attention to collectively emergent properties, and the naturalism with which such collective traumas are conceived, are evident in the following passage.

> By individual trauma I mean a *blow* to the psyche that *breaks through* one's defenses *so suddenly and with such brutal force that one cannot react to it effectively.* . . .
> By collective trauma, on the other hand, I mean a *blow* to the basic tissues of social life that *damages* the bonds attaching people together and impairs the prevailing sense of communality. The collective trauma works it's way slowly and even insidiously into the awareness of those who suffer from it, so it does not have the quality of suddenness normally associated with "trauma." *But it is a form of shock all the same*, a gradual realization that the community *no longer exists* as an effective source of support and that *an important part of the self has disappeared*. . . . "We" no longer exist as a connected pair or as linked cells in a larger communal body. (Erikson, 1976: 153–4, italics added)

As Smelser suggests (Alexander et al., forthcoming), trauma theory began to enter ordinary language and scholarly discussions alike in the efforts to understand the "shell shock" that affected so many soldiers during World War I, and it became expanded and elaborated in relation to other wars that followed in the course of the twentieth century. When Glen Elder created "life course analysis" to trace the cohort effects on individual identity of these and other cataclysmic social events in the twentieth century, he and his students adopted a similar Enlightenment mode of trauma (Elder, 1974). Similar understandings have long informed approaches in other disciplines, for example the vast historiography devoted to the far-reaching effects on nineteenth-century Europe and the United States of the "trauma" of the French Revolution. Elements of the lay Enlightenment perspective have also informed contemporary thinking about the Holocaust (see chapter 2, above) and responses to other episodes of mass murder in the twentieth century.

## PSYCHOANALYTIC THINKING

Such realist thinking continues to permeate everyday life and scholarly thought alike. Increasingly, however, it has come to be filtered through a psychoanalytic perspective that has become central to both contemporary lay common sense and academic thinking. This approach places a model of unconscious emotional fears and cognitively distorting mechanisms of psychological defense between the external shattering event and the actor's internal traumatic response. When bad things happen to good people, according to this academic version of lay theory, they can become so frightened that they can actually repress the experience of trauma itself. Rather than direct cognition and rational understanding, the traumatizing event becomes distorted in the actor's imagination and memory. The effort to accurately attribute responsibility for the event, and the progressive effort to develop an ameliorating response, are undermined by displacement. This psychoanalytically mediated perspective continues to maintain a naturalistic approach to traumatic events, but it suggests a more complex understanding about the human ability consciously to perceive them. The truth about the experience is perceived, but only unconsciously. In effect, truth goes underground, and accurate memory and responsible action are its victim. Traumatic feelings and perceptions, then, come not only from the originating event but from the anxiety of keeping it repressed. Trauma will be resolved, not only by setting things right in the world, but by setting things right in the self.[4] According to this perspective, the truth can be recovered, and psychological equanimity restored only, as the Holocaust historian Saul Friedlander once put it, "when memory comes."

This phrase actually provides the title of Friedlander's memoir about his childhood during the Holocaust years in Germany and France. Recounting, in evocative literary language, his earlier experiences of persecution and displacement, Friedlander suggests that conscious perception of highly traumatic events can emerge only after psychological introspection and "working through" allows actors to recover their full capacities for agency (Friedlander, 1978, 1992b). Emblematic of the intellectual framework that has emerged over the last three decades in response to the Holocaust experience, this psychoanalytically informed theorizing particularly illuminated the role of collective memory, insisting on the importance of working backward through the symbolic residues that the originating event has left on contemporary recollection.[5]

Much as these memory residues surface through free association in psychoanalytic treatment, they appear in public life through the creation of literature. It should not be surprising, then, that literary interpretation, with its hermeneutical approach to symbolic patterns, has been offered as a kind of academic counterpart to the psychoanalytic intervention. In fact, the major theoretical and empirical statements of the psychoanalytic version of lay trauma theory have been produced by scholars in the various disciplines of the humanities. Because within the psychoanalytic tradition it has been Lacan who has emphasized the importance of language in emotional formation, it has been Lacanian theory, often in combination with Derridean deconstruction, that has informed these humanities-based studies of trauma.

Perhaps the most influential scholar in shaping this approach has been Cathy Caruth, in her own collection of essays, *Unclaimed Experience: Trauma, Narrative, and History,* and in her edited collection *Trauma: Explorations in Memory* (Caruth, 1995, 1996).[6] Caruth focuses on the complex permutations that unconscious emotions impose on traumatic reactions, and her work has certainly been helpful in my own thinking about cultural trauma. In keeping with the psychoanalytic tradition, however, Caruth roots her analysis in the power and objectivity of the originating traumatic event, saying that "Freud's intuition of, and his passionate fascination with, traumatic experiences" related traumatic reactions to "the unwitting reenactment of an event that one cannot simply leave behind" (Caruth, 1995: 2). The event cannot be left behind because "the breach in the mind's experience," according to Caruth, "is experienced too soon." This abruptness prevents the mind from fully cognizing the event. It is experienced "too unexpectedly . . . to be fully known and is therefore not available to consciousness." Buried in the unconscious, the event is experienced irrationally, "in the nightmares and repetitive actions of the survivor." This shows how the psychoanalytic version of lay trauma theory goes beyond the Enlightenment one: "Trauma is not locatable in the simple violent or original event in an individual's past, but rather in the way its very unassimilated nature—the way it was precisely *not known* in the first instance—returns to haunt the survivor later on." When Caruth describes these traumatic symptoms, however, she returns to the theme of objectivity, suggesting that they "tell us of a reality or truth that is not otherwise available" (3–4).[7]

The enormous influence of this psychoanalytic version of lay trauma theory can be seen in the way it has informed the recent efforts by Latin American scholars to come to terms with the traumatic brutalities of their recent dictatorships. Many of these discussions, of course, are purely empirical investigations of the extent of repression and/or normative arguments that assign responsibilities and demand reparations. Yet there is an increasing body of literature that addresses the effects of the repression in terms of the traumas it caused.

The aim is to restore collective psychological health by lifting societal repression and restoring memory. To achieve this, social scientists stress the importance of finding—through public acts of commemoration, cultural representation, and public political struggle—some collective means for undoing repression and allowing the pent-up emotions of loss and mourning to be expressed. While thoroughly laudable in moral terms, and without doubt also very helpful in terms of promoting public discourse and enhancing self-esteem, this advocacy literature typically is limited by the constraints of lay common sense. The traumatized feelings of the victims, and the actions that should be taken in response, are both treated as the unmediated, common-sense reactions to the repression itself. Elizabeth Jelin and Susana Kaufman, for example, directed a large-scale project on "Memory and Narrativity" sponsored by the Ford Foundation, involving a team of investigators from different South American countries. In their powerful report on their initial findings, "Layers of Memories: Twenty Years After in Argentina,"[8] they contrast the victims' insistance on recognizing the reality of traumatizing events and experiences with the denials of the perpetrators and their conservative supporters, denials that insist on looking to the future and forgetting the past: "The confrontation is between the voices of those who call for commemoration, for remembrance of the disappearances and the torment, for denunciation of the repressors, and those who make it their business to act 'as if nothing has happened here.'" Jelin and Kaufman call these conservative forces the "bystanders of horror" who claim they "did not know" and "did not see." But because the event—the traumatizing repression—was real, these denials will not work: "The personalized memory of people cannot be erased or destroyed by decree or by force." The efforts to memorialize the victims of the repression are presented as efforts to restore the objectivity reality of the brutal events, to separate them from the unconscious distortions of memory: "Monuments, museums and memorials are . . . attempts to make statements and affirmations [to create] a materiality with a political, collective, public meaning [and] a physical reminder of a conflictive political past" (unpublished, 5–7).

## THE NATURALISTIC FALLACY

It is through these Enlightenment and psychoanalytic approaches that trauma has been translated from an idea in ordinary language into an intellectual concept in the academic languages of diverse disciplines. Both perspectives, however, share the "naturalistic fallacy" of the lay understanding from which they derive. It is on the rejection of this naturalistic fallacy that my own approach rests. First and foremost, I maintain that events do not, in and of themselves, create collective trauma. Events are not inherently traumatic. Trauma is a socially mediated attribution. The attribution may be made in real time, as an event unfolds; it may also be made before the event occurs, as an adumbration, or after the event has concluded, as a post hoc reconstruction. Sometimes, in fact, events that are deeply traumatizing may not actually have occurred at all; such imagined events, however, can be as traumatizing as events that have actually occurred.

This notion of an "imagined" traumatic event seems to suggest the kind of process that Benedict Anderson describes in *Imagined Communites* (Anderson, 1991). Anderson's concern, of course, is not with trauma per se but with the kinds of self-consciously ideological narratives of nationalist history. Yet these collective beliefs often assert the existence of some national trauma. In the course of defining national identity, national histories are constructed around injuries that cry out for revenge. The twentieth century was replete with examples of angry nationalist groups and their intellectual and media representatives asserting that they were injured or traumatized by agents of some putatatively antagonistic ethnic and political group, which must then be battled against in turn. The Serbians inside Serbia, for example, contended that ethnic Albanians in Kosovo did them traumatic injury, thus providing justification for their own "defensive" invasion and ethnic cleansing. The type case of such militarist construction of primordial national trauma was Adolph Hitler's grotesque assertion that the international Jewish conspiracy had been responsible for Germany's traumatic loss in World War I.

But what Anderson means by "imagined" is not, in fact, exactly what I have in mind here. For he makes use of this concept in order to point to the completely illusory, nonempirical, nonexistent quality of the original event. Anderson is horrified by the ideology of nationalism, and his analysis of imagined national communities partakes of "ideology critique." As such, it applies the kind of Enlightenment perspective that mars lay trauma theory, which I am criticizing here. It is not that traumas are never constructed from nonexistent events. Certainly they are. But it is too easy to accept the imagined dimension of trauma when the reference is primarily to claims like these, which point to events that either never did occur or to events whose representation involve exaggerations that serve obviously aggressive and harmful political force. Our approach to the idea of "imagined" is more like what Durkheim meant in *The Elementary Forms of Religious Life* when he wrote of the "religious imagination." Imagination is intrinsic to the very process of representation. It seizes on an inchoate experience from life and forms it, through association, condensation, and aesthetic creation, into some specific shape.

Imagination informs trauma construction just as much when the reference is to something that has actually occurred as to something that has not. It is only through the imaginative process of representation that actors have the sense of experience. Even when claims of victimhood are morally justifiable, politically democratic, and socially progressive, these claims still cannot be seen as automatic, or natural, responses to the actual nature of an event itself. To accept the constructivist position in such cases may be difficult, for the claim to verisimilitude is fundamental to the very sense that a trauma has occurred. Yet, while every argument about trauma claims ontological reality, as cultural sociologists we are not primarily concerned with the accuracy of social actors' claims, much less with evaluating their moral justification. We are concerned only with how and under what conditions the claims are made, and with what results. It is neither ontology nor morality, but with epistemology, that we are concerned.

Traumatic status is attributed to real or imagined phenomena, not because of their actual harmfulness or their objective abruptness, but because these phenomena are believed to have abruptly, and harmfully, affected collective identity. Individual security is anchored in structures of emotional and cultural expectations that provide a sense of security and capability. These expectations and capabilities, in turn, are rooted in the sturdiness of the collectivities of which individuals are a part. At issue is not the stability of a collectivity in the material or behavioral sense, although this certainly plays a part. What is at stake, rather, is the collectivity's identity, its stability in terms of meaning, not action.

Identity involves a cultural reference. Only if the patterned meanings of the collectivity are abruptly dislodged is traumatic status attributed to an event. It is the meanings that provide the sense of shockingness and fear, not the events in themselves. Whether or not the structures of meaning are destabilized and shocked is not the result of an event but the effect of a sociocultural process. It is the result of an exercise of human agency, of the successful imposition of a new system of cultural classification. This cultural process is deeply affected by power structures and by the contingent skills of reflexive social agents.

## THE SOCIAL PROCESS OF CULTURAL TRAUMA

At the level of the social system, societies can experience massive disruptions that do not become traumatic. Institutions can fail to perform. Schools may fail to educate, failing miserably even to provide basic skills. Governments may be unable to secure basic protections and may undergo severe crises of delegitimation. Economic systems may be profoundly disrupted, to the extent that their allocative functions fail even to provide basic goods. Such problems are real and fundamental, but they are not, by any means, necessarily traumatic for members of the affected collectivities—much less for the society at large. For traumas to emerge at the level of the collectivity, social crises must become cultural crises. Events are one thing, representations of these events quite another. Trauma is not the result of a group experiencing pain. It is the result of this acute discomfort entering into the core of the collectivity's sense of its own identity. Collective actors "decide" to represent social pain as a fundamental threat to their sense of who they are, where they came from, and where they want to go. In this section I lay out the processes that the nature of these collective actions and the cultural and institutional processes that mediate them.

### Claim-Making: The Spiral of Signification

The gap between event and representation can be conceived as the "trauma process." Collectivities do not make decisions as such; rather, it is agents who do (Alexander, 1987; Alexander, Giesen, Munch, & Smelser, 1987; Sztompka, 1991, 1993). The persons who compose collectivites broadcast symbolic representations—characterizations—of ongoing social events, past, present, and future. They broadcast these representations as members of a social group. These group representations can be seen as "claims" about the shape of social reality, its causes, and the responsibilities for action such causes imply. The cultural construction of trauma begins with such a claim (Thompson, 1998).[9] It is a claim to some fundamental injury, an exclamation of the terrifying profanation of some sacred value, a narrative about a horribly destructive social process, and a demand for emotional, institutional, and symbolic reparation and reconstitution.

### Carrier Groups

Such claims are made by what Max Weber, in his sociology of religion, called "carrier groups" (Weber, 1968: 468–517).[10] the collective agents of the trauma process. Carrier groups have both ideal and material interests; they are situated in particular places in the social structure; and they have particular discursive talents for articulating their claims—for what might be called "meaning making"—in the public sphere. Carrier groups may be elites, but they may also be denigrated and marginalized classes. They may be prestigious religious leaders or groups whom the majority has designated as spiritual pariahs. A carrier group can be generational, representing the perspectives and interests of a younger generation against an older one. It can be national, pitting one's own nation against a putative enemy. It can be institutional, representing one particular social sector or organization against others in a fragmented and polarized social order.

### Audience and Situation: Speech Act Theory

The trauma process can be likened, in this sense, to a speech act (Austin, 1962; Habermas, 1984; Pia Lara, 1998; Searle, 1969).[11] Traumas, like speech acts, have the following elements:

1. *Speaker*: the carrier group
2. *Audience:* the public, putatively homogeneous but sociologically fragmented
3. *Situation:* the historical, cultural, and institutional environment within which the speech act occurs

The goal of the speaker is persuasively to project the trauma claim to the audience-public. In doing so, the carrier group makes use of the particularities of the historical situation, the symbolic resources at hand, and the constraints and opportunites provided by institutional structures. In the first place, of course, the speaker's audience must be members of the carrier group itself. If there is illocutionary success, the members of this originating collectivity become convinced that they have been traumatized by a singular event. Only with this success can the audience for the traumatic claim be broadened to include other publics within the "society at large."

### Cultural Classification: The Creation of Trauma as a New Master Narrative

Bridging the gap between event and representation depends on what Kenneth Thompson has called, in reference to the topic of moral panics, a "spiral of signification" (Thompson, 1998: 20–4).[12] Representation of trauma depends on constructing a compelling framework of cultural classification. In one sense, this is simply telling a new story. Yet this story-telling is, at the same time, a complex and multivalent symbolic process that is contingent, highly contested, and sometimes highly polarizing. For the wider audience to become persuaded that they, too, have become traumatized by an experience or an event, the carrier group needs to engage in successful meaning work.

Four critical representations are essential to the creation of a new master narrative. While I will place these four dimensions of representations into an analytical sequence, I do not mean to suggest temporality. In social reality, these representations unfold in an interlarded manner that is continuously crossreferential. The causality is symbolic and aesthetic, not sequential or developmental but "value-added" (Smelser, 1963).

The questions to which a successful process of collective representation must provide compelling answers are as follows.

*The nature of the pain.* What actually happened—to the particular group and to the wider collectivity of which it is a part?

- Did the denouement of the Vietnam War leave a festering wound on the American psyche or was it incorporated in a more or less routine way? If there was a shattering wound, in what exactly did it consist? Did the American military lose the Vietnam War or did the Vietnam trauma consist of the pain of having the nation's hands "tied behind its back"?[13]
- Did hundreds of ethnic Albanians die in Kosovo, or was it tens and possibly even hundreds of thousands? Did they die because of starvation or displacement in the course of a civil war, or were they deliberately murdered?
- Was slavery a trauma for African Americans? Or was it, as some revisionist historians have claimed, merely a highly profitable mode of economic production? If the latter, then slavery may not have produced traumatic pain. If the former, it certainly involved brutal and traumatizing physical domination (Eyerman, 2002).
- Was the internecine ethnic and religious conflict in Northern Ireland, these last thirty years, "civil unrest and terrorism," as Queen Elizabeth once described it, or a "bloody war," as claimed by the IRA (quoted in Maillot, unpublished manuscript)?
- Did less than a hundred persons die at the hands of Japanese soldiers in Nanking, China, in 1938, or three hundred thousand? Did these deaths result from a one-sided "massacre" or a "fierce contest" between opposing armies? (Chang, 1997: 206)

*The nature of the victim.* What group of persons was affected by this traumatizing pain? Were they particular individuals or groups, or the much more all-encompassing "people" as such? Did one singular and delimited group receive the brunt of the pain, or were several groups involved?

- Were the German Jews the primary victims of the Holocaust or did the victim group extend to the Jews of the Pale, European Jewry, or the Jewish people as a whole? Were the millions of Polish people who died at the hands of German Nazis also victims of the Holocaust? Were communists, socialists, homosexuals, and handicapped persons also victims of the Nazi Holocaust?

- Were Kosovar Albanians the primary victims of ethnic cleansing, or were Kosovar Serbs also significantly, or even equally victimized?
- Are African-American blacks the victims of the brutal, traumatizing conditions in the desolate inner cities of the United States, or are the victims of these conditions members of an economically defined "underclass"?
- Were North American Indians the victims of European colonizers or were the victims particularly situated, and particularly "aggressive," Indian nations?
- Are non-Western or third world nations the victims of globalization, or only the least developed, or least well equipped, among them?

*Relation of the trauma victim to the wider audience.* Even when the nature of the pain has been crystallized and the identity of the victim established, there remains the highly significant question of the relation of the victim to the wider audience. To what extent do the members of the audience for trauma representations experience an identity with the immediately victimized group? Typically, at the beginning of the trauma process, most audience members see little if any relation between themselves and the victimized group. Only if the victims are represented in terms of valued qualities shared by the larger collective identity will the audience be able to symbolically participate in the experience of the originating trauma.

- Gypsies are acknowledged by contemporary Central Europeans as trauma victims, the bearers of a tragic history. Yet insofar as large numbers of central Europeans represent the "Roman people" as deviant and uncivilized, they have not made that tragic past their own.
- Influential groups of German and Polish people have acknowledged that Jews were victims of mass murder, but they have often refused to experience their own national collective identities as being affected by the Jews' tragic fate.
- Did the police brutality that traumatized black civil rights activists in Selma, Alabama, in 1965, create identification among the white Americans who watched the events on their televisions in the safety of the nonsegregated North? Is the history of white American racial domination relegated to an entirely separate time, or is it conceived, by virtue of the reconstruction of collective memory, as a contemporary issue?

*Attribution of responsibility.* In creating a compelling trauma narrative, the identity of the perpetrator—the "antagonist"—is critical to establish. Who actually injured the victim? Who caused the trauma? This issue is always a matter of symbolic and social construction.

- Did "Germany" create the Holocaust or was it the Nazi regime? Was the crime restricted to special SS forces or was the Werhmacht, the entire Nazi army, also deeply involved? Did the crime extend to ordinary soldiers, to ordinary citizens, to Catholic as well as Protestant Germans? Was it only the older generation of Germans who were responsible, or later generations as well?

## Institutional Arenas

This representational process creates a new master narrative of social suffering. Such cultural (re)classification is critical to the process by which a collectivity becomes traumatized.[14] But it does not unfold in what Habermas would call a transparent speech situation (Habermas, 1984).[15] The notion of transparency is posited by Habermas as a normative ideal essential to the democratic functioning of the public sphere, not as an empirical description. In actual social practice, speech acts never unfold in an unmediated way. Linguistic action is powerfully mediated by the nature of the institutional arenas within which it occurs. While by no means exhaustive, some examples of this institutional mediation are provided here.

1. If the trauma process unfolds inside the *religious* arena, its concern will be to link trauma to theodicy.

- The Torah's story of Job, for example, asks "why did God allow this evil?" The answers to such questions will generate searching discussions about whether and how human beings strayed from divinely inspired ethics and sacred law, or whether the existence of evil means that God does not exist.

2. Insofar as meaning work takes place in the *aesthetic* realm, it will be channeled by specific genres and narratives that aim to produce imaginative identification and emotional catharsis.

- In the early representations of the Holocaust, for example, the tragic *Diary of Anne Frank* played a vital role, and in later years an entirely new genre called "survivor literature" developed (Hayes, 1999, and chapter 2, above).
- In the aftermath of ethnocide in Guatemala, in which two hundred thousand Mayan Indians were killed and entire villages destroyed, an ethnographer recorded how, in the town of Santa Maria Tzeja, theatre was "used to publicly confront the past."

"A group of teenagers and . . . a North American teacher and director of the community's school write a play that documents what Santa Maria Tzeja has experienced. They call the play, *There Is Nothing Concealed That Will Not Be Disclosed Matthew (10:26)*, and the villagers themselves perform it. The play not only recalls what happened in the village in a stark, unflinching manner but also didactially lays out the laws and rights that the military violated. The play pointedly and precisely cites articles of the Guatemalan constitution that were trampled on, not normally the text of great drama. But in

Guatemala, reading the constitution can be a profoundly dramatic act. Peformances inevitably lead to moving and at times heated discussions. [The production] had a cathartic impact on the village. (Manz, 2002)

As this example suggests, mass media are significant, but not necessary, in this aesthetic arena.

- In the aftermath of the 80-day NATO bombing that forced Yugoslavian Serbs to abandon their violent, decade-long domination of Albanian Kosovo, Serbian films provided mass channels for reexperincing the period of suffering even while they narrated the protagonists, the victims, and the very nature of the trauma in strikingly different ways.

It is hard to see why anyone who survived 78 traumatic days of air-strikes in 1999 would want to relive the experience in a theater, bringing back memories as well of a murderous decade that ended in October with the fall of President Slobodan Milosevic. Yet Yugoslavia's feature film industry has done little else in the past year but turn out NATO war movies [some of which] have begun to cut through the national façade that Milsoevic's propagandists had more than 10 years to build. [In one movie, the protagonist recounts that] "it is dead easy to kill. . . . They stare at you, weep and wail, and you shoot 'em and that's the end—end of story. Later, of course, they all come back and you want to set things right, but it's too late. That's why the truth is always returning to judge men. (Paul Watson, "War's Over in Yugoslavia, but Box-Office Battles Have Begun," *Los Angeles Times,* January 3, 2001, A1–6)

3. When the cultural classification enters the *legal* realm, it will be disciplined by the demand to issue a definitive judgment of legally binding responsibilities and to distribute punishments and material reparations. Such a demonstration may have nothing at all to do with the perpetrators themselves accepting responsibility or a broader audience identifying with those who suffered as the trauma drama plays out.

- In regard to binding definitions of war crimes and crimes against humanity, the 1945 Nuremberg trials were critical. They created revolutionary new law and resulted in dozens of successful prosecutions, yet they did not, by any means, succeed in compelling the German people themselves to recognize the existence of Nazi traumas, much less their responsibilities for them. Nonetheless, the legal statutes developed at Nuremberg were elaborated in the decades following, laying the basis for dozens highly publicized lawsuits that in recent years have created significant dramaturgy and unleashed profound moral effects. These trials for "crimes against humanity" have implicated not only individuals but national organizations.

- Because neither postwar Japanese governments nor the most influential Japanese publics have even recognized the war crimes committed by its Imperial war policies, much less taken moral responsibility for them, no suit seeking damages for Imperial atrocities has, until recently, ever made any substantial headway in Japan's courts. In explaining why one suit against the Imperial government's biological warfare unit has finally made substantial progress, observers have pointed to the specificity and autonomy of the legal arena.

  As a member of the Japanese biological warfare outfit, known as United 731, Mr. Shinozuka was told that if he ever faced capture by the Chinese, his duty to Emperor Hirohito was to kill himself rather than compromise the secrecy of a program that so clearly violated international law. . . . Now, 55 years later, he is a hale 77-year-old. But still haunted by remorse, he has spoken—providing the first account before a Japanese court by a veteran about the workings of the notorious unit. . . . That this case, now in its final stages, has not been dismissed like so many others is due in part to painstaking legal research and to cooperation over strategy by some of Japan's leading lawyers. Lawyers who have sued the government say the fact that this case has become the first in which a judge has allowed the extensive introduction of evidence instead of handing down a quick dismissal may also attest to an important shift under way on the issue of reparations. (Howard W. French, "Japanese Veteran Testifies in War Atrocity Lawsuit," *New York Times,* December 21, 2000: A3)

4. When the trauma process enters the *scientific* world, it becomes subject to evidentiary stipulations of an altogether different kind, creating scholarly controversies, "revelations," and "revisions." When historians endeavor to define an historical event as traumatic, they must document, by acceptable scholarly methods, the nature of the pain, the victims, and the responsibility. In doing so, the cultural classification process often triggers explosive methodological controversies.

- What were the causes of World War I? Who was responsible for initiating it? Who were its victims?
- Did the Japanese intend to launch a "sneak" attack on Pearl Harbor, or was the late-arriving message to Washington, D.C., from the Japanese Imperial government, delayed by inadvertance and diplomatic confusion?
- The German *Historichstreit* controversy captured international attention in the 1980s, questioning the new scholarly conservatives' emphasis on anticommunism as a motivation for the Nazi seizure of power and its anti-Jewish policies. In the 1990s, Daniel Goldhagen's book *Hitler's Willing Executioners* was attacked by mainstream historians for overemphasizing the uniquess of German anti-Semitism.

5. When the trauma process enters the *mass media,* it is gains opportunities and at the same time becomes subject to distinctive kinds of restrictions. Mediated mass communication allows traumas to be expressively dramatized, and some of the competing interpretations to gain enormous persuasive power over others. At the same time, however, these representational processes become subject to the restrictions of news reporting, with their demands for concision, ethical neutrality, and perspectival balance. Finally, there is the competition for readership that often inspires the sometimes exaggerated and distorted production of "news" in mass circulation newspapers and magazines. As an event comes to be reported as a trauma, a particular group as "traumatized," and another group as the perpetrators, politicians and other elites may attack the media, its owners, and often the journalists whose reporting established the trauma facts.

- During the traumas of the late 1960s, American television news brought evocative images of terrible civilian suffering from the Vietnam War into the living rooms of American citizens. These images were seized on by antiwar critics. The conservative American politician, vice-president Spiro Agnew, initiated virulent attacks against the "liberal" and "Jewish-dominated" media for their insistence that the Vietnamese civilian population was being traumatized by the American-dominated war.

6. When the trauma process enters into the *state bureaucracy,* it can draw on the governmental power to channel the representational process. Decisions by the executive branches of governments to create national commissions of inquiry, votes by parliaments to establish investigative committees, the creation of state-directed police investigations and new directives about national priorities—all such actions can have decisive effects on handling and channeling the spiral of signification that marks the trauma process (Smelser, 1963).[16] In the last decade, blue-ribbon commissions have become a favored state vehicle for such involvement. By arranging and balancing the participation on such panels, forcing the appearance of witnesses, and creating carefully choreographed public dramaturgy, such panels tilt the interpretive process in powerful ways, expanding and narrowing solidarity, creating or denying the factual and moral basis for reparations and civic repair.

- Referring to hundreds of thousands of Mayan Indians who died at the hands of Guatemalan counterinsurgency forces between 1981 and 1983, an ethnographer of the region asserts that "without question, the army's horrific actions ripped deep psychological wounds into the consciousness of the inhabitants of this village [who were also] involved in a far larger trauma" (Manz, 2002: 294). Despite the objective status of the trauma, however, and the pain and suffering it had caused, the ability to collectively recognize and process it was inhibited because the village was "a place hammered into silence and accustomed to impunity." In 1994, as part of the negotiation between the Guatemalan government and the umbrella group of insurgent forces, the *Commission for Historical Clarification* (CEH) was created to hear testimony from the affected parties and to present an interpretation. Five years later, its published conclusion declared that "agents of the State of Guatemala . . . committed acts of genocide against groups of Mayan people" (quoted in Manz, 2002: 293). According to the ethnographer, the report "stunned the country." By publicly representing the nature of the pain, defining victim and perpetrator, and assigning responsibility, the trauma process was enacted within the governmental arena: "It was as if the whole country burst into tears, tears that had been repressed for decades and tears of vindication" (Manz, 2002: 294).

• In the middle 1990s, the post-apartheid South African government established the *Truth and Reconciliation Commission.* Composed of widely respected blacks and whites, the group called witnesses and conducted widely broadcast hearings about the suffering created by the repression that marked the preceding Afrikaner government. The effort succeeded, to some significant degree, in generalizing the trauma process beyond racially polarized audiences, making it into a shared experience of the new, more solidary, and more democratic South African society. Such a commission could not have been created until blacks became enfranchised and became the dominant racial power.

• By contrast, the postfascist Japanese government has never been willing to create official commissions investigate the war crimes committed by its Imperial leaders and soldiers against non-Japanese during World War II. In regard to the Japanese enslavement of tens and possibly hundreds of thousands of "comfort women," primarily Korean, who provided sexual services for Imperial solidiers, the Japanese government finally agreed in the late 1990s to disperse relatively token monetary reparation to the Korean women still alive. Critics have continued to demand that an officially sanctioned commission hold public hearings into the trauma, a dramaturgical and legally binding process that, despite its ambiguous, and brief, public apology to the "comfort women," the Japanese government has never been willing to allow. It is revealing of the significance of such a governmental arena that these critics eventually mounted an unofficial tribunal themselves.

Last week in Tokyo, private Japanese and international organizations convened a war tribunal that found Japan's military leaders, including Emperor Hirohito, guilty of crimes against humanity for the sexual slavery imposed on tens of thousands of women in countries controlled by Japan during World War II. The tribunal has no legal power to exact reparations for the survivors among those so-called comfort women. But with its judges and lawyers drawn from official international tribunals for the countries that once were part of Yugoslavia and for Rwanda, it brought unparalleled moral authority to an issue scarcely discussed or taught about in Japan. (Howard W. French, "Japanese

Veteran Testifies in War Atrocity Lawsuit," *New York Times,* December 21, 2000: A3)

## Stratificational Hierarchies

The constraints imposed by institutional arenas are themselves mediated by the uneven distribution of material resources and the social networks that provide differential access to them.

1. Who owns the newspapers? To what degree are journalists independent of political and financial control?
2. Who controls the religious orders? Are they internally authoritarian or can congregants exercise independent influence?
3. Are courts independent? What is the scope of action available to entrepreneurical legal advocates?
4. Are educational policies subject to mass movements of public opinion or are they insulated by bureaucratic procedures at more centralized levels?
5. Who exercizes controls over the government?

As I have indicated in my earlier reference to the governmental arena, local, provincial, and national governments deploy significant power over the trauma process. What must be considered here is that these bodies might occupy a positon of dominance over the traumatized parties themselves. In these cases, the commissions might whitewash the perpetrators' actions rather than dramatize them.

- In the 1980s, the conservative American and British governments of Ronald Reagan and Margaret Thatcher initially did little to dramatize the dangers of the virulent AIDS epidemic because they did not wish to create sympathy or identification with the homosexual practices their ideologies so stigmatized. The failure allowed the epidemics to spread more rapidly. Finally, the Thatcher government launched a massive public education campaign about the dangers of HIV. The effort quickly took the steam out of the moral panic over the AIDS epidemic that had swept through British society and helped launch appropriate public health measures (Thompson, 1998).
- In 2000, reports surfaced in American media about a massacre of several hundred Korean civilians by American soliders at No Gun Ri early in the Korean War. Suggestions from Korean witnesses, and newfound testimony from some American soldiers, suggested the possibility that the firings had been intentional, and allegations about racism and war crimes were made. In response, President Clinton assigned the U.S. army itself to convene its own official, in-house investigation. While a senior army official claimed "we

have worked closely with the Korean government to investigate the circumstances surrounding No Gun Ri," the power to investigate and interpret the evidence clearly rested with the perpetrators of the trauma alone. Not surprisingly, when its findings were announced several months later, the U.S. army declared itself innocent of the charges that had threatened its good name:

We do not believe it is appropriate to issue an apology in this matter. [While] some of those civilizan casualties were at the hand of American solider[s], that conclusion is very different from the allegation that was made that this was a massacre in the classic sense that we lined up innocent people and gunned them down. (New York Times, December 22, 2000: A5)

### Identity Revision, Memory, and Routinization

"Experiencing trauma" can be understood as a sociological process that defines a painful injury to the collectivity, establishes the victim, attributes responsibility, and distributes the ideal and material consequences. Insofar as traumas are so experienced, and thus imagined and represented, the collective identity will become significantly revised. This identity revision means that there will be a searching re-remembering of the collective past, for memory is not only social and fluid but deeply connected to the contemporary sense of the self. Identities are continuously constructed and secured not only by facing the present and future but also by reconstructing the collectivity's earlier life.

Once the collective identity has been so reconstructed, there will eventually emerge a period of "calming down." The spiral of signification flattens out, affect and emotion become less inflamed, preoccupation with sacrality and pollution fades. Charisma becomes routinized, effervescence evaporates, and liminality gives way to reaggregation. As the heightened and powerfully affecting discourse of trauma disappears, the "lessons" of the trauma become objectified in monuments, museums, and collections of historical artifacts.[17] The new collective identity will be rooted in sacred places and structured in ritual routines. In the late 1970s, the ultra-Maoist Khmer Rouge government was responsible for the deaths of more than one-third of Cambodia's citizens. The murderous regime was deposed in 1979. While fragmentation, instability, and authoritarianism in the decades following prevented the trauma process from fully playing itself out, the processes of reconstruction, representation, and working-through produced significant commemoration, ritual, and reconstruction of national identity.

Vivid reminders of the DK [Khmer Rouge]'s horrors are displayed in photographs of victims, paintings of killings, and implements used for torture at the Tuol Sleng Museum of Genocidal Crimes, a former school that had become a deadly interrogation center's . . . as well as in a monumental display of skulls and bones at Bhhoeung Ek, a former killing field where one can still see bits of bone and cloth in the soil of what had been mass graves. The PRK [the new Cambodian government] also instituted an annual observance called The Day of Hate, in which people were gathered at various locales to hear invectives heaped on the Khmer Rouge. State propaganda played on this theme with such slogans as: "We must absolutely prevent the return of this former black darkness" and "We must struggle ceaselessly to protect against the return of the . . . genocidal clique." These formulaic and state-sanctioned expressions were genuine and often expressed in conversations among ordinary folk. (Ebihara & Ledgerwood in Hinton, 2002: 282–3)

In this routinization process, the trauma process, once so vivid, can become subject to the technical, sometimes dessicating attention of specialists who detach affect from meaning. This triumph of the mundane is often noted with regret by audiences that had been mobilized by the trauma process, and it is sometimes forcefully opposed by carrier groups. Often, however, it is welcomed with a sense of public and private relief. Created to remember and commemorate the trauma process, efforts to institutionalize the lessons of the trauma will eventually prove unable to evoke the strong emotions, the sentiments of betrayal, and the affirmations of sacrality that once were so powerfully associated with it. No longer deeply preoccupying, the reconstructed collective identity remains, nevertheless, a fundamental resource for resolving future social problems and disturbances of collective consciousness.

The inevitability of such routinization processes by no means neutralizes the extraordinary social significance of cultural traumas. Their creation and routinization have, to the contrary, the most profound normative implications for the conduct of social life. By allowing members of wider publics to participate in the pain of others, cultural traumas broaden the realm of social understanding and sympathy, and they provide powerful avenues for new forms of social incorporation.[18]

The elements of the trauma process I have outlined in this section can be thought of as social structures, if we think of this term in something other than its materialist sense. Each element plays a role in the social construction and deconstuction of a traumatic event. Whether any or all of these structures actually come into play is not itself a matter of structural determination. It is subject to the unstructured, unforeseeable contingencies of historical time. A war is lost or won. A new regime has entered into power or a discredited regime remains stubbornly in place. Hegemonic or counterpublics may be empowered and enthusiastic or undermined and exhausted by social conflict and stalemate. Such contingent historical factors exercise powerful influence on whether a consensus will be generated that allows the cultural classification of trauma to be set firmly in place.

## TRAUMA CREATION AND PRACTICAL-MORAL ACTION: THE NON-WESTERN RELEVANCE

In the preceding pages, I have elaborated a middle-range theory of the complex causes propeling the trauma process. In illustrating this analytical argument, I have referred to traumatic situations in Western and non-Western, developed and less-developed societies—in Northern Ireland and Poland, the United Kingdom and Cambodia, Japan and Yugoslavia, South Africa, Guatemala, and Korea.

It would be a serious misunderstanding if trauma theory were restricted in its reference to Western social life. True, it has been Western societies that have recently provided the most dramatic apologias for traumatic episodes in their national histories; yet the victims of these traumas have disproportionately been members of subaltern and marginalized groups. It should hardly be surprising, in other words, that the theory developed in relation to these empirical cases can so fluidly be extended to the experiences of trauma outside of Western societies. In the course of this introduction, I have mentioned also gypsies, Mayan Indians, American Indians, Kosovar Albanians, Chinese city dwellers, and Cambodian peasants. In fact, it is clear that the non-Western regions of the world, and the most defenseless segments of the world's population, that have recently been subjected to the most terrifying traumatic injuries.

The anthropologist Alexander Hinton has suggested that "while the behaviors it references have an ancient pedigree, the concept of genocide . . . is thoroughly modern." (Hinton, 2002: 27). Indeed, it is the very premise of the contributions he and his fellow anthropologists make to their collective work, *Annihilating Difference: The Anthropology of Genocide*, that by the latter half of the twentieth century this modern framework had thoroughly penetrated non-Western societies (Hinton, 2002). "On the conceptual level," Hinton writes,

> terms like *trauma, suffering,* and *cruelty* are linked to the discourses of modernity . . . (Hinton, 2002: 25). Furthermore, in the mass media, the victims of genocide are frequently condensed into an essentialized portrait of the *universal* sufferer, an image that can be . . . (re)broadcast to *global* audiences who see their own potential trauma reflected in this simulation of the modern subject.
> Refugees frequently epitomize this modern trope of human suffering; silent and anonymous, they signify both a *universal humanity* and the threat of the premodern and uncivilized, which they have supposedly barely survived. . . . Particularly in the *global* present, as such diverse populations and images flow rapidly across national borders, genocide . . . creates diasporic communities that threaten to undermine its culminating political incarnation. (26, italics added)

There is no more excruciating example of the universal relevance of trauma theory than the way it can help illuminate the tragic difficulties that non-

Western societies have often experienced in coming to terms with genocide. Because genocide is more likely to occur in collective arenas that are neither legally regulated and democratic nor formally egalitarian (Kuper, 1981),[19] it is hardly surprising that, in the last half century, the most dramatic and horrifying examples of mass murder have emerged from within the more fragmented and impoverished areas of the non-Western world: the Hutu massacre of more than five hundred thousand Tutsis in less than three weeks in Rwanda, the Guatemalan military's ethnocide of two hundred thousand Mayan Indians during the dirty civil war in the early 1980s, the Maoist Khmer Rouge's elimination of almost one-third of Cambodia's entire population in its revolutionary purges in the late 1970s.

The tragic reasons for these recent outpourings of mass murder in the non-Western world cannot be our concern here. A growing body of social scientific work is devoted to this question, although a great deal more needs to be done (Kleinman, Das, & Lock, 1997). What cultural trauma theory helps us understand, instead, is a central paradox, about not the causes of genocide but its aftereffects: Why have these genocidal actions, so traumatic to their millions of immediate victims, so rarely branded themselves on the consciousness of the wider populations? Why have these horrendous phenomena of mass suffering not become compelling, publicly available narratives of collective suffering to their respective nations, let alone to the world at large? The reasons, I suggest, can be found in the complex patterns of the trauma process I have outlined here.

In fact, several years before the Nazi massacre of the Jews, which eventually branded Western modernity as the distinctive bearer of collective trauma in the twentieth century, the most developed society outside the West had itself already engaged in systematic atrocities. In early December 1938, invading Japanese soldiers slaughtered as many as three hundred thousand Chinese residents of Nanking, China. Under orders from the highest levels of the Imperial government, they carried out this massacre in six of the bloodiest weeks of modern history, without the technological aids later developed by the Nazis in their mass extermination of the Jews. By contrast with the Nazi massacre, this Japanese atrocity was not hidden from the rest of the world. To the contrary, it was carried out under the eyes of critical and highly articulate Western observers and reported on massively by respected members of the world's press. Yet in the sixty years that have transpired since that time, the memorialization of the "rape of Nanking" has never extended beyond the regional confines of China, and eventually barely beyond the confines of Nanking itself. The trauma contributed scarcely at all to the collective identity of the People's Republic of China, let alone to the self-conception of the postwar democratic government of Japan. As the most recent narrator of the massacre puts it, "even by the standards of history's most destructive war, the Rape of Nanking represents one of the worst instances of mass extermination." Yet, though extraordinarily traumatic for the contemporary residents of Nanking, it became "the forgotten

Holocaust of World War II." It remains an "obscure incident" today (Chang, 1997: 5–6), the very existence of which is routinely and successfully denied by some of Japan's most powerful and esteemed public officials.

As I have suggested in this chapter, such failures to recognize collective traumas, much less to incorporate their lessons into collective identity, do not result from the intrinsic nature of the original suffering. This is the naturalistic fallacy that follows from lay trauma theory. The failure stems, rather, from an inability to carry through what I have called here the trauma process. In Japan and China, just as in Rwanda, Cambodia, and Guatemala, claims have certainly been made for the central relevance of these "distant sufferings" (Boltanski, 1999).[20] But for both social-structural and culture reasons, carrier groups have not emerged with the resources, authority, or interpretive competence to powerfully disseminate these trauma claims. Sufficiently persuasive narratives have not been created, or they have not been successfully broadcast to wider audiences. Because of these failures, the perpetrators of these collective sufferings have not been compelled to accept moral responsibility, and the lessons of these social traumas have been neither memorialized nor ritualized. New definitions of moral responsibility have not been generated. Social solidarities have not been extended. More primordial and more particularistic collective identities have not been changed.

In this concluding section, I have tried to underscore my earlier contention that the theory presented here is not merely technical and scientific. It is normatively relevant and significantly illuminates processes of moral-practical action. However tortuous the trauma process, it allows collectivities to define new forms of moral responsibility and to redirect the course of political action. This open-ended and contingent process of trauma creation, and the assigning of collective responsibility that goes along with it, is as relevant to non-Western as Western societies. Collective traumas have no geographical or cultural limitations. The theory of cultural trauma applies, without prejudice, to any and all instances when societies have, or have not, constructed and experienced cultural traumatic events, and to their efforts to draw, or not to draw, the moral lessons that can be said to emanate from them.

4

# A CULTURAL SOCIOLOGY OF EVIL

In the course of the last two decades, there has emerged a new recognition of the independent structuring power of culture. Yet it turns out that this new disciplinary self-consciousness has not been any more successful in addressing evil than its reductionist predecessor. In thinking about culture—values and norms, codes and narratives, rituals and symbols—"negativity" has been set off to one side and treated as a residual category. While it has not been treated naturalistically, it has been presented merely as a deviation from cultural constructions of the good. Thus, in social scientific formulations of culture, a society's "values" are studied primarily as orientations to the good, as efforts to embody ideals.[1] Social notions of evil, badness, and negativity are explored only as patterned deviations from normatively regulated conduct. If only this were the case! It seems to me that this cultural displacement of evil involves more moralizing wish fulfillment than empirical realism. Not only does it detract from our general understanding of evil but it makes the relation of evil to modernity much more difficult to comprehend. Thinking of evil as a residual category camouflages the destruction and cruelty that has accompanied enlightened efforts to institutionalize the good and the right. The definition of social evil and the systematic effort to combat it have everywhere accompanied the modern pursuit of reason and moral right. That is the central and most legitimate meaning of Michel Foucault's lifework, despite its simplifications, one-sidedness, and undermining relativism. It is the salvageable, saving remnant of the postmodern critique of modernity.

Culture cannot be understood only as value and norm, which can be defined as conceptual glosses on social efforts to symbolize, narrate, code, and ritualize the good. Culturalizing evil is, in sociological terms, every bit as important as such efforts to define and institutionalize the good. In semiotic terms, evil is the necessary cognitive contrast for "good."[2] In moral terms, exploring heinous evil is the only way to understand and experience the pure and the upright.[3] In terms of narrative dynamics, only by creating antiheroes can we implot the dramatic tension between protagonist and antagonist that is transformed by *Bildung* or resolved by catharsis.[4] In ritual terms, it is only the crystallization of evil, with all its stigmatizing and polluting potential, that makes rites of purification culturally necessary and sociologically possible.[5] Religiously, the sacred is incomprehensible without the profane, the promise of salvation meaningless without the threat of damnation.[6] What I am suggesting here, in other words, is that for every value there is an equal and opposite antivalue, for every norm an antinorm. For every effort to institutionalize comforting and inspiring images of the socially good and right, there is an interlinked and equally determined effort to construct social evil in a horrendous, frightening, and equally realistic way. Drawing Durkheim back to Nietzsche, and writing under the impact of the trauma of early twentieth-century modernity, Bataille articulated this point in a typically pungent and literary way.

> Evil seems to be understandable, but only to the extent to which Good is the key to it. If the luminous intensity of Good did not give the night of Evil its blackness, Evil would lose its appeal. This is a difficult point to understand. Something flinches in him who faces up to it. And yet we know that the strongest effects on the sense are caused by contrasts. . . . Without misfortune, bound to it as shade is to light, indifferences would correspond to happiness. Novels describe suffering, hardly ever satisfaction. The virtue of happiness is ultimately its rarity. Were it easily accessible it would be despised and associated with boredom. . . . Would truth be what it is if it did not assert itself generously against falsehood? (Bataille, 1990 [1957]: 14)[7]

Actors, institutions, and societies systematically crystallize and elaborate evil. They do so, ironically, in pursuit of the good. To these paradoxical and immensely depressing facts attention must be paid.

## THE INTELLECTUAL ROOTS
## OF THE DISPLACEMENT OF EVIL

To appreciate the pervasiveness of this truncated conception of culture, it is important to recognize that, while deeply affecting contemporary social science, it is rooted in earlier forms of secular and religious thought.[8] From the Greeks onward, moral philosophy has been oriented to justifying and sustaining the good and to elaborating the requirements of the just society. Plato associated his ideal forms with goodness. To be able to see these forms, he believed, was to be able to act in accordance with morality. In dramatizing Socrates' teachings in the *Re-*

*public*, Plato made use of the figure of Thrasymachus to articulate the evil forces that threatened ethical life. Rather than suggesting that Thrasymachus embodied bad values, Plato presented Thrasymachus as denying the existence of values as such: "In all states alike, 'right' has the same meaning, namely what is for the interest of the party established in power, and that is the strongest." Thrasymachus is an egoist who calculates every action with an eye not to values but to the interests of his own person. Plato makes a homology between self/collectivity, interest/value, and evil/good. In doing so, he establishes the following analogical relationship:

Self:collectivity::interest:value::evil: good
Self is to collectivity, as interest is to value, as evil is to good.

The commitment to values is the same as the commitment to collective beliefs; beliefs and values are the path to the good. Evil should be understood not as the product of bad or negatively oriented values but as the failure to connect to collective values. Evil comes from being self-interested.

In elaborating what came to be called the republican tradition in political theory, Aristotle followed this syllogism, equating a society organized around values with an ethical order: "The best way of life, for individuals severally, as well as for states collectively, is the life of goodness duly equipped with such a store of requisites as makes it possible to share in the activities of goodness" (Aristotle, 1962: 7. 1. 13).[9] Republics contained virtuous citizens, who were defined as actors capable of orienting to values outside of themselves. As individuals become oriented to the self rather than the collectivity, republics are endangered; desensitized to values, citizens become hedonistic and materialistic. According to this stark and binary contrast between morality and egoism, value commitments in themselves contribute to the good; evil occurs not because there are commitments to bad values but because of a failure to orient to values per se. While it is well known that Hegel continued the Aristotelian contrast between what he called the system of needs and the world of ethical regulation, it is less widely appreciated that pragmatism endorsed the same dichotomy in its own way. For Dewey, to value is to value the good. Interpersonal communication is bound to produce altruistic normative orientation. Crass materialism and selfishness occur when social structures prevent communication.[10]

This philosophical equation of values with goodness and the lack of values with evil informs contemporary communitarianism, which might be described as a marriage between republican and pragmatic thought. Identifying contemporary social problems with egoism and valuelessness, communitarians ignore the possibility that communal values are defined by making pejorative contrasts with other values, with others' values, and, in fact, often with the values of "the other."[11] Empirically, I want to suggest that the issue is not values versus interests or having values as compared with not having them. There are always "good" values and "bad." In sociological terms, good values can be crystallized only in relation to values that are feared or considered repugnant. This is not to recommend that values should be relativized in a moral sense, to suggest that they can or should be "transvalued" or inverted in Nietzschean terms. It is rather to insist that social thinkers recognize how the social construction of evil has been, and remains, empirically and symbolically necessary for the social construction of good.[12]

In the Enlightenment tradition, most forcefully articulated by Kant, concern about the parochial (we would today say communitarian) dangers of an Aristotelian "ethics" led to a more abstract and universalistic model of a "moral" as compared to a good society.[13] Nonetheless, one finds in this Kantian tradition the same problem of equating value commitments in themselves with positivity in the normative sense.[14] To be moral is to move from selfishness to the categorical imperative, from self-reference to a collective orientation resting on the ability to put yourself in the place of another. What has changed in Kantianism is, not the binary of value-versus-no-value, but the contents of the collective alternative; it has shifted from the ethical to the moral, from the particular and local to the universal and transcendent. The range of value culture has been expanded and generalized because more substantive and more metaphysical versions came to be seen as particularist, antimodern, and antidemocratic.

If communitarianism is the contemporary representation of the republican and pragmatic traditions, Habermas's "theory of communicative action" represents—for social theory at least—the most influential contemporary articulation of this Kantian approach. Underlying much of Habermas's empirical theory one can find a philosophical anthropology that reproduces the simplistic splitting of good and evil. Instrumental, materialistic, and exploitative "labor," for example, is contrasted with altruistic, cooperative, ideal-oriented "communication." These anthropological dichotomies in the early writings are linked in Habermas's later work with the sociological contrast between system and lifeworld, the former producing instrumental efficiency, domination, and materialism, the latter producing ideals and, therefore, making possible equality, community, and morality. According to Habermas's developmental theory, the capacity for communication and moral self-regulation is enhanced with modernity, which produces such distinctive values as autonomy, solidarity, rationality, and criticism. The possibility of connecting to such values, indeed of maintaining value commitments per se, is impeded by the systems-rationality of modern economic and political life, the materialism of which "colonizes" and undermines the culture-creating, solidarizing possibilities of the lifeworld.[15] In arguing that it is recognition, not communication, that creates value commitments and mutual respect, Axel Honneth (1995) similarly ignores the possibility that pleasurable and cooperative interaction can be promoted by immoral and particularistic values that are destructive of ethical communities.[16]

This deracinated approach to culture-as-the-good can also be linked, in my view, to the Western religious tradition of Judaism and Christianity. In order to achieve salvation, the believer must overcome the temptations of the earthly, the material, and the practical in order to establish transcendental relations with an otherworldly source of goodness. According to this dualistic consciousness, evil is presented as an alternative to the transcendental commitments that establish value. As Augustine put it, "evil is the absence of the good."[17] The "original sin" that has marked humanity since the Fall was stimulated by the earthly appetites, by lust rather than idealism and value commitment. This sin can be redeemed only via a religious consciousness that connects human beings to higher values, either those of an ethical, law-governed community (Judaism) or the moral universalism of a church (Christianity). In this religious universe, in other words, evil is connected to nonculture, to passions and figures associated with the earth in contrast with the heavens. According to recent historical discussions (e.g., Macoby, 1992) in fact, devil symbolism first emerged as a kind of iconographic residual category. Radical Jewish sects created it as a deus ex machina to explain the downward spiral of Jewish society, allowing these negative developments to be attributed to forces outside the "authentic" Jewish cultural tradition. This nascent iconography of evil was energetically elaborated by early Christian sects who were similarly attracted to the possibility of attributing evil to forces outside their own cultural system. The Christian devil was a means of separating the "good religion" of Jesus from the evil (primarily Jewish) forces from which it had emerged.

## THE DISPLACEMENT OF EVIL IN CONTEMPORARY SOCIAL SCIENCE

Given these philosophical and religious roots,[18] it is hardly surprising that, as I have indicated earlier, contemporary social science has conceived culture as composed of values that establish highly esteemed general commitments and norms as establishing specific moral obligations to pursue the good. This is as true for social scientists, such as Bellah (1985) and Lasch (1978), who engage in cultural criticism as it is in more mainstream work. While issuing withering attacks on contemporary values as degenerate, narcissistic, and violent, such culture critics conceive these values as misguided formulations of the good—stupid, offensive, and pitiable but at the same time fundamentally revealing of how "the desirable" is formulated in the most debased modern societies.

On the basis of the identification of values with the good, mainstream social scientists and culture critics alike assume that a shared commitment to values is positive and beneficial to society. Functionalism is the most striking example of this tendency, and Talcott Parsons its classic representative. According to Parsons, value internalization leads not only to social equilibrium but to mutual respect, solidarity, and cooperation. If common values are not internalized, then the social system is not regulated by value, and social conflict, coercion, and even violence are the probable results.[19] In this sociological version of republicanism, Parsons follows the early- and middle-period Durkheim, who believed that shared values are essential to solidarity and social health. The lack of attachment to values marks the condition Durkheim defined as egoism, and it was by this standard that he defined social pathology. Durkheim emphasized education because he regarded it as the central means for attaching individuals to values. Since the simple attachment to culture is valued so highly, it is clear that neither Durkheim nor Parsons seriously considered the theoretical or empirical possibility that evil might be valued as energetically as the good.[20]

Because sociological folklore has so often pitted the functionalist "equilibrium" theory against the more critical "conflict" theory, it is well to ask whether, in fact, Parsonian functionalism is the only guilty party here. Have the theoretical alternatives to functionalism provided a truly different approach to the problem of evil? Let us consider, as a case in point, how Marx conceptualized the depravity of capitalism. Rather than pointing to the social effects of bad values, Marx argued that capitalism destroyed their very possibility. As he put it so eloquently in the *Communist Manifesto*, "All that is holy is profaned, all that is solid melts into air." The structural pressures of capitalism create alienation and egoism; they necessitate an instrumental and strategic action orientation that suppresses values and destroys ideals. Because materialism destroys normativity, there is no possibility for shared understanding, solidarity, or community. Only after socialism removes the devastating forces of capitalist competition and greed does value commitment become possible and solidarity flourish.

The notion that it is not evil values but the absence of values that creates a bad society continues to inform the neo-Marxism of the early Frankfurt School. For Horkheimer and Adorno (e.g., 1972 [1947]), late capitalism eliminates authentic values. Culture exists only as an industry; it is a completely contingent set of expressive symbols, subject to continuous manipulation according to materialistic exigencies. While Habermas's later theory of discourse ethics avoids this kind of mechanism and reduction, it continues to be organized around the pragmatic notion that communicatively generated value commitment leads to mutual understanding, toleration, and solidarity.

The apotheosis of this "critical" approach to evil-as-the-absence-of-value—evil as the displacement of culture by power—is Zygmunt Bauman's explanation of the Holocaust in his highly praised book *Modernity and the Holocaust* (1989). He writes that Nazi genocide has largely been ignored by social theory, suggesting that it has troubling implications for any positive evaluation of modernity. Bauman is right about this, but for the wrong reasons. He attributes the social evil of the Holocaust not to motivated cultural action but to the efficiency of the Nazis' bureaucratic killing machine. There is no indication in his explanation that this genocide was also caused by valuations of evil, by general representations of the polluted other that were culturally fundamental to Germany and its folkish, romantic traditions, and more specifically by representations of the Jewish other that were endemic not just to German but to Christian society. Yet only if this possibility is seriously entertained can the Holocaust be seen as an intended action, as something that was desired rather than merely imposed, as an event that did indeed grow out of systematic tendencies in the culture of modernity. It seems important, both morally and empirically, to emphasize, along with, Goldhagen (1996), that the Nazis and their German supporters wanted to kill Jews.[21] They worked hard to establish Judaism as a symbol of evil, and in turn they annihilated Jews to purge themselves of this evil. The act of murdering millions of Jewish and non-Jewish people during the Holocaust must be seen as something valued, as something desired. It was an evil event motivated not by the absence of values—an absence created by the destructive colonization of lifeworld by economic and bureaucratic systems—but by the presence of heinous values. These polluted cultural representations were as integral as the positive idealizations on which it pretended exclusively to rest.

## GIVING EVIL ITS DUE

We need to elaborate a model of social good and evil that is more complex, more sober, and more realistic than the naturalistic or idealistic models. Symbolically, evil is not a residual category, even if those who are categorized by it are marginalized socially. From the merely distasteful and sickening to the truly heinous, evil is deeply implicated in the symbolic formulation and institutional maintenance of the good.[22] Because of this, the institutional and cultural vitality of evil must be continually sustained. The line dividing the sacred from profane must be drawn and redrawn time and time again; this demarcation must retain its vitality, or all is lost.[23] Evil is not only symbolized cognitively but experienced in a vivid and emotional way—as I am suggesting in virtually every chapter of this book. Through such phenomena as scandals, moral panics, public punishments, and wars, societies provide occasions to reexperience and recrystallize the enemies of the good.[24] Wrenching experiences of horror, revulsion, and fear create opportunities for purification that keep what Plato called "the memory of justice" alive. Only through such direct experiences—provided via interaction or symbolic communication —do members of society come to know evil and to fear it. The emotional-cum-moral catharsis that Aristotle described as the basis for tragic experience and knowledge is also at the core of such experiences of knowing and fearing evil. Such knowledge and fear triggers denunciation of evil in others and confession about evil intentions in oneself, and rituals of punishment and purification in collectivities. In turn, these renew the sacred, the moral, and the good.

Evil is produced, in other words, not simply to maintain domination and power, as Foucault and Marx would argue, but in order to maintain the possibility of making positive valuations. Evil must be coded, narrated, and embodied in every social sphere—in the intimate sphere of the family, in the world of science, in religion, in the economy, in government, in primary communities.

In each sphere, and in every national society considered as a totality, there are deeply elaborated narratives about how evil develops and where it is likely to appear, about epochal struggles that have taken place between evil and the good, and about how good can triumph over evil once again.

This perspective has profound implications for the way we look at both cultural and institutional processes in contemporary societies. In the various substantive essays in this book, I discuss the former in terms of "binary representations." I would like at this point to discuss the latter—the institutional processes of evil—in terms of "punishments."

## PUNISHMENT: SOCIAL PROCESS AND INSTITUTIONS

If it is vital to understand the cultural dimension of society as organized around evil as much as around good, this by no means suggests that the problem of social evil can be understood simply in discursive terms. On the contrary, organizations, power, and face-to-face confrontations are critical in determining how and to whom binary representations of good and evil are applied. While these social processes and institutional forces do not invent the categories of evil and good—that they are not responsive purely to interest, power, and need has been one of my central points—they do have a strong influence on how they are understood. Most important, however, they determine what the "real" social effects of evil will be in time and space.

The social processes and institutional forces that specify and apply representations about the reality of evil can be termed "punishment." In the *Division of Labor in Society,* (1933), Durkheim first suggested that crime is "normal" and necessary because it is only punishment that allows society to separate normative behavior from that which is considered deviant. In my terms, I can suggest that punishment is the social medium through which the practices of actors, groups, and institutions are meaningfully and effectively related to the category of evil. It is through punishment that evil is naturalized. Punishment "essentializes" evil, making it appear to emerge from actual behaviors and identities rather than being culturally and socially imposed on them.[25]

Punishment takes both routine and more spontaneous forms. The bureaucratic iterations of evil are called "crimes." In organizational terms, the situational references of criminal acts are precisely defined by civil and criminal law, whose relevance to particular situations is firmly decided by courts and police. Polluting contact with civil law brings monetary sanctions; stigmatization by contact with criminal law brings incarceration, radical social isolation, and sometimes even death.

The nonroutine iterations of evil are less widely understood and appreciated. They refer to processes of "stigmatization" rather than to crimes.[26] What Cohen first identified as moral panics represent fluid, rapidly formed crystallizations of evil in relation to unexpected events, actors, and institutions. Historical witch trials and more contemporary anticommunist witch hunts, for example, are stimulated by the sudden experience of weakness in group boundaries. Panics over "crime waves," by contrast, develop in response to the chaotic and disorganizing entrance of new, formerly disreputable social actors into civil society.[27] Whatever their specific cause, and despite their evident irrationality, moral panics do have a clear effect, both in a cultural and a social sense. By focusing on new sources of evil, they draw an exaggerated line between social pollution and the good. This cultural clarification prepares the path for a purging organizational response, for trials of transgressors, for expulsion, and for incarceration.

*Scandals* represent a less ephemeral but still nonroutine form of social punishment. Scandals are public degradations of individuals and groups for behavior that is considered polluting to their status or office. In order to maintain the separation between good and evil, the behavior of an individual or group is "clarified" by symbolizing it as a movement from purity to danger. The religious background of Western civil society makes such declension typically appear as a "fall from grace," as a personal sin, a lapse created by individual corruption and the loss of individual responsibility. In the discourse of civil society, the greatest "sin" is the inability to attain and maintain one's autonomy and independence.[28] In terms of this discussion, scandal is created because civil society demands more or less continuous "revivifications" of social evil. These rituals of degradation range from the apparently trivial—the gossip sheets that, nonetheless, demand systematic sociological consideration—to the kinds of deeply serious, civil-religious events that create national convulsions: The Dreyfus Affair that threatened to undermine the Third Republic in France and the Watergate affair that toppled the Nixon regime in the United States represented efforts to crystallize and punish social evil on this systematic level. Once again, scandals, like moral panics, have not only cultural but fundamental institutional effects, repercussions that range from the removal of specific persons from status or office to deep and systematic changes in organizational structure and regime.

There is nothing fixed or determined about scandals and moral panics. Lines of cultural demarcation are necessary but not sufficient to their creation. Whether or not this or that individual or group comes to be punished is the outcome of struggles for cultural power, struggles that depend on shifting coalitions and the mobilization of resources of a material and not only ideal kind. This applies not only to the creation of panics and scandals but to their denouements. They are terminated by purification rituals reestablishing the sharp line between evil and good, a transition made possible by the act of punishment.

## TRANSGRESSION AND THE AFFIRMATION OF EVIL AND GOOD

Once we understand the cultural and institutional "autonomy" of evil, we can see how the experience and practice of evil become, not simply frightening and repulsive, but also desirable. The sociological creation of evil results not only in the avoidance of evil but also in the pursuit of it. Rather than a negative that directs people toward the good, in other words, social evil can be and often is sought as an end in itself. As Bataille (1990: 29, 21) observed, "evil is always the object of an ambiguous condemnation"; it is "not only the dream of the wicked" but "to some extent the dream of [the] Good."

Attraction to the idea and experience of evil motivates the widespread practice that Bataille called transgression and that Foucault, following Bataille, termed the "limit experience."[29]

> *Sacred* simultaneously has two contradictory meanings. . . . The taboo gives a
> negative definition of the sacred object and inspires us with awe. . . . Men are
> swayed by two simultaneous emotions: they are driven away by terror and
> drawn by an awed fascination. Taboo and transgression reflect these two con-
> tradictory urges. The taboo would forbid the transgression but the fascination
> compels it. . . . The sacred aspect of the taboo is what draws men towards it
> and transfigures the original interdiction. (Bataille, 1986 [1957]: 68)

In particular situations, evil comes to be positively evaluated, creating a kind of inverted liminality. Transgression takes place when actions, associations, and rhetoric—practices that would typically be defined and sanctioned as serious threats to the good—become objects of desire and sometimes even social legitimation. Bataille believed that transgression occurred mainly in the cultural imagination, that is, in literature, although he also wrote extensively about eroticism and was personally motivated by a desire to comprehend the dark social developments of the early and midcentury period—Nazism, war, and Stalinism.[30] Transgression, however, also takes a decidedly social-structural form. In criminal activity and popular culture, evil provides the basis of complex social institutions that provide highly sought-after social roles, careers, and personal identities. Without evoking the term, Jack Katz certainly was investigating transgression in his profound phenomenological reconstruction of the "badass syndrome," as was Richard Strivers in his earlier essay on the apocalyptic dimension of 1960s rock and roll concerts. The latter embodied the long-standing "noir" strain of popular culture that has transmogrified into the "bad rapper" phenomenon of today.[31]

It seems that every social thinker and artist who sets out to explore the attractions of this dark side, whether in the moral imagination or in social action and structure, risks being tarred by self-proclaimed representatives of social morality with a polluting brush. This tendency is fueled by the apparent fact that those who are personally attracted to transgressive practices are those who are most drawn to exploring them in art and social thought. The analysis set forth in this book suggests, however, that those who are seriously interested in maintaining moral standards should refrain from this kind of knee-jerk response. It confuses causes with effects. Societies construct evil so that there can be punishment; for it is the construction of, and the response to, evil that defines and revivifies the good. One should not, then, confuse the aesthetic imagining of evil, the vicarious experiencing of evil, much less the intellectual exploration of evil with the actual practice of evil itself.

Modern and postmodern societies have always been beset by a socially righteous fundamentalism, both religious and secular. These moralists wish to purge the cultural imagination of references to eros and violence; they condemn frank discussions of transgressive desires and actions in schools and other public places; they seek to punish and sometimes even to incarcerate those who practice "victimless" crimes on the grounds that they violate the collective moral conscience. The irony is that, without the imagination and the social identification of evil, there would be no possibility for the attachment to the good that these moralists so vehemently uphold. Rather than undermining conventional morality, trangression underlines and vitalizes it. Bataille, whom James Miller pejoratively called the *philosophe maudit* of French intellectual life, never ceased to insist on this point. "Transgression has nothing to do with the primal liberty of animal life. It opens the door into what lies beyond the limits usually observed, but it maintains these limits just the same. Transgression is complementary to the profane [i.e., the mundane] world, exceeding its limits but not destroying it" (Bataille, 1986 [1957]: 67).

*Amnesty International*, winner of the Nobel Peace Prize, has been one of the world's most effective nongovernmental democratic organizations, exposing and mobilizing opposition against torture and other heinous practices of authoritarian and even democratic governments. It is all the more relevant to note, therefore, that at the heart of the internal and external discourse of this prototypically "do-gooder" organization one finds an obsessive concern with defining, exploring, and graphically presenting evil, the success of which efforts allows members and outsiders vicariously to experience evil's physical and emotional effects.[32] In the Amnesty logo, good and evil are tensely intertwined. At the core is a candle, representing fervent attention, patience, and the sacrality of Amnesty's commitment to life. Surrounding the candle is barbed wire, indicating concentration camps and torture. This binary structure is iterated throughout the persuasive documents that Amnesty distributes to the public and also in the talk of Amnesty activists themselves. They revolve around narratives that portray, often in graphic and gothic detail, the terrible things that are done to innocent people and, in a tone of almost uncomprehending awe, the heroism of the prisoner to endure unspeakable suffering and remain in life and at the point of death a caring, dignified human being. Amnesty's attention to evil, to constructing the oppressor and graphically detailing its actions, in this way contributes to maintaining the ideals of moral justice and sacralizing the human spirit, not only in thought but in practice. It is in order to explain and illuminate such a paradox that a cultural sociology of evil must be born.

# THE DISCOURSE OF AMERICAN
# CIVIL SOCIETY

(with Philip Smith)

Civil society consists of actors, relationships between actors, and institutions. At the very heart of the *culture* of American civil society is a set of binary codes that discuss and interrelate these three dimensions of social-structural reality in a patterned and coherent way. In the United States, there is a "democratic code" that creates the discourse of liberty. It specifies the characteristics of actors, social relationships, and institutions that are appropriate in a democratically functioning society. Its antithesis is a "counterdemocratic code" that specifies the same features for an authoritarian society. The presence of two such contrasting codes is no accident: the elements that create the discourse of liberty can signify democracy only by virtue of the presence of antonymic "partners" in an accompanying discourse of repression.

In reconstructing the "discourse of civil society," we draw on historical notions of civilization and civility (e.g., Elias, 1978; Freud, 1961 [1930], Shils, 1975; Walzer, 1970) and also on the tradition of liberal political theory in which democracy is defined by the distinction between the state and an independent, legally regulated civil order (e.g., Cohen & Arato, 1992; Keane, 1988a, b). Civil society has institutions of its own—parliaments, courts, voluntary associations, and the media—through which moral regulation is administered. These institutions provide a public forum in which crises are defined and problems are resolved. Their decisions are not only binding but also exemplary. Most important from our perspective, however, is the fact that the institutions of civil society, and their decisions, are informed by a unique set of cultural codes.[1]

These codes show marked similarities from one national society to another; not only broad pressures of Western cultural history but also the very structures of civil society, and its ability to interpenetrate with other social spheres, mandate a cultural structure that regulates civil life in similar ways. Such a homogeneity of core structures, however, does not preclude substantial and important variations in national form. Every civil society develops in a historically specific way. The terms *Bürgerliche Geselischaft, société,* and "society" name variations in the relations among state, economy, culture, and community in different national civil societies, just as they can be seen to suggest variations on widely shared cultural themes (e.g., Brubaker, 1992). In this chapter, we concentrate on the discourse of civil society as it is articulated in American society. We concentrate on America for two reasons. First, detailed, thick description tends to be the most persuasive in cultural sociology; one must fight against the tendency (tempting in comparative work) for interpretation to engage in a broad-brushstroke portrayal of general themes. Second, America has typically been considered the closest approximation to a democratic nation-state. Here, if anywhere, we would expect to find the discourse of civil society in its most pristine form.

In the discourse of American civil society, democratic and counterdemocratic codes provide radically divergent models of actors and their motivations. Democratically minded persons are symbolically constructed as rational, reasonable, calm, and realistic in their decision-making and are thought to be motivated by conscience and a sense of honor. In contrast, the repressive code posits that antidemocratically minded persons are motivated by pathological greed and self-interest. They are deemed incapable of rational decision making and conceived of as exhibiting a tendency toward hysterical behavior by virtue of an excitable personality from which unrealistic plans are often born. Whereas the democratic person is characterized by action and autonomy, the counterdemocratic person is perceived of as having little free will, and, if not a leader, as a passive figure who follows the dictates of others.[2]

Accompanying this discourse on actors and their motivations is another directed to the social relationships that are presumed to follow from such personal needs. The qualities of the democratic personality are constructed as those that permit open, trusting, and straightforward relationships. They encourage critical and reflective rather than deferential relations among people. In contrast, counterdemocratic persons are associated with secretive, conspirational dealings in which deceit and Machiavellian calculation play a key role. The irrational and essentially dependent character of such persons, however, means that they still tend to be deferential toward authority.

Given the discursive structure of motives and civil relationships, it should not be surprising that the implied homologies and antimonies extend to social, political, and economic institutions. Where members of the community are irrational in motivation and distrusting in their social relationships, they will "naturally" create institutions that are arbitrary rather than rule governed, that use brute power rather than law, and that exercise hierarchy over equality. Such institutions will tend to be exclusive rather than inclusive and to promote per-

*Table 5.1*  The discursive structure of actors

| Democratic code | Counterdemocratic code |
|---|---|
| Active | Passive |
| Autonomous | Dependent |
| Rational | Irrational |
| Reasonable | Hysterical |
| Calm | Excitable |
| Controlled | Passionate |
| Realistic | Unrealistic |
| Sane | Mad |

*Table 5.2*  The discursive structure of social relationships

| Democratic code | Counterdemocratic code |
|---|---|
| Open | Secret |
| Trusting | Suspicious |
| Critical | Deferential |
| Truthful | Deceitful |
| Straightforward | Calculating |
| Citizen | Enemy |

sonal loyalty over impersonal and contractual obligations. They will tend to favor the interests of small factions rather than the needs of the community as a whole.

The elements in the civil discourses on motives, relationships, and institutions are tied closely together. "Common sense" seems to dictate that certain kinds of motivations are associated with certain kinds of institutions and relationships. After all, it is hard to conceive of a dictator who trusts his minions, is open and honest, and rigorously follows the law in an attempt to extend equality to all his subjects. The semiologics of the codes, then, associate and bind individual ele-

*Table 5.3*  The discursive structure of social institutions

| Democratic code | Counterdemocratic code |
|---|---|
| Rule regulated | Arbitrary |
| Law | Power |
| Equality | Hierarchy |
| Inclusive | Exclusive |
| Impersonal | Personal |
| Contractual | Ascriptive |
| Groups | Factions |
| Office | Personality |

ments on each side of a particular code to the other elements on the same side of the discourse as a whole. "Rule regulated," for example, is considered homologous with "truthful" and "open," terms that define social relationships, and with "reasonable" and "autonomous," elements from the symbolic set that stipulate democratic motives. In the same manner, any element from any set on one side is taken to be antithetical to any element from any set on the other side. Thus hierarchy is thought to be inimical to "critical" and "open" and also to "active" and "self-controlled."

The formal logic of homology and opposition through which meaning is created, and which we have just outlined, is the guarantor of the autonomy of the cultural codes—despite the fact that they are associated with a particular social-structural domain. However, despite the formal grammars at work in the codes, which turn the arbitrary relationships[3] between the elements into a set of relationships characterized by what Lévi-Strauss (1967) has termed an "a posteriori necessity," it would be a mistake to conceive of the discourse of civil society as merely an abstract cognitive system of quasi-mathematical relationships. To the contrary, the codes have an evaluative dimension that enables them to play a key role in the determination of political outcomes. In American civil society, the democratic code has a sacred status, whereas the counterdemocratic code is considered profane. The elements of the counterdemocratic code are dangerous and polluting, held to threaten the sacred center (Shils, 1975) of civil society, which is identified with the democratic code. To protect the center, and the sacred discourse that embodies its symbolic aspirations, the persons, institutions, and objects identified with the profane have to be isolated and marginalized at the boundaries of civil society, and sometimes even destroyed.

It is because of this evaluative dimension that the codes of civil society become critical in determining the outcomes of political processes. Actors are obsessed with sorting out empirical reality and, typifying from code to event, with attributing moral qualities to concrete "facts." Persons, groups, institutions, and communities who consider themselves worthy members of the national community identify themselves with the symbolic elements associated with the sacred side of the divide. Their membership in civil society is morally assured by the homology that they are able to draw between their motives and actions and the sacred elements of the semiotic structure. Indeed, if called on, members who identify themselves as in good standing in civil society must make all their actions "accountable" in terms of the discourse of liberty. They must also be competent to account for those who are thought to be unworthy of civic membership—who are or should be excluded from it—in terms of the alternative discourse of repression. It is through the concept of accountability that the strategic aspects of action come back into the picture, for differing accounts of actors, relationships and institutions can, if successfully disseminated, have powerful consequences in terms of the allocation of resources and power. Strategically, this dual capacity will typically result in efforts by competing actors to tar each other with the brush of the counterdemocratic code while attempting to shield themselves behind the discourse of democracy. This process is clearest in the courts, where lawyers attempt to sway the opinion of the jury by providing differing accounts of the plaintiffs and defendants in terms of the discourses of civil society.

Before turning to our empirical investigation of this code, it is necessary to clarify the relationship between our theory and other work on American civic culture. Scholars such as Bellah (1985) and Huntington (1981) have argued that American political culture is characterized by fundamentally conflicting ideals and values. In contrast, our approach argues for a semantic commensurability between contrasting themes in American culture. Our claim that there is an underlying consensus as to the key symbolic patterns of American civic society, and a relationship of complementarity between differing components of the cultural system, reinforces earlier arguments by scholars such as Hartz (1955) and Myrdal (1944). In recognizing the existence of a shared culture in the civil society we do not, of course, claim that differing traditions and subcultures do not exist in America. The communitarian tradition, for example, has a very different conception of civility.

Discussions among intellectual and cultural historians have also been characterized by sharp disagreement over the nature of the basic ideas that underlie American political thought. Scholars have argued intensely (e.g., Bailyn, 1967; Bercovitch, 1978; Pocock, 1975) over the comparative merits of civic republicanism, Lockean liberalism, and Protestant Christianity in accounting for both the ideal and material forms of American political culture at different times. Our approach claims that these traditions, while importantly different in themselves, rest on a single more basic symbolic framework. Bailyn, for example, argues that fear of negative elements such as power and conspiracy were at the heart of American ideology. In contrast, Hartz highlights positive values such as individual autonomy and contractual relations. Others, in the republican tradition, emphasize more collectivist elements such as honesty, trust, cooperation and egalitarianism. We suggest that the binary organization of America's civic codes enables these competing interpretations to be seen as complementary rather than competing. Indeed, we would argue that our model provides less an alternative than a reunderstanding of the various particular claims that have been advanced by other scholars. As we understand the discourse of civil society, it constitutes a general grammar on which historically specific traditions draw to create particular configurations of meanings, ideology and belief. We are not arguing, in other words, that all understandings of American civil society can be reduced to a single discourse. Rather we assert that this broad discourse provides the possibility for the variety of specific cultural traditions, or rhetorical themes, that have historically characterized American political debate.

Finally, we should emphasize that we do not claim that this scheme provides the only level at which political and social debate is conducted. Although the discursive structure we identify is continuously drawn on in constructing cultural understandings from contingent political events, the structure becomes the key foundation for public debate only in times of tension, unease, and crisis. Smelser and Parsons (1956) have argued that in periods of social tension communication becomes more generalized and abstract, shifting away from the mundane concerns with means and ends that characterize the discourse of everyday life. Writing from within an earlier functionalist medium, these theorists ascribed generalization to a combination of psychological strain and adaptive pressure for conflict resolution. We take a more cultural approach, conceiving of such crises as liminal, quasi-ritualized periods in which fundamental meanings are also at stake (Turner, 1974). When we examine conflicts over civic discourse, we are looking at generalized accounts in such liminal times.

How modern societies or subsets of these societies enter into such liminal periods of intense social drama, which groups or audiences are more influential or heavily involved, how and by what means these crises are eventually resolved, whether they polarize society or clear the ground for a new consensus—these are not questions that can be answered by interpretive analysis as such. We would argue, nonetheless, that the discursive dimension of civil conflict is fundamentally important. Habermas has argued that democratic authority must stand the test of thematization. Citizens must be able to defend the rationality of their actions by invoking the fundamental criteria according to which their decisions are made. That they do so in terms of "arbitrary" or conventional symbolic codes rather than the rationalistic, developmental frameworks that Habermas invokes makes the process no less important and, in fact, much more challenging from the perspective of a social science. As political language must inevitably contain a structured and symbolic dimension, the entirely rational conduct of politics—to which Habermas aspires—becomes an impossibility. Precisely because the processes that generate crises of democratic authority are less predictably rational than Habermas and other democratic theorists suppose, it is necessary to explore the codes of civil society in a much more complex and dynamic way.

## HISTORICAL ELABORATIONS OF AMERICA'S CIVIL DISCOURSE

We propose to illustrate the plausibility of our approach by examining a series of crises and scandals in the past two hundred years of American history. Although in qualitative (and often also in quantitative) research rigorous falsification is impossible, we believe that by showing the pervasive nature of the same culture structure across time, types of events, and differing political groups our model can be established as a powerful explanatory variable in its own right. To this end, our historical discussion is more general and iterative than specific and detailing. Once again, we stress that we do not intend to explain any particular historical outcome; in order to accomplish this, extremely detailed case studies are necessary. We offer, rather, the groundwork for such studies by demonstrating the continuity, autonomy, and internal organization of a particular cultural structure across time.

## ATTACKS ON U.S. PRESIDENTS

As conspicuous individuals, presidents tend to be evaluated in the public discourse in terms of the discourse of actors. However, civil society rarely limits its discourse to only one subset of codes. As we will show, the types of relationships that U.S. presidents are thought to be involved in, and the institutions they are often attributed responsibility for, provide important contextual material for the evaluation of their motives.

Two speeches of no extraordinary historical significance provide a useful starting point for our empirical investigations. The first was delivered in the Senate by the Massachusetts senator Charles Sumner on May 31, 1872, and amounted to an attack on President Ulysses S. Grant. The second, delivered three days later, was a defense of Grant by the Illinois senator John Logan. In these speeches we can see how two individuals hold to the same discursive codes yet sharply differ in the way they apply them to the same referent, in this case President Grant.

According to Sumner, Grant was not a fit individual for the presidency. He argued in Congress that Grant was more interested in personal profit and pleasure than the public good. "The presidential office is treated as little more than [a] plaything and a perquisite. . . . Palace cars fast horses and seaside loiterings figure more than duties. . . . From the beginning this exalted trust has dropped to be a personal indulgence."[4]

Not only does Grant fail to live up to the republican ideal of duty—note the contrast between public "trust" and "personal" indulgence—but he is unable to conduct himself rationally. Sumner argues that Grant is not able fully to control and command his own actions. He is under the spell of uncontrollable psychic forces and treats people as enemies.

Any presentment [sic] of the President would be imperfect which did not show how this ungovernable personality breaks forth in quarrel, making him the great presidential quarreler of our history. . . . To him a quarrel is not only a constant necessity, but a perquisite of office. To nurse a quarrel, like tending a horse, is in his list of presidential duties.[5]

Sumner saw Grant's irrational and selfish personality as tempting him to establish a government founded on counterdemocratic principles. Through personal whim, Grant has set up a government based on nepotism and militarism. This arbitrary organization displays a hierarchical structure and depends on secretive relationships and passive members.

[Grant's various] assumptions have matured into a personal government, semi-military in character and breathing of the military spirit, being a species of caesarism or personalism abhorrent to republican institutions, where subservience to the President is the supreme law.[6]

In maintaining this subservience he has operated by a system of combinations, military, political and even senatorial, having their orbits about him, so that, like the planet Saturn, he is surrounded by rings.[7]

In view of the fact that Grant's government was characterized by a "Quixotism of personal pretension," it is hardly surprising that the president was also seen by Sumner as acting outside the boundary of the law, most especially in his attempts to annex Santo Domingo to the United States. Notice also here how Sumner attempts to ally himself with the democratic discourse by stressing his own rationality.

In exhibiting this autocratic pretension, so revolutionary and unrepublican in character, I mean to be moderate in language and to keep within the strictest bounds. The facts are indisputable, and nobody can deny the gross violation of the Constitution and of International law with insult to the Black Republic—the whole case being more reprehensible, as also plainly more unconstitutional and more illegal than anything alleged against Andrew Johnson on his mpeachment.[8]

In defending Grant, Senator Logan demonstrates a very different understanding of the appropriate arrangement of characters against the background of civil codes. He argues that it is Senator Sumner, not President Grant, who is best characterized by the counterdemocratic discourse. Sumner is denounced as not living up to the ethical demand for rational conduct and thought, as a complex intellectual elitist, as a liar, and as a selfish egotistical soul with an inability to act as an autonomous senator with a realistic worldview.

I was sorry to see a Senator . . . lower himself as he did on this occasion, for the purpose of venting his spleen and vindictive feeling against a President and those who stand by him.[9]

His statesmanship has consisted for twenty-four years in high-sounding phrases, in long drawn out sentences, in paragraphs taken from books of ancient character. . . . It consists of plagiarism, in declamation, in egotism.[10]

Let us compare the tanner President with the magnificently educated Senator from Massachusetts, who has accomplished so much, and see how he will stand in comparison. The Senator from Massachusetts has lived his life without putting upon the records of this country a solitary act of his own origination without amendment of other men having more understanding than himself in reference to men and things. General Grant, the President of the United States, a tanner from Galena, has . . . written his history in deeds which will live.[11]

Logan not only pollutes Sumner by identifying him in terms of the elements of the counterdemocratic code but argues that Grant is best typified by the democratic ones. He does this by asking rhetorical questions that distance the president from the charges Sumner made. "In what respect has the President violated the law? I ask the Senator from Massachusetts to tell this country in what has he violated the constitution, in what particular.[12] . . . With whom has the President quarrelled? I do not know."[13]

Finally, Logan positively identifies President Grant with critical elements of the discourse of liberty, demonstrating that his honesty and good faith have allowed the legal order to be sustained, and cooperation and civility to rule. "President Grant has made an honest President. He has been faithful. The affairs of the world are in good condition. We are at peace with the civilized world, we are at war with none. Every State in this Union is quiet; the laws have been faithfully executed and administered; we have quiet and peace throughout our land."[14]

In the speeches of Sumner and Logan we see how two individuals are able to typify and legitimate the same persons and events in sharply different ways. Yet to see this process in purely individualistic terms would be a mistake. While every individual typifies, ad hocs, and accounts for events, they perform these activities with reference to cultural codes that are collectively held.

In the case of the impeachment of Andrew Johnson we see an attack on a president that was similar to Sumner's attack on Grant but was more severe and more widely shared. This is explicable in terms of Johnson's uncanny ability to alienate himself from large segments of the political community through his extensive (mis)use of executive powers, his antagonism toward Congress, and his soft line on the question of Reconstruction. The issue that led directly to his impeachment, however, was his attempt, without congressional permission, to remove Howard Stanton from his post in control of the War Office and to replace him with a personal friend, Lorenzo Thomas.

Andrew Johnson's opponents argued that he had a defective personality structure. He was held to be both calculative, selfish, and Machiavellian, as well as irrational, emotive, and foolish. The seeming contradiction between these two lines of attack is not apparent to "practical reasoners" who are embedded in the binary oppositions of America's central codes. Thus the *New York Daily Tribune* was able to reconstruct Johnson's Machiavellian strategy in an editorial of February 7, 1868, and to argue against Johnson later in the same month on the grounds that he had little self-control.

We can almost imagine the President's reasoning. I have had good use of Grant. He is an amiable man, easily bullied. He did well by me. . . . Now I've got

Stanton out. Before Congress meets the country will have forgotten all about him. Grant will go back to the army. I'll give some of the Radical Senators a tax collector or two, and get Steedman and Black through the Senate, just as I got Rousseau through. So I'll have Stanton out of the way and Grant a dead duck, for the Radicals will call him my decoy bird and not trust him. With the Tenure of Office Bill thus blown to atoms, things will be lovely all around.

American gentlemen blushed when they remembered that a drunken Vice President had shaken his fist in the face of the ambassadors of foreign countries. . . . We saw the President bandying words with a mob in Cleveland, defending a riot and murder in St. Louis, and making wild, incoherent speeches at every station. . . . It is well to remember that morally he was long since tried by the common sense of his countrymen. (*New York Daily Tribune*, editorial, February 24, 1868)

Johnson displays drunkenness and bad temper; he is associated with riots, mobs, wildness, incoherence, and murder—the most anticivil act of all. These traits are counterposed to morality and common sense and to the fraternal term "countrymen."

Given these serious character flaws, it was inevitable that other aspects of the counterdemocratic discourse would be applied to Johnson. It was argued that he had a master plan to set up a network of passive toadies in the place of active and critical public servants. In a crucial debate one congressman argued, for example, that Johnson had attempted to replace Stanton in the War Office with "some fawning sycophant, who, for the sake of his patron, will consent to become the pliant tool in his hands for the accomplishment of his base purpose." The result of such acts, he goes on to argue, could only be the destruction of the institution of office and, eventually, of democracy itself. "If [Johnson] may exercise such a power in this case [the Stanton removal] he has only to remove every civil officer who will not consent to be a fawning slave to his will, obedient to his power and destroy the Republic."[15]

More generally, it was argued in Congress that Johnson's intention was to break the law. This institutional violation was inevitable, considering his fatally flawed character.

In his maddened zeal to accomplish his evil designs, he has set at defiance the laws and law making power of the land.

Andrew Johnson . . . deliberately and intentionally strikes at the majesty of the law and attempts to trample it beneath his feet. This act . . . removed the mask from the man who was made President by the act of an assassin and proclaimed . . . that Andrew Johnson would not hesitate to set the laws at defiance where they interfered with his plans, and if an opportunity offered to proclaim himself dictator upon the ruins of the Republic.[16]

Note that these simple arguments are built on a series of interlaced antinomies. The alternative to sacred civility is evil calculation, to decent law-making madness and defiance. The nation will be taken from majesty to ruin, from republic to dictatorship.

Those who were opposed to President Johnson argued for his exclusion from civil society on the basis of his counterdemocratic motives, arguing that he was attempting to establish repressive relationships and institutions in the place of the existing system, which was seen as essentially democratic. Those who supported Johnson saw events in a completely different light, though they employed the same code. First, they opposed the rhetoric of moral confrontation itself, arguing in effect that the climate of symbolic generalization that had demanded the application of morally sanctioned codes was overblown. Suggesting that events should be understood not in terms of transcendental values but rather in the more mundane framework of detailed legal technicalities, Johnson's supporters claimed that what we would today call a "realpolitik" attitude was necessary in order to sustain the national interest in the demanding period of Reconstruction. Among Johnson's most influential supporters was the *New York Times*:

> Congress has on its hands already quite as many subjects of grave and pressing importance as it can dispose of wisely. To throw into the political arena now, so exciting a subject as impeachment . . . would be not only to postpone a wise and beneficient restoration of the Union and peace, but to invite a renewal of the dangers from which we have just escaped. (editorial, February 14, 1868)

> In our judgement the impeachment of the President is wholly out of place so long as the constitutionality of the law is in controversy. (editorial, February 24, 1868)

But a more direct confrontation with the polluting categories of Johnson's indictment was also necessary. In his own defense, Johnson argued that his efforts to remove Stanton from the War Office without congressional permission had been designed to test a point of law rather than to usurp power. Accepting this typification, the *New York Times* wrote: "Mr. Johnson's method of carrying out his purposes has always been more objectionable than the purposes themselves. His present controversy is a case in point" (editorial, February 24, 1868).

Because the actual relationship between the "method of carrying out one's purposes" and the "purposes themselves" is unknowable, readers and political actors are being asked to fill in the missing links through a kind of "documentary method."[17] In principle, differing opinions of the same events and personalities can be formed, or "documented," by persons with the same raw information. In practice, however, the information of public life is cooked, not raw: it is itself shaped by collective, cultural logics that permit only certain combinations of interpretations to make sense. It is not possible for Johnson to attempt to usurp power and at the same time to be seen as a rational, morally concerned person. It is possible, however, for Johnson to test the constitutionality of the law regarding the Tenure of Office Act and to remain a democratically minded individual. Because the *New York Times* believes in the worthiness of Johnson's intentions in removing Stanton from office, it is bound to argue that those who seek his impeachment are constituted by the counterdemocratic code. "Reason, judgement or patriotism has nothing to do with the purpose now proclaimed [impeachment]. In its inception and in its exercise it is partisanship worked up to the point of frenzy and aggravated with a personal hate, of which many who yesterday voted for impeachment will shortly be ashamed" (editorial, February 25, 1868).

Given these particularistic and irrational motivations, it should by now come as little surprise that those opposed to Johnson were accused in Congress not only of attacking the President, but also the fabric of democratic society. On the one side there is tyranny, fury, fanaticism, and usurpation; on the other the constructive activities of the patriots and their constitution. "Mr. Chairman, in the brief time allowed me under the tyrannical rule of the majority of this House, I can but glance at the topics which present themselves for consideration now that a partisan caucus has determined to complete the usurpation of the Government by the impeachment and removal of the President."[18] "This attack is directed against the walls of our Government, which were reared by the patriot fathers, and whose foundations were laid deep down in the constitution of our country—the fear is that they will not be able to resist the fury of this tornado of fanaticism."[19]

It should also come as little surprise that the type of social relationship invoked in this attack was considered to be repressive, involving the use of secrecy and calculation along with the brutal use of power.

> In the name of the larger liberty the American people are asked to consent to the embrace of a monster whose hidden mechanism is managed by the unprincipled Stanton, aided and abetted by the controlling men in the Radical party. . . .
> The efforts of Mr. Stanton have been directed to establish an armed despotism in this country. . . . This plot is reaching its culmination in the recent action of this body in impeaching the President of the United States.[20]

## EVALUATING INSTITUTIONS AND BUSINESS

One might suppose that the economic sphere is understood and evaluated merely in terms of its efficiency in providing for the generation, safekeeping, and distribution of wealth. However, this is not the case. Even economic institutions and transactions are liable to the process of generalization, through which they become understood via the semiotic and moral distinctions that we have outlined in this chapter. The so-called Bank War of the 1830s provides a case in point. The issue at hand was the renewal of the charter of the Bank of the United States, which was due to expire in 1836. The bank had been chartered and endowed with various unusual rights and privileges by Congress in 1816. Those opposed to the renewal of the charter were led by the president, Andrew Jackson. In the case of presidents, as we have shown, their high individual visibility leads to a focus on psychological motivations. In contrast, attacks on institutions such as the bank, which tend to be more diffuse, usually focus on social and institutional relationships and activities.

A recurring theme in the assaults of the opponents of the bank are gothic images reminiscent of the macabre aspects of the literature of the time. In congressional debates images abound of darkness, intrigue, and strange uncontrollable powers threatening to the civil society. "The bank was an institution whose arms extended into every part of the community. . . . An institution like this, which by the mere exertion of its will could rise or sink the value of any and every commodity, even of the bread we ate, was to be regarded with a jealous watchfulness."[21]

> And what is that influence? Boundless—incalculable. Wielding a capital of
> sixty million dollars, with power to crush every state bank in the Union; having
> thereby in its iron clamp the press, the counting house the manufactory and the
> workshop; its influence penetrates into every part of this vast country, concen-
> trating and directing its energies as it pleases.[22]

The bank had such a polluting power that it could transform democratic into counterdemocratic social relationships.

> We moreover view it as one of the most stupendous engines of political power
> that was ever erected; capable of being exerted not only against the head, but
> every branch of the government, corrupting by its money, and awing by its
> power the virtuous and independent action of the representatives of the people
> in prostituting them to its base and sinister purposes.[23]

Associated with this corrupt and awesome power—which prostitutes and debases once autonomous citizens—was an aura of secrecy antithetical to the type of relationships that would have characterized a democratic institution. Important evidence for this was the opposition of the bank's supporters to an open public enquiry. The bank's opponents argued that an open and rational investigation of the bank would be necessary to discover the truth.

> Our debate is set on the supposition that the charter has dissolved . . . that
> the bank is no longer a living power but a cadaver—a dead subject, which we
> should examine with the dispassionate scrutiny of a surgeon who lets no piece

of corrupted flesh, no bone or muscle, however monstrous, escape the edge of this knife.[24]

Dispassionate fairness implies not only rationality and objectivity but vitality and life itself; the sinister and secretive bank, in contrast, is identified with death, with the pollution of corrupted, monstrous flesh.

Given the bank's secretive nature and power, it is only to be expected that its opponents would also find evidence that it was a particular institution favoring the interests of the enemies of civil society, of foreigners and the domestic elite over those of the American people. Therefore, on returning the Bank Bill, President Jackson included in his message to Congress the argument that "the stock will be worth more to foreigners than to citizens of this country."

> If we must have a bank with private stockholders, every consideration of sound policy, and every impulse of American feeling, admonishes that it should be purely American. Its stockholders should be composed exclusively of our own citizens. . . . If we cannot, at once, in justice to interests vested under improvident legislation, make our government what it ought to be, we can, at least, take a stand against all new grants of monopolies and exclusive privileges, against any prostitution of our government to the advancement of the few at the expense of the many.[25]

Supporters of the bank perceived things differently. As with the supporters of Johnson, they tried to prevent the application of moral categories altogether by arguing that events had not reached a symbolic crisis point and that the bank could, consequently, be evaluated on utilitarian grounds.

> Sir, it is the highest eulogium [sic] that can be provided on the Bank of the United States that it provides the Government with a sound currency of a perfectly uniform value, at all places, for all its fiscal operations, and at the same time enables that Government to collect and disburse its immense revenues in the mode least oppressive to the community. If the same functions were exclusively devolved upon the state banks . . . the absolute distresses and necessities of the country would drive those banks into the fatal policy of suspending specie payments in twelve months.[26]

Insofar as they accepted symbolic generalization as inevitable, the bank was also, but less often, justified in terms of the specific details of the democratic discourse. For example, one supporter argued against the assertion that it was a secretive institution, claiming that, to the contrary, the bank was open and honest. "Bank checks are in circulation everywhere, and are seen every day. The amount issued by the bank is known, the bank has furnished the information."[27]

Defenses of the bank's moral status were less often resorted to, however, than attacks on the bank's opponents, who were portrayed as themselves counter-democratic. In rebutting one Congressman's allegations of corruption, one of the bank's most important supporters remarks: "Has he not received some admonitions on the subject of yielding his ear too credulously to those suspicions which are whispered by anonymous and irresponsible informers. . . . I have no doubt that some dark insinuation has been poured into the gentleman's ear."[28]

Criticisms of the bank are discredited through their association with anonymity, which is suspicious because it allows people not to take responsibility for their statements. The rationality of the critics' thought processes, and the integrity of their motivations, are also called into question.

> I have no doubt that the gentleman regards the Bank of the United States as a great national curse, and I can, therefore, very well conceive that his mind will give credence to much slighter evidence against the bank than would satisfy a mind differently prepossessed, or having no prepossessions of any kind.[29]

> To destroy the existing bank . . . would be an act rather of cruelty and caprice, than of justice and wisdom.[30]

Caprice speaks of irrationality and lack of control, cruelty of a lack of conscience and good will. These motives are themselves polluting; they make it seem unlikely that the "curse" on the nation could have come only from the actions of the bank itself. President Jackson too came under attack via the counterdemocratic rubric. His highhanded dealings in the Bank War, including the firing of the secretary who refused to follow his orders to withdraw federal deposits from the Bank of the United States and place them in the state banks, were taken as important evidence of despotic inclinations. Seizing the moment, Henry Clay, Jackson's main political opponent, argued that the president had "assumed the exercise of power over the Treasury of the United States not granted to him by the Constitution and laws, and dangerous to the liberties of the people."[31] Given this lawlessness, Clay is also able to assert that Jackson was determined to rule by power and to set up a network of repressive relationships within the government.

> We are in the midst of a revolution, which, although bloodless, yet we are advancing to a concentration of all powers of Government in the hands of one man. By the exercise of the power assumed by the President of the United States in his letter to this cabinet, the powers of congress are paralyzed except where they are in compliance with his own will.[32]

Thus, while the opponents of the bank were inclined to perceive its activities in a highly generalized framework, the proponents of the bank employed a mixture of a mundane means-ends interpretation of its activities with a generalized interpretation of the motives and methods of its detractors. This would seem to suggest that in a given crisis the two levels of discourse are not mutually exclusive. The level of generalization will vary according to the objects being typified and the strategic positions and interests of the participants.

The Teapot Dome scandal of the mid-1920s provides the second example of how the legitimacy of institutions and their transactions can be determined only in their relationship to codes. Teapot Dome was one of several scandals involving President Harding's administration that had only just begun to come to light when he died. He was succeeded by his vice-president, Calvin Coolidge, under whose administration the investigations were conducted. Teapot Dome was the name of a geological structure in Wyoming that contained a reserve of oil set aside by Congress for the exclusive use of the navy. Along with other reserves, it was intended to provide an emergency supply in case of war. In 1924 a scandal arose when it became public knowledge that an executive order had been issued by Harding transferring jurisdiction over the reserve from the secretary of the Navy to the secretary of the Interior. It also became known that the secretary of the Interior, Albert Fall, had negotiated a sale of some of the reserves to the oil magnates Harry F. Sinclair and Edward L. Doheny, the former having purchased Teapot Dome, the latter the Elk Hills reserve in California. Proceeds from the sale were not placed in the Treasury but went directly to the navy to be used for improvements to bases, which amounted to $102 million spent without congressional authorization. Moreover, Fall received various gifts and undisclosed sums of money.

Those attacking the Teapot Dome deals saw them as strongly counterdemocratic, as secretive, illegal transactions that had been entered into for selfish reasons using Machiavellian calculation. As in the case of the Bank War, we see the opponents of the deals exhibiting a strong suspicion of the corrupting nature of large financial institutions and identifying themselves with the protection of the democratic ideals.

> See the marvelous cunning with which this thing was done. It is perfectly plain that for years these precious oil reserves had been watched with covetous eyes by these greedy exploiters. It was the vigilance and the courage and honesty of preceding administrations which held them off as they endeavored to encroach day after day, creeping and crawling and hungering for the gold hidden there, even though they had to betray and imperil a nation to get it.[33]

The oilmen are identified by the terms *cunning*, *greed*, *covetousness* (selfishness), and *exploitation*. These terms establish them as outside of civil society, which they appear to imperil and betray, much as the creeping and crawling serpent had once betrayed Eve. Against these amoral and nonhuman creatures, courageous, honest, and vigilant citizens seek to defend the nation.

We are the immediate guardians of the Government. Are we going to stand off and permit big looters on the outside who have accumulated millions, maybe in questionable ways, to come and lay their tempting offers before unfit public officials hungry for the ill-gotten gain of corrupt transactions to open the doors to the nations natural resources and brazenly barter them like sheep in the market place.[34]

The image of rapacious leaders demands passive and deferential followers. Once again, an image emerges of networks of actors behaving like puppets under the control of manipulative leaders. Although the leaders are seen actively as "combining and confederating,"[35] the mass of the people involved are depicted as passive and under the control of the leaders.

It is perfectly amazing that in three great law departments, with many learned experts and many thousands of men, every one of whom knew or ought to have known that this thing was fraught with evil, there was not a voice raised. Cabinet officers, learned lawyers, shrewd experts were moved around like pawns upon a chessboard by unseen and cunning hands or by the avaricious of Fall. . . . I cannot understand how one wise Iago could delude all these trusting Othellos about him, how one cunning and avaricious soul could exercise a kind of hideous hypnosis over hundreds of men.[36]

To combat the evils of Teapot Dome, two strategies presented themselves. The first was for an investigation to be carried out that would exemplify the discourse of liberty. Thus, in an important speech, President Coolidge counterposes the repressive associations and growing pollution of the scandal with promises of immediate punishment, which is attached to the antonymic set of openness and clarity, nonpartisanship, and the interests of the civil community. "For us we propose to follow the clear, open path of justice. There will be immediate, adequate, unshrinking prosecution, criminal and civil, to punish the guilty and to protect every national interest. In this effort there will be no politics, no partisanship."[37]

The second strategy was to ignore the niceties of the legal system and simply to declare the contracts null and void before the issue went to court. This strategy is particularly illuminating because it reveals the compromises with repressive codes that authorities often declare to be necessary if democracy is to be protected and repaired. "I do not care what legal phrases are used in fraudulently transferring the property of the Government of the United States to a band of marauders with their millions. I am ready to set a precedent by saying that these deals shall be declared off the minute the Government discovers the scandal and the crime."[38]

By this point in our discussion the reader will probably be able to guess the kinds of strategies used by those few who wished to defend the deals. They are well illustrated by a statement issued by the oil speculator Doheny. He argued that those investigating the deal were motivated by selfish political concerns rather than high ideals.

> The election in November—not the legality of the oil leases—is the sole factor now controlling the politicians who are conducting the so-called oil investigation. . . . The American people send senators and representatives to Washington to legislate. But some of the latter find they can gain far more publicity by acting as gum-shoe detectives than in trying to act as statesmen. (statement in *Washington Post*, March 3, 1924: 1)

Due to this selfish attitude, it is the investigators and not Doheny who pose a threat to law and constitutionality. "The attempt is now being made to destroy the leases and convict myself and other citizens in an atmosphere deliberately prejudiced and poisoned. Such an attempt cannot succeed without destroying the sacred constitutional right to a fair and impartial trial" (statement in *Washington Post*, March 3, 1924: 2).

Doheny accuses his accusers of failure to observe their official duties and of being not only vain and prejudiced but farcical in their destructive pursuits. Constructing the oilmen as citizens, he argues that the efforts to punish them threaten to pollute (poison) the values of fairness and impartiality, that form part of the sacred center of democratic life.

Finally, Doheny argues that his own actions were in accordance with the democratic code. Far from being treasonous, he asserts, his leases were undertaken for the common good. He goes on to contrast his own noble and self-sacrificing gesture with the dirty tactics of his opponents, who have deceived the civil society as to his true generosity and patriotism.

> Admiral Robinson, Chief of Engineers of the Navy, and other experts, have testified that the Dehony leases, including the construction of the tankage at Pearl Harbor, were essential to the protection of the Pacific Coast. . . . Senator Walsh and his Democratic colleagues know full well that in order to make the Pacific coast safe against enemy attack my company has actually advanced to the government nearly $5 million for which we will have to wait for payment for an indefinite period. But by insinuations of scandal and actual scandal mongering, they have successfully obscured that fact from the public. (statement in *Washington Post*, March 3 1924: 2)

It is one of the many ironies of the Teapot Dome affair that the facilities constructed by Doheny at Pearl Harbor as part of his Elk Hills deal later helped prevent the total collapse of the U.S. Pacific Fleet after the Japanese attack.

## DISSENT OVER STATE POLICIES

Whether policies are understood as a threat to the values and unity of the American nation or accepted as legitimate depends crucially on the coding that is made of them. In this section, we briefly demonstrate how differing opinions about policy are shaped by the democratic and counterdemocratic codes.

The Nullification Crisis of 1832 provides a miniature of the political understandings that characterized America on its way to the Civil War. The rhetoric of states' rights was a territorially and historically specific version of the democratic code, and it was on this basis that a convention in South Carolina nullified acts approved by Congress imposing high tariffs on imported manufactured goods. The South Carolinians argued that these were prejudicial to their interests, that the tariffs would raise the cost of living for those in the South while favoring the northern manufacturing states. These objections were not couched in a mundane means-ends idiom, however; they were pitched in an intensely moral discourse. The Nullification Ordinance itself begins with an indictment of Congress as a repressive institution, characterized by counterdemocratic social relationships and motivations.

> Whereas the Congress of the United States, by various acts, purporting to be
> acts laying duties and impost on foreign imports, but in reality intended for the
> protection of domestic manufactures, and giving of bounties to classes and individuals engaged in particular employments, at the expense and to the injury and
> oppression of other classes and individuals, and by wholly exempting from taxation certain foreign commodities, such as are not produced or manufactured in
> the United States, to afford a pretext from imposing higher and excessive duties
> on articles similar to those to be protected, hath exceeded its just powers under
> the Constitution, which confer on it no authority to afford such protection, and
> hath violated the true meaning and intent of the constitution, which provides
> for equality in imposing the burdens of taxation upon the several states and portions of the confederacy.[39]

South Carolina is associated with equality and the Constitution, Congress with particularity, oppression, and foreign threat. As was the case in the Bank Crisis and Teapot Dome, the aggrieved party sees itself as coolly, openly, and rationally opposing the insidious corruption creeping into American society.

> A disposition is manifested in every section of the country to arrest, by some
> means or other, the progress of the intolerable evil. This disposition having
> arisen from no sudden excitement, but from the free temperate discussion of the
> press, there is no reason to believe it can ever subside by any means short of the
> removal of the urgent abuse.[40]

If the federal government used force against South Carolina, it would be but more evidence of the its repressive character. "Unless the President is resolved to disregard all constitutional obligations, and to trample the laws of his country under his feet he has no authority whatever to use force against the States of South Carolina."[41]

South Carolina represented itself not as attacking the Union but as attempting to rejuvenate it—as closer to the symbolic center of America than was the institutional center itself. It identified itself with rationality, law, and constitutionality against oppression, tyranny, and force. Those opposed to nullification, naturally, inverted this relationship between South Carolina and the democratic code. President Jackson, to take one example, argued that South Carolina was guilty of selfishly challenging the rule of law, accusing it of provoking violent rather than rational behavior.

> This solemn denunciation of the laws and authority of the United States, has
> been followed up by a series of acts, on the part of the authorities of the state,
> which manifest a determination to render inevitable a resort to those measures
> of self-defense which the paramount duty of the federal Government requires.
> . . . In fine she has set her own will and authority above the laws, has
> made herself arbiter in her own cause, and has passed at once over all inter-
> mediate steps to measures of avowed resistance, which, unless they be sub-
> mitted to, can be enforced only by the sword. . . . The right of the peo-
> ple of a single State to absolve themselves at will and without the consent
> of the other states, from their most solemn obligations and hazard the
> liberties and happiness of the millions composing this union, cannot be
> acknowledged.[42]

The president's message is clear: the arbitrary will and coercive force characteristic of South Carolina endanger the consent, liberty, and the rule of law prevalent in the wider civil community. Violent action is therefore justified in order to protect the integrity of that civil community.

## AMERICA'S CIVIL DISCOURSE IN ITS CONTEMPORARY FORM

Critical social science, whether issuing from the left or from the right, tends to argue that modernization strips individual and institutional actions of their ethical moorings, creating anomie and chaos, and allowing a shallow world dominated by instrumental rationality. From this perspective, it might be objected that the examples of intense public valuation we have discussed thus far relate only to earlier, more "traditional" epochs in American history. It could be argued that in the course of this century, social evolution—rationalization, capitalism, secularization—has intensified, producing a tendency for discourse that is less excited and more mundane and "rational." In this final section of this chapter we present evidence for the contrary view: late twentieth-century American society continues to be permeated by the discourse we have described. We do not claim here that nothing has changed. Clearly, discourses at more specific, intermediate levels reflect the historical conditions and controversies in which they arise. In the twentieth century, for example, the discourse of states' rights has faded in importance while that of civil rights for individuals has grown. What we do claim is that there is a continuity in the deep structure from which these discourses are derived and to which they must appeal.

Unfortunately for social science, history never repeats itself exactly. We are thus unable to provide precise "controls" for our antihistoricist experiment by investigating crises that are exactly parallel to the ones we have analyzed earlier. Still, there are broad similarities between the issues involved in the following cases and the previous examples. The case of Richard Nixon's fall in the early 1970s demonstrates many affinities with the impeachment of Johnson one hundred years earlier. The Iran-Contra affair of the late 1980s demonstrates that the structures of civil discourse are as relevant to the understanding of today's executive scandals as they were during Teapot Dome. Indeed, we would maintain that the correspondence between more contemporary and earlier discussion is at times so remarkable that one could swap statements from earlier and later crises without altering the substantive thrust of either argument.

Yet, although the similarities are fundamental to one side of our argument, the differences from case to case are important to another. The postwar examples show yet again the astonishing malleability of the codes that are applied contingently to a wide and scattered array of issues. Indeed, in the final example we discuss, we expand the scope of this chapter to show how America's civil discourse is used to understand foreigners and foreign powers, not only domestic forces and events.

## RICHARD NIXON AND WATERGATE

The discourse involved in the push for the impeachment of President Nixon in 1974 is remarkably similar to that of the impeachment of President Johnson some one hundred years earlier. Although the particular issues in hand (in the Watergate break-in and coverup, the misuse of surveillance powers of the FBI, CIA, and the IRS, the president's failure to obey various subpoenas to hand over documents and tapes, and the secret bombing of Cambodia) contrast with those of Johnson's impeachment (the Tenure of Office Act, the Stanton Removal, and various statements opposing Congress), the generalized understandings made by the impeachers were shaped by the logic of the same symbolic structure. As was the case with Johnson, Nixon's motivations were perceived by many in terms of the counterdemocratic discourse. As deliberations by the congressional committee on the impeachment of Nixon made clear, central to this perception was an image of the president as a selfish and fractious person who was interested in gaining wealth and power at the expense of the civil community. "The evidence is overwhelming that Richard Nixon has used the Office of President to gain political advantage, to retaliate against those who disagreed with him, and to acquire personal wealth."[43] "He created a moral vacuum in the Office of the Presidency and turned that great office away from the service of the people toward the service of his own narrow, selfish interests."[44]

True to the codes, this self-centered attitude was understood to have arisen from an irrational, unrealistic, slightly paranoid motivational structure. Because of these personality needs, it was argued, Nixon evaluated others, without reasonable cause, in terms of the counterdemocratic rhetoric of social relationships. "Once in the White House, Mr. Nixon turned on his critics with a vengeance, apparently not appreciating that others could strenuously disagree with him without being either subversive or revolutionary."[45]

Irrational, selfish, and narrow motives are connected to sectarian rather than cooperative and communal relations. They cannot form the basis for an inclusive, conflict-containing, civil society. Time and again Nixon was described as deceitful, calculating, suspicious, and secretive—unacceptable characteristics in a democracy. These perversities, it was believed, led him to resort to counterdemocratic and illegal political practices. Nixon had covered up his dark deeds by making false excuses for himself. He had acted in a calculating rather than honorable manner to maximize his own advantage regardless of morality and legality. "To defend both the bombing [of Cambodia] and the wire-tapping, he invoked the concept of national security. . . . The imperial presidency of Richard Nixon came to rely on this claim as a cloak for clandestine activity, and as an excuse for consciously and repeatedly deceiving the Congress and the people."[46]

> We have seen that the President authorized a series of illegal wire-taps for his own political advantage, and not only did he thereby violate the fundamental constitutional rights of the people of this country but he tried to cover up those illegal acts in the very same way that he tried to cover up Watergate. He lied to the prosecutors. He tried to stop investigations. He tried to buy silence, and he failed to report criminal conduct.[47]

These procedures and relationships were viewed by Nixon's accusers as a dangerous source of pollution, a disease that had to be stopped before it could infect the rest of the civil society, destroying the very tissues of social solidarity. "Mr. Nixon's actions had attitudes and those of his subordinates have brought us to verge of collapse as a Nation of people who believe in its institutions and themselves. Our people have become cynical instead of skeptical. They are beginning to believe in greater numbers that one must look out only for himself and not worry about others."[48]

The president's motivations and relationships were seen as subversive of democracy. His administration had developed into an arbitrary, personalistic organization bent on concentrating power. The institutional aim was, as the *New York Times* argued, dictatorship and an authoritarian coup d'etat.

> One coherent picture emerges from the evidence. . . . It is the picture of a White House entirely on its own, operating on the assumption that it was accountable to no higher authority than the wishes of and the steady accretion of power by the President. It is the picture of a Presidency growing steadily more sure that it was above and beyond the reaches of the law. (editorial, July 31, 1974)

Yet, despite the mounting tide of evidence against Nixon in the early summer of 1974, he still had significant support. Those who continued to support him did not counter the discourse of repression with the picture of a flawless, pristine paragon of democratic morality; they tended to argue, rather, that in the messy world of political reality, Nixon's personal behavior and political achievements were not inconsistent with that discourse broadly conceived.

> The President's major contribution to international peace must be recognized to compensate for other matters, to a substantial degree. (letter to the editor, *New York Times*, August 1, 1974)

> As has been written to many representatives on the Judiciary Committee, President Nixon's lengthy list of accomplishments rules out impeachment. Let us be grateful we have such a fine leader, doing his utmost to establish world peace. (letter to the editor, *New york Times*, july 31, 1974)

> As in the case of the evidence relating to the Plumbers' operation they show a specific Presidential response to a specific and serious problem: namely, the public disclosure by leaks of highly sensitive information bearing upon the conduct of American foreign policy during that very turbulent period both domestically and internationally.[49]

These statements suggested that in a world characterized by realpolitik, it would be unwise to punish Nixon's peccadillos when, on balance, he had supported and advanced the cause of the good. Especially important in this equation were Nixon's foreign policy initiatives with the Soviets and Chinese, as well as his ending the Vietnam War, all of which were presented as having advanced the cause of "peace," a state of affairs analogous with inclusive social relationships. Related to this argument was another that focused not on the impact of the president but on the consequences of impeachment itself. These consequences, it is suggested, militate against a prolonged period of distracting, generalized discourse. "Certain members of Congress and the Senate urge the President's removal from office despite the impact such a disastrous decision would have on America's political image and the economy." (letter to the editor, *New York Times*, August 1, 1974)

> We would do better to retain the President we in our judgment elected to office, for the balance of his term, and in the meantime place our energies and spend our time on such pressing matters as a real campaign reform, a sound financial policy to control inflation, energy and the environment, war and peace, honesty throughout Government, and the personal and economic rights and liberties of the individual citizen against private agglomerations of power in the monolithic state.[50]

The message is that, because of political realities, both mundane political and wider moral goals can be effectively attained only by avoiding impeachment.

The use of these arguments, however, did not preclude Nixon's supporters in Congress from also understanding events in a more generalized manner. They held the impeachment inquiry and its committee members strictly accountable in terms of the two antithetical moral discourses. They linked the lack of hard, irrefutable evidence of the commission to their concern that the inquiry measure up to the highest ethical standards. In principle, therefore, they were compelled to refuse to consider Nixon guilty of an impeachable offense until his accusers could produce a "smoking gun" proof of his direct, personal, and willful involvement in an indictable crime. "To impeach there must be direct Presidential involvement, and the evidence thus far has failed to produce it."[51] "Now many wrongs have been committed, no question about it, but were those wrongs directed by the President? Is there direct evidence that said he had anything to do with it? Of course there is not."[52]

Nixon's supporters pointedly contrasted their hard line on the issue of proof with that of his detractors. They described these opponents in terms of the discourse of repression: Nixon's critics were willing to support impeachment on the basis of evidence that a rational and independent thinker would not accept. Indeed, the critics' motive was greed, their social relationships manipulative. They were the very paradigm of a counterdemocratic group: a bloodthirsty and suggestible mob unable to sustain the dispassionate attitude on which civility depends. "I join in no political lynching where hard proof fails as to this President or any other President."[53] "I know that the critics of the President want their pound of flesh. Certainly they have achieved that in all the convictions that have taken place. However, they now want the whole body, and it is self-evident that it is Mr. Nixon who must supply the carcass" (letter to the editor, *New York Times*, July 31, 1974). "Yes, the cries of impeachment, impeachment, impeachment are getting louder. . . . For the past year allegation after allegation has been hurled at the President. Some of them have been stated so often many people have come to accept them as facts, without need of proof."[54]

This evaluation of the impeachers' motives and social relationships was accompanied by a negative evaluation of the institution involved in the impeachment process. They were described as performing in an arbitrary manner, treating Nixon as an enemy rather than as a fellow citizen, and trying to maximize their own power rather than the power of right. This disregard for the law endangered the democratic foundations of society; it could, indeed, create an antidemocratic revolution.

[We are] each convinced of the serious threat to our country, caused by the bias and hate pumped out daily by the media. (letter to the editor, *New York Times*, July 31, 1974)

The Supreme Court decision that President Nixon must turn over Watergate-related tapes . . . can make any President virtually a figurehead whose actions can be overturned by any arbitrary high court order. . . . The Court has, in effect, ignored the Constitution, written its own law, and demanded it be considered the law of the land. (letter to the editor, *New York Times*, July 29, 1974)

Five members of the committee have made public statements that Mr. Nixon should be impeached and they have not been disqualified from voting. Leaks detrimental to the President appear almost daily in the media. . . . When public hearings begin, I fully expect women to appear with their knitting, each a modern Madame Defarge, clicking their needles as they wait for Richard Nixon's head to roll. (letter to the editor, *New York Times*, July 2, 1974)

## A MODERN SCANDAL: THE IRAN-CONTRA AFFAIR

The Iran-Contra affair of the late 1980s provides evidence of the continuing importance of the cultural codes that we have identified as central in the social definition of scandal. As was the case with Teapot Dome, this more recent incident involved the evaluation of transactions and activities undertaken by members of the executive branch without the knowledge or consent of Congress. In late 1986, information emerged that a small team in the Reagan administration, spearheaded by Lieutenant-Colonel Oliver North, had sold arms to Iran, in return for which Iran was to use its influence to obtain the release of American hostages held by various Islamic groups in the Middle East. As a further twist in the tale, the money raised from the sale was used to support a secret operation in Central America backing the anticommunist "contra" guerrillas in Nicaragua. Once the action came to light, a process of generalization rapidly occurred in which the motivations, relationships, and institutions of North and his associates became the subject of intense public scrutiny.

The weeklong session of the joint congressional inquiry in which North was the key witness is a useful place to examine this cultural process, which centered around dramatically different interpretations by North and his detractors of the same empirical events. Of the greatest importance to those who denounced the affair were the social relationships involved, which they described in terms of the counterdemocratic code. The administration officials involved were perceived by their critics as an elite "secret team," operating clandestinely and furthering their own particularistic and illegal aims through a web of lies.

> Foreign policies were created and carried out by a tiny circle of persons, apparently without the involvement of even some of the highest officials of our government. The administration tried to do secretly what the Congress sought to prevent it from doing. The administration did secretly what it claimed to all the world it was not doing.[55]

> But I am impressed that policy was driven by a series of lies—lies to the Iranians, lies to the Central Intelligence Agency, lies to the Attorney General, lies to our friends and allies, lies to the Congress, and lies to the American people.[56]

> It has been chilling, and, in fact, frightening. I'm not talking just about your part in this, but the entire scenario—about government officials who plotted and conspired, who set up a straw man, a fall guy [North]. Officials who lied, misrepresented and deceived. Officials who planned to superimpose upon our government a layer outside of our government, shrouded in secrecy and only accountable to the conspirators.[57]

Such "conspirators" could not be expected to trust other institutions and persons in government; according to the semiotic foundations of common-sense reasoning, they could treat them only as enemies, not as friends. This attitude was understood as antithetical to the democratic ideal. "Your opening statement made the analogy to a baseball game. You said the playing field here was uneven and the Congress would declare itself the winner. [But we] are not engaged in a game of winners and losers. That approach, if I may say so, is self-serving and ultimately self-defeating. We all lost. The interests of the United States have been damaged by what happened."[58]

These kinds of relationships not only were taken to confound the possibility of open and free political institutions but also were perceived as leading to inevitably foolish and self-defeating policies.

> A great power cannot base its policy on an untruth without a loss of credibility.
> . . . In the Middle-East, mutual trust with some friends was damaged, even shattered. The policy of arms for hostages sent a clear message to the States of the Persian Gulf, and that message was, that the United States is helping Iran in its war effort, and making an accommodation with the Iranian revolution, and Iran's neighbors should do the same. The policy provided the Soviets with an

opportunity they have now grasped, with which we are struggling to deal. The policy achieved none of the goals it sought. The Ayatollah got his arms, more Americans are held hostage today than when this policy began, subversion of U.S. interests throughout the region by Iran continues. Moderates in Iran, if any there were, did not come forward.[59]

In dealing with attacks on his motives and the relationships in which he was involved, North used several strategies. At a mundane level he denied the illegality of his actions, pointing not only to various historical precedents but also to the legal justification of the "Hostage Act," which had given the American executive vast autonomy over policy in recovering American hostages. North also drew on aspects of the generalized codes to defend and interpret not only his own actions but those of Congress. First, he argued that while the methods he employed and the relationships he developed could be characterized within the discourse of repression, they were necessary means in order more effectively to promote the cause of the good. Second, North argued that his own motivations were, in fact, compatible with the discourse of liberty. Finally, North suggested that it was actually the policies of Congress that could best be construed in terms of the discourse of repression, not the Administration's own.

In defending the secrecy of his operations and his lies to Congress, North denied particularistic motivations and drew attention to his higher, more universal aims. He argued in strongly patriotic terms that secrecy and lies were necessary in a world threatened by antidemocratic Soviet power, that dealings with polluted terrorist parties were necessary in order to protect the purity of American civic life, and that his policies in Central America had the extension of democracy as their noble aim.

If we could [find] a way to insulate with a bubble over these hearings that are being broadcast in Moscow, and talk about covert operations to the American people without it getting into the hands of our adversaries, I'm sure we would do that. But we haven't found the way to do it.[60]

Much has been made of, "How callous could North be, to deal with the very people who killed his fellow Marines?" The fact is we were trying to keep more Marines in places like El Salvador from being killed.[61]

I worked hard on the political military strategy for restoring and sustaining democracy in Central America, and in particular El Salvador. We sought to achieve the democratic outcome in Nicaragua that this administration still supports, which involved keeping the Contras together in both body and soul.[62]

As long as democratically motivated, rational individuals were involved, North argued, counterdemocratic methods would be legitimate and safe. "There are certainly times for patience and prudence, and there are certainly times when one has to cut through the tape. And I think the hope is that one can find that there are good and prudent men who are judicious in the application of their understanding of the law, and understanding of what was right. And I think we had that."[63]

With great success North argued that he was just such a man. Public discourse before the trial had portrayed North as a counterdemocratic figure. It was argued on the one hand that he was a passive zombie blindly following the dictates of his superiors and on the other that he was a Machiavellian maverick pursuing his own "gung-ho" policies. In the symbolic work of the hearings, North managed to refute these characterizations, drawing attention to his dynamic patriotism and the autonomy of his White House role, while at the same time demonstrating a sense of his officially regulated position on the White House team.

> I did not engage in fantasy that I was President or Vice President or Cabinet member, or even Director of the National Security Council. I was simply a staff member with a demonstrated ability to get the job done. My authority to act always flowed, I believe, from my superiors. My military training inculcated in me a strong belief in the chain of command. And so far as I can recall, I always acted on major matters with specific approval, after informing my superiors of the facts, as I knew them, the risks, and the potential benefits. I readily admit that I was counted upon as a man who got the job done. . . . There were times when my superiors, confronted with accomplishing goals or difficult tasks, would simply say, "Fix it, Ollie," or "Take care of it."[64]

Although he was a "patriot" who understood his own actions and motivations as informed by the discourse of liberty, North did not feel that the actions of some other Americans could be constituted in the same way. Notably, he asserted that he had been driven to his own actions by a weak and uncertain Congress, which had first decided to support and then to withdraw support from the "Contras," North described this congressional action as arbitrary and irrational, as a betrayal of persons who were fighting for liberty and against repression in Central America.

> I suggest to you that it is the Congress which must accept at least some of the blame in the Nicaraguan freedom fighters matter. Plain and simple, the Congress is to blame because of the fickle, vacillating, unpredictable, on-again off-again policy toward the Nicaraguan Democratic Resistance—the so-called Contras. I do not believe that the support of the Nicaraguan freedom fighters can be treated as the passage of a budget. . . . [They] are people—living, breathing, young men and women who have had to suffer a desperate struggle for liberty with sporadic and confusing support from the United States of America.[65]

North understood Congress to be repressive not only in its treatment of the Contras but also in its investigation of himself and his associates. In denying that he would receive a fair hearing North drew attention to what he saw as the arbitrary use of power by Congress and its deceit in making the executive branch into a scapegoat for its own foolish policies. Far from being the case that he had treated Congress without trust, it was members of the congressional investigation who had treated him as an enemy, declaring him to be guilty and announcing that they would refuse to believe his testimony even before he had spoken. The actions of the congressional committee were threatening to pollute the universal, timeless rules of the American "game."

> You dissect that testimony to find inconsistencies and declare some to be truthful and others to be liars. You make the rulings as to what is proper and what is not proper. You put the testimony which you think is helpful to your goals up before the people and leave others out. It's sort of like a baseball game in which you are both the player and the umpire.[66]

> The Congress of the United States left soldiers in the field unsupported and vulnerable to their communist enemies. When the executive branch did everything possible within the law to prevent them from being wiped out by Moscow's surrogates in Havana and Managua, you then had this investigation to blame the problem on the executive branch. It does not make sense to me.[67]

> As a result of rumor and speculation and innuendo, I have been accused of almost every crime imaginable—wild rumours have abound.[68]

## MODERN FOREIGN POLICY: MAKING SENSE OF GORBACHEV AND GLASNOST

Earlier in this chapter we demonstrated how the discourses of liberty and repression underlie debates in which U.S. presidents and domestic threats to American civil society are evaluated. In this final section we show that these symbolic structures also underpin the typifications that actors deploy in evaluating foreign persons and threats.

Throughout the Cold War, public discourse represented on the Soviet Union and its leaders as paradigmatic of the repressive code. The Soviet Union was framed as a secretive state controlled by an unfathomable oligarchy of party cadre, which was forever scheming and plotting in murky ways to extend its power both within the Soviet Union and without. This image remained unqualified until the death of Chernenko and the rise of Mikhail Gorbachev to the position of general secretary in 1985. Soon after his assumption of power, many in America began to argue that both Gorbachev himself, and a reborn Soviet Union, could be understood in terms of the discourse of liberty rather than that of repression. This typification gradually grew in strength until even hardline anticommunists such as Ronald Reagan and George Bush were persuaded that Gorbachev was deserving of American support, a trustworthy person with whom one could negotiate.

Part of the reason for this transformation lay in what were perceived as Gorbachev's personal characteristics. In contrast to dour, frumpy, and frequently ailing Kremlin apparatchiks such as Chernenko, Brezhnev, and Gromyko (who was described by the media as "Grim Grom" and by President Reagan as "Mr. Nyet"), Gorbachev was seen as outgoing, honest, charismatic, young and healthy. Bush, for example, said he was impressed by Gorbachev's candor, and the American president characterized the Soviet leader in terms of the discourse of liberty. "I asked him if he would take a sleeping pill? And he said: 'I've just been thinking about that.' You know," Bush added, "I can't imagine any of his predecessors being so open as that." (*Los Angeles Times*, December 12, 1987: n.p.).

Jesse Jackson mentioned Gorbachev's realism and rational behavior, in order to prevent him from being infected by comparison with a Nikita Krushchev, who lacked rational self-control. "He'll not be beating shoes on tables like Khrushchev. . . . [He is] very well-versed academically and experientially" (*Los Angeles Times*, December 12, 1987: n.p.).

Even more important than Gorbachev's motives, however, was his effort to transform the Soviet's domestic and foreign policy. His reformist domestic policies of *glasnost* and *perestroika* were seen as implying a radical break with the earlier structure of Soviet institutions and relationships, shifts that would parallel the new perception of Soviet motives. These policies, it was increasingly believed, offered the prospect of an open society in which free discussion would replace censorship, where decentralization would lead to the evolution of a rational and nonhierarchical society. In foreign policy, for example, Gorbachev's arms control initiatives were seen as belying the traditional image of the Soviets as aggressors hell-bent on world domination.

Supporters of Gorbachev's new discursive status argued that his pronouncements were more than mere rhetoric. They pointed to concrete evidence through which Gorbachev's Russia could be distinguished from the totalitarian Russia and asserted that he was involved in a righteous struggle to bring about the transformation from repression to freedom, and from madness and ideology to trust and realism. These shifts allow the restoration not only of criticism but of civil humanism as well.

> Gorbachev has gone much further than many expected in his pursuit of glasnost, or openness. It is not only in some decentralization in economic controls, the release of Andrei D. Sakharov from internal exile and the permission for emigration extended to certain dissidents. It is particularly noticeable in the press. For the first time since Josef Stalin came to power, one can now see significant criticism and public debate.[69]

The Soviet Union is softening its ideology of global struggle into a vision of pragmatic humanism. It has replaced Stalin's paranoia with a spectacular call for mutual trust backed by a series of largely unilateral concessions, including withdrawal from Afghanistan and the promise to demobilize half a million troops.[70]

In order to account for those who did not share their typification of Gorbachev, his American supporters invoked the discourse of repression. One commentator, for example, identifies some of Gorbachev's detractors as powerful, self-interested elites, such as "the military-industrial complex, legions of professional cold-warriors and self-described national security intellectuals, certain Jewish organizations and an array of other special interests." He goes on to argue that while these factions are unable to accept a realistic interpretation of the situation because it would damage their own particularistic interests, American opposition to Gorbachev can be understood more generally as an irrational pathology akin to what psychoanalysts term "projection."

> Any acknowledged improvement in the Soviet system threatens their political, economic and ideological well-being. For many of them the necessity of eternal cold war against the Soviet Union is theological rather than analytical. . . . America seems to have developed a deep psychological need for an immutably ugly Soviet Union in order to minimize or obscure its own imperfections.[71]

Despite the growing power and influence of the pro-Gorbachev typification through 1987, many still believed that he should be considered, and treated, in the manner appropriate to a counterdemocratic person. The assault of these persons on what was increasingly becoming the dominant typification of Gorbachev took on several strands. They argued that there was a substantial continuity between Gorbachev's Russia and previous Soviet regimes. They pointed to continuing secrecy and repression and argued from this that the Soviet Union should continue to be treated by America in the skeptical manner appropriate for dealings with a counterdemocratic power. They interpreted Gorbachev's thought as traditional, fanatical, and amoral Marxist-Leninist dogma, cunningly wrapped up in a devious and guileful disguise.

> If the Soviet Union will not trust its own citizens to travel freely to other countries, or to read foreign publications, or to know the truth about how much their government spends on weapons, or to express their skepticism about the party line and official policy, how then can the Soviet leaders expect outsiders, including Americans, to trust the Soviet Union?[72]

> The Gorbachev who wrote "Perestroika" is a classical Leninist—flexible, adaptable, skillful in the pursuit and use of power, absolutely committed to "the revolution," to socialism, to a one party state, and not at all disturbed about the high human cost of past Soviet policy.[73]

This gap between appearance and substance was a recurring leitmotif in diverse comments. Attention was drawn to Gorbachev's public relations skills. He was denounced as merely a "master of propaganda," a criminal trickster cynically manipulating the media in order to subvert democracy and further his own mysterious power over the American public. In this way it was argued that, like all previous Soviet leaders, he was "really" proposing an inscrutable, and counterdemocratic, agenda.

> The Gorbachev regime, more worldly-wise and media wise, acts more skillfully to exploit network rivalry. Incentives are created to temper coverage in order to win favor. If these subtle pressures are not resisted, the Soviets will have succeeded in manipulating American television, and thus the American people.
> . . . his larger aim is to influence American opinion in ways that will make it harder for anyone who succeeds Reagan to impose unwanted choices on the Soviet Union. It will be fascinating to watch Gorbachev go about his work. He is very good. So keep your eyes open—and your hand on your wallet.[74]

In addition to discrediting Gorbachev's motivations, his detractors attempted to discredit those who argued that he was democratically minded. They gave tit for tat, asserting that belief in Gorbachev could only have come about from personal vanity or defective and emotive thinking. Those who trusted him, therefore, could be understood in terms of the discourse of repression.

> It is very difficult to credit Reagan's somewhat mystical sense that a new era has dawned with Gorbachev. Instead his change of heart can be accounted for only in other, less rational, terms. . . . One explanation may lie in the effect that nearly eight years at the pinnacle of power have had on an elderly and not terribly well-educated mind. There is considerable evidence that Reagan's ego has expanded in the twilight of his presidency as he gropes for a place in history.[75]

> Gorbachev has fulfilled the Western yearning for some automatic nostrum promising relief from tension.[76]

## CONCLUSIONS

In this chapter, we have suggested that the culture of civil society should be conceived as a system of symbolic codes that specify good and evil. Conceptualizing culture in this way allows it causal autonomy—by virtue of its internal semiologics—and also affords the possibility for generalizing from and between specific localities and historical contexts. Yet at the same time our formulation allows for individual action and social-structural factors to be included in the analytical frame. The codes, we have argued, inform action in two ways. First, they are internalized, hence provide the foundations for a strong moral imperative. Second, they constitute publicly available resources against which the actions of particular individual actors are typified and held morally accountable. By acknowledging the importance of phenomenological processes in channeling symbolic inputs, our model shows that it is precisely these contingent processes that allow codes to make sense in specific situations for specific actors and their interests.

In addition to this claim about action, our model takes account of social structure. We have argued, in theoretical terms, that relatively autonomous cultural codes are specified vis-à-vis subsystems and institutions. Their content, we have suggested, reflects and refracts the empirical dimensions in which institutions are embedded. Our studies, indeed, provide crucial empirical insights into the relationship between culture and social structure and, more specifically, into the relationship between civil society and the state in American society. They demonstrate that conflicts at the social-structural level need not necessarily be accompanied by divergent values, or "ideologies," at the ideational level. To the contrary, in the American context at least, conflicting parties within the civil society have drawn on the same symbolic code to formulate their *particular* understandings and to advance their *competing* claims.

The very structured quality of this civil culture, and its impressive scope and breadth, help to underscore a paradoxical fact: differences of opinion between contending groups cannot be explained simply as the automatic product of divergent subcultures and value sets. In many cases, especially those that respond to new historical conditions, divergent cultural understandings are, to the contrary, an emergent property of individual and group-level typifications from code to event. This is not to posit a radically individualist theory but rather to suggest a more interactive conception of the link between cultural and social structures on the one hand and the actors, groups, and movements who have to improvise understandings always for "another first time" on the other. Because worthiness can be achieved only by association to the discourse of liberty or by active opposition to the discourse of repression, political legitimacy and political action in the "real world" are critically dependent on the processes by which contingent events and persons are arrayed in relation to the "imagined" one. In light of these relations among culture, structure, and typification, we can credit the role of political tactics and strategies without falling into the instrumentalist reductions of "institutionalism" on the one hand or elusive concepts like "structuration" or "habitus" on the other.

Although in this chapter our studies were drawn from spheres of life that may be considered political in a narrow sense, we are confident that the discourses and processes we have discovered provide insights into other domains in which questions of citizenship, inclusion, and exclusion within civil society are at stake. Women and African-Americans, for example, were for a long time excluded from full citizenship (and to some extent still are) in part because of a negative coding. In these cases the discourse of motivations was mobilized to identify purported intellectual deficiencies. These deficiencies were variously attributed to a naturally emotive and fickle disposition and to a lack of the education necessary to become an informed and responsible member of the civil society.[77] Similarly, schizophrenics and the mentally ill, to take another example, have long been marginalized on the basis of alleged qualities such as lack of self-control, deficient moral sensibility, inability to function autonomously, and the lack of a realistic and accurate world view. Since the 1960s their champions have asserted that this view is mistaken (Laing, 1967). They argue that the mentally ill have a unique insight into the true condition of society. In general this counterattack has used the discourse of institutions and relationships to assault the psychiatric professions and their practices. As a final example, during the 1950s in the United States the persecution and marginalization of "communists" was legitimated through a discourse that drew on the counterdemocratic codes of relationships and institutions.

Our studies have established the remarkable durability and continuity of a single culture structure over time that is able to reproduce itself discursively in various highly contingent contexts. On the basis of this discovery, it seems plausible to suggest that this culture structure must be considered a *necessary* cause in all political events that are subject to the scrutiny of American civil society. The wide-ranging nature of our survey, however, also has distinctive drawbacks, for only by developing a more elaborated case study would we be able to detail the shifts in typifications that allow culture to operate not only as a generalized input but also as an *efficient* cause. Even if we could show this to be the case, however, we would not wish to suggest that cultural forces are cause enough alone. We merely argue that to understand American politics, one must understand the culture of its civil society, and that the best way to understand that political culture is to understand its symbolic codes.

# WATERGATE AS
# DEMOCRATIC RITUAL

In June 1972, employees of the Republican party made an illegal entry and burglary into the Democratic party headquarters in the Watergate Hotel in Washington, D.C. Republicans described the break-in as a "third-rate burglary," neither politically motivated nor morally relevant. Democrats said it was a major act of political espionage, a symbol, moreover, of a demagogic and amoral Republican president, Richard Nixon, and his staff. Americans were not persuaded by the more extreme reaction. The incident received relatively little attention, generating no real sense of outrage at the time. There were no cries of outrage. There was, in the main, deference to the president, respect for his authority, and belief that his explanation of this event was correct, despite what in retrospect seemed like strong evidence to the contrary. With important exceptions, the mass news media decided after a short time to play down the story, not because they were coercively prevented from doing otherwise but because they genuinely felt it to be a relatively unimportant event. Watergate remained, in other words, part of the profane world in Durkheim's sense. Even after the national election in November of that year, after Democrats had been pushing the issue for four months, 80 percent of the American people found it hard to believe that there was a "Watergate crisis"; 75 percent felt that what had occurred was just plain politics; 84 percent felt that what they had heard about it did not influence their vote. Two years later, the same incident, still called "Watergate," had initiated the most serious peacetime political crisis in American history. It had become a riveting moral symbol, one that initiated a long passage through sacred time and space and wrenching conflict between pure and impure sacred forms. It was responsible for the first voluntary resignation of a president.

How and why did this perception of Watergate change? To understand this one must see first what this extraordinary contrast in these two public perceptions indicates, namely that the actual event, "Watergate," was in itself relatively inconsequential. It was a mere collection of facts, and, contrary to the positive persuasion, facts do not speak. Certainly, new "facts" seem to have emerged in the course of the two-year crisis, but it is quite extraordinary how many of these "revelations" actually were already leaked and published in the preelection period. Watergate could not, as the French might say, tell itself. It had to be told by society; it was, to use Durkheim's famous phrase, a social fact. It was the context of Watergate that had changed, not so much the raw empirical data themselves.

To understand how this telling of a crucial social fact changed, it is necessary to bring to the sacred/profane dichotomy the Parsonian concept of generalization. There are different levels at which every social fact can be told (Smelser, 1959, 1963). These levels are linked to different kinds of social resources, and the focus on one level or another can tell us much about whether a system is in crisis—and subject, therefore, to the sacralizing process—or is operating routinely, or profanely, and in equalibrium.

First and most specific is the level of goals. Political life occurs most of the time in the relatively mundane level of goals, power, and interest. Above this, as it were, at a higher level of generality, are norms—the conventions, customs, and laws that regulate this political process and struggle. At still a higher point there are values: those very general and elemental aspects of the culture that inform the codes that regulate political authority and the norms within which specific interests are resolved. If politics operates routinely, the conscious attention of political participants is on goals and interests. It is a relatively specific attention. Routine, "profane" politics means, in fact, that these interests are not seen as violating more general values and norms. Nonroutine politics begins when tension between these levels is felt, either because of a shift in the nature of political activity or a shift in the general, more sacred commitments that are held to regulate them. In this situation, a tension between goals and higher levels develops. Public attention shifts from political goals to more general concerns, to the norms and values that are now perceived as in danger. In this instance we can say there has been the generalization of public consciousness that I referred to earlier as the central point of the ritual process.

It is in light of this analysis that we can understand the shift in the telling of Watergate. It was first viewed merely as something on the level of goals, "just politics," by 75 percent of the American people. Two years after the break-in, by summer 1974, public opinion had sharply changed. Now Watergate was regarded as an issue that violated fundamental customs and morals, and eventually—by 50 percent of the population—as a challenge to the most sacred values that sustained political order itself. By the end of this two-year crisis period, almost half of those who had voted for Nixon changed their minds, and two-thirds of all voters thought the issue had now gone far beyond politics.[1] What had happened was a radical generalization of opinion. The facts were not that different, but the social context in which they were seen had been transformed.

If we look at the two-year transformation of the context of Watergate, we see the creation and resolution of a fundamental social crisis, a resolution that involved the deepest ritualization of political life. To achieve this "religious" status, there had to be an extraordinary generalization of opinion vis-à-vis a political threat that was initiated by the very center of established power and a successful struggle not just against that power in its social form but against the powerful cultural rationales it mobilized. To understand this process of crisis creation and resolution, we must integrate ritual theory with a more muscular theory of social structure and process. Let me lay these factors out generally before I indicate how each relates to Watergate.

What must happen for an entire society to experience fundamental crisis and ritual renewal?

First, there has to be sufficient social consensus so that an event will be considered polluting (Douglas, 1966), or deviant, by more than a mere fragment of the population. Only with sufficient consensus, in other words, can "society" itself be aroused and indignant.

Second, there has to be the perception by significant groups who participate in this consensus that the event is not only deviant but threatens to pollute the "center" (Shils, 1975: 3–16) of society.

Third, if this deep crisis is to be resolved, institutional social controls must be brought into play. However, even legitimate attacks on the polluting sources of crisis are often viewed as frightening. For this reason, such controls also mobilize instrumental force and the threat of force to bring polluting forces to heel.

Fourth, social control mechanisms must be accompanied by the mobilization and struggle of elites and publics that are differentiated and relatively autonomous (e.g., Eisenstadt, 1971; Keller, 1963) from the structural center of society. Through this process there the formation of countercenters begins.

Finally, fifth, there has to be effective processes of symbolic interpretation, that is, ritual and purification processes that continue the labeling process and enforce the strength of the symbolic, sacred center of society at the expense of a center that is increasingly seen as merely structural, profane, and impure. In so doing, such processes demonstrate conclusively that deviant or "transgressive" qualities are the sources of this threat.

In elaborating how each one of these five factors came into play in the course of Watergate, I will indicate how, in a complex society, reintegration and symbolic renewal are far from being automatic processes. Durkheim's original ritual theory was developed in the context of simple societies. The result was that "ritualization" was confidently expected. In contemporary fragmented societies, political reintegration and cultural renewal depend on the contingent outcomes of specific historical circumstances. The successful alignment of these forces is very rare indeed.

First, there must emerge the capacity for consensus. Between the Watergate break-in in June 1972 and the Nixon-McGovern election contest in November, the necessary social consensus did not emerge. This was a time during which Americans experienced intense political polarization, though most of the actual social conflicts of the 1960s had significantly cooled. Nixon had built his presidency, in part, on a backlash against these 1960s conflicts, and the Democratic candidate, George McGovern, was the very symbol of this "leftism" to many. Both candidates thought that they, and the nation, were continuing the battles of the 1960s. McGovern's active presence during this period, therefore, allowed Nixon to continue to promote the authoritarian politics that could justify Watergate. One should not suppose, however, because there was not significant social reintegration during this period that no significant symbolic activity occurred. Agreement in complex societies occurs at various levels. There may be extremely significant cultural agreement (e.g., complex and systematic agreement about the structure and content of language) while more socially or structurally related areas of subjective agreement (e.g., rules about political conduct) do not exist. Symbolic agreement without social consensus can exist, moreover, within more substantive cultural arenas than language.

During the summer of 1972 one can trace a complex symbolic development in the American collective conscience, a consensual development that laid the basis for everything that followed even while it did not produce consensus at more social levels.[2] It was during this four-month period that the meaning complex "Watergate" came to be defined. In the first weeks that followed the break-in at the Democratic headquarters, "Watergate" existed, in semiotic terms, merely as a sign, as a denotation. This word simply referred, moreover, to a single event. In the weeks that followed, the sign "Watergate," became more complex, referring to a series of interrelated events touched off by the break-in, including charges of political corruption, presidential denials, legal suits, and arrests. By August 1972, "Watergate" had become transformed from a mere sign to a redolent symbol, a word that rather than denoting actual events connotated multifold moral meanings.

Watergate had become a symbol of pollution, embodying a sense of evil and impurity. In structural terms, the facts directly associated with Watergate— those who were immediately associated with the crime, the office and apartment complex, the persons implicated later—were placed on the negative side of a system of symbolic classification. Those persons or institutions responsible for ferreting out and arresting these criminal elements were placed on the other, positive side. This bifurcated model of pollution and purity was then superimposed onto the traditional good/evil structure of American civil discourse, whose relevant elements appeared in the form indicated in table 6.1. It is clear, then, that while significant symbolic structuring had occurred, the "center" of the American social structure was in no way implicated.

This symbolic development, it should be emphasized, occurred in the public

*Table 6.1*    Symbolic classification system as of August 1972

| The Watergate "structure" | |
| --- | --- |
| Evil | Good |
| Watergate Hotel | Nixon and staff/White House |
| The burglars | FBI |
| Dirty Tricksters | Courts/Justice Department's prosecution team |
| Money raisers | Federal "watchdog" bureaucracy |

| American Civil Culture | |
| --- | --- |
| Evil | Good |
| Communism/fascism | Democracy |
| Shadowy enemies | White House—Americanism |
| Crime | Law |
| Corruption | Honesty |
| Personalism | Responsibility |
| Bad presidents (e.g., Harding/Grant) | Great presidents (e.g., Lincoln/Washington) |
| Great scandals (e.g., Teapot Dome) | Heroic reformers |

mind. Few Americans would have disagreed about the moral meanings of "Watergate" as a collective representation. Yet while the social basis of this symbol was widely inclusive, the symbol just about exhausted the meaning complex of Watergate as such. The term identified a complex of events and people with moral evil, but the collective consciousness did not connect this symbol to significant social roles or institutional behaviors. Neither the Republican party nor President Nixon's staff nor, least of all, President Nixon himself had yet been polluted by the symbol of Watergate. In this sense, it is possible to say that some *symbolic* generalization had occurred but that value generalization within the social system had not.

It had not because the social and cultural polarization of American society had not yet sufficiently abated. Because there was continued polarization, there could be no movement upward toward shared social values; because there was no generalization, there could be no societal sense of crisis. Because there was no sense of crisis, in turn, it became impossible for the other forces I have mentioned to come into play. There was no widespread perception of a threat to the center, and because there was none there could be no mobilization against the center. Against a powerful, secure, and legitimate center, social control forces like investigative bodies, courts, and congressional committees were afraid to act. Similarly, there was no struggle by differentiated elites against the threat to (and by) the center, for many of these elites were divided, afraid, and immobilized. Finally, no deep ritual processes emerged—that could have happened only in response to tensions generated by the first four factors.

Yet in the six months following the election the situation began to be reversed. First, consensus began to emerge. The end of an intensely divisive election period allowed a realignment that had been building at least for two years prior to Watergate. The social struggles of the 1960s had long been over, and many issues had been taken over by centrist groups.[3]

In the 1960s struggles, the Left had invoked critical universalism and rationality, tying these values to social movements for equality and against institutional authority, including, of course, the authority of the patriotic state itself. The Right, for its part, evoked particularism, tradition, and the defense of authority and the state. In the postelection period, critical universalism could now be articulated by centrist forces without being likened to the specific ideological themes or goals of the Left; indeed, such criticism could now be raised in defense of American national patriotism itself. With this emerging consensus, the possibility for a common feeling of moral violation emerged, and with it began the movement toward generalization vis-à-vis political goals and interests. Once this first resource of consensus had become available, the other developments I have mentioned could be activated.

The second and third factors were anxiety about the center and the invocation of institutional social control. Because the postelection developments described above provided a much less "politicized" atmosphere, it became safer to exercise social control. Such institutions as the courts, the Justice Department, various bureaucratic agencies, and special congressional committees could issue regulations in a more legitimate way. The very effectiveness of these social control institutions legitimated the media's efforts, in turn, to spread Watergate pollution closer to central institutions. The exercise of social control and the greater approximation to the center reinforced public doubt about whether Watergate was, in fact, only a limited crime, forcing more "facts" to surface. While the ultimate generality and seriousness of Watergate remained open, fears that Watergate might pose a threat to the center of American society quickly spread to significant publics and elites. The question about proximity to the center preoccupied every major group during this early postelection Watergate period. Senator Baker, at a later time, articulated this anxiety with the question that became famous during the summertime Senate hearings: "How much did the President know, and when did he know it?" This anxiety about the threat to the center, in turn, intensified the growing sense of normative violation, increased consensus, and contributed to generalization. It also rationalized the *invocation* of coercive social control. Finally, in structural terms, it began to realign the "good" and "bad" sides of the Watergate symbolization. Which side of the classification system were Nixon and his staff really on?

The fourth factor was elite conflict. Throughout this period, the generalization process—pushed by consensus, by the fear for the center, and by the activities of new institutions of social control—was fueled by a desire for revenge against Nixon by alienated institutional elites. These elites had represented "leftism" or simply "sophisticated cosmopolitanism" to Nixon during his first four years in office, and they had been the object of his legal and illegal attempts at suppression or control. They included journalists and newspapers, intellectuals, universities, scientists, lawyers, religionists, foundations, and, last but not least, authorities in various public agencies and the U.S. Congress. Motivated by a desire to get even, to reaffirm their threatened status, and to defend their universalistic values, these elites moved to establish themselves as countercenters in the years of crisis.

By May 1973, almost one year after the break-in and six months after the election, all of these forces for crisis creation and resolution were in motion. Significant changes in public opinion had been mobilized, and powerful structural resources were being brought into play. It is only at this point that the fifth crisis factor could emerge. Only now could there emerge deep processes of ritualization—sacralization, pollution, and purification—though there had certainly already been important symbolic developments.

The first fundamental ritual process of the Watergate crisis involved the Senate Select Committee's televised hearings, which began in May 1973 and continued through August. This event had tremendous repercussions on the symbolic patterning of the entire affair. The decision to hold and to televise the Senate's hearings was a response to the anxiety that had built up within important segments of the population. The symbolic process that ensued functioned to canalize this anxiety in certain distinctive, more generalized, and more consensual directions. The hearings constituted a kind of civic ritual that revivified very general yet nonetheless very crucial currents of critical universalism and rationality in the American political culture. It recreated the sacred, generalized morality on which more mundane conceptions of office are based, and it did so by invoking the mythical level of national understanding in a way that few other events have in postwar history.

These hearings were initially authorized by the Senate on specific political and normative grounds, their mandate being to expose corrupt campaign practices and to suggest legal reforms. The pressure for ritual process, however, soon made this initial mandate all but forgotten. The hearings became a sacred process by which the nation could reach a judgment about the now critically judged Watergate crime. The consensus-building, generalizing aspect of the process was to some extent quite conscious. Congressional leaders assigned membership to the committee on the basis of the widest possible regional and political representation and excluded from the committee all potentially polarizing political personalities. Most of the generalizing process, however, developed much less consciously in the course of the event itself. The developing ritual quality forced committee members to mask their often sharp internal divisions behind commitments to civic universalism. Many of the committee staff, for example, had been radical or liberal activists during the 1960s. They now had to assert patriotic universalism without any reference to specific left-wing issues. Other staffers, who had been strong Nixon supporters sympathetic to backlash politics, now had to forsake entirely that justification for political action.

The televised hearings, in the end, constituted a liminal experience (Turner, 1969), one radically separated from the profane issues and mundane grounds of everyday life. A ritual *communitas* was created for Americans to share, and within this reconstructed community none of the polarizing issues that had generated the Watergate crisis, or the historical justifications that had motivated it, could be raised. Instead, the hearings revivified the civic culture on which democratic conceptions of "office" have depended throughout American history. To understand how a liminal world could be created it is necessary to see it as a phenomenological world in the sense that Schutz has described. The hearings succeeded in becoming a world "unto itself." It was *sui generis,* a world without history. Its characters did not have rememberable pasts. It was in a very real sense "out of time." The framing devices of the television medium contributed to the deracination that produced this phenomenological status. The in-camera editing and the repetition, juxtaposition, simplification, and other techniques that allowed the story to appear mythical were invisible. Add to this "bracketed experience" the hushed voices of the announcers, the pomp and ceremony of the "event," and we have the recipe for constructing, within the medium of television, a sacred time and sacred space.[4]

At the level of mundane reality, two ferociously competitive political forces were at war during the Watergate hearings. These forces had to translate themselves into the symbolic idioms of the occasion; as a result, they were defined and limited by cultural structures even as they struggled to define and limit these structures in turn. For Nixon and his political supporters, "Watergate" had to be defined politically: what the Watergate burglars and coveruppers had done was "just politics," and the anti-Nixon senators on the Watergate committee (a majority of whom, after all, were Democratic) were characterized simply as engaged in a political witch hunt. For Nixon's critics on the committee, by contrast, this mundane political definition had to be opposed. Nixon could be criticized and Watergate legitimated as a real crisis only if the issues were defined as being above politics and involving fundamental moral concerns. These issues, moreover, had to be linked to forces near the center of political society.

The first issue was whether the hearings were to be televised at all. To allow something to assume the form of a ritualized event is to give participants in a drama the right to forcibly intervene in the culture of the society; it is to give to an event, and to those who are defining its meaning, a special, privileged access to the collective conscience. In simple societies, ritual processes are ascribed: they occur at preordained periods and in preordained ways. In more complex societies, ritual processes are achieved, often, against great odds. Indeed, in a modern society the assumption of ritual status often poses a danger and a threat to vested interests and groups. We know, in fact, that strenuous efforts were made by the White House to prevent the Senate hearings from being televised, to urge that less television time be devoted to them, and even to pressure the networks to cut short their coverage after it had begun. There were also efforts to force the committee to consider the witnesses in a sequence that was far less dramatic than the one eventually followed.

Because these efforts were unsuccessful, the ritual form was achieved.[5] Through television, tens of millions of Americans participated symbolically and emotionally in the deliberations of the committee. Viewing became morally obligatory for wide segments of the population. Old routines were broken, new ones formed. What these viewers saw was a highly simplified drama—heroes and villains formed in due course. But this drama created a deeply serious symbolic occasion.

If achieving the form of modern ritual is contingent, so is explicating the content, for modern rituals are not nearly so automatically coded as earlier ones. Within the context of the sacred time of the hearings, administration witnesses and senators struggled for moral legitimation, for definitional or ritual superiority and dominance. The end result was in no sense preordained. It depended on successful symbolic work. To describe this symbolic work is to embark on the ethnography, or hermeneutics, of televised ritual.

The Republican and Administration witnesses who were "called to account for themselves" pursued two symbolic strategies during the hearings. First, they tried to prevent public attention from moving from the political/profane to the value/sacred level at all. In this way, they repeatedly tried to rob the event of its phenomenological status as a ritual. They tried to cool out the proceedings by acting relaxed and casual. For example, H. R. Haldeman, the president's chief of staff who was compared to a Gestapo figure in the popular press, let his hair grow long so he would look less sinister and more like "one of the boys." These administrative witnesses also tried to rationalize and specify the public's orientation to their actions by arguing that they had acted with common sense according to pragmatic considerations. They suggested that they had decided to commit their crimes only according to standards of technical rationality. The secret meetings that had launched a wide range of illegal activities, and considered many more, were described not as evil, mysterious conspiracies but as technical discussions about the "costs" of engaging in various disruptive and illegal acts.

Yet the realm of values could not really be avoided. The symbol of Watergate was already quite generalized, and the ritual form of the hearings was already in place. It was within this value realm, indeed, that the most portentous symbolic struggles of the hearings occurred, for what transpired was nothing less than a struggle for the spiritual soul of the American republic. Watergate had been committed and initially justified in the name of cultural and political backlash, values that in certain respects contradicted the universalism, critical rationality, and tolerance on which contemporary democracy must be based. Republican and Administration witnesses evoked this subculture of backlash values. They urged the audience to return to the polarized climate of the 1960s. They sought to justify their actions by appealing to patriotism, to the need for stability, to the "un-American" and thereby deviant qualities of McGovern and the Left. They also justified it by arguing against cosmopolitanism, which in the minds of backlash traditionalists had undermined respect for tradition and neutralized the universalistic constitutional rules of the game. More specifically, Administration witnesses appealed to loyalty as the ultimate standard that should govern the relationship between subordinates and authorities. An interesting visual theme that summed up both of these appeals was the passive reference by Administration witnesses to family values. Each witness brought his wife and children if he had them. To see them lined up behind him, prim and proper, provided symbolic links to the tradition, authority, and personal loyalty that symbolically bound the groups of backlash culture.

The anti-Nixon senators, for their part, faced an enormous challenge. Outside of their own constituencies they were not well known; arrayed against them were representatives of an administration that six months before had been elected by the largest landslide vote in American history. This gigantic vote had been, moreover, partly justified by the particularistic sentiments of the backlash, the very sentiments that the senators were now out to demonstrate were deviant and isolated from the true American tradition.

What was the symbolic work in which the senators engaged? In the first instance, they denied the validity of particularist sentiments and motives. They bracketed the political realities of everyday life, and particularly the critical realities of life in the only recently completed 1960s. At no time in the hearings did the senators ever refer to the polarized struggles of that day. By making those struggles invisible, they denied any moral context for the witnesses' actions. This strategy of isolating backlash values was supported by the only positive explanation the senators allowed, namely, that the conspirators were just plain stupid. They poked fun at them as utterly devoid of common sense, implying that no normal person could ever conceive of doing such things.

This strategic denial, or bracketing in the phenomenological sense, was coupled with a ringing and unabashed affirmation of the universalistic myths that are the backbone of the American civic culture. Through their questions, statements, references, gestures, and metaphors, the senators maintained that every American, high or low, rich or poor, acts virtuously in terms of the pure universalism of civil society. Nobody is selfish or inhumane. No American is concerned with money or power at the expense of fair play. No team loyalty is so strong that it violates common good or makes criticism toward authority unnecessary. Truth and justice are the basis of American political society. Every citizen is rational and will act in accordance with justice if he is allowed to know the truth. Law is the perfect embodiment of justice, and office consists of the application of just law to power and force. Because power corrupts, office must enforce impersonal obligations in the name of the people's justice and reason.

Narrative myths that embodied these themes were often invoked. Sometimes these were timeless fables, sometimes they were stories about the origins of English common law, often they were the narratives about the exemplary behavior of America's most sacred presidents. John Dean, for example, the most compelling anti-Nixon witness, strikingly embodied the American detective myth (Smith, 1970). This figure of authority is derived from the Puritan tradition and in countless different stories is portrayed as ruthlessly pursuing truth and injustice without emotion or vanity. Other narratives developed in a more contingent way. For Administration witnesses who confessed, the committee's "priests" granted forgiveness in accord with well-established ritual forms, and their conversions to the cause of righteousness constituted fables for the remainder of the proceedings.

These democratic myths were confirmed by the senators' confrontation with family values. Their families were utterly invisible throughout the hearings. We didn't know if they had families, but they certainly were not presented. Like the committee's chairman, Sam Ervin, who was always armed with the Bible and the Constitution, the senators embodied transcendent justice divorced from personal or emotional concerns. Another confrontation that assumed ritual status was the swearing-in of the witnesses. Raising their right hands, each swore to tell the truth before God and man. While this oath did have a formal legal status, it also served the much more important function of ensuring moral degradation. It reduced the famous and powerful to the status of everyman. It placed them in subordinate positions vis-à-vis the overpowering and universalistic law of the land.

In terms of more direct and explicit conflict, the senators' questions centered on three principle themes, each fundamental to the moral anchoring of a civic democratic society. First, they emphasized the absolute priority of office obligations over personal ones: "This is a nation of laws not men" was a constant refrain. Second, they emphasized the embeddedness of such office obligations in a higher, transcendent authority: "The laws of men" must give way to the "laws of God." Or as Sam Ervin, the committee chairman, put it to Maurice Stans, the ill-fated treasurer of Nixon's Committee to Re-Elect the President (CRETP), "Which is more important, not violating laws or not violating ethics?" Finally, the senators insisted that this transcendental anchoring of interest conflict allowed America to be truly solidaristic—in Hegel's terms, a true "concrete universal." As Senator Wiecker famously put it: "Republicans do not cover up, Republicans do not go ahead and threaten . . . and God knows Republicans don't view their fellow Americans as enemies to be harassed [but as] human being[s] to be loved and won."

In normal times many of these statements would have been greeted with derision, with hoots and cynicism. In fact, many of them were lies in terms of the specific empirical reality of everyday political life and especially in terms of the political reality of the 1960s. Yet they were not laughed at or hooted down.

The reason was because this was not everyday life. This had become a ritualized and liminal event, a period of intense generalization that had powerful claims to truth. It was a sacred time, and the hearing chambers had become a sacred place. The committee was evoking luminescent values, not trying to describe empirical fact. On this mythical level, the statements could be seen and understood as true—as, indeed, embodying the normative aspirations of the American people. They were so seen and understood by significant portions of the population.

The hearings ended without making law or issuing specific judgments of evidence, but they nevertheless had profound effects. They helped to establish and fully legitimate a framework that henceforth gave the Watergate crisis its meaning. They accomplished this by continuing and deepening the cultural process that had begun before the election itself. Actual events and characters in the Watergate episode were organized in terms of the higher antitheses between the pure and the impure elements of America's civil culture. Before the hearings, "Watergate" was already a symbol redolent with the structured antitheses of American mythical life, antitheses that were implicitly linked by the American people to the structure of their civil codes. What the hearings accomplished, first, was to make this cultural linkage explicit and pronounced. The "good guys" of the Watergate process—their actions and motives—were purified in the resacralization process through their identification with the Constitution, norms of fairness, and citizen solidarity. The perpetrators of Watergate, and the themes which they evoked as justification, were polluted by association with symbols of civil evil: sectarianism, self-interest, particularistic loyalty. As this description implies, moreover, the hearings also restructured the linkages between Watergate elements and the nation's political center. Many of the most powerful men surrounding President Nixon were now implacably associated with Watergate evil, and some of Nixon's most outspoken enemies were linked to Watergate good. As the structural and symbolic centers of the civil religion were becoming so increasingly differentiated, the American public found the presidential party and the elements of civic sacredness more and more difficult to bring together (see table 6.2).

While this reading of the events is based on ethnography and interpretation, the process of deepening pollution is also revealed by poll data. Between the 1972 election and the very end of the crisis in 1974, there was only one large increase in the percentage of Americans who considered Watergate "serious." This occurred during the first two months of the Watergate hearings, April through early July 1973. Before the hearings, only 31 percent of Americans considered Watergate a "serious" issue. By early July, 50 percent did, and this figure remained constant until the end of the crisis.

Although a fundamental kind of ritual experience had clearly occurred, any contemporary application of cultural theory acknowledges that such modern rituals are never complete. In the first place, the symbols evoked by ritual process must be carefully differentiated. Despite the frequent references to presi-

*Table 6.2* Symbolic classification system as of August 1973

### The Watergate "Structure"

| Evil | Good |
|---|---|
| Watergate Hotel | White House |
| Burglars | FBI |
| Dirty Tricksters | Justice Department |
| Money raisers | |
| Employees of CRETP and Republican party | Special Prosecutor Archibald Cox |
| Former U.S. attorney John Mitchell | |
| and secretary of Treasury | Senators Ervin, Weicker, Baker |
| President's closest aides | Federal "Watchdog" Bureaucracy |
| | President Nixon |

### American Civil Culture

| Evil | Good |
|---|---|
| Communism/fascism | Democracy |
| Shadowy enemies | White House—Americanism |
| Crime | Law |
| Corruption | Honesty |
| Personalism | Responsibility |
| Bad presidents (e.g., Harding/Grant) President Nixon | Great presidents (e.g., Lincoln/Washington) |
| Great scandals (e.g., Watergate) | Heroic reformers (e.g., Sam Ervin) |

dential involvement, and despite the president's shadow throughout the hearings, poll data reveal that most Americans did not emerge from the ritual experience convinced of President Nixon's involvement. In the second place, the ritual effects of the hearings were unevenly felt. The Senate hearings were most powerful in their effect on certain centrist and left-wing groups: (1) among McGovern voters whose outrage at Nixon was splendidly confirmed; (2) among moderate Democrats who even if they had voted for Nixon were now outraged at him, particularly after many had crossed party lines to vote for him; (3) among moderate or liberal Republicans and independents who, while disagreeing with many of Nixon's positions, had voted for him anyway. The latter two groups were particularly important to the entire process of Watergate. They were prototypically crosspressured, and it was the crosspressured groups who, along with radical McGovern supporters, became most deeply involved in the hearings. Why? Perhaps they needed the hearings to sort out confused feelings, to clarify crucial issues, to resolve their uncomfortable ambivalence. Certainly such a relative stake can be found in the poll data. In the period mid-April 1973 to late June 1973—the period of the hearings' beginnings and their most dramatic revelations—the growth among Republicans who thought Watergate "serious" was 20 percent and among independents 18 percent; for Democrats, however, the percentage growth was only 15 percent.[6]

The year-long crisis that followed the hearings, from August 1973 to August 1974, was punctuated by episodes of moral convulsion and public anger, by renewed ritualization, by the further shifting of symbolic classification to include the structural center—the Nixon presidency—and by the further expansion of the solidarity base of this symbolism to include most of the significant segments of American society. In the wake of the Senate hearings, the Special Prosecutor's Office was created. It was staffed, though not chaired, almost entirely by formerly alienated members of the left-wing opposition to Nixon, who with their assumption of office made publicly accepted professions of their commitments to impartial justice, a process that further demonstrated the powerful generalizing and solidarizing phenomenon underway. The first special prosecutor was Archibald Cox, whose Puritan and Harvard background made him the ideal embodiment of the civil religion. Nixon fired Cox in October 1973 because Cox had asked the courts to challenge the president's decision to withhold information from the Special Prosecutor's Office. In response there was a massive outpouring of spontaneous public anger, which newspaper reporters immediately dubbed the "Saturday Night Massacre."

Americans seemed to view Cox's firing as a profanation of the attachments they had built up during the Senate hearings, commitments to newly revivified sacred tenets and against certain diabolical values and tabooed actors. Because Americans had identified their positive values and hopes with Cox, his firing made them fear pollution of their ideals and themselves. This anxiety caused public outrage, an explosion of public opinion during which three million protest letters were sent to the White House over a single weekend. These letters were labeled a "flash flood," a metaphor that played on the precrisis signification of the word "Watergate." The metaphor suggested that the scandal's polluted water had finally broken the river gates and flooded surrounding communities. The term "Saturday Night Massacre" similarly intertwined deeper rhetorical themes. In the 1920s a famous mob killing in gangland Chicago had been called the "St. Valentine's Day Massacre." "Black Friday" was the day in 1929 when the American stock market fell, shattering the hopes and trust of millions of Americans. Cox's firing, then, produced the same kind of symbolic condensation as dream symbolism, but on a mass scale. The anxiety of the citizenry was deepened, moreover, by the fact that pollution had now spread directly to the very figure who was supposed to hold American civil religion together, the president himself. By firing Cox, President Nixon came into direct contact with the molten lava of sacred impurity. The pollution that "Watergate" carried had now spread to the very center of American social structure. While support for Nixon's impeachment had gone up only a few points during the Senate hearings, after the "Saturday Night Massacre" it increased by fully 10 points. From this flash flood came the first congressional motions for impeachment and the instauration of the impeachment process in the House of Representatives.

Another major expansion of pollution occurred when the transcripts of White House conversations secretly taped during the Watergate period were released in April and May 1974. The tapes contained numerous examples of presidential deceit, and they were also laced with presidential expletives and ethnic slurs. Once again, there was tremendous public indignation at Nixon's behavior. By his words and recorded actions he had polluted the very tenets that the entire Watergate process had revivified: the sacredness of truth and the image of America as an inclusive, tolerant community. The symbolic and structural centers of American society were further separated, with Nixon (the representative of the structural center) increasingly pushed into the polluted, evil side of the Watergate dichotomies. This transcript convulsion helped define the symbolic center as a distinct area, and it demonstrated that this center was neither liberal nor conservative. Indeed, most of the indignation over Nixon's foul language was informed by conservative beliefs about proper behavior and civil decorum, beliefs that had been flagrantly violated by Nixon's enemies, the Left, during the polarized period that preceded the Watergate crisis.

In June and July of the year following, legal proceedings began against Nixon in the House of Representatives. These impeachment hearings were conducted by the House Judiciary Committee, and they marked the most solemn and formalized ritual of the entire Watergate episode. This proved to be the closing ceremony, a rite of expulsion in which the body politic rid itself of the last and most menacing source of sacred impurity. By the time of these hearings the symbolization of Watergate was already highly developed; in fact, Watergate had become not only a symbol with significant referents but also a powerful metaphor whose self-evident meaning itself served to define unfolding events. The meaning structure associated with "Watergate," moreover, now unequivocally placed a vast part of White House and "center" personnel on the side of civil pollution and evil. The only question that remained was whether President Nixon himself would finally be placed alongside them as well. The House hearings recapitulated the themes that had appeared in the Senate hearings one year before. The most pervasive background debate was over the meaning of "high crimes and misdemeanors," the constitutional phrase that set forth the standard for impeachment. Nixon's supporters argued for a narrow interpretation that held that an officer had to have committed an actual civil crime. Nixon's opponents argued for a broad interpretation that would include issues of political morality, irresponsibility, and deceit. Clearly, this was a debate over the level of system crisis: were merely normative, legal issues involved, or did this crisis reach all the way to the most general value underpinnings of the entire system? Given the highly ritualized format of the hearings, and the tremendous symbolization that had preceded the committee's deliberations, it hardly seems possible that the committee could have adopted anything other than the broad interpretation of "high crimes and misdemeanors."

This generalized definition set the tone for the hearings' single most distinctive quality: the ever-recurring emphasis on the members' fairness and the objectivity of its procedures. Journalists frequently remarked on how congressmen rose to the sense of occasion, presenting themselves not as political representatives of particular interests but as embodiments of sacred civil documents and democratic mores. This transcendence of wide partisan division was echoed by the cooperation among the Judiciary Committee's staff, which, in fact, had actually set the tone for the committee's formal, televised deliberations. Key members of the staff had, in the 1960s, been critics of establishment activities like the Vietnam War and supporters of antiestablishment movements like civil rights. Yet this partisan background never publicly surfaced during the vast journalistic coverage of the committee's work; even right-wing conservatives never made an issue of it. Why not? Because this committee, like its Senate counterpart one year before, existed in a liminal, detached place. They, too, operated within sacred time, their deliberations continuous not with the immediate partisan past but with the great constitutive moments of the American republic. They were framed the great patriots who had signed the Declaration of Independence, created the Constitution, and resolved the crisis of the Union that had started the Civil War.

This aura of liminal transcendence moved many of the most conservative members of the committee, southerners whose constituents had voted for Nixon by landslide proportions, to act out of conscience rather than political expediency. The southern bloc, indeed, formed the key to the majority coalition that emerged to support three articles of impeachment. Revealingly, this same coalition purposefully eschewed a fourth article, earlier proposed by liberal Democrats, that condemned Nixon's secret bombing of Cambodia. Though this earlier article did refer to a real violation of law, it was an issue that was interpreted by most Americans in specifically political terms, terms about which they still widely *disagreed*. The final three impeachment articles, by contrast, referred only to fully generalized issues. At stake was the code that regulated political authority, the question of whether impersonal obligations of office can and should control personal interest and behavior. It was Nixon's violation of the obligations of his office that made the House vote his impeachment.

After Nixon resigned from office, the relief of American society was palpable. For an extended period the political community had been in a liminal state, a condition of heightened anxiety and moral immersion that scarcely allowed time for the mundane issues of political life. When Vice-President Ford ascended to the presidency, there were a series of symbolic transformations that indicated ritualistic reaggregation. President Ford, in his first words after taking office, announced that "our long national nightmare is over." Newspaper headlines proclaimed that the sun had finally broken through the clouds, that a new day was being born. Americans effused about the strength and unity of the country. Ford himself was transformed, through these reaggregating rites, from a rather bumbling partisan leader into a national healer, the incarnation of a "good guy" who embodied the highest standards of ethical and political behavior.

Before continuing with my account of the symbolic process after this reaggregation, I would like to return, once again, to the fact that modern rituals are never complete. Even after the ritual ceremony that consensually voted articles of impeachment and the ritual renewal with President Ford, poll data reveal that a significant segment of American society remained unconvinced. Between 18 and 20 percent of Americans did not find President Nixon guilty, either of a legal crime or of moral turpitude. These Americans, in other words, did not participate in the generalization of opinion that drove Nixon from office. They interpreted the Watergate process, rather, as stimulated by political vengeance by Nixon's enemies. The demographics of this loyalist group are not particularly revealing. They were of mixed education and from every class and occupation. One of the few significant structural correlations was their tendency to be from the South. What did, apparently, really distinguish this group was their political values. They held a rigid and narrow idea of political loyalty, identifying the belief in God, for example, with commitment to Americanism. They also held a deeply personalized view of political authority, tending much more than other Americans to express their allegiance to Nixon as a man and to his family as well. Finally, and not surprisingly, this group had reacted much more negatively than other Americans to the left-wing social movements of the 1960s. The fact that they were committed to a polarized and exclusivist vision of political solidarity reinforced their reluctance to generalize from specifically political issues to general moral concerns. Such generalization would have involved not only criticism of Nixon but the restoration of a wider, more inclusive political community. In voting for Nixon they had supported a candidate who promised to embody their backlash sentiments and who had appeared, during his first years in office, inclined to carry out their wishes for a narrow and primordial political community.

The period of social reaggregation after Watergate's liminal period—the closure of the immediate ritual episode—raises, once again, the problem of the dichotomizing nature of Western social theory, for it involves the relationship between such categories as charisma/routine, sacred/profane, generalization/institutionalization. (See "The Dilemma of Uniqueness," chapter 2.) On the one hand, it is clear that with Ford's ascension a much more routine atmosphere prevailed. Institutional actors and the public in general seemed to return to the profane level of goal and interest conflict. Political dissensus once again prevailed. Conflicts over the inflationary economy captured the news for the first time in months, and this issue, along with America's dependence on foreign oil, loomed large in the congressional elections of autumn 1974.

According to the theories of routinization and specification, or institutionalization, the end of ritualization ushers in a new, postsymbolic phase, in which there is the institutionalization or crystallization of ritual spirit in a concrete form. The most elaborated theory of this transition is found in the works of Smelser (1959, 1963) and Parsons (Parsons & Bales, 1955: 35–132). Here, postcrisis structures are described as evolving because they are better adapted to deal with the source of initial disequilibrium. Generalization is ended, then, because of the efficiency with which newly created structures deal with concrete role behavior. Now, to a certain extent, such new and more adaptive institution-building did occur in the course of the Watergate process. New structures emerged that allowed the political system to be more differentiated, or insulated, from interest conflict and allowed universalism to be more strongly served. Conflict-of-interest rules were developed and applied to presidential appointments; congressional approval of some of the president's key staff appointments, like director of the Office of Management and Budget, was instituted; a standing special prosecutor's office was created, the attorney general being required to decide within thirty days of any congressional report on impropriety whether a prosecutor should actually be called; finally, federal financing of presidential election campaigns was passed into law. There were, in addition, a range of more informally sanctioned institutional innovations: the post of chief of staff became less powerful; the doctrine of executive privilege was used much more sparingly; Congress was consulted on important matters.

Durkheim and Weber would tend to support this dichotomous picture of crisis resolution. Weber, of course, saw most political interaction not as cultural but as instrumental. When charismatic episodes did occur, they would be deflated by an inevitable process of routinization triggered by the demands for control exerted by the leader's self-interested staff after his "death (Weber, 1968: 246–55)[7]." Durkheim's understanding is more complex. On the one hand, Durkheim saw the nonritual world as thoroughly profane, as nonvaluational, as political or economic, as conflictual, and even in a certain sense as nonsocial (Alexander, 1982: 292–306). At the same time, however, Durkheim clearly overlaid this sharp distinction with a more continuous theory, for he insisted that the effervescence from rituals continued to infuse postritual life for some time after the immediate period of ritual interaction.

Though the crisis model of generalization-specification has been taken from functionalist analysis, the notion of generalization as ritual has been drawn from Durkheim. The analysis of social crisis presented here, therefore, has given much more autonomy to symbolic process than would a purely functionalist one. Generalization and ritualization are not engaged, in my view, purely for psychological or social-structural reasons—either because of anxiety or the inefficiency of social structures—but also because of the violation of ardently adhered-to moral beliefs. Symbolic processes occur as much to work out issues on this level as to provide more efficient structures for addressing specific, "real" disequilibriating problems. It is for this reason that ritualization is succeeded not by merely structural change but also by continued cultural effervescence. The recharged antinomies of the cultural order, and the emotional intensity that underlies them continue to create moral conflict and, often, to support significantly different cultural orientations.

As compared, for example, to the aftershocks of the Dreyfus Affair, the effervescence of Watergate must be understood in terms of *relative* cultural integration. "Watergate" came to be viewed—and this is extraordinarily significant in comparative terms—not as an issue of the Left or the Right but rather as a national issue about which most parties agreed (see Schudson, 1992). There were, it was universally agreed, certain "lessons of Watergate" from which the nation had to learn. American talked incessantly in the period between 1974 and 1976 about the imperatives of what was referred to as "post-Watergate morality." They experienced this as an imperious social force that laid waste to institutions and reputations. "Post-Watergate morality" was the name given to the effervescence from the ritual event. It named the revivified values of critical rationality, antiauthoritarianism, and civil solidarity, and it named the polluted values of conformity, personalistic deference, and factional strife. For several years after the end of liminality, Americans applied these highly charged moral imperatives to group and interest conflict and to bureaucratic life, demanding radical universalism and heightened solidarity at every turn.

For the adult population, therefore—the case seems to have been somewhat different for children—the effect of Watergate was not increased cynicism or political withdrawal. Quite the opposite. Ritual effervescence increased faith in the political "system" even while the distrust it produced continued to undermine public confidence in particular institutional actors and authorities. Institutional distrust is different from the delegitimation of general systems per se (Lipset & Schneider, 1983). If there is trust in the norms and values that are conceived of as regulating political life, there may actually be more contention over the wielding of power and force (see Barber, 1983). In this sense, political democracy and political efficiency may be opposed, for the first lends itself to conflict while the second depends on order and control.

In the immediate post-Watergate period, a heightened sensitivity to the general meaning of office and democratic responsibility did indeed lead to heightened conflict and to a series of challenges to authoritative control. Watergate became more than ever before a highly charged metaphor. It was no longer simply a referent for naming events that objectively occurred but a moral standard that helped subjectively to create them. Members of the polity, inspired by its symbolic power, sought out sinful behavior and tried to punish it. The result was a series of scandals: "Koreagate" and "Billygate" on the American scene, for example, and "Winegate" abroad. Indeed, the symbolic power of the metaphor has proved remarkably durable up to today. It set the narrative framework within which President Clinton's actions during "Monicagate" were judged.

The giant explosion of Watergate into the American collective conscience in 1973 and 1974 produced aftershocks of populist antiauthoritarianism and critical rationality.

1. Almost immediately after the reaggregation ceremonies, there unfolded in close succession a series of unprecedented congressional investigations. Nelson Rockefeller, Ford's vice-presidential nominee, was subjected to a long and heated televised inquiry into the possible misuses of his personal wealth. Enormous televised investigations were also launched by the Congress into the secret, often antidemocratic working of the CIA and the FBI, institutions whose patriotic authority had previously been unquestioned. This outpouring of these "little Watergates," as they were called, extended well into the Carter administration of 1976–80. Carter's chief assistant, Bert Lance, was forced out of office after highly publicized hearings that badly impugned his financial and political integrity. Each of these investigations created a scandal in its own right; each followed, often down to the smallest detail and word, the symbolic form established by Watergate.

2. Whole new reform movements were generated from the Watergate spirit. There The Society for Investigative Reporting emerged, a new organization that responded to the spurt of morally inspired, critical journalism by those journalists who had internalized the Watergate experience and sought to externalize its model. Federal crime investigators—lawyers and policemen—formed white-collar crime units throughout the United States. For the first time in American history significant prosecutorial resources were shifted away from the conventionally defined, often lower-class criminals to high-status office-holders in the public and private domains. Inspired by the Watergate model, it became the established, a priori conviction of many city, state, and federal prosecutors that

office-holders might well commit crimes against the public. By ferreting them out and prosecuting them, they tried to maintain the moral alertness of all authorities to the responsibility of office as such.

3. In the months subsequent to reaggregation, authority was critically examined at every institutional level of American society, even the most mundane. The Boy Scouts, for example, rewrote their constitution to emphasize not just loyalty and obedience but critical questioning. The judges of the Black Miss America beauty pageant were accused of personalism and bias. Professional groups examined and rewrote their codes of ethics. Student-body officers of high schools and universities were called to task after little scandals were created. City councillors and mayors were "exposed" in every city, great and small. Through most of these controversies, specific issues of policy and interest were not significantly considered. It was the codes of office themselves that were at stake.

These mundane institutional events, in other words, were actually motivated by the heightened symbolic polarities of post-Watergate culture. This reverberation is further demonstrated by the continuation of other, less specifically Watergate-related themes. There were continuous assertions, for example, that America was morally unified. Groups that had been previously excluded or persecuted, most particularly those associated with the Communist Party, were publicly cleansed. I have already mentioned that those institutions most responsible for political witch hunts, particularly the FBI, were reprimanded for their un-Americanism. Books, articles, movies, and television shows appeared about the immorality and tragedies associated with "McCarthyism," painting persecuted fellow-travelers and communists in a sympathetic and familiar light. The antiwar movement assumed, through the same retrospective refiguring process, a respectable, even heroic light. No doubt inspired by this rebirth of community, fugitive leaders of New Left underground organizations began to give themselves up, trusting the state but particularly the American opinion-making process to give them a fair hearing. It was within the context of this same spirit of re-integration that the first elected president after Watergate, Jimmy Carter, issued a full and complete pardon to those who had illegally but peacefully resisted the Vietnam war.

Through it all the vividness of Watergate's impure symbols remained strikingly intact. Trials of the Watergate conspirators, former cabinet officers, and high-ranking aides generated large headlines and great preoccupation. Their published confessions and *mea culpas* were objects of intensely moral, even spiritual dispute. Richard Nixon, the very personification of evil, was viewed by alarmed Americans as a continuing source of dangerous pollution. Still a source of symbolic power, his name and his person became representations of evil (chapter 4), forms of what Durkheim called the "liquid impure." Americans tried to protect themselves from this polluting Nixonian lava by building walls. They sought to keep Nixon out of "good society" and isolated in San Clemente, his former presidential estate. When Nixon tried to buy an expensive apartment in New York, the building's tenants voted to bar the sale. When he traveled around the country, crowds followed to boo him and politicians shunned him. When he reappeared on television, viewers sent indignant, angry letters. Indeed, Nixon could escape this calumny only by traveling to foreign countries, though even some foreign leaders refused to associate with him in public. For Americans, there was an extraordinary fear of being touched by Nixon or his image. Such contact was believed to lead to immediate ruin. When President Ford pardoned Nixon several months after assuming office, Ford's honeymoon with the public abruptly ended. Tarnished by this (however brief) association with Nixon, he alienated such a large body of the electorate that it cost him the subsequent presidential election.

The spirit of Watergate did eventually subside. Much of the structure and process that had stimulated the crisis reappeared, although it did so in a significantly altered form. Nixon had ridden a backlash against leftist modernity into office, and after his departure this conservative movement continued. It now, however, assumed a much more antiauthoritarian form. Social movements like the tax revolt and the antiabortion movement combined the post-Watergate spirit of critique and challenge with particularistic and often reactionary political themes. Only six years after Watergate ended, Ronald Reagan was swept into office on many of the old backlash issues, yet on the Reagan presidency too there continued to be a noticeable post-Watergate effect. For if Reagan was even more conservative than Nixon, he was committed to carrying out his reaction against the Left in a democratic and consensual way. This commitment may not have been a personal one, but it was enforced unequivocally by the public mood and by the continuing vitality of the potential countercenters to presidential power.

Not only did the rightward movement of American politics reappear, but the authoritarianism of the "imperial presidency" regained much of its earlier force. As the distance from Watergate increased, concrete economic and political problems assumed greater importance. Solving foreign crises, inflation, energy problems—the American people focused more and more on attaining these elusive "goals." These generated demands for specificity and efficacy, not for generalized morality. Given the structure of the American political system, these demands for efficacy necessitated a stronger executive. The concern about the morality of authority became increasingly blunted by demands for strong and effective authority. Jimmy Carter began his presidency by promising the American people "I will never lie to you." He ended it by making a strong presidency his principal campaign slogan. By the time Reagan became president, he could openly disdain some conflict-of-interest laws, reemploy some of the less-polluted Watergate figures, and move to wrap executive authority once again in a cloak of secrecy and charisma. These later developments do not mean that Watergate had no effect. The codes rgulating political authority in America had been forcibly renewed, codes that, even when they are latent, continue to affect concrete political activity. Politics in America had simply, and finally, returned to the "normal" level of interests and roles.

The Iran-Contra affair of 1986–87 demonstrated both sides of the Watergate denouement—social normalization and political conservatism on the one hand and continuing normative vitality and broad democratic conventions on the other. Like Nixon and other presidents who were confronted with institutional blockages, Reagan subverted office obligations to attain his conservative foreign policy goals by illegal means. When the Democrats took back control of the Congress in November 1986, and the conservative mood of American public opinion began to change, the polarized social environment that had legitimated Regan's actions weakened. It was in this changed context that "Contragate" crystallized and institutional barriers against the President's Central American forays put in place. In the midst of the furor in the public media and contentious congressional hearings, Reagan's actions were transformed for many Americans from a questionable political strategy into an abuse, even usurpation, of power. Because this attack on earthly power was intertwined, once again, with a renewal of ideal codes, this usurpation was described as a dangerous, polluting deviation from the democratic discourse of civil society (chapter 6). These events never reached the crisis proportions of Watergate; few events in a nation's history ever do. Yet without the "memory of justice" provided by that earlier crisis, it is doubtful that the Administration's actions would so easily and quickly have been transformed into an affair. Ten years later, another American President learned this lesson again, in a much harder way.

Scandals are not born, they are made.

# 7

# THE SACRED AND PROFANE
# INFORMATION MACHINE

The oldest prejudice that social theory has held about modern life is that it is not prejudiced at all. Modernity will make people rational because it is scientific, and because it is so scientific, the institutions of and processes of modern society have become "purely technological." This venerable story can be pessimistic or optimistic, but it is always anticultural, for it stresses the utter materialism of the contemporary world. But this is a just-so story. The modern world is indeed technological, but technology is hardly purely material in form. It is religion and antireligion, our god and our devil, the sublime and the accursed. Technology is rooted in the deepest resources and abysses of our imagination. We can penetrate these depths only with the tools of cultural sociology that I have been developing here.

The gradual permeation of the computer into the pores of modern life deepened what Max Weber called the rationalization of the world. The computer converts every message, regardless of its substantive meaning, metaphysical remoteness, or emotional allure, into a series of numerical bits and bytes. These series are connected to others through electrical impulses. Eventually these impulses are converted back into the media of human life.

Can there be any better example of the subjection of worldly activity to impersonal rational control? Can there be any more forceful illustration of the disenchantment of the world that Weber warned would be the result? Much depends on the answer to this portentous question, for discourse about the meaning of advanced technology demarcates one of the central ideological penumbra of the age. If the answer is yes, we are not only trapped inside of Weber's cage of iron but also bound by the laws of exchange that Marx asserted would eventually force everything human into a commodity form.

This query about the rationalization of the world poses theoretical questions, not just existential ones. Can there really exist a world of purely technical rationality? Although this question may be ideologically compelling for critics of the modern world, I will argue that the theory underlying such a proposition is not correct. Because both human action and its environments are indelibly interpenetrated by the nonrational, a pure technically rational world cannot exist. Certainly the growing centrality of the digital computer is an empirical fact. This fact, however, remains to be interpreted and explained.

## SOCIOLOGICAL ACCOUNTS OF TECHNOLOGY AS UNMEANINGFUL

Considered in its social reference—its economic and scientific forms—technology is a thing that can be touched, observed, interacted with, and calculated in an objectively rational way. Analytically, however, technology is also part of the cultural order. It is a sign, both a signifier and a signified, in relation to which actors cannot entirely separate their subjective states of mind. Social scientists have not usually considered technology in this more subjective way. Indeed, they have not typically considered it as a cultural object at all. It has appeared as the material variable par excellence, not as a point of sacrality but as the most routine of the routine, not a sign but an antisign, the essence of a modernity that has undermined the very possibility for cultural understanding itself.

In the postmodern era, Marx has become infamous for his effusive praise in the *Communist Manifesto* of technology as the embodiment of scientific rationality. Marx believed that modern industrial technique, as the harbinger of progress, was breaking down the barriers of primitive and magical thought. Stripped of its capitalist integument, Marx predicted, advanced technology would be the mainspring of industrial communism, which he defined as the administration of *things* rather than *people*.[1] Despite the central role he gives to technology, for Marx it is not a form of knowledge, even of the most rational sort. It is a material variable, a "force of production" (Marx, 1962). As an element of the base, technology is something actors relate to mechanistically. It is produced because the laws of the capitalist economy force factory owners to lower their costs. The effects of this incorporation are equally objective. As technology replaces human labor, the organic composition of capital changes and the rate of profit falls; barring mitigating factors, this falling rate causes the collapse of the capitalist system.

While neo-Marxism has revised the determining relationship Marx posits between economy and technology, it continues to accept Marx's view of technology as a purely material fact. In Rueschemeyer's work on the relation between power and the division of labor, for example, neither general symbolic patterns nor the internal trajectory of rational knowledge are conceived of as affecting technological growth. "It is the inexorability of interest and power constellations," Rueschemeyer (1986: 117–8) argues, "which shape even fundamental research and which determine translations of knowledge into new products and new ways of production." We might expect modern functionalism, the political and theoretical antithesis to Marxism, to view technology very differently, but this is true in an only limited sense. Of course, Parsons (1967) criticized Marx for putting technology into the base; functionalists recognized that technology belongs in a more intermediate position in the social system. Still, they never looked at it as anything other than the product of rational knowledge, and they have often conceived of its efficient causes and specific effects in material terms.

In *Science, Technology, and Society in Seventeenth-Century England,* Merton does emphasize the role that puritanism played in inspiring scientific inventions. Within the context of this inventive climate, however, the immediate cause of technology is economic benefit. The "relation between a problem raised by economic development and technologic endeavor is clear-cut and definite," Merton argues (1970: 144), suggesting that "importance in the realm of technology is often concretely allied with economic estimations." It was the "vigorous economic development" of the time that led to effective inventions, because it "posed the most imperative problems for solution" (146). In Smelser's (1959) later account of the industrial revolution, the perspective is exactly the same. Methodist values form a background input to technological innovation, but they are not involved in the creation or the effects of technology itself. Innovation is problem driven, not culture driven, and the immediate cause is economic demand. The effect of technology is also concrete and material. By resolving strain at the social system level, innovation allows collective behavior to leave the level of generalized behavior—wish fulfillment, fantasy, utopian aspirations—and return to the more mundane and rational attitudes of the everyday (Smelser, 1959: 21–50).

Parsons himself was more sensitive to the subjective environment of technology. While acknowledging that it is "a product of productive processes," he insists (1960: 135) that it depends ultimately on cultural resources. Yet, in a characteristic move, he turns his discussion of technology from economic issues to a focus on the origins of "usable knowledge." He describes the latter as "produced by two processes which, though economic factors play a part, are clearly predominantly noneconomic, namely research and education" (135). In other words, while Parsons recognizes that technology is, in the most important sense, a product of subjective knowledge rather than material force, this recognition leads him not to the analysis of symbolic processes but to the study of institutional processes, namely research and education. When Parsons and Platt explore these processes in *The American University* (1973), they take the input from culture—the "rationality value"—as a given, focusing instead on how this value becomes institutionalized in the social system.

Frankfurt School critical theory, drawing from Weber's rationalization theme, differs from orthodox Marxism in its attention to the relation between technology and consciousness. But whereas Weber (e.g., 1946b) viewed the machine as the objectification of discipline, calculation, and rational organization, critical theorists reverse the causal relation, asserting that it is technology that creates rationalized culture by virtue of its brute physical and economic power. "If we follow the path taken by labour in its development from handicraft [to] manufacture to machine industry," writes Lukács (1971: 88), the school's most significant precursor, "we can see a continuous trend toward greater rationalization [as] the process of labour is progressively broken down into abstract, rational, specialized operations." This technologically driven rationalization eventually spreads to all social spheres, leading to the objectification of society and the "reified mind" (93). Lukács insists that he is concerned "with the *principle* at work here" (88, italics in original), but the principle is that technology is conceived as a material force.

This shift toward the pivotal ideological role of technology, without giving up its materialist conceptualization or its economic cause, culminates in Marcuse's later work. To explain the reasons for "one-dimensional society," Marcuse actually focuses more on technological production per se than on its capitalist form. Again, that technology is a purely instrumental, rational phenomenon Marcuse takes completely for granted. Its "sweeping rationality," he writes (1963: xiii), "propels efficiency and growth." The problem, once again, is that this "technical progress [is] extended to a whole system of domination and coordination" (xii). When it is, it institutionalizes throughout the society a purely formal and abstract norm of rationality. This technological "culture" suppresses any ability to imagine social alternatives. As Marcuse says (xvi), "technological rationality has become political rationality."

New class and postindustrial theories make this critical theory more nuanced and sophisticated, but they do not overcome its fatal anticultural flaw. Gouldner claims that scientists, engineers, and government planners have a rational worldview because of the technical nature of their work. Technocratic competence depends on higher education, and the expansion of higher education depends in the last analysis on production driven by technology. Indeed, Gouldner finds no fault with technocratic competence in and of itself; he takes it as a paradigm of universalism, criticism, and rationality. When he attacks the technocrats' false consciousness, he does so because they extend this rationality beyond their sphere of technical competence: "The new ideology holds [that] the *society's* problems are solvable on a technological basis, with the use of educationally acquired technical competence" (1979: 24, italics added). By pretending to understand society at large, the new class can provide a patina of rationality for the entire society. Gouldner also emphasizes, of course, that this very expansion of technical rationality can create a new kind of class conflict and thus become unwittingly a "rational" source of social change. But this is simply the old contradiction between the technological forces and the social relations of production, dressed in postindustrial garb. When Szelenyi and Martin (1987) criticize Gouldner's theory as economistic, they have touched its theoretical core.

Using similar theoretical distinctions, conservative theorists have reached different ideological conclusions. In his postindustrial theory, Bell (1976) also emphasizes the growing cultural rationality of modern societies, a cultural pattern that he, too, ties directly to technological and productive demands. In order to produce and maintain the advanced technologies that are at the basis of postindustrial economic and political institutions, scientific values and scientific education have become central to modern life. In the political and economic spheres of modern societies, therefore, sober, rational, and instrumental culture is the rule. It is only in reaction against this technological sphere that according to Bell (1976), irrational, postmodern values develop, which create the cultural contradictions of capitalist society. Here the old contradiction between (technological) forces and relations is dressed in new garb. Because Ellul, the other, more conservative, theorist of "technological society," wrote before the 1960s, he views the social effects of technology as more thoroughly instrumental and rational than does Bell. Propelled by "the search for greater efficiency" (Ellul, 1964: 19), technique "clarifies, arranges, and rationalizes" (5). It exists in "the domain of the abstract" (5) and has no relation to cultural values or to the real needs of human life.

It is fitting to close this section with Habermas, for the distinction between the world of technique (variously defined as work, organization, or system) and the world of humanity (communication, norms, or lifeworld) has marked a fateful contrast throughout his work. Habermas (1968a: 57) defines technology in the familiar manner. He believes it to be the "scientifically rationalized control of objectified processes" and contrasts it with phenomena that are related to "the practical question of how men can and want to live." With the increasing centrality of technology, the meaningful organization of the world is displaced by purposive-rational organization. "To the extent that technology and science permeate social institutions and thus transform them," Habermas (1968b: 81) insists, "old legitimations are destroyed."

These old legitimations were based on tradition, "the older mythic, religious, and metaphysical worldviews" that addressed "the central questions of men's collective existence [for example] justice and freedom, violence and oppression, happiness and gratification . . . love and hate, salvation and damnation (1968b: 96)." After technology has done its work, however, these questions can no longer be asked: "The culturally defined self-understanding of a social lifeworld is replaced by the self-reification of men under categories of purposive-rational action and adaptive behavior" (105–6). There has ensued a "horizontal extension of subsystems of purposive-rational action" such that "traditional structures are increasingly subordinated to conditions of instrumental or strategic rationality" (98). In this particular sense, Habermas argues, the ideology of technology has displaced all previous ideologies. Because it is so stubbornly rationalistic, this new ideology does not exhibit "the opaque force of a delusion" or a "wish-fulfilling fantasy"; nor is it "based in the same way [as earlier ideologies] on the causality of dissociated symbols and unconscious motives." This new, technological ideology, Habermas believes, has abandoned any attempt to "express a projection of the 'good life.'"

In the discussion that follows I will demonstrate that these suppositions about technological consciousness are false. Only because Habermas has accepted the possibility of a radical historicization of consciousness can he believe them to be true. My own discussion begins from quite the opposite understanding. It is impossible for a society to be dominated by technical rationality because the mental structures of humankind cannot be radically historicized; in crucial respects, they are unchanging. Human beings continue to experience the need to invest the world with metaphysical meaning and to experience solidarity with objects outside the self. Certainly, the ability to calculate objectively and impersonally is perhaps the clearest demarcation of modernity. But this remains one institutionalized complex (Parsons, 1951) of motives, actions, and meanings among many others. Individuals can exercise scientifically rational orientations in certain situations, but even in these instances their actions are not scientifically rational as such. Objectivity is a cultural norm, a system of social sanctions and rewards, a motivational impulse of the personality. It remains nested, however, within deeply irrational systems of psychological defense and cultural systems of an enduringly primordial kind.

This is not to deny that technological production has become more central with the advent of postindustrial society. There has been a quickening in the substitution of information for physical energy, which Marx described as a shift in the organic composition of capital, with dramatic consequences. The shift from manual to mental labor has transformed the class structure and the typical strains of capitalist and socialist societies. The increased capacity for storing information has strengthened the control of bureaucracy over the information that it constantly needs. But the sociological approaches to technology, which I have examined in this section, extend much further than such empirical observations. The stronger version of Marxist and critical theory describes a technologically obsessed society whose consciousness is so narrowed that the meaningful concerns of traditional life are no longer possible. The weaker versions of functionalist and postindustrial theory describe technology as a variable that has a merely material status and orientations to technology as cognitively rational and routine. From my point of view, neither of these positions is correct. The ideas that inform even the most modern societies are not cognitive repositories of verified facts; they are symbols that continue to be shaped by deep emotional impulses and molded by meaningful constraints.

# TECHNOLOGICAL DISCOURSE AND SALVATION

We must learn to see technology as a discourse, as a sign system that is subject to semiotic constraints even as it is responsive to social and emotional demands. The first step to this alternative conception of modern technology is to reconceptualize its historical emergence in metaphysical terms. Ironically, Weber still provides the best indication of how this can be done.

Weber argued that those who created modern industrial society did so in order to pursue salvation. The Puritan capitalists practiced what Weber (1958) called this-worldly asceticism. Through hard work and self-denial, they produced wealth as proof that God had predestined them to be saved. Weber (1964) demonstrated, indeed, that salvation has been a central concern of humankind for millennia. Whether it be heaven or nirvana, the great religions have promised human beings an escape from toil and suffering and a release from earthly constraints—only if humans conceived of the world in certain terms and strove to act in certain ways. In order to historicize this conception of salvation and to allow comparative explanation of it, Weber developed the typology of this worldly versus otherworldly paths to salvation, which he interwove with the distinction between ascetic and mystical. The disciplined, self-denying, and impersonal action on which modernization depended, Weber argued, could be achieved only by acting in a this-worldly, ascetic way. Compared to Buddhist or Hindu holy men, the Puritan saints focused their attention much more completely on this world. Rather than allowing themselves the direct experience of God and striving to become vessels of his spirit, they believed that they would be saved by becoming practical instruments for carrying out his will. This-worldly salvation was the cultural precursor for the impersonal rationality and objectivism that, in Weber's view (1958: 181–3), eventually dominated the world.

While Weber's religious theory is of fundamental importance, it has two substantial weaknesses. First, Weber conceived the modern style of salvation in a caricatured way. It has never been as one-sidedly ascetic as he suggests. This-worldly activity is permeated by desires to escape from the world, just as the ascetic self-denial of grace is punctuated by episodes of mystical intimacy (Alexander 2000b). In an anomalous strain in his writing about modernity (Alexander, 1986), Weber acknowledged that industrial society is shot through with what he called "flights from the world," in which category he included things such as the surrender by moderns to religious belief or ideological fanaticism and the escape provided by eroticism or aestheticism. Although Weber condemned these flights as morally irresponsible, he was never able to incorporate them into his empirical sociology of modern life. They represented a force with which his historicist and overly ideal-typical theory could not contend.

In truth, modern attempts to pursue salvation in purely ascetic ways have always short-circuited, not only in overtly escapist forms but also in the everyday world itself. We would never know from Weber's account, for example, that the Puritans conceived of their relationship to God in terms of the intimacies of holy matrimony (Morgan, 1958); nor would we be aware that outbursts of mystical "antinomianism" were a constant, recurring danger in Puritan life. The post-Puritan tradition of evangelical Protestantism, which developed in Germany, England, and the United States in the late eighteenth and early nineteenth centuries, was distinguished by its significant opening to mystical experience. One of its cultural offshoots, the modern ideology of romantic love (Lewis, 1983), reflected the continuing demand for immediate, transformative salvation in the very heart of the industrial age.

This last example points to the second major problem in Weber's religious theory, its historicism. Weber believed that a concern with salvation could permeate and organize worldly experience only so long as scientific understanding had not undermined the possibility of accepting an extramundane, divine telos for progress on earth. As I suggested previously, this mistaken effort to rationalize contemporary discourse can be corrected by incorporating the more structural understandings of what Durkheim called his "religious sociology." Durkheim believed that human beings continue to divide the world into sacred and profane and that even modern men and women need to experience mystical centers directly through ritual encounters with the sacred. In the modern context, then, Weber's salvation theory can be elaborated and sustained only by turning to Durkheim. The fit can be made even tighter if we make the alteration in Durkheim's theory suggested by Caillois (1959 [1939]), who argued that alongside sacred and profane there was a third term, *routine*. Whereas routine life does not partake of ritual experience, sacred and profane experiences are both highly charged. Whereas the sacred provides an image of the good with which social actors seek community and strive to protect, the profane defines an image of evil from which human beings must be saved. This conception allows us to be more true to Weber's understanding of theodicy, even when we shift it onto the modern state. Secular salvation "religions" provide escape not only from earthly suffering in general but also more specifically from evil. Every salvation religion has conceived not only God and death, in other words, but also the devil.

It is in terms of these reconstructed arenas for symbolic discourse that my examination of the introduction of technology will proceed.

## THE SACRED AND PROFANE INFORMATION MACHINE

Expectations for salvation were inseparable from the technological innovations of industrial capitalism. Major inventions like the steam engine, railroad, telegraph, and telephone (Pool, 1983) were hailed by elites and masses as vehicles for secular transcendence. Their speed and power, it was widely proclaimed, would undermine the earthly constraints of time, space, and scarcity. In their early halcyon days, they became vessels for experiencing ecstatic release, instruments for bringing the glories of heaven down to earth. The technicians and engineers who understood this new technology were elevated to the status of worldly priests. In this technological discourse, however, the machine has been not only God but also the devil. In the early nineteenth century, Luddites lashed out at spinning machines as if they were the idols that the Hebrew fathers had condemned. William Blake decried "dark Satanic mills." Mary Shelley wrote *Frankenstein, or, the Modern Prometheus,* about the terrifying results of Victor Frankenstein's effort to build the world's most "gigantic" machine. The gothic genre presented a revolt against the Age of Reason and insisted that dark forces were still brewing, forces that were often embodied by the engine of technology itself. It was, ironically, from such forces that the modern age had to be saved. There is a direct line from that gothic revival to George Lukas's wildly popular movie *Star Wars* (Pynchon, 1984). Today's science fiction mixes technology with medieval gothic themes, pits evil against good, and promises salvation from space, from time, even from mortality itself.

The computer is the newest and certainly one of the most potent technological innovations of the modern age, but its symbolization has been much the same. The culture structure of technological discourse has been firmly set. In theoretical terms, the introduction of the computer into Western society resembled the much more tumultuous entrance of Captain Cook into the Sandwich Islands. It was an event, in Sahlins's (1981: 31) words, "given significance and effect by the system in place."

While there were certainly routine assessments of the computer from 1944 to 1975—assessments that talked about it in rational, scientific, and "realistic" tones—they paled in comparison to the transcendental and mythical discourse that was filled with wish-fulfilling rhetoric of salvation and damnation.[2] In a *Time* magazine report on the first encounter between computer and public in 1944, the machine was treated as a sacred and mysterious object. What was "unveiled" was a "bewildering 50-foot panel of knobs, wires, counters, gears and switches." The connection to higher, even cosmic, forces immediately suggested itself. *Time* described it as having been unveiled "in the presence of high officers in the Navy" and promised its readers that the new machine would solve problems "on earth as well as those posed by the celestial universe" (T8/44). This sacred status was elaborated in the years that followed.

To be sacred, an object must be sharply separated from contact with the routine world. Popular literature continually recounted the distance that separated the computer from the lay public and the mystery attendant on this. In another report on the 1944 unveiling, *Popular Science*, a leading lay technology magazine, described the first computer as an electrical brain whirring "behind its polished panels" and secluded in "an air-conditioned basement" (PS10/44). Twenty years later the image had not changed. In 1965, a new and far more powerful computer was conceptualized in the same way, as an "isolated marvel" working in "the air-conditioned seclusion of the company's data-programming room." In unmistakable terms, *Time* elaborated this discourse of the sacred technology: "Arranged row upon row in air-conditioned rooms, waited upon by crisp young white-shirted men who move softly among them like priests serving in a shrine, the computers go about their work quietly and, for the most part, unseen from the public" (T4/65).

Objects are isolated because they are thought to possess mysterious power. The connection between computer and established centers of charismatic power is repeated constantly in the popular literature. Occasionally, an analogy is made between the computer and sacred things on earth. Reporting on the unveiling of a new and more sophisticated computer in 1949, *Newsweek* called it "the real hero" of the occasion and described it, like royalty, as "holding court in the computer lab upstairs" (N11/49). Often, however, more direct references to the computer's cosmic powers and even to its extrahuman status were made. In an article about the first computer, *Popular Science* reported that "everybody's notion of the universe and everything in it will be upset by the columns of figures this monster will type out" (PS10/44). Fifteen years later, a famous technical expert asserted in a widely circulated feature magazine that "forces will be set in motion whose ultimate effects for good and evil are incalculable" (RD3/60).

As the machine became more sophisticated, and more awesome, references to godly powers were openly made. The new computers "render unto Caesar by sending out the monthly bills and . . . unto God by counting the ballots of the world's Catholic bishops" (T4/65). A joke circulated to the effect that a scientist tried to stump his computer with the question: Is there a God? "The computer was silent for a moment. Then it answered: 'Now there is'" (N1/66). After describing the computer in superhuman terms—"infallible in memory, incredibly swift in math [and] utterly impartial in judgment"—a mass weekly made the obvious deduction: "This transistorized prophet can help the church adapt to modern spiritual needs" (T3/68). A leader of one national church described the Bible as a "distillation of human experience" and asserted that computers arc capable of correlating an even greater range "of experience about how people ought to behave." The conclusion that was drawn underscored the deeply established connection between the computer and cosmic power: "When we want to consult the deity, we go to the computer because it's the closest thing to God to come along" (T3/68).

If an object is sacred and sealed off from the profane world, gaining access to its powers becomes a problem in itself. Priests emerge as intermediaries between divinity and laity. As one leading expert suggested, while there were many who appreciated the computer, "only specialists yet realize how these elements will all be combined and [the] far-reaching social, economic, and political implications" (RD5/60). Typically, erroneous predictions about the computer were usually attributed to "nonspecialists" (BW3/65). To possess knowledge of computing, it was emphasized time and again, requires incredible training and seclusion. Difficult new procedures must be developed. To learn how to operate

a new computer introduced in 1949, specialists "spent months literally studying day and night" (N8/49). The number of people capable of undergoing such
rigorous training was highly restricted. The forging of "links between human
society and the robot brain" (N9/49) called for "a new race of scientists." The
"new breed of specialists [which] has grown up to tend the machines," *Time*
wrote sixteen years later, "have formed themselves into a solemn priesthood of
the computer, purposely separated from ordinary laymen [and] speak[ing] an
esoteric language that some suspect is just their way of mystifying outsiders"
(T4/65). The article predicted: "There will be a small, almost separate society of
people in rapport with the advanced computer. They will have established a relationship with their machines that cannot be shared with the average man.
Those with talent for the work will have to develop it from childhood and will
be trained as intensively as the classical ballerina." Is it surprising that, reporting on computer news ten years later, *Time* (1/74) decided its readers would be
interested in learning that among this esoteric group of programmers there had
emerged a new and wildly popular computer game called "the game of life"?
The identification of the computer with God and of computer operators with
sacred intermediaries signifies culture structures that had not changed in forty
years.

   The contact with the cosmic computer that these technological priests provided would, then, certainly transform earthly life. Like the revolutionary technologies that preceded it, however, the computer embodied within itself both
superhuman evil and superhuman good. As Lévi-Strauss (1963) emphasized, it
is through naming that the cultural codes defining an object are first constructed. In the years immediately following the introduction of the computer,
efforts to name this new thinking machine were intense, and they followed the
binary pattern that Durkheim and Lévi-Strauss described.

   The result was a similitude of signifiers, an amplified series of sacred and profane associations that created for technological discourse a thick semantic field.
One series revealed dreadful proportions and dire implications. The computer
was called a "colossal gadget" (T8/44, N8/49), a "figure factory" (PS 10/44), a
"mountain of machinery" (PS10/44), a "monster" (PS10/44, SEP2/50), a "mathematical dreadnought" (PS10/44), a "portentous contrivance" (PS10/44), a "giant"
(N8/49), a "math robot" (N8/49), a "wonderworking robot" (SEP2/50), the "Ma-
niac" (SEP2/50), and the "Frankenstein-monster" (SEP2/50). In announcing a
new and bigger computer in 1949, *Time* (9/49) hailed the "great machines that eat
their way through oceans of figures like whale grazing on plankton" and described them as roaring like "a hive of mechanical insects."

   In direct opposition to this profane realm, journalists and technicians also
named the computer and its parts through analogies to the presumptively innocent and assuredly sacred human being. It was called a "super-brain" (PS10/44)
and a "giant brain" (N8/49). Attached to an audio instrument, it was described
as "a brain child with a temporary voice" and as "the only mechanical brain with

a soft heart" (N10/49). Its "physiology" (SEP2/50) became a topic of debate. Computers were given an "inner memory" (T9/49), "eyes," a "nervous system" (SEP2/50), a "spinning heart" (T2/51), and a "female temperament" (SEP2/50) in addition to the brain with which they were already endowed. It was announced that they were to have "descendants" (N4/50), and in later years "families" and "generations" (T4/65) emerged. Finally, there were the developmental phrases. "Just out of its teens," *Time* announced (T4/65), the computer was about to enter a "formidable adulthood." It might do so, however, in a neurotic way, for its designers had "made a pampered and all but adored child" out of it.[3]

The period of compulsive naming quickly abated, but the awesome forces for good and evil that the names symbolized have been locked in deadly combat to this day. Salvation rhetoric overcomes this dualism in one direction, apocalyptic rhetoric in another. Both moves can be seen in structural terms as overcoming binary opposition by providing a third term. But more profound emotional and metaphysical issues are also at stake. Computer discourse was eschatological because the computer was seen as involving matters of life and death.

At first, salvation was defined in narrowly mathematical terms. The new computer would "solve in a flash" (T9/49) problems that had "baffled men for years" (PS10/44). By 1950, salvation had already become much more broadly defined. "Come the Revolution!" read the headline to a story about these new predictions (T11/50). A broad and visionary ideal of progress was laid out: "Thinking machines will bring a healthier, happier civilization than any known heretofore" (SEP2/50). People would now be able to "solve their problems the painless electronic way" (N7/54). Airplanes, for example, would be able to reach their destinations "without one bit of help from the pilot" (PS1/55).

By 1960, public discourse about the computer had become truly millennial. "A new age in human relations has opened," a reigning expert announced (RD3/60). Like all eschatological rhetoric, the timing of this promised salvation is imprecise. It has not yet occurred, but it has already begun. It is coming in five years or ten, its effects will be felt soon, the transformation is imminent. Whatever the timing, the end result is certain. "There will be a social effect of unbelievable proportions" (RD3/60). "By surmounting the last great barrier of distance," the computer's effect on the natural world will be just as great (RD3/60). Most human labor will be eliminated, and people will finally be set "free to undertake completely new tasks, most of them directed toward perfecting ourselves, creating beauty, and understanding one another" (Mc5/65).[4]

The convictions were confirmed in still more sweeping tones in the late 1960s and early 1970s. The new computers had such "awesome power" (RD5/71) that, as God was recorded in the book of Genesis, they would bring "order out of chaos" (BW7/71). That "the computer age is dawning" was certain. One sign of this millennium will be that "the common way of thinking in terms of cause and effect [will be] replaced by a new awareness" (RD5/71). That this was the stuff of which "dreams are made" (USN6/67) cannot be denied. Computers would transform all natural forces. They would cure diseases and guarantee long life. They would allow everyone to know everything at all times. They would allow all students to learn easily and the best to learn perfectly. They would produce a world community and end war. They would overturn stratification and allow equality to reign. They would make government responsible and efficient, business productive and profitable, work creative, and leisure endlessly satisfying.

As for apocalypse, there was also much to say. Machines have always embodied not only the transcendental hopes but also the fear and loathing generated by industrial society. Regarding this new technological machine, *Time* once articulated this deep ambiguity in a truly gothic way. Viewed from the front, computers exhibit a "clean, serene dignity." This is deceptive, however, for "behind there hides a nightmare of pulsing, twitching, flashing complexity" (9/49).

Whereas contact with the sacred side of the computer is the vehicle for salvation, the profane side threatens destruction. It is something from which human beings must be saved. First, the computer creates the fear of degradation. "People are scared" (N8/68) because the computer has the power to "blot or diminish man" (RD3/60). People feel "rage and helpless frustration" (N9/69). The computer degrades because it objectifies; this is the second great fear. It will "lead to mechanical men who replace humans" (T11/50). Students will be "treated as impersonal machines" (RD 1/71). Computers are inseparable from "the image of slavery" (USN11/67). It is because they are seen as objectifying human beings that computers present a concrete danger. In 1975, one popular author described his personal computer as a "humming thing poised to rip me apart" (RD 11/75). More typically the danger is not mutilation but manipulation. With computers "markets can be scientifically rigged . . . with an efficiency that would make dictators blush" (SEP2/50). Their intelligence can turn them into "instruments for massive subversion" (RD3/60). They could "lead us to that ultimate horror—chains of plastic tape" (N8/66).

Finally, there is the cataclysm, the final judgment on earthly technological folly that has been predicted from 1944 until the present day. Computers are "Frankenstein [monsters] which can . . . wreck the very foundations of our society" (T11/50). They can lead to "disorders [that may] pass beyond control" (RD4/60). There is a "storm brewing" (BW1/68). There are "nightmarish stories" about the "light that failed" (BW7/71). "Incapable of making allowances for error," the "Christian notion of redemption is incomprehensible to the computer" (N8/66). The computer has become the antichrist.

I have taken the computer story to 1975. This was the eve of the so-called personal computer, the very name of which demonstrates how the battle between human and antihuman continued to fuel the discourse that surrounded the computer's birth. In the decades of discussion that followed, utopian and antiutopian themes have remained prominent (for example, Turkle, 1984: 165–96). Disappointment and "realism," however, also became more frequently expressed. Yet, even as computer news passed from the cover of *Time* to advertisements in the sports pages of daily newspapers, eschatological speculations about the Internet revolution and the new e-world have frothed to the bubbling surface of cultural life.

## CONCLUSION

Let us return to the socioscientific understandings of technology I have recounted here. We can now see that, far from being empirical accounts based on objective observations and interpretations, they represent simply another version of technocratic discourse itself. The apocalyptic strain of that discourse fears degradation, objectification, slavery, and manipulation. Has not critical theory merely translated this evaluation into the empirical language of social science? The same goes for those sociol-theoretical analyses that take a more benign form: they provide social scientific translations of the discourse about salvation.[5]

At stake is more than the accuracy or the distortion of social scientific statements. That the rationalization hypothesis is wrong does not make technology a benign force. The great danger that technology poses to modern life is neither the flattening-out of human consciousness nor its enslavement to economic or political reality. To the contrary, it is because technology is lodged in the fantasies of salvation and apocalytse that its dangers are real. Only by understanding the omnipresent shaping of technological consciousness by discourse can we hope to gain control over technology in its material form. World War II was brought to an end on August 10, 1945, by the surrender of Japan, which followed quickly on American atomic bomb attacks on Hiroshima and Nagasaki. The very next day in the *Times* of London an article by Niels Bohr appeared that presented a prescient perspective on how efforts to control the bomb might proceed. Even while he notes the apocalyptic strain in the public's comprehension of this terrible technological achievement, Bohr warns that, above all, a distance from this fantasy is necessary if rational control efforts are to be made. "The grim realities which are being revealed to the world in these days will no doubt, in the minds of many, revive terrifying prospects forecast in fiction. With all admiration for such imagination, it is, however, most essential to appreciate the contrast between these fantasies and the actual situation confronting us" (1985 [1945]: 264).

# 8

## MODERN, ANTI, POST, AND NEO

### How Intellectuals Explain "Our Time"

Karl Marx once famously opined that while intellectuals have traditionally sought to understand the world, our task is to change it. From the hermeneutic, cultural perspective I have been developing in this book, understanding and changing the world simply cannot be separated in this way. If the world is itself based on collective understandings, then changing the world always involves, in some large part, changing these understandings in turn.

Intellectual understanding must itself be reunderstood as well. For Marx and other moderns, the task of intellectuals was one of rational reconstruction. Even the broadest theories of history were seen as factual, either descriptive or explanatory. From the perspective of cultural sociology, however, what intellectuals actually do is something very different from this. The really broad and influential thinkers are prophets and priests. Their ability to be critical, to explain, to historicize, even to describe their own time emerges from a depth of commitment to ethics and feelings that form, and emerge from, simplified binary structures and fiction-like narratives. They involve leaps of faith and faith in leaps. Intellectuals divide the world into the sacred and profane and weave stories about the relationship in between. It is less interesting to examine these tapestries for their factual meaning than to deconstruct their symbolic meaning in a cultural sociological way.

Sometime during the mid-1970s, at the annual meeting of the American Sociological Association, a major debate erupted around modernization theory that crystallized a decade of social and intellectual change. Two speakers were featured, Alex Inkeles and Immanuel Wallerstein. Inkeles reported that his studies of "modern man" (Inkeles & Smith, 1974) had demonstrated that personality shifts toward autonomy and achievement were crucial and predictable results of social modernization, which revolved most centrally around the industrialization of society. The response to Inkeles was appreciative from many of the senior members of the audience, skeptical from the younger. Wallerstein responded to Inkeles in a manner that pleased the younger generation more. "We do not live in a modernizing world but in a capitalist world," he proclaimed (1979: 133), asserting that "what makes this world tick is not the need for achievement but the need for profit." When Wallerstein went on to lay out "an agenda of intellectual work for those who are seeking to understand the world *systemic transition from capitalism to socialism in which we are living*" (135, italics in original), he literally brought the younger members of the audience to their feet.[1]

Fifteen years later, the lead article in the *American Sociological Review* was entitled "A Theory of Market Transition: From Redistribution to Markets in State Socialism." The transition referred to in this chapter was rather different from the one Wallerstein had in mind. Written by Victor Nee, once inclined to Maoism and now a rational choice theorist specializing in China's burgeoning market economy, the article suggested that the only hope for organized socialism was capitalism. In fact, Nee portrayed socialism exactly as Marx had depicted capitalism and his predictions for the future formed a mirror image of Marx's own. State socialism, he wrote, was an archaic, outdated mode of production, one whose internal contradictions were leading to capitalism. Employing the class conflict analytic of Marx to the productive system that Marx believed would end such conflict for all time, Nee argued that it is state socialism, not capitalism, that "appropriates surplus directly from the immediate producers and creates and structures social inequality through the processes of its reallocation" (1989: 665). Such expropriation of surplus—exploitation—can be overcome only if workers are given the opportunity to own and sell their own labor power. Only with markets, Nee insisted, could workers develop the power to "withhold their product" and protect their "labor power" (666). This movement from one mode of production to another would shift power to the formerly oppressed class. "The transition from redistribution to markets," he concluded, "involves a transfer of power favoring direct producers" (666).

## A NEW "TRANSITION"

In the juxtaposition between these formulations of modernity, socialism, and capitalism there lies a story. They describe not only competing theoretical positions but deep shifts in historical sensibility. We must understand both together, I believe, if either contemporary history or contemporary theory is to be properly understood.

Social scientists and historians have long talked about "the transition." A historical phrase, a social struggle, a moral transformation for better or for worse, the term referred, of course, to the movement from feudalism to capitalism. For

Marxists, the transition initiated the unequal and contradictory system that produced its antithesis, socialism and equality. For liberals, the transition represented an equally momentous transformation of traditional society but created a set of historical alternatives—democracy, capitalism, contracts, and civil society—that did not have a moral or social counterfactual like socialism ready to hand. By the late 1980s, for the first time in the history of social science, "the transition" had come to mean something that neither of these earlier treatments could have foreseen. It was the transition from communism to capitalism, a phrase that still seems oxymoronic to our chastened ears even today. In this new transition, the sense of world-historical transformation remains, but the straight line of history seems to be running in reverse.

In this recent period we have witnessed one of the most dramatic spatially and temporally contiguous social transformations in the history of world. The more contemporary meaning of transition may not have entirely eclipsed the earlier one, yet there is no doubt that it has already diminished its significance and will arouse significantly more intellectual interest for a long time to come.

This second great transformation, to redirect Polanyi's (1957) famous phrase, has produced an unexpected, and for many an unwelcome, convergence in both history and social thought. It is impossible even for already committed intellectuals to ignore the fact that we are witnessing the death of a major alternative not only in social thought but in society itself.[2] In the foreseeable future, it is unlikely that either citizens or elites will try to structure their primary allocative systems in nonmarket ways.[3]

For their part, social scientists will be far less likely to think of antimarket "socialist societies" as counterfactual alternatives with which to explain their own. They will be less likely to explain economic stratification by implicitly comparing it with an egalitarian distribution produced by publicly rather than privately held property, a "plausible world" (Hawthorn, 1991) that inevitably seems to suggest that economic inequality is produced by the existence of private property itself. Social scientists will, perhaps, also be less likely to explain status stratification by postulating the counterfactual tendency to communal esteem in a world that is uncorrupted by individualism of a bourgeois rather than socialist kind. Similarly, it will become much more difficult to speak about the emptiness of formal democracy or to explain its limitations by pointing merely to the existence of a dominant economic class, for these explanations, too, require counterfactuals of a traditionally "socialist" kind. In brief, it will be much less easy to explain contemporary social problems by pointing to the capitalist nature of the societies of which they are a part.

In this essay, I do not propose a return to "convergence" or modernization theories of society as such, as have some reinvigorated proponents of the early tradition (Inkeles, 1991; Lipset, 1990). I will propose, however, that contemporary social theory must be much more sensitive to the apparent reconvergence of the world's regimes and that, as a result, we must try to incorporate some broad sense of the universal and shared elements of development into a critical, undogmatic, and reflexive theory of social change. Indeed, in the conclusion of this essay I will demonstrate that a growing range of widely diverse contemporary social theorists, from literary radicals and rational choice theorists to postcommunists, are in fact developing a new language of convergence, and I will address the challenging question, raised so trenchantly by Muller (1992), of whether this emerging conversation can avoid the relatively simplistic and totalizing form that obliterated the complexities of earlier societies and the particularisms of our own.

Despite this new and more sophisticated form, however, what I will later call neomodern theory will remain as much myth as science (Barbour, 1974), as much narrative as explanation (Entrikin, 1991). Even if one believes, as I do, that such a broader and more sophisticated theory of social development is now historically compelling, it remains the case that every general theory of social change is rooted not only in cognition but also in existence—that it possesses a surplus of meaning, in Ricoeur's (1977) deeply suggestive phrase. Modernity, after all, has always been a highly relativist term (Bourricaud, 1987; Habermas, 1981; Pocock,1987). It emerged in the fifth century when newly Christianized Romans wished to distinguish their religiosity from two forms of barbarians, the heathens of antiquity and the unregenerate Jews. In medieval times, modernity was reinvented as a term implying cultivation and learning, which allowed contemporary intellectuals to identify backward with the classical learning of the Greek and Roman heathens themselves. With the Enlightenment, modernity became identified with rationality, science, and forward progress, a semantically arbitrary relationship that seems to have held steady to this day. Who can doubt that, sooner or later, a new historical period will displace this second "age of equipoise" (Burn, 1974) into which we have so inadvertently but fortuitously slipped. New contradictions will emerge and competing sets of world-historical possibilities will arise, and it is unlikely that they will be viewed in terms of the emerging neomodernization frame.

It is precisely this sense of the instability, of the imminent transitoriness of the world, that introduces myth into social theory. Despite the fact that we have no idea what our historical possibilities will be, every theory of social change must theorize not only the past but the present and future as well. We can do so only in normative and expressive ways, in relation not only to what we know but to what we believe, hope, and fear. Every historical period needs a narrative that defines its past in terms of the present and suggests a future that is fundamentally different from and, typically, "even better" than contemporary time. For this reason there is always an eschatology, not merely an epistemology, in theorizing about social change.

I proceed now to examine early modernization theory, its contemporary reconstruction, and the vigorous intellectual alternatives that arose in the period between. I will insist throughout on the relation of these theoretical developments to social and cultural history, for only in this way can we understand social theory not only as science but also as an ideology in the sense made famous by Geertz (1973 [1964]). Unless we recognize the interpenetration of science and ideology in social theory, neither element can be evaluated or clarified in a rational way. With this stricture in mind, I delineate four distinctive theoretical-cum-ideological periods in postwar social thought: modernization theory and romantic liberalism; antimodernization theory and heroic radicalism; postmodern theory and comic detachment; and the emerging phase of neomodernization or reconvergence theory, which seems to combine the narrative forms of each of its predecessors on the postwar scene.

While I will be engaging in genealogy, locating the historical origins of each phase of postwar theory in an archeological way, it is vital to keep in mind that each one of the theoretical residues of the phases that I examine remains vitally alive today. My archeology, in other words, is an investigation not only of the past but of the present. Because the present is history, this genealogy will help us to understand the theoretical sedimentation within which we live.

## MODERNIZATION: CODE, NARRATIVE, AND EXPLANATION

Drawing from a centuries-long tradition of evolutionary and Enlightenment-inspired theories of social change, "modernization" theory as such was born with the publication of Marion Levy's book on Chinese family structure (1949) and died sometime in the mid-1960s, during one of those extraordinarily heated rites of spring that marked student uprising, antiwar movements, and newly humanist socialist regimes and that preceded the long hot summers of the race riots and the black consciousness movement in the United States. Modernization theory can and certainly should be evaluated as a scientific theory, in the postpositivist, *wissenschaftliche* sense.[4] As an explanatory effort, the modernization model was characterized by the following ideal-typical traits:[5]

1. Societies were conceived as coherently organized systems whose subsystems were closely interdependent.
2. Historical development was parsed into two types of social systems, the traditional and the modern, statuses that were held to determine the character of their societal subsystems in determinate ways.
3. The modern was defined with reference to the social organization and culture of specifically Western societies, which were typified as individualistic, democratic, capitalist, scientific, secular, and stable and as dividing work from home in gender-specific ways.
4. As a historical process, modernization was held to involve nonrevolutionary, incremental change.
5. The historical evolution to modernity—modernization—was viewed as

likely to succeed, thus assuring that traditional societies would be provided with the resources for what Parsons (1966) called a general process of adaptive "upgrading," including economic takeoff to industrialization, democratization via law, and secularization and science via education.

There were important aspects of truth in these models, which were articulated by thinkers of considerable historical and sociological insight. One truth, for example, lay in the insight that there are functional, not merely idealistic exigencies that push social systems toward democracy, markets, and the universalization of culture, and that shifts toward "modernity" in any subsystem create considerable pressures on the others to respond in a complementary way.[6] This understanding made it possible for the more sophisticated among them to make prescient predictions about the eventual instability of state socialist societies, thus avoiding the rational-is-the-real embarrassments encountered by theorists of a more leftist kind. Thus, Parsons (1971: 127) insisted long before *perestroika* "that the processes of democratic revolution have not reached an equilibrium in the Soviet Union and that further developments may well run broadly in the direction of Western types of democratic government, with responsibility to an electorate rather than to a self-appointed party." It should perhaps also be emphasized that, whatever their faults, modernization theorists were not provincials. Despite their ideological intent, the most important of them rarely confused functional interdependence with historical inevitability. Parsons's theorizing, for example (1964: 466, 474), stressed that systemic exigencies actually opened up the possibility of historical choice.

> Underneath the ideological conflicts [between capitalism and communism] that have been so prominent, there has been emerging an important element of very broad consensus at the level of values, centering in the complex we often refer to as "modernization." . . . Clearly, definite victory for either side is not the only possible choice. We have another alternative, namely, the eventual integration of both sides—and of uncommitted units as well—in a wider system of order.[7]

Despite these important insights, however, the historical judgment of subsequent *social* thought has not erred its evaluation of modernization theory as a failed explanatory scheme. Neither non-Western nor precontemporary societies can be conceptualized as internally homogeneous (see Mann, 1986). Their subsystems are more loosely coupled (e.g., Alexander & Colomy, 1990; Meyer & Rowan, 1977) and their cultural codes more independent (e.g., Hall, 1985). Nor is there the kind of dichotomized historical development that can justify a single conception of traditional or modern, as Eisenstadt's (e.g., 1964) extensive investigations of "Axial Age" civilizations make clear. Even the concept "Western society," built on spatial and historical contiguity, fails sufficiently to recognize historical specificity and national variation. Social systems, moreover, are not as internally homogeneous as was supposed, nor are there necessarily grounds for optimism that modernization will succeed. In the first place, universalizing change is neither imminent nor developmental in an idealist sense; it is often abrupt, involving contingent positions of power, and can have murderous results.[8] In the second place, even if one were to accept a linear conceptual scheme, one would have to acknowledge Nietzsche's observation that historical regression is as possible as progress, indeed, perhaps more likely. Finally, modernization, even if it does triumph, does not necessarily increase social contentment. It may be that the more highly developed a society, the more it produces, encourages, and relies on strident and often utopian expressions of alienation and criticism (Durkheim, 1937 [1897]).

When we look back on a "scientifically invalidated" theory that dominated the thinking of an entire intellectual stratum for two decades, those of us who are still committed to the project of a rational and generalizing social science will be inclined to ask ourselves: Why was it believed? While we would ignore at our peril the partial truths of modernization theory, we would not be wrong to conclude that there were extrascientific reasons involved. Social theory (Alexander & Colomy, 1995) must be considered not only as a research program but as a generalized discourse, one very important part of which is ideology. It is as a meaning structure, as a form of existential truth, that social scientific theory functions effectively in an extrascientific way.[9]

To understand modernization theory and its fate, then, we must examine it not only as a scientific theory but as an ideology—not in the mechanistic Marxist or more broadly Enlightenment sense (e.g., Boudon, 1984) of "false consciousness" but in the Geertzian (1973 [1964]) one. Modernization theory was a symbolic system that functioned not only to explain the world in a rational way but also to interpret the world in a manner that provided "meaning and motivation" (Bellah, 1970). It functioned as a metalanguage that instructed people how to live.

Intellectuals must interpret the world, not simply change or even explain it. To do so in a meaningful, reassuring, or inspiring manner means that intellectuals must make distinctions. They must do so especially in regard to phases of history. If intellectuals are to define the "meaning" of their "time," they must identify a time that preceded the present, offer a morally compelling account of why it was superseded, and tell their audiences whether or not such a transformation will be repeated vis-à-vis the world they live in. This is, of course, merely to say that intellectuals produce historical narratives about their own time.[10]

The ideological dimension of modernization theory is further illuminated by thinking of this narrative function in a structuralist, or semiotic, way (Barthes, 1977). Because the existential unit of reference is one's own time, the empirical unit of reference must be totalized as one's own society. It must, in other words, be characterized as a whole regardless of the actual nature of its divisions and inconsistencies. Not only one's own time, then, but one's own society must be characterized by a single linguistic term, and the world that preceded the present must be characterized by another single broad term as well. In light of these considerations, the important ideological, or meaning-making, function that modernization theory served seems fairly clear. For Western but especially American and American-educated intellectuals, modernization theory provided a telos for postwar society by making it "historical." It did so by providing postwar society with a temporal and spatial identity, an identity that could be formed only in a relation of difference with another, immediately preceding time and place. As Pocock has emphasized, "modernity" must be understood as the "consciousness" rather than the condition of being "modern." Taking a linguistic model of consciousness, he suggests that such consciousness must be defined as much by difference as identification. The modern is a "signifier" that functions as an "excluder" at the same time. "We call something (perhaps ourselves) modern in order to distance that of which we speak from some antecedent state of affairs. The antecedent is most unlikely to be of neutral effect in defining either what is to be called 'modern' or the 'modernity' attributed to it" (Pocock, 1987: 48).

If I may give to this approach a late Durkheimian turn—a turn that has been elaborated throughout this book—I would like to suggest that we think of modernity as constructed on a binary code. This code serves the mythological function of dividing the known world into the sacred and profane, thereby providing a clear and compelling picture of how contemporaries must act to maneuver the space in between.[11] In this sense, the discourse of modernity bears a striking resemblance to metaphysical and religious salvation discourse of diverse kinds (Walzer, 1965; Weber, 1964 [1922]). It also resembles the more secular dichotomizing discourses that citizens employ to identify themselves with, and to distance themselves from, the diverse individuals, styles, groups, and structures in contemporary societies (Bourdieu, 1984; Wagner-Pacifici, 1986).

It has been argued, in fact (see chapter 4), that a "discourse of civil society" provides a structured semiotic field for the conflicts of contemporary societies, positing idealized qualities like rationality, individuality, trust, and truth as essential qualities for inclusion in the modern, civil sphere, while identifying qualities such as irrationality, conformity, suspicion, and deceit as traditional traits that demand exclusion and punishment. There is a striking overlap between these ideological constructions and the explanatory categories of modernization theory, for example Parsons's pattern variables. In this sense, modernization theory may be seen as a generalizing and abstracting effort to transform a historically specific categorial scheme into a scientific theory of development applicable to any culture around the entire world.

Because every ideology is carried by an intellectual cadre (Eisenstadt, 1986; Konrad & Szelenyi, 1979), it is important to ask why the intellectual cadre in a particular time and place articulated and promoted a particular theory. In regard to modernization theory, despite the importance of a small number of influential Europeans like Raymond Aron (e.g., Aron, 1962), we are speaking primarily about American and American-educated intellectuals.[12] Following some work by Eyerman (1992; see Jamison & Eyerman, 1994) on the formation of American intellectuals in the 1950s, I would begin by emphasizing the distinctive social characteristics of the postwar period in the United States, particularly the sharpness of the transition to the postwar world. This transition was marked by massive suburbanization and the decline of culturally bounded urban communities, a dramatic reduction in the ethnicity of American life, an extraordinary lessening of labor-capital conflict, and unprecedented long-term prosperity.

These new social circumstances, coming as they did at the end of two decades of massive national and international upheaval, induced in postwar American intellectuals a sense of a fundamental historical break.[13] On the left, intellectuals like C. Wright Mills and David Riesman issued jeremiads against what they feared was the massification of society. In the liberal center, theorists like Parsons suggested how the same transition had created a more egalitarian, more inclusive, and significantly more differentiated society.[14] On the right, there were cries of alarm about the disappearance of the individual in an authoritarian and bureaucratic welfare state (Buckley, 1951; Rand, 1957). On every side of the political spectrum, in other words, American intellectuals were motivated by a sense of dramatic and bifurcating social change. This was the social basis for constructing the traditional/modern binary code, an experience of bifurcation that demanded an interpretation of present anxieties, and future possibilities, in relation to the imagined past.

To fully understand the interrelation between history and theory that produced the new intellectuals, however, we must think about narrativity in addition to symbolic structure. In order to do so, I will draw on the dramaturgical terms of genre theory, which stretches from Aristotle's poetics to the path-setting literary criticism of Frye (1971 [1957]), which inspired the "negative hermeneutics" of such historically oriented literary critics as White (1987), Jameson (1980), Brooks (1984), and Fussell (1975).[15]

In such dramaturgical terms we can characterize the historical period that preceded the era of modernization theory as one in which intellectuals "inflated" the importance of actors and events by emplotting them in a heroic narrative. The 1930s and the war years that followed defined a period of intense social conflict that generated millennial, world-historical hopes for utopian social transformation, either through communist and fascist revolutions or the construction of an unprecedented kind of "welfare state." Postwar American intellectuals, by contrast, experienced the social world in more "deflationary" terms. With the failure of revolutionary proletarian movements in Europe and the headlong rush to normalization and demobilization in the United States, the heroic "grand narratives" of collective emancipation seemed less compelling.[16] The present was no longer perceived primarily as a way station to an alternative social order but, rather as more or less the only possible system there ever could be.

Such a deflationary acceptance of "this world" was not necessarily dystopian, fatalistic, or conservative. In Europe and America, for example, there emerged a principled anticommunism that wove together the bare threads of a collective narrative and committed their societies to social democracy. Yet even for such social-democratic and reformist groups the deflation of prewar social narratives had strong effects, effects that were very widely shared. Intellectuals as a group became more "hardheaded" and "realistic." Realism diverges radically from the heroic narrative, inspiring a sense of limitation and restraint rather than idealism and sacrifice. Black-and-white thinking, so important for social mobilization, is replaced by "ambiguity" and "complexity," terms favored by New Critics like Empson (1935) and particularly Trilling (1950), and by "skepticism," a position exemplified in Niebuhr's writings (e.g., Niebuhr, 1952). The conviction that one has been "born again"—this time to the social sacred—which inspires utopian enthusiasm is succeeded by the "thrice-born," chastened soul described by Bell (1962) and by an acute sense that the social God has failed (Crossman, 1950). Indeed, this new realism convinced many that narrative itself—history—had been eclipsed, which produced the representations of this newly "modern" society as the "end of ideology" (Bell,1962) and the portrayal of the postwar world as "industrial" (Aron, 1962; Lipset & Bendix, 1960) rather than capitalistic.

Yet, while realism was a significant mood in the postwar period, it was not the dominant narrative frame through which postwar social science intellectuals charted their times. Romanticism was.[17] Relatively deflated in comparison with heroism, romanticism tells a story that is more positive in its evaluation of the world as it exists today. In the postwar period it allowed intellectuals and their audiences to believe that progress would be more or less continuously achieved, that improvement was likely. This state of grace referred, however, more to individuals than to groups and to incremental rather than revolutionary change. In the new world that emerged from the ashes of war, it had finally become possible to cultivate one's own garden. This cultivation would be an enlightened, modernist work, regulated by the cultural patterns of achievement and neutrality (Parsons & Shils, 1951), culminating in the "active" (Etzioni, 1968) and "achieving" (McClelland, 1953) society.

Romanticism, in other words, allowed America's postwar social science intellectuals, even in a period of relative narrative deflation, to continue to speak the language of progress and universalization. In the United States, what differentiates romantic from heroic narratives is the emphasis on the self and private life. In America's social narratives, heroes are epochal; they lead entire peoples to salvation, as collective representations like the American Revolution and the civil rights movement indicate. Romantic evolution, by contrast, is not collective; it is about Tom Sawyer and Huck Finn (Fiedler, 1955), the yeoman farmer (Smith,

1950), and Horatio Alger. American intellectuals, then, articulated modernization as a process that freed the self and made society's subsystems responsive to its needs. In this sense modernization theory was behavioral and pragmatic; it focused on real individuals rather than on a collective historical subject like nation, ethnic group, or class.

Existentialism was basic to the romantic American ideology of "modernism." American intellectuals, indeed, developed an idiosyncratic, optimistic reading of Sartre. In the milieu saturated with existentialism, "authenticity" became a central criterion for evaluating individual behavior, an emphasis that was central to Trilling's (1955) modernist literary criticism but also permeated social theory that ostensibly did not advocate modernization, for example Goffman's (1956) microsociology, with its equation of freedom with role distance and its conception of back-versus-front stage,[18] and Riesman's (1950) eulogy for the inner-directed man.

These individualistic romantic narratives stressed the challenge of being modern, and they were complemented by an emphasis on irony, the narrative Frye defines as deflationary vis-à-vis romance but not downright negative in its effects. In the 1950s and early 1960s, the modernist aesthetic in Britain and America stressed irony, introspection, ambiguity. The dominant literary theory, so-called New Criticism, while tracing its origins back to Empson's book *Seven Types of Ambiguity* (1935), came into its own only after the heroic and much more historicist criticism of the 1930s. The key contemporary figure in American letters was Lionel Trilling, who defined the psychological and aesthetic goal of modernity as the expansion of complexity and tolerance for ambiguity. Psychoanalysis was a major critical approach, interpreted as an exercise in introspection and moral control (Rieff, 1959). In visual art, "modern" was equated with abstraction, the revolt against decoration, and minimalism, all of which were interpreted as drawing attention away from the surface and providing pathways into the inner self.

It is evidently difficult, at this remove, for contemporary postmodern and post-postmodern intellectuals to recapture the rich and, indeed, often ennobling aspects of this intellectual and aesthetic modernism, almost as difficult as it is for contemporaries to see the beauty and passion of modernist architecture that Pevsner (1949) so effectively captured in his epoch-defining book *Pioneers of Modern Design*. The accounts of intellectual-cum-aesthetic modernism proffered by contemporary postmodernists—from Bauman (1989), Seidman (1991a), and Lash (1985) to Harvey (1989) and Jameson (1988)—is a fundamental misreading. Their construction of it as dehumanizing abstraction, mechanism, fragmentation, linearity, and domination, I will suggest below, says much more about the ideological exigencies that they and other contemporary intellectuals are experiencing today than it does about modernism itself. In culture, in theory, and in art, modernism represented a spareness that devalued artifice not only as decoration but as pretension and undercut utopianism as a collective delusion that was homologous with neurosis of an individual kind (Fromm, 1956). It was precisely such admirable qualities that Bell (1976) designated as early or "classical modernity" in his attack on the 1960s in *The Cultural Contradictions of Capitalism.*

This picture was not, of course, an entirely homogeneous one. On the right, engagement in the Cold War provided for some intellectuals a new field for collective heroism, despite the fact that America's most influential modernist thinkers were not as a rule Cold Warriors of the most righteous kind. On the left, both within and outside the United States, there were important islands of social criticism that made self-conscious departures from romanticism of both a social democratic and individualist ironic sort.[19] Intellectuals influenced by the Frankfurt School, like Mills and Riesman, and other critics, like Arendt, refused to legitimate the humanism of this individualist turn, criticizing what they called the new mass society as forcing individuals into an amoral, egotistical mode. They inverted modernization theory's binary code, viewing American rationality as instrumental rather than moral and expressive and big science as technocratic rather than inventive. They saw conformity rather than independence; power elites rather than democracy; and deception and disappointment rather than authenticity, responsibility, and romance.

In the 1950s and early 1960s, these social critics did not become highly influential. To do so they would have had to pose a compelling alternative, a new heroic narrative to describe how the sick society could be transformed and a healthy one put in its place.[20] This was impossible to do in the deflationary times. Fromm's *Art of Loving* (1956) followed his denunciation in *The Sane Society* (1955); in the fifties, social solutions often were contained in individual acts of private love. No social program issued from Adorno, Frankel-Brunswick, Levinson, and Sanford's *Authoritarian Personality* (1950). Not only did C. Wright Mills fail to identify any viable social alternatives in his stream of critical studies (see n. 32), but he went out of his way to denounce the leaders of the social movements of the thirties and forties as "the new men of power" (Mills, 1948). After nearly twenty years of violence-producing utopian hopes, collective heroics had lost their sheen. The right-wing populism of Joe McCarthy reinforced the withdrawal from public life. Eventually, however, Americans and western Europeans did catch their breath, with results that must be related, once again, to history and social theory alike.

## ANTIMODERNIZATION THEORY: THE HEROIC REVIVAL

Sometime in the 1960s, between the assassination of President Kennedy and the San Francisco "summer of love" of 1967, modernization theory died. It died because the emerging younger generation of intellectuals could not believe it was true.

Even if we regard social theory as semiotic code rather than pragmatically inducted generalization, it is a sign system whose signifieds are empirical reality in a rather strictly disciplined sense. So it is important to recognize that, during this second postwar period, serious "reality problems" began to intrude on modernization theory in a major way. Despite the existence of capitalist markets, poverty persisted at home (Harrington, 1962) and perhaps was even increasing in the third world. Revolutions and wars continually erupted outside of Europe and North America (Johnson, 1983) and sometimes even seemed to be produced by modernization itself. Dictatorship, not democracy, was spreading throughout the rest of the world (Moore, 1966); postcolonial nations seem to require an authoritarian state (Huntington, 1968) and a command economy to be modern, not only in the economy and state but in other spheres as well. New religious movements (Bellah & Glock, 1976) emerged in Western countries and in the developing world, with sacralization and ideology gaining ground over secularization, science, and technocracy. These developments strained the central assumptions of modernization theory, although they did not necessarily refute it.[21]

Factual problems, however, are not enough to create scientific revolutions. Broad theories can defend themselves by defining and protecting a set of core propositions, jettisoning entire segments of their perspective as only peripherally important. Indeed, if one looks closely at modernization theory during the middle and late 1960s, and even during the early 1970s, one can see an increasing sophistication as it geared up to meet its critics and to address the reality problems of the day. Dualistic simplifications about tradition and modernity were elaborated—not replaced by—notions that portrayed a continuum of development, as in the later neoevolutionary theories of Parsons (1964, 1966, 1971), Bellah (1970), and Eisenstadt (1964). Convergence was reconceptualized to allow parallel but independent pathways to the modern (e.g., Shils, 1972) on India, Eisenstadt (1963) on empires, Bendix (1964) on citizenship. Notions like diffusion and functional substitutes were proposed to deal with the modernization of non-Western civilizations in a less ethnocentric manner (Bellah, 1957; Cole, 1979). The postulate of tight subsystem links was replaced by the notion of leads and lags (Smelser, 1968), and the insistence on interchange became modified by notions of paradoxes (Schluchter, 1979), contradictions (Eisenstadt, 1963), and strains (Smelser, 1963). Against the metalanguage of evolution, notions about developmentalism (Schluchter & Roth, 1979) and globalism (Nettl & Robertson, 1968) were suggested. Secularity gave way to ideas about civil religion (Bellah, 1970) and to references to "the tradition of the modern" (Gusfield, 1966).

Against these internal revisions, antagonistic theories of antimodernization were proposed on the grounds that they were more valid explanations of the reality problems that emerged. Moore (1966) replaced modernization and evolution with revolution and counter revolution. Thompson (1963) replaced abstractions about evolving patterns of industrial relations with class history and consciousness from the bottom up. Discourse about exploitation and inequality (e.g., Goldthorpe, Lockwood, Beckhofer, & Platt, 1969; Mann, 1973) contended with, and eventually displaced, discussions of stratification and mobility. Conflict theories (Coser, 1956; Dahrendorf, 1959; Rex, 1961) replaced functional ones; state-centered political theories (Bendix 1968; Collins, 1976; Evans, Rueschemeyer, & Skocpol, 1985; Skocpol, 1979) replaced value-centered and multidimensional approaches; and conceptions of binding social structures were challenged by microsociologies that emphasized the liquid, unformed, and negotiated character of everyday life.

What pushed modernization theory over the edge, however, were not these scientific alternatives in and of themselves. Indeed, as I have indicated, the revisers of the earlier theory had themselves begun to offer coherent, equally explanatory theories for many of the same phenomena. The decisive fact in modernization theory's defeat, rather, was the destruction of its ideological, discursive, and mythological core. The challenge that finally could not be met was existential. It emerged from new social movements that were increasingly viewed in terms of collective emancipation—peasant revolutions on a worldwide scale, black and Chicano national movements, indigenous people's rebellions, youth culture, hippies, rock music, and women's liberation. Because these movements (e.g., Weiner, 1984), profoundly altered the zeitgeist—the experienced tempo of the times—they captured the ideological imaginations of the rising cadre of intellectuals.

In order to represent this shifting empirical and existential environment, intellectuals developed a new explanatory theory. Equally significant, they inverted the binary code of modernization and "narrated the social" (Sherwood, 1994) in a new way. In terms of code, "modernity" and "modernization" moved from the sacred to the profane side of historical time, with modernity assuming many of the crucial characteristics that had earlier been associated with traditionalism and backwardness. Rather than democracy and individualization, the contemporary modern period was represented as bureaucratic and repressive. Rather than a free market or contractual society, modern America became "capitalist," no longer rational, interdependent, modern, and liberating but backward, greedy, anarchic, and impoverishing.

This inversion of the sign and symbols associated with modernity polluted the movements associated with its name. The death of liberalism (Lowi, 1969) was announced, and its reformist origins in the early twentieth century dismissed as a camouflage for extending corporate control (Kolko, 1967; Weinstein, 1968). Tolerance was associated with fuzzy-mindedness, immorality, and repression (Wolff, Marcuse, & Moore, 1965). The asceticism of Western religion was criticized for its repressive modernity and Eastern and mystical religious were sacralized instead (Brown, 1966; see Brown, 1959). Modernity was equated with the mechanism of the machine (Roszak, 1969). For the third world, democracy was defined as a luxury, strong states a necessity. Markets were not luxuries but enemies, for capitalism came to be represented as guaranteeing underdevelopment and backwardness. This inversion of economic ideals carried into the first world as well. Humanistic socialism replaced welfare state capitalism as the ultimate symbol of the good. Capitalist economies were held to produce only great poverty and great wealth (Kolko, 1962), and capitalist societies were viewed as sources of ethnic conflict (Bonacich, 1972), fragmentation, and alienation (Ollman, 1971). Not market society but socialism would provide wealth, equality, and a restored community.

These recordings were accompanied by fundamental shifts in social narratives. Intellectual myths were inflated upward, becoming stories of collective triumph and heroic transformation. The present was reconceived, not as the denouement of a long struggle but as a pathway to a different, much better world.[22] In this heroic myth, actors and groups in the present society were conceived as being "in struggle" to build the future. The individualized, introspective narrative of romantic modernism disappeared, along with ambiguity and irony as preferred social values (Gitlin, 1987: 377–406). Instead, ethical lines were sharply drawn and political imperatives etched in black and white. In literary theory, the new criticism gave way to the new historicism (e.g., Veeser, 1989). In psychology, the moralist Freud was now seen as antirepressive, erotic, and even polymorphously perverse (Brown, 1966). The new Marx was sometimes a Leninist and other times a radical communitarian; he was only rarely portrayed as a social democrat or humanist in the earlier, modernist sense.[23]

The historical vignette with which I opened this essay provides an illustration of this shift in sensibility. In his confrontation with Inkeles, Wallerstein portentously announced that "the time has come to put away childish things, and look reality in the face" (1979: 133). He was not adopting here a realist frame but rather donning a heroic guise. For it was emancipation and revolution that marked the narrative rhetoric of the day, not, as Weber might have said, the hard, dreary task of facing up to workaday demands. To be realistic, Wallerstein suggested, was to realize that "we are living in the transition" to a "socialist mode of production, our future world government" (136). The existential question he put to his listeners was "How are we relating to it?" He suggested that there were only two alternatives: They could relate to the imminent revolution "as rational militants contributing to it or as clever obstructors of it (whether of the malicious or cynical variety)." The rhetorical construction of these alternatives demonstrates how the inversion of binary coding (the clear line between good and bad, with modernity being polluted) and the creation of a newly heroic narrative (the militantly millennial orientation to future salvation) were combined.[24] Wallerstein made these remarks, it will be recalled, in a scientific presentation, later published as "Modernization: *Requiescat in Pace.*" He was one of the most influential and original social scientific theorists of the antimodernization theory phase.

The social theories that this new generation of radical intellectuals produced can and must be considered in scientific terms (see, e.g., Alexander, 1987; van den Berg, 1980). Their cognitive achievements, indeed, became dominant in the 1970s and remained hegemonic in contemporary social science long after the ideological totalities in which they were initially embedded disappeared.[25] Yet to study the decline of a mode of knowledge, I would insist once again, demands broader, extrascientific considerations as well. Theories are created by intellectuals in their search for meaning. In response to continuing social change, generational shifts occur that can make the scientific and ideological efforts of earlier intellectual generations seem not only empirically implausible but psychologically shallow, politically irrelevant, and morally obsolete.

By the end of the 1970s, the energy of the radical social movements of the preceding period had dissipated. Some of their demands became institutionalized; others were blocked by massive backlash movements that generated conservative publics and brought right-wing governments to power. The cultural-cum-political shift was so rapid as to seem, once again, to represent some kind of historical-cum-epistemological break.[26] Materialism replaced idealism among political influentials, and surveys reported increasingly conservative views among young people and university students. Marxist ideologues—one thinks of Bernard-Henri Levy (1977) in Paris and David Horowitz (Horowitz & Collier, 1989) in the United States—became anticommunist *nouvelles philosophes* and, some of them, neoconservatives. Yippies became yuppies. For many intellectuals who had matured during the radicalism of the 1960s and 1970s, these new developments brought unbearable disappointment. Parallels with the 1950s were evident. The collective and heroic narrative of socialism once again had died, and the end of ideology seemed once again to be at hand.

## POSTMODERNIZATION THEORY: RESIGNATION AND COMIC DETACHMENT

Postmodernism can be seen as an explanatory social theory that has produced new middle-range models of culture (Foucault, 1977; Huyssen, 1986; Lyotard, 1984), science and epistemology (Rorty, 1979), class (Hall, 1993), social action (Crespi,1992), gender and family relations (Halpern,1990; Seidman, 1991b), and economic life (Harvey, 1989; Lash, 1985). In each of these areas, and others, postmodern theories have made original contributions to the understanding of reality.[27] It is not as a theory of the middle range, however, that postmodernism has made its mark. These discussions have become significant only because they are taken to exemplify broad new trends of history, social structure, and moral life. Indeed, it is by intertwining the levels of structure and process, micro and macro, with strong assertions about the past, present, and future of contemporary life that postmodernism has formed a broad and inclusive general theory of society, one that, like the others I have considered here, must be considered in extrascientific terms, not only as an explanatory source.

If we consider postmodernism as myth—not merely as cognitive descriptions but as their coding and narration into a "meaningful" frame—we must deal with it as the successor ideology to radical social theory, animated by the failure of reality to unfold in a manner that was consistent with the expectations generated by that antimodernization creed. From this perspective, we can see that while postmodernism seems to be coming to grips with the present and future, its horizon is fixed by the past. It was initially (at least) an ideology of intellectual disappointment, Marxist and post-Marxist intellectuals articulated postmodernism in reaction to the fact that the period of heroic and collective radicalism seemed to be slipping away.[28] They redefined this exalted collective present, which had been held to presage an even more heroic imminent future, as a period that was now passed. They declared that it had been superseded not for reasons of political defeat but because of the structure of history itself.[29] The defeat of utopia had threatened a mythically incoherent possibility, namely that of historical retrogression. It threatened to undermine the meaning structures of intellectual life. With postmodern theory, this imminent defeat could be transformed into an immanent one, a necessity of historical development itself. The heroic "grand narratives" of the Left had merely been made irrelevant by history; they were not actually defeated. Myth could still function. Meaning was preserved.

The most influential early attributions of postmodernism were filled with frank revelations of theoretical perplexity, testimonies to dramatic shifts in reality, and expressions of existential despair.[30] Fredric Jameson (1988: 25), for example, identified a "new and virtually unimaginable quantum leap in technological alienation." Despite his methodological commitments, Jameson resists the impulse to fall back on the neo-Marxist certainties of the earlier age. Asserting that shifts in the productive base of society had created the superstructural confusions of a transitional time, he bemoaned "the incapacity of our minds, at least at present, to map the great global multinational and decentered communication network in which we find ourselves caught as individual subjects" (15). Referring to the traditional role of art as a vehicle for gaining cultural clarity, Jameson complained that this meaning-making reflex had been blocked: we are "unable to focus our own present, as though we have become incapable of achieving aesthetic representations of our own current experience" (20).[31]

Yet the intellectual meaning-making triumph of mature postmodernism is already visible in Jameson's depiction of this new order as privatized, fragmented, and commercial. With these terms, the perplexities and blockages of rationality that Jameson succeeded in articulating can be explained not as personal failure but as historical necessities based on reason itself. What threatened meaninglessness now becomes the very basis for meaning; what has been constructed is a new present and a new past. No wonder that Jameson described (1988: 15) postmodernism as first and foremost a "periodizing concept," suggesting that the term was created so that intellectuals and their audiences could make sense of these new times: "The new postmodernism expresses the inner truth of that newly emergent social order of late capitalism" (15).

Postmodern theory, then, may be seen, in rather precise terms, as an attempt to redress the problem of meaning created by the experienced failure of "the sixties." Only in this way can we understand why the very dichotomy between modern and postmodern was announced and why the contents of these new historical categories are described in the ways they are. From the perspective developed here, the answers seem clear enough. Continuity with the earlier period of antimodern radicalism is maintained by the fact that postmodernism, too, takes "the modern" as its explicit foe. In the binary coding of this intellectual ideology, modernity remains on the polluted side, representing "the other" in postmodernism's narrative tales.

Yet in this third phase of postwar social theory, the contents of the modern are completely changed. Radical intellectuals had emphasized the privacy and particularism of modern capitalism, its provinciality, and the fatalism and resignation it produced. The postmodernization alternative they posited was not postmodern but public, heroic, collective, and universal. It is precisely the latter qualities, of course, that postmodernization theory has condemned as the very embodiment of modernity itself. In contrast, it has coded privacy, diminished expectations, subjectivism, individuality, particularity, and localism as the embodiments of the good. As for narrative, the major historical propositions of postmodernism—the decline of the grand narrative and the return to the local (Lyotard, 1984),the rise of the empty symbol, or simulacrum (Baudrillard, 1983), the end of socialism (Gorz, 1982), the emphasis on plurality and difference (Seidman, 1991a, 1992)—are transparent representations of a deflationary narrative frame. They are responses to the decline of "progressive" ideologies and their utopian beliefs.

The resemblances to radical antimodernism, then, are superficial and misleading. In fact, there is a much more significant connection between postmodernism and the period that preceded radicalism, that is, modernization theory itself. Modernization theory, we recall, was itself a deflationary ideology following an earlier heroic period of radical quest. It, too, contained emphases on the private, the personal, and the local.

While these similarities reveal how misleading the intellectual self-representations of intellectual ideologies can be, it is obviously true that the two approaches differ in fundamental ways. These differences emerge from their positions in concrete historical time. The postwar liberalism that inspired modernization theory followed on a radical movement that understood transcendence within a progressivist frame, one that, while aiming to radicalize modernism hardly rejected it. Thus while the romantic and ironic dimensions of postwar liberalism deflated heroic modernism, its movement away from radicalism made central aspects of modernism even more accessible.

Postmodernism, by contrast, followed on a radical intellectual generation that had condemned not only liberal modernism but also key tenets of the very notion of modernization as such. The New Left rejected the Old Left in part because it was wedded to the modernization project; they preferred the Frankfurt School (e.g., Jay, 1973), whose roots in German Romanticism coincided more neatly with its own, antimodernist tone. While postmodernism, then, is indeed a deflationary narrative vis-à-vis heroic radicalism, the specificity of its historical position means that it must place both heroic (radical) and romantic (liberal) versions of the modern onto the same negative side. Successor intellectuals tend to invert the binary code of the previously hegemonic theory. For postmodernism, the new code, *modernism: postmodernism*, implied a larger break with "universalist" Western values than did the *traditionalism: modernism* of the immediate postwar period or the capitalist *modernism: socialist antimodernization* dichotomy that succeeded it.[32]

In narrative terms as well, there are much greater deflationary shifts. Although there remains, to be sure, a romantic tenor in some strands of postmodernist thought, and even collectivist arguments for heroic liberation, these "constructive" versions (Rosenau, 1992; Thompson, 1992) focus on the personal and the intimate and tend to be offshoots of social movements of the 1960s, for example gay and lesbian "struggles," the women's "movement," and the ecology activists like the Greens. Insofar as they do engage public policy, such movements articulate their demands much more in the language of difference and particularism (e.g., Seidman,1991a, 1992) than in the universalistic terms of the collective good. The principal and certainly the most distinctive thrust of the postmodern narrative, moreover, is strikingly different. Rejecting not only heroism but romanticism as well, it tends to be more fatalistic, critical, and resigned, in short more comically agnostic, than these more political movements of uplift and reform suggest. Rather than upholding the authenticity of the individual, postmodernism announced, via Foucault and Derrida, the death of the subject. In Jameson's (1988: 15) words, "the conception of a unique self and private identity is a thing of the past." Another departure from the earlier, more romantic version of modernism is the singular absence of irony. Rorty's political philosophy is a case in point. Because he espouses irony and complexity (e.g., Rorty, 1985, 1989), he maintains a political if not an epistemological liberalism, and because of these commitments he must distance himself from the postmodernist frame.

Instead of romance and irony, what has emerged full-blown in postmodernism is the comic frame. Frye calls comedy the ultimate equalizer. Because good and evil cannot be parsed, the actors—protagonists and antagonists—are on the same moral level, and the audience, rather than being normatively or emotionally involved, can sit back and be amused. Baudrillard (1983) is the master of satire and ridicule, as the entire Western world becomes Disneyland at large. In the postmodern comedy, indeed, the very notion of actors is eschewed. With tongue in cheek but a new theoretical system in his mind, Foucault announced the death of the subject, a theme that Jameson canonized with his announce-ment that "the conception of a unique self and private identity is a thing of the past." Postmodernism is the play within the play, a historical drama designed to convince its audiences that drama is dead and that history no longer exists. What remains is nostalgia for a symbolized past.

Perhaps I may end this discussion with a snapshot of Daniel Bell, the intellec-tual whose career neatly embodies each of the scientific-cum-mythical phases of history I have thus far described. Bell came to intellectual self-consciousness as a Trotskyist in the 1930s. For a time after World War II he remained in the heroic anticapitalist mode of figures like C. Wright Mills, whom he welcomed as a colleague at Columbia University. His famous essay on the assembly line and deskilled labor (1963 [1959]) demonstrated continuity with prewar leftist work. By insisting on the concept of alienation, Bell committed himself to "cap-italism" rather than "industrialism," thus championing epochal transformation and resisting the postwar modernization line. Soon, however, Bell made the transition to realism, advocating modernism in a more romantically individual-ist than radical socialist way. Although *The Coming of Post-Industrial Society* ap-peared only in 1973, Bell had introduced the concept as an extension of Aron's industrialization thesis nearly two decades before. Postindustrial was a peri-odization that supported progress, modernization, and reason while undermin-ing the possibilities for heroic transcendence and class conflict. Appearing in the midst of antimodernist rebellion, *The Coming of Post-Industrial Society* was re-viewed with perplexity and disdain by many intellectuals on the antimodernist left, although its oblique relationship with theories of postscarcity society were sometimes noted as well.

What is so striking about this phase of Bell's career, however, is how rapidly the modernist notion of postindustrial society gave way to postmodernism, in content if not explicit form. For Bell, of course, it was not disappointed radical-ism that produced this shift but his disappointments with what he came to call late modernism. When Bell turned away from this degenerate modernism in *The Cultural Contradictions of Capitalism* (1976), his story had changed. Post-industrial society, once the epitome of modernism, now produced not reason and progress but emotionalism and irrationalism, categories alarmingly embodied in sixties youth culture. Bell's solution to this imminent self-destruction of Western society was to advocate the return of the sacred (1977), a solution that exhibited the nostalgia for the past that Jameson would later diagnose as a cer-tain sign of the coming of the postmodern age.

The comparison of Bell's postindustrial argument with Harvey's post-Fordism (1989) is revealing in this regard. Harvey takes similar developments in the pro-ductive arrangements of high-information capitalism but draws a far different conclusion about their effects on the consciousness of the age. Bell's anti-Marxism—his (1978) emphasis on the asynchronicity of systems—allows him to posit rebellion in the form of youth culture and to posit cultural salvation in the ideal of "the sacred return" (see Eliade, 1954). Harvey's continued commitment to orthodox base-superstructure reasoning, by contrast, leads him to postulate fragmentation and privatization as inevitable, and unstoppable, results of the post-Fordist productive mode. Bell's conservative attack on modernism embraces nostalgia; Harvey's radical attack on postmodernism posits defeat.

Postmodern theory is still, of course, very much in the making. As I have already mentioned, its middle-range formulations contain significant truths. Evaluating the importance of its general theorizing, by contrast, depends on whether one places poststructuralism under its wing.[33] Certainly theorists of the strong linguistic turn—thinkers like Foucault, Bourdieu, Geertz, and Rorty—began to outline their understandings long before postmodernism appeared on the scene. Nevertheless, their emphasis on relativism and constructivism, their principled antagonism to an identification with the subject, and their skepticism regarding the possibility of totalizing change make their contributions more compatible with postmodernism than either modernism or radical antimodernization. Indeed, these theorists wrote in response to their disappointment with modernism (Geertz and Rorty vis-à-vis Parsons and Quine) on the one hand and heroic antimodernism (Foucault and Bourdieu vis-à-vis Althusser and Sartre) on the other. Nonetheless, Geertz and Bourdieu can scarcely be called postmodern theorists, and strong culturalist theories cannot be identified with the broad ideological sentiments that the term postmodernism implies.

I would maintain here, as I have earlier in this essay, that scientific considerations are insufficient to account for shifts either toward or away from an intellectual position. If, as I believe to be the case, the departure from postmodernism has already begun, we must look closely, once again, at extrascientific considerations, at recent events and social changes that seem to demand yet another new "world-historical frame."

## NEOMODERNISM: DRAMATIC INFLATION AND UNIVERSAL CATEGORIES

In postmodern theory, intellectuals have represented to themselves and to society at large their response to the defeat of the heroic utopias of radical social movements, a response that while recognizing defeat did not give up the cognitive reference to that utopic world. Every idea in postmodern thought is a reflection on the categories and false aspirations of the traditional collectivist narrative, and for most postmodernists the dystopia of the contemporary world is the semantic result. Yet while the hopes of leftist intellectuals were dashed by the late 1970s, the intellectual imagination of others was rekindled. For when the Left lost, the Right won and won big. In the 1960s and 1970s, the right was a backlash, reactive movement. By 1980 it had become triumphant and began to initiate far-reaching changes in Western societies. A fact that has been conveniently overlooked by each of the three intellectual generations I have considered thus far—and most grievously by the postmodernist movement that was historically coterminous with it—is that the victory of the neoliberal Right had, and continues to have, massive political, economic, and ideological repercussions around the globe.

The most striking "success" for the Right was, indeed, the defeat of communism, which was not only a political, military, and economic victory but, as I suggested in the introduction to this essay, also a triumph on the level of the historical imagination itself. Certainly there were objective economic elements in the bankruptcy of the Soviet Union, including growing technological deficiencies, sinking export proceeds, and the impossibility of finding desperately needed capital funds by switching to a strategy of internal growth (Muller, 1992: 139). Yet the final economic breakdown had a political cause, for it was the computer-based military expansion of America and its NATO allies, combined with the right-wing-inspired technology boycott, that brought the Soviet party dictatorship to its economic and political knees. While the lack of access to documents makes any definitive judgment decidedly premature, there seems no doubt that these policies were, in fact, among the principal strategic goals of the Reagan and Thatcher governments and that they were achieved with signal effect.[34]

This extraordinary, and almost completely unexpected triumph over what once seemed not only a socially but an intellectually plausible alternative world had the same kind of destabilizing, deontologizing effects on many intellectuals as the other massive historical "breaks" I have discussed earlier. It created, as well, the same sense of imminence and the conviction that the "new world" in the making (see Kumar, 1992) demands a new and very different kind of social theory.[35]

This negative triumph over state socialism was reinforced, morever, by the dramatic series of "positive successes" during the 1980s of aggressively capitalist market economies. This was most often remarked on (most recently by Kennedy, 1993) in connection with the newly industrialized, extraordinarily dynamic Asian economies that arose in what was once called the third world. It is important not to underestimate the ideological effects of this world-historical fact: high-level, sustainable transformations of backward economies were achieved not by socialist command economies but by zealously capitalist states.

What has often been overlooked, however, is that during this same time frame the capitalist market was also reinvigorated, both symbolically and objectively, in the capitalist West. This transpired not only in Thatcherite Britain and Reaganite America but perhaps even more dramatically in the more "progressive" and state-interventionist regimes like France and, subsequently, in countries like Italy, Spain, and Scandinavia itself. There was not only, in other words, the ideologically portentous bankruptcy of most of the world's communist economies but also the marked privatization of nationalized capitalist economies in both authoritarian-corporatist and socialist-democratic states. Clinton's centrist liberalism, British New Labour, and the movement of German social democrats toward the market similarly marked the new vitality of capitalism for egalitarian ideology. In the late 1960s and 1970s, the intellectual successors to modernization theory, neo-Marxists like Baran and Sweezy (1966) and Mandel (1968), announced the imminent stagnation of capitalist economies and an inevitably declining rate of profit.[36] History has proved them wrong, with far-reaching ideological results (Chirot, 1990).

"Rightward" developments on the more specifically political plane have been as far-reaching as those on the economic. As I mentioned earlier, during the late 1960s and 1970s it had become ideologically fashionable, and empirically justifiable, to accept political authoritarianism as the price of economic development. In the last two decades, however, events on the ground seem to have challenged this view, and a radical reversal of conventional wisdom is now underway. It is not only communist tyrannies that have opened up since the mid-1980s but the very Latin American dictatorships that seemed so "objectively necessary" only an intellectual generation before. Even some African dictatorships have recently begun to show signs of vulnerability to this shift in political discourse from authoritarianism to democracy.

These developments have created social conditions—and mass public sentiment—that would seem to belie the postmodern intellectuals' coding of contemporary (and future) society as fatalistic, private, particularistic, fragmented, and local. They also would appear to undermine the deflated narrative frame of postmodernism, which has insisted either on the romance of difference or, more fundamentally, on the idea that contemporary life can only be interpreted in a comic way. Indeed, if we look closely at recent intellectual discourse, we can observe a return to many earlier modernist themes.

Because the recent revivals of market and democracy have occurred on a worldwide scale and because they are categorically abstract and generalizing ideas, universalism has once again become a viable source for social theory. Notions of commonality and institutional convergence have reemerged and with them the possibilities for intellectuals to provide meaning in a utopian way.[37] It seems, in fact, that we have been witness to the birth of a fourth postwar version of myothopoeic social thought. "Neomodernism" (see Tiryakian, 1991) will serve as a rough-and-ready characterization of this phase of postmodernization theory until a term appears that represents the new spirit of the times in a more imaginative way.

In response to economic developments, different groupings of contemporary intellectuals have reinflated the emancipatory narrative of the market, in which they inscribe a new past (antimarket society) and a new present/future (market transition, full-blown capitalism) that makes liberation dependent on privatization, contracts, monetary inequality, and competition. On one side a much enlarged and more activist breed of intellectual conservatives has emerged. Although their policy and political concerns have not, as yet, greatly affected the discourse of general social theory, there are exceptions that indicate the potential is there. James Coleman's massive *Foundations of Social Theory* (1990), for example, has a self-consciously heroic cast; it aims to make neomarket, rational choice the basis not only for future theoretical work but for the re-creation of a more responsive, law-abiding, and less degraded social life.

Much more significant is the fact that within liberal intellectual life, among the older generation of disillusioned utopians and the younger intellectual groups as well, a new and positive social theory of markets has reappeared. For many politically engaged intellectuals, too, this has taken the theoretical form of the individualistic, quasi-romantic frame of rational choice. Employed initially to deal with the disappointing failures of working-class consciousness (e.g., Przeworski, 1985; Wright, 1985; see Elster, 1989), it has increasingly served to explain how state communism, and capitalist corporatism, can be transformed into a market-oriented system that is liberating, or at least substantively rational (Moene & Wallerstein, 1992; Nee, 1989; Przeworski, 1991). While other politically engaged intellectuals have appropriated market ideas in less restrictive and more collectivist ways (e.g., Blackburn, 1991b; Friedland & Robertson, 1990; Szelenyi, 1988), their writings, too, betray an enthusiasm for market processes that is markedly different from the attitude of the left-leaning intellectuals of earlier times. Among the intellectual advocates of "market socialism" there has been a similar change. Kornai (1990), for example, has expressed distinctly fewer reservations about free markets in his more recent writings than in the pathbreaking works of the 1970s and 1980s that brought him to fame.

This neomodern revival of market theory is also manifest in the rebirth and redefinition of economic sociology. In terms of research program, Granovetter's (1974) earlier celebration of the strengths of the market's "weak ties" has become a dominant paradigm for studying economic networks (e.g., Powell, 1991), one that implicitly rejects postmodern and antimodern pleas for strong ties and local communities. His later argument for the "imbeddedness" (1985) of economic action has transformed (e.g., Granovetter & Swedberg, 1992) the image of the market into a social and interactional relationship that has little resemblance to the deracinated, capitalist exploiter of the past. Similar transformations can be seen in more generalized discourse. Adam Smith has been undergoing an intellectual rehabilitation (Boltanski, 1999: 35–95; Boltanski & Thevenot, 1991: 60–84; Hall, 1985; Heilbroner, 1986). Schumpeter's "market realism" has been revived; the individualism of Weber's marginalist economics has been celebrated (Holton & Turner, 1986); and so has the market acceptance that permeates Parsons's theoretical work (Holton, 1992; Holton & Turner, 1986).

In the political realm, neomodernism has emerged in an even more powerful way, as a result, no doubt, of the fact that it has been the political revolutions of the last decade that have reintroduced narrative in a truly heroic form (contra

Kumar, 1992: 316) and challenged the postmodern deflation in the most direct way. The movements away from dictatorship, motivated in practice by the most variegated of concerns, were articulated mythically as a vast, unfolding "drama of democracy" (Sherwood, 1994), literally as an opening up of the spirit of humanity. The melodrama of social good triumphing, or almost triumphing, over social evil—which Peter Brooks (1984) placed at the roots of the nineteenth-century narrative form—populated the symbolic canvas of the late twentieth-century West with heroes and conquests of truly world-historical scope. This drama started with the epochal struggle of Lech Walesa and what seemed to be virtually the entire Polish nation (Tiryakian, 1988) against Poland's coercive party-state. The day-to-day dramaturgy that captured the public imagination ended initially in Solidarity's inexplicable defeat. Eventually, however, good did triumph over evil, and the dramatic symmetry of the heroic narrative was complete. Mikhail Gorbachev began his long march through the Western dramatic imagination in 1984. His increasingly loyal worldwide audience fiercely followed his epochal struggles in what eventually became the longest-running public drama in the postwar period. This grand narrative produced cathartic reactions in its audience, which the press called "Gorbymania" and Durkheim would have labeled the collective effervescence that only symbols of the sacred inspire. This drama was reprised in what the mass publics, media, and elites of Western countries construed as the equally heroic achievements of Nelson Mandela and Václav Havel, and later Boris Yeltsin, the tank-stopping hero who succeeded Gorbachev in Russia's postcommunist phase. Similar experiences of exaltation and renewed faith in the moral efficacy of democratic revolution were produced by the social drama that took place in 1989 in Tiananmen Square, with its strong ritualistic overtones (Chan, 1994) and its classically tragic denouement.

It would be astonishing if this reinflation of mass political drama did not manifest itself in equally marked shifts in intellectual theorizing about politics. In fact, in a manner that parallels the rise of the "market," there has been the powerful reemergence of theorizing about democracy. Liberal ideas about political life, which emerged in the eighteenth and nineteenth centuries and were displaced by the "social question" of the great industrial transformation, seem like contemporary ideas again. Dismissed as historically anachronistic in the anti- and postmodern decades, they became quite suddenly à la mode.

The reemergence took the form of the revival of the concept of "civil society," the informal, nonstate, and noneconomic realm of public and personal life that Tocqueville defined as vital to the maintenance of the democratic state. Rising initially from within the intellectual debates that helped spark the social struggles against authoritarianism in eastern Europe (see Cohen & Arato, 1992) and Latin America (Stepan, 1985), the term was "secularized" and given more abstract and more universal meaning by American and European intellectuals connected with these movements, like Cohen and Arato (1992) and Keane (1988a,

1988b). They utilized the concept to begin theorizing in a manner that sharply demarcated their own "left" theorizing from the antimodernization, antiformal democracy writings of an earlier day.

Stimulated by these writers and also by the English translation (1989 [1962]) of Habermas's early book on the bourgeois public sphere, debates about pluralism, fragmentation, differentiation, and participation became the new order of the day. Frankfurt theorists, Marxist social historians, and even some postmodernists became democratic theorists under the sign of the "public sphere"(see, e.g., the essays by Moishe Postone, Mary P. Ryan, and Geoff Eley in Calhoun [1993] and the more recent writings of Held, e.g. 1987).[38] Communitarian and internalist political philosophers, like Walzer (1992a, 1992b), took up the concept to clarify the universalist yet nonabstract dimensions in their theorizing about the good. For conservative social theorists (e.g., Banfield, 1991; Shils, 1991a, 1991b; Wilson, 1991), civil society is a concept that implies civility and harmony. For neofunctionalists (e.g., Mayhew, 1990; Sciulli, 1990), it is an idea that denotes the possibility of theorizing conflicts over equality and inclusion in a less anticapitalist way. For old functionalists (e.g., Inkeles, 1991), it is an idea that suggests that formal democracy has been a requisite for modernization all along.

But whatever the particular perspective that has framed this new political idea, its neomodern status is plain to see. Theorizing in this manner suggests that contemporary societies either possess, or must aspire to, not only an economic market but a distinctive political zone, an institutional field of universal if contested domain (Touraine, 1994). It provides a common empirical point of reference, which implies a familiar coding of citizen and enemy and allows history to be narrated, once again, in a teleological manner that gives the drama of democracy full force.

## NEOMODERNISM AND SOCIAL EVIL: POLLUTING NATIONALISM

This problem of the demarcation of civil as opposed to uncivil society points to issues that go beyond the narrating and explanatory frameworks of neomodern theory that I have described thus far. Romantic and heroic narratives that describe the triumph, or possible triumph, of markets and democracies have a reassuringly familiar form. When we turn to the binary coding of this emerging historical period, however, certain problems arise. Given the resurgence of universalism, of course, one can be confident that what is involved is a specification of the master code, described earlier as the discourse of civil society. Yet while this almost archetypical symbolization of the requisites and antonyms of democracy establishes general categories, historically specific "social representations" (Moscovici, 1984) must also be developed to articulate the concrete categories of good and evil in a particular time and place. In regard to these secondary elaborations, what strikes one is how difficult it has been to develop a set of binary categories that is semantically and socially compelling, a black-versus-white contrast that can function as a successor code to the *postmodern: modern* or, for that matter, the *socialist: capitalist* and *modern: traditional* symbolic sets that were established by earlier intellectual generations and that by no means have entirely lost their efficacy today.

To be sure, the symbolization of the good does not present a real problem. Democracy and universalism are key terms, and their more substantive embodiments are the free market, individualism, and human rights. The problem comes in establishing the profane side. The abstract qualities that pollution must embody are obvious enough. Because they are produced by the principle of difference, they closely resemble the qualities that were opposed to modernization in the postwar period, qualities that identified the polluting nature of "traditional" life. But despite the logical similarities, earlier ideological formulations cannot simply be taken up again. Even if they effectuate themselves only through differences in second-order representations, the distances between present-day society and the immediate postwar period are enormous.

Faced with the rapid onrush of "markets" and "democracy" and the rapid collapse of their opposites, it has proven difficult to formulate equally universal and far-reaching representations of the profane. The question is this: Is there an oppositional movement or geopolitical force that is a convincingly and fundamentally dangerous—that is a "world-historical"—threat to the "good"? The once powerful enemies of universalism seemed to be historical relics, out of sight and out of mind, laid low by a historical drama that seems unlikely soon to be reversed. It was for this semantic reason that, in the interim period after "1989," many intellectuals, and certainly broad sections of Western publics, experienced a strange combination of optimism and self-satisfaction without an energetic commitment to any particular moral repair.

In comparison with the modernization theory of the postwar years, neomodern theory involves fundamental shifts in both symbolic time and symbolic space. In neomodern theory, the profane can neither be represented by an evolutionarily preceding period of traditionalism nor identified with the world outside of North America and Europe. In contrast with the postwar modernization wave, the current one is global and international rather than regional and imperial, a difference articulated in social science by the contrast between early theories of dependency (Frank, 1966) and more contemporary theories of globalization (Robertson, 1992). The social and economic reasons for this change center on the rise of Japan, which this time around has gained power not as one of Spencer's military societies—a category that could be labeled backward in an evolutionary sense—but as a civilized commercial society.

Thus, for the first time in five hundred years (see Kennedy, 1987; Huntington 1996), it is becoming impossible for the West to dominate Asia, either economically or culturally. When this objective factor is combined with the pervasive de-Christianization of Western intellectuals, we can understand the remarkable fact that "orientalism"—the symbolic pollution of Eastern civilization that Said (1978) articulated so tellingly scarcely two decades ago—seems no longer to be a forceful spatial or temporal representation in Western ideology or social theory, although it has by no means entirely disappeared.[39] A social scientific translation of this ideological fact, which points the way to a postpostmodern, or neomodern, code is Eisenstadt's (1987: vii) call for "a far-reaching reformulation of the vision of modernization, and of modern civilizations." While continuing to code the modern in an overly positive way, this conceptualization explains it not as the end of an evolutionary sequence but as a highly successfully globalizing movement.

> Instead of perceiving modernization as the final stage in the fulfillment of the evolutionary potential common to all societies—of which the European experience was the most important and succinct manifestation and paradigm— modernization (or modernity) should be viewed as one specific civilization or phenomenon. Originating in Europe, it has spread in its economic, political and ideological aspects all over the world. . . . The crystallization of this new type of civilization was not unlike the spread of the great religions, or the great imperial expansions, but because modernization almost always combined economic, political, and ideological aspects and forces, its impact was by far the greatest. (vii)

Original modernization theory transformed Weber's overtly Western-centric theory of world religions into a universal account of global change that still culminated in the social structure and culture of the postwar Western world. Eisenstadt proposes to make modernization itself the historical equivalent of a world religion, which relativizes it on the one hand and suggests the possibility of selective indigenous appropriation (Hannerz, 1987, 1989) on the other.

The other side of this decline of orientalism among Western theorists is what seems to be the dimunition of "third world-ism"—what might be called occidentalism—from the vocabulary of intellectuals who speak from within, or on behalf of, developing countries. One indication of this discursive shift can be found in an opinion piece that Edward Said published in the *New York Times* protesting the imminent allied air war against Iraq in early 1991. While reiterating the familiar characterization of American policy toward Iraq as the result of an "imperialist ideology," Said justified his opposition not by pointing to the distinctive worth of national or political ideology but by upholding universality: "A new world order has to be based on authentically general principles, not on the selectively applied might of one country" (Said, 1991). More significant, Said denounced the Iraqi president Saddam Hussein and the "Arab world," representing them in particularizing categories that polluted them as the enemies of universalism itself.

The traditional discourse of Arab nationalism, to say nothing of the quite decrepit state system, is inexact, unresponsive, anomalous, even comic. . . .
Today's Arab media are a disgrace. It is difficult to speak the plain truth in the Arab world. . . . Rarely does one find rational analysis—reliable statistics, concrete and undoctored descriptions of the Arab world today with its . . . crushing mediocrity in science and many cultural fields. Allegory, complicated symbolism and innuendo substitute for common sense.

When Said concludes that there appears to be a "remorseless Arab propensity to violence and extremism," he suggests the end of occidentalism. If anything, this trend has deepened with the post–September 11 "war" on terrorism, in which intellectuals from East and West have made elaborate efforts—contra Huntington (1996)—to represent the action as a defense of universalism and to separate it from the orientalist bias of modernist thought.

Because the contemporary recoding of the antithesis of universalism can be geographically represented neither as non-Western nor as temporally located in an earlier time, the social sacred of neomodernism cannot, paradoxically, be represented as "modernization." In the ideological discourse of contemporary intellectuals, it would seem almost as difficult to employ this term as it is to identify the good with "socialism." Not modernization but democratization, not the modern but the market—these are the terms that the new social movements of the neomodern period employ. These difficulties in representation help to explain the new saliency of supranational, international organizations (Thomas & Lauderdale, 1988), a salience that points, in turn, to elements of what the long-term representation of a viable ideological antinomy might be. For many critically placed European and American intellectuals (e.g., Held, 1995), the United Nations and European Community have taken on new legitimacy and reference, providing institutional manifestations of the new universalism that transcend earlier great divides.

The logic of these telling institutional and cultural shifts is that "nationalism"—not traditionalism, communism, or the "East"—is coming to represent the principal challenge to the newly universalized discourse of the good. *Nationalism* is the name intellectuals and publics are now increasingly giving to the negative antinomies of civil society. The categories of the "irrational," "conspiratorial," and "repressive" are taken to be synonymous with forceful expressions of nationality and equated with primordiality and uncivilized social forms. That civil societies have always themselves taken a national form is being conveniently neglected, along with the continuing nationalism of many democratic movements themselves.[40] It is true, of course, that in the geopolitical world that has so suddenly been re-formed, it is the social movements and armed rebellions for national self-determination that trigger military conflicts that can engender large-scale wars (Snyder, 2000).

Is it any wonder, then, that nationalism came to be portrayed as the successor of communism, not only in the semantic but in the organizational sense? This equation is made by high intellectuals, not only in the popular press. "Far from extinguishing nationalism," Liah Greenfeld (1992) wrote in the *New Republic,* "communism perpetuated and reinforced the old nationalist values. And the intelligentsia committed to these values is now turning on the democratic regime it inadvertently helped to create." It does not seem surprising that some of the most promising younger generation of social scientitsts have shifted from concerns with modernization, critical theory, and citizenship to issues of identity and nationalism. In addition to Greenfeld, one might note the new work of Rogers Brubaker, whose studies of central European and Russian nationalism (e.g., Brubaker, 1994) make similar links between Soviet communism and contemporary nationalism and whose current pessimistic interests in nationalism seems to have displaced an earlier preoccupation with citizenship and democracy (see Calhoun, 1993).

In winter 1994, *Theory and Society,* a bellwether of intellectual currents in Western social theory, devoted a special issue to nationalism. In their introduction to the symposium, Comaroff and Stern make particularly vivid the link between nationalism-as-pollution and nationalism-as-object-of-social-science.

> Nowhere have the signs of the quickening of contemporary history, of our misunderstanding and misprediction of the present, been more clearly expressed than in the . . . assertive renaissance of nationalisms. . . . World events over the past few years have thrown a particularly sharp light on the darker, more dangerous sides of nationalism and claims to sovereign identity. And, in so doing, they have revealed how tenuous is our grasp of the phenomenon. Not only have these events confounded the unsuspecting world of scholarship. They have also shown a long heritage of social theory and prognostication to be flatly wrong. (Comaroff & Stern, 1994: 35)

While these theorists do not, of course, deconstruct their empirical argument by explicitly relating it to the rise of a new phase of myth and science, it is noteworthy that they do insist on linking the new understanding of nationalism to the rejection of Marxism, modernization theory, and postmodern thought (35–7). In their own contribution to this special revival issue, Greenfeld and Chirot insist on the fundamental antithesis between democracy and nationalism in the strongest terms. After discussing Russia, Germany, Romania, Syria, Iraq, and the Cambodian Khmer Rouge, they write:

> The cases we discuss here show that the association between certain types of nationalism and aggressive, brutal behavior is neither coincidental nor inexplicable. Nationalism remains the world's most powerful, general, and primordial basis of cultural and political identity. Its range is still growing, not diminishing, throughout the world. And in most places, it does not take an individualistic or civic form. (Greenfeld & Chirot, 1994: 123)

The new social representation of nationalism and pollution, based on the symbolic analogy with communism, has also permeated the popular press. Serbia's expansionist military adventures provided a crucial field of collective representation. See, for example, the categorial relationships established in this editorial from the *New York Times:*

> Communism can pass easily into nationalism. The two creeds have much in common. Each offers a simple key to tangled problems. One exalts class, the other ethnic kinship. Each blames real grievances on imagined enemies. As a Russian informant shrewdly remarked to David Shipler in *The New Yorker:* "They are both ideologies that liberate people from personal responsibility. They are united around some sacred [read profane] goal." In varying degrees and with different results, old Bolsheviks have become new nationalists in Serbia and many former Soviet republics.

The *Times* editorial writer further codes the historical actors by analogizing the 1990s breakup of Czechoslovakia to the kind of virulent nationalism that followed on the First World War.

> And now the same phenomenon has surfaced In Czechoslovakia. . . . There is a . . . moral danger, described long ago by Thomas Masaryk, the founding president of Czechoslovakia, whose own nationalism was joined inseparably to belief in democracy. "Chauvinism is nowhere justified," he wrote in 1927, "least of all in our country. . . . To a positive nationalism, one that seeks to raise a nation by intensive work, none can demur. Chauvinism, racial or national intolerance, not love of one's own people, is the foe of nations and of humanity." Masaryk's words are a good standard for judging tolerance on both sides. (June 16, 1992: reprinted in the *International Herald Tribune*)

The analogy between nationalism and communism, and their pollution as threats to the new internationalism, is even made by government officials of formerly communist states. For example, in late September 1992, Andrei Kozyrev, Russia's foreign minister, appealed to the United Nations to consider setting up international trusteeships to oversee the move to independence by former Soviet non-Slavic republics. Only a UN connection, he argued, could prevent the newly independent states from discriminating against national minorities. The symbolic crux of his argument is the analogy between two categories of pollution. "Previously, victims of totalitarian regimes and ideologies needed protection," Kozyrev told the UN General Assembly. "Today, ever more often one needs to counter aggressive nationalism that emerges as a new global threat."[41]

Since the murder and social havoc wreaked by Al Qaeda in New York City on September 11, 2001, this already strenuous effort to symbolize the darkness that threatens neo-modern hopes has become even more intense. "Terror" has become the ultimate, highly generalized negative quality. It is not only associated with anticivil murder but with religious fundamentalism, which in the wake of the tragedy has displaced nationalism as representing the essence of antimodernity. *Terror* was a term that postwar modern employed to represent the facist and communist others against which it promised relief. Fundamentalism, however, is new. Religiosity was not associated with totalitarianism. But is it fundamentalism per se or only Islamic versions that are employed to mark the current alternative to civil society? Is terrorism such a broad negative that militant movements against antidemocratic, even murderous regimes will be polluted in turn? Will opposing "terrorism" and "fundamentalism" make the neomodern vulnerable to the conservatism and chauvinism of modernization theory in its earlier form? (Alexander, forthcoming).

## MODERNIZATION REDUX? THE HUBRIS OF LINEARITY

In 1982, when Anthony Giddens confidently asserted that "modernization theory is based upon false premises" (144), he was merely reiterating the common social scientific sense of the day, or at least his generation's version of it. When he added that the theory had "served . . . as an ideological defense of the dominance of Western capitalism over the rest of the world," he reproduced the common understanding of why this false theory had once been believed. Today both these sentiments seem anachronistic. Modernization theory (e.g., Parsons, 1964) stipulated that the great civilizations of the world would converge toward the institutional and cultural configurations of Western society. Certainly we are witnessing something very much like this process today, and the enthusiasm it has generated cannot be explained simply by citing Western or capitalist domination.

The sweeping ideological and objective transformations described in the preceding section have begun to have their theoretical effect. The gauntlet that the various strands of neomodernism have thrown at the feet of postmodern theory are plain to see. Shifting historical conditions have created fertile ground for such post-postmodern theorizing, and intellectuals have responded to these conditions by revising their earlier theories in far-reaching ways. Certainly, it would be premature to call neomodernism a "successor theory" to postmodernism. It has only recently become crystallized as an intellectual alternative, much less emerged as the victor in this ideological-cum-theoretical fight. It is unclear, further, whether the movement is nourished by a new generation of intellectuals or by fragments of currently competing generations who have found in neomodernism a unifying vehicle to dispute the postmodern hegemony over the contemporary field. Despite these qualifications, however, it must be acknowledged that a new and very different current of social theorizing has emerged on the scene.

With this success, however, there comes the grave danger of theoretical amnesia about the problems of the past, problems that I have alluded to in my brief discussion of September 11. Retrospective verifications of modernization theory have begun in earnest. One of the most acute reappraisals was written by Muller (1992), who offered fulsome praise for the once-disgraced perspective even while suggesting that any current version must be fundamentally revised (see Muller, 1994). "With an apparently more acute sense of reality," Muller (1992: 111) writes, "the sociological theory of modernity had recorded the long-term developments within the Eastern European area, currently taking place in a more condensed form, long before they were empirically verifiable." Muller adds, for good measure, that "the *grand theory* constantly accused of lacking contact with reality seemingly proves to possess predictive capacity—the classical sociological modernization theory of Talcott Parsons" (111, italics in original). Another sign of this reappraisal can be found in the return to modernization theory made by distinguished theorists who were once neo-Marxist critics of capitalist society. Bryan Turner (1986), for example, now defends Western citizenship against radical egalitarianism and lauds (Holton & Turner, 1986) Parsons for his "antinostalgic" acceptance of the basic structures of modern life. While Giddens's (1990, 1991, 1992) position is more ambiguous, his later work reveals an unacknowledged yet decisive departure from the conspicuously antimodernization stance that marked his earlier ideas. A portentous tone of crisis frames this new work, which Giddens conspicuosly anchors in the abrupt emergence of social developments that in his view could not have been foreseen.

> In the social sciences today, as in the social world itself, we face a new agenda. We live, as everyone knows, at a time of endings . . . *Fin de siècle* has become widely identified with feelings of disorientation and malaise . . . We are in a period of evident transition—and the "we" here refers not only to the West but to the world as a whole. (Giddens, 1994: 56; see Beck, 1994: 1, Lash, 1994: 110)

The new and historically unprecedented world that Giddens discovers—the world he came eventually to characterize as "beyond left and right"—however, turns out to be nothing other than modernity itself. Even among former communist apparatchiks themselves, there is growing evidence (i.e., Borko, cited in Muller, 1992: 112) that similar "retrodictions" about the convergence of capitalist and communist societies are well underway, tendencies that have caused a growing number of "revisits" to Schumpeter as well.

The theoretical danger here is that this enthusiastic and long overdue reappreciation of some of the central thrusts of postwar social science might actually lead to the revival of convergence and modernization theories in their earlier forms. In his reflections on the recent transitions in eastern Europe, Habermas (1990: 4) employed such evolutionary phrases as "rewinding the reel" and "rectifying revolution." Inkeles's (1991) tractatus to American policy agencies is replete with such convergence homilies as that a political "party should not seek to advance its objectives by extrapolitical means." Sprinkled with advice about "the importance of locating . . . the distinctive point where additional resources can provide greatest leverage" (69), his article displays the kind of over-confidence in controlled social change that marked the hubris of postwar modernization thought. When Lipset (1990) claims the lesson of the second great transition as the failure of the "middle way" between capitalism and socialism, he is no doubt correct in an important sense, but the formulation runs the danger of reinforcing the tendentious, either/or dichotomies of earlier thinking in a manner that could justify not only narrow self-congratulation but unjustified optimism about imminent social change. Jeffrey Sachs and other simpliste expositors of the "big bang" approach to transition seemed to be advocating a rerun of Rostow's earlier "takeoff" theory. Like that earlier species of modernization idea, this new monetarist modernism throws concerns of social solidarity and citizenship, let alone any sense of historical specificity, utterly to the winds (see Leijonhofvud [1993] and the perceptive comments by Muller, 1994: 17–27).

Giddens's enthusiastic return to the theory of modernity provides the most elaborate case in point. Despite the qualifying adjectives he employs to differentiate his new approach from the theories he once rejected—he speaks at different points of "high," "late," and "reflexive" modernity—his model rests on the same simplistic set of binary oppositions as did earlier modernization theory in its most banal forms. Giddens (1994a: 63–5, 79, 84, 104–5) insists on a clear-cut and decisive polarity between traditional and modern life. "Traditional order," he claims, rests on "formulaic notions of truth," which conflate "moral and emotional" elements, and on "ritual practices," organized by "guardians" with unchallengeable power. These beliefs and practices, he declares, create a "status"-based, "insider/outsider" society. By contrast, in the period of "reflexive modernity" everything is different. Ritual is displaced by "real" and "pragmatic" action, formulaic ideas by "propositional" ones, guardians by "skeptical" experts, and status by "competence."

From this familiar conceptual binarism there follows the equally familiar empirical conclusion; tradition, Giddens discovers, has been completely "evacuated" from the contemporary phase of social life. To provide some distance from earlier postwar theory, Giddens suggests that these earlier versions were naive; they had not realized that their own period, which they took to be thoroughly modern, actually remained firmly rooted in the past –"for most of its history, modernity has rebuilt tradition as it has dissolved" (1994a: 56; see Beck, 1994: 2). What Giddens has really done, however, is to historicize the present by invoking the alternatives of modernization theory in an even more arbitrary way. Indeed, his renewal of the tradition/modern divide is much more reductive than the complex and nuanced, if ultimately contradictory, arguments that emerged from within classical modernization theory in its terminal phase, arguments about which Giddens seems completely unaware. Nor does Giddens appear to have learned anything from the debates that so successfully persuaded postmodernization intellectuals to abandon the historically arbitrary, Western-centered, and theoretically tendentious approach to tradition he now takes up. Only by ignoring the implications of the linguistic turn, for example, can he conceive modernity in such an individualistic and pragmatic way (see Lash's [1994] similar criticism). Finally, Giddens's version of neomodernism is impoverished in an ideological and moral sense. The problem is not only that he fails to provide a compelling alternative vision of social life—a failure rooted in the forced-choice nature of the binary categories themselves—but also that his arguments give credence to the "end of ideology" argument in a new way. In the face of the changes wrought by reflexive modernization, Giddens suggests (1994b), the very difference between reformism and conservatism has become passé. Contemporary empirical developments demonstrate not only that politics must go beyond the traditional alternatives of capitalism and socialism but beyond the very notions of "left" and "right." Such is the intellectual amnesia that the new historical disjuncture has produced and on which its continued misunderstanding depends.

While many of the recent social scientific formulations of market and democracy avoid such egregious distortions, the universalism of their categories, the heroism of their zeitgeist, and the dichotomous strictures of their codes make the underlying problems difficult to avoid. Theories of market transition sometimes suggest a linearity and rationality that historical experience belies. Civil society theory too often seems unable to theorize empirically the demonic, anti-civil forces of cultural life (see Sztompka, 1991).

If there is to be a new and more successful effort at constructing a social theory about the fundamentally shared structures of contemporary societies (see Sztompka, 1993: 136–41), it will have to avoid these tendencies, which resurrect modernization ideas in their simplistic form. Institutional structures like democracy, law, and market are institutional requisites if certain social competencies are to be achieved and certain resources to be acquired. They are not, however, either historical inevitabilities or linear outcomes; nor are they social panaceas for the problems of noneconomic subsystems or groups (see, e.g., Rueschemeyer, 1993). Social and cultural differentiation may be an ideal-typical pattern that can be analytically reconstructed over time; however, whether or not any particular differentiation occurs—market, state, law, or science—depends on the normative aspirations (e.g., Sztompka, 1991), strategic position, history, and powers of particular social groups.

No matter how socially progressive in itself, moreover, differentiation displaces as much as it resolves and can create social upheaval on an enormous scale. Social systems may well be pluralistic and the causes of change multidimensional; at any given time and in any given place, however, a particular subsystem and the group that directs it—economic, political, scientific, or religious—may successfully dominate and submerge the others in its name. Globalization is, indeed, a dialectic of indigenization and cosmopolitanism, but cultural and political asymmetries remain between more and less developed regions, even if they are not inherent contradictions of some imperialistic fact. While the analytic concept of civil society must by all means be recovered from the heroic age of democratic revolutions, it should be deidealized so that the effects of "anticivil society"—the countervailing processes of decivilization, polarization, and violence—can be seen also as typically "modern" results. Finally, these new theories must be pushed to maintain a decentered, self-conscious reflexivity about their ideological dimensions even while they continue in their efforts to create a new explanatory scientific theory. For only if they become aware of themselves as moral constructions—as codes and as narratives—will they be able to avoid the totalizing conceit that gave early modernizing theory its bad name. In this sense, "neo-" must incorporate the linguistic turn associated with "post-" modern theory, even while it challenges its ideological and more broadly theoretical thrust.

In one of his last and most profound theoretical meditations, François Bourricaud (1987: 19–21) suggested that "one way of defining modernity is the way in which we define solidarity." The notion of modernity can be defended, Bourricaud believed, if rather than "identify[ing] solidarity with equivalence" we understand that the "general spirit" is both "universal and particular." Within a group, a generalizing spirit "is universal, since it regulates the intercourse among members of the group." Yet if one thinks of the relations between nations, this spirit "is also particular, since it helps distinguish one group from all others." In this way, it might be said that 'the "general spirit of a nation" assures the solidarity of individuals, without necessarily abolishing all their differences, and even establishing the full legitimacy of some of them. What of the concept of universalism? Perhaps, Bourricaud suggested, "modern societies are characterized less by what they have in common or by their structure with regard to well-defined universal exigencies, than by the fact of their involvement in the issue of universalization" as such.

Perhaps it is wise to acknowledge that it is a renewed sense of involvement in the project of universalism rather than some lipid sense of its concrete forms that marks the character of the new age in which we live. Beneath this new layer of the social topsoil, moreover, lie the tangled roots and richly marbled subsoil of earlier intellectual generations, whose ideologies and theories have not ceased to be alive. The struggles between these interlocutors can be intimidating and confusing, not only because of the intrinsic difficulty of their message but because each presents itself not as form but as essence, not as the only language in which the world makes sense but as the only real sense of the world. Each of these worlds does make sense, but only in a historically bounded way. A new social world is coming into being. We must try to make sense of it. For the task of intellectuals is not only to explain the world; they must interpret it as well.

# NOTES

<br>

*Chapter 1.*

1. Alexander (1996a) posited this dichotomy. This chapter builds on that earlier work.

2. Here lies the fundamental difference between a cultural sociology and the more instrumental and pragmatic approach to culture of the new institutionalism, whose emphasis on institutional isomorphism and legitimation would otherwise seem to place it firmly in the cultural tradition. See the forceful critique of this perspective "from within" by Friedland and Alford (1991).

3. It is unfortunate that the connection between Geertz and Dilthey has never been understood, since it has made Geertz seem "without a home" philosophically, a position his later antitheoreticism seems to welcome (see Alexander, 1987, 316–29).

4. Smith (1998a) makes this point emphatically in his distinction between American and European versions of cultural sociology.

5. It is ironic that in an article published the year before *Communities of Discourse,* Wuthnow (1988) had begun working toward this precise point, suggesting that differences between fundamentalist and liberal religious discourses should be understood as expressions of divergent structural logics rather than as situated ideologies.

<br>

*Chapter 2.*

1. In the inaugural conference of the United States Holocaust Research Institute, the Israeli historian Yehuda Bauer made a critical observation and posted a fundamental question to the opening session.

> About two decades ago, Professor Robert Alter of California published a piece in *Commentary* that argued that we had had enough of the Holocaust, that a concentration of Jewish intellectual and emotional efforts around it was counterproductive, that the Holocaust should always be remembered, but that there were new agendas that to be confronted. . . . Elie Wiesel has expressed the view that with the passing on of the generation of Holocaust survivors, the Holocaust may be forgotten. . . . But the memory is not

going away; on the contrary, the Holocaust has become a cultural code, a symbol of evil in Western civilization. Why should this be so? There are other genocides: Hutu and Tutsi in Rwanda, possibly Ibos in Nigeria, Biharis in Bangladesh, Cambodia, and of course the dozens of millions of victims of the Maoist purges in China, the Gulag, and so forth. Yet it is the murder of the Jews that brings forth a growing avalanche of films, plays, fiction, poetry, TV series, sculpture, paintings, and historical, sociological, psychological and other research. (Berenbaum & Peck, 1998: 12)

The same opening session was also addressed by Raul Hilberg. As the editors of the subsequent book suggest, Hilberg's "magisterial work, *The Destruction of the European Jews*," which had been "written in virtual isolation and in opposition to the academic establishment nearly four decades earlier," had since "come to define the field" of Holocaust studies (Berenbaum & Peck, 1998: 1). Hilberg began his address as follows:

> When the question is posed about where, as academic researchers of the Holocaust, we stand today, the simple answer is: in the limelight. Never before has so much public attention been lavished on our subject, be it in North America or in Western Europe.
>
> . . . Interest in our topic is manifest in college courses, which are developed in one institution or another virtually every semester; or conferences, which take place almost every month; or new titles of books, which appear practically every week. The demand for output is seemingly inexhaustible. The media celebrate our discoveries, and when an event in some part of the world reminds someone of the Holocaust, our researchers are often asked to explain or supply a connection instantaneously. (Berenbaum & Peck, 1998: 5)

This essay may be viewed as an effort to explain where the "limelight" to which Hilberg refers has come from and to answer Bauer's question "Why should this be so?"

2. As we will show, to be defined as a traumatic event for all humankind does not mean that the event is literally experienced or even represented as such by all humankind. As I suggest in the conclusion of this essay, indeed, only one part of contemporary humankind has even the normative aspiration of experiencing the originating event as a trauma—the "Western" versus the "Eastern" part of humankind—and this cultural-geographical difference itself may have fateful consequences for international relations, definitions of legal-moral responsibility, and the project of global understanding today.

3. Once an "atrocity" had involved murderous actions against civilians, but this definition was wiped out during the course of World War II.

4. The report continued in a manner that reveals the relation between such particularistic, war-and-nation-related definitions of atrocity and justifications for nationalistic military escalation of brutality in response: "Even though the truth of Japan's tribal viciousness had been spattered over the pages of history down through the centuries and repeated in the modern slaughters of Nanking and Hong Kong, word of this new crime had been a shock . . ." Secretary of State Cordell Hull speaking with bitter self-restraint [sic] excoriated the "demons" and "fiendishness" of Japan. Senator Alben W. Barkley exclaimed: "Retribution [must] be meted out to these heathens—brutes and beasts in the form of man." Lister Hill of Alabama was practically monosyllabic: "Gut the heart of Japan with fire!" The connection of such attributions of war atrocity to pledges of future military revenge illuminates the lack of indignation that later greeted the atomic bombing of Hiroshima and Nagaski. This kind of particularistic framing of mass civilian murder would be lifted only decades later—after the Jewish mass murder had itself become generalized as a crime that went beyond national and war-related justifications. I discuss this later.

5. For a detailed "thick description" of these first encounters, see Robert Abzug, *Inside the Vicious Heart* (Abzug, 1985).

6. During April, under the entry "German Camps," the *New York Times Index* (1945: 1184) employed the noun eight times.

7. For a broad discussion of the role played by such analogies with alleged German World War I atrocities in creating initial unbelief, see Laqueur (1980). The notion of moral panic suggests, of course, a fantasied and distorted object or belief (Thompson, 1997). In this sense, trauma is different from panic. I discuss these issues in a forthcoming book on cultural trauma.

8. This is not to say that the fact of the Nazis' anti-Jewish atrocities was accepted all at once but that the Allies' discovery of the concentration camps, relayed by reporters and photographers, soon did put an end to the doubts, which had not been nearly as thoroughly erased by revelations about the Majdanek death camp liberated by Soviets months earlier. For a detailed discussion of this changing relationship between acceptance and doubt, see Zelizer (1998: 49–140).

9. In early October 1945, General George Patton, the much-heralded chief of the U.S. Third Army, became embroiled in controversy over what were taken to be anti-Semitic representations of the Jewish survivors in the camps Patton administered. The general had contrasted them pejoratively with the German and other non-German camp prisoners and given them markedly worse treatment. In light of the argument I will make hereafter, it is revealing that what was represented as intolerable about this conspicuous mistreatment of Jewish survivors was its implied equation of American and Nazi relations to Jews. The *New Republic* headlined its account of the affair "The Same as the Nazis."

> Only on the last day of September did the nation learn that on the last day of August, President Truman had sent a sharp letter to General Eisenhower regarding the treatment of Jews in Germany. The President told the General bluntly that according to a report made by his special investigator, Earl Harrison, "we appear to be treating the Jews as the Nazi treated them, except that we do not exterminate them." Thousands of displaced Jews are still crowded in badly run concentration camps, improperly fed, clothed and housed, while comfortable homes nearby are occupied by former Nazis or Nazi sympathizers. These Jews are still not permitted to leave the camps except with passes, which are doled out to them on the absolutely incomprehensible policy that they should be treated as prisoners. . . . Americans will be profoundly disturbed to learn that anti-Semitism is rife in the American occupation forces just as is tenderness to Nazis.
> (October 8, 1945: 453)

*Time* reported the event in the same way:

> Plain G.I.s had their problems, too. Ever since they had come to Germany, the soldiers had fraternized—not only with *Fraulein* but with a philosophy. Many now began to say that the Germans were really O.K., that they had been forced into the war, that the atrocity stories were fakes. Familiarity with the eager German women, the free-faced German young, bred forgetfulness of Belsen and Buchenwald and Oswieczim. (October 8, 1945: 31–2)

In a story headlined "The Case of General Patton," the *New York Times* wrote that Patton's transfer from his Barvarian post "can have and should have just one meaning," which was that the U.S. government "will not tolerate in high positions . . . any officers, however brave, however honest, who are inclined to be easy on known Nazis and indifferent or hard to the surviving victims of the Nazi terror" (October 3, 1945: 18). For more details on Patton's treatment of the Jewish camp survivors, see Abzug (1985).

10. In "Radical Evil: Kant at War with Himself" (Bernstein, 2001) Richard Bernstein has provided an illuminating discussion of Kant's use of this term. While Kant intended the term to indicate an unusual, and almost unhuman, desire not to fulfill the imperatives of moral behavior, Bernstein demonstrates that Kant contributed little to the possibility of providing standards of evaluation for what, according to post-Holocaust morality, is called radical evil today. Nonetheless, the term itself was in im-

portant addition to moral philosophy. I want to emphasize here that I am speaking about social representations of the Holocaust, not its actual nature. I do not intend, in other words, either here or elsewhere in this chapter, to enter into the debate about the uniqueness of the Holocaust in Western history. As Norman Naimark (2001) and many others have usefully pointed out, there have been other terrible ethnically inspired bloodlettings that arguably can be compared with it, for example, the Armenian massacre by the Turks, the killing fields in Cambodia, which claimed three million of a seven million person population, the Rwanda massacre. My point here is not to make claims about the objective reality of what would later come to be called the "Holocaust" but about the sociological processes that allowed estimations of its reality to shift over time. For a specific discussion of the discourse about uniqueness, see the section on "The Dilemma of Uniqueness."

11. I am drawing here from a new approach to collective drama that has been developed collectively by Bernhard Giesen, Ron Eyerman, Piotr Sztompka, Neil J. Smelser, and myself during 1998–99 at the Center for Advanced Studies in the Behavioral Sciences in Palo Alto. This special project was funded, in part, by the Hewlett Foundation, to which I would like to record my gratitude here. My own understanding of this collective effort, which follows in Chapter 3, below, will be published as the introductory essay to our collective publication, *Cultural Trauma and Collective Identity* (Berkeley: University of California Press, forthcoming). The essay that compromises this chapter will also be published in that collective effort, as well as, in much reduced form, in Roger Friedland and John Mohr, eds., *The Cultural Turn* (Cambridge: Cambridge University Press, forthcoming). I would like to record my gratitude to my colleagues in this joint project for their contributions to my thinking not only about cultural trauma in general but about the Holocaust in particular.

12. This common-sense link is repeated time and again, exemplifying not empirical reality but the semantic exigencies of what I will call the progressive narrative of the Holocaust. In his pathbreaking article on the postwar attack on anti-Semitism, for example, Leonard Dinnerstein (1981–82) suggests that "perhaps the sinking in of the knowledge that six million Jews perished in the Holocaust" was a critical factor in creating the identification with American Jews. A similarly rationalist approach is exhibited by Edward Shapiro (1992) in his book-length study of the changing position of Jews in postwar America. Shapiro observes that "after the Holocaust, anti-Semitism meant not merely the exclusion of Jews from clubs [etc.] but mass murder." The issue here is what "meant" means. It is not obvious and rational but highly contextual, and that context is culturally established. The distinguished historian of American history John Higham represents this Enlightenment version of lay trauma theory when he points to the reaction to the Holocaust as explaining the lessening of prejudice in the United States between the mid-1930s and the mid-1950s, which he calls "the broadest, most powerful movement for ethnic democracy in American history." Higham suggests that "in the 30s and 40s, the Holocaust in Germany threw a blazing light on every sort of bigotry," thus explaining the "traumatic impact of Hitlerism on the consciousness of the Western world" (Higham, 1981–82: 154). Movements for ethnic and religious tolerance in the U.S., Higham adds, came only later, "only as the war drew to a close and the full horrors of the nazi concentration camp spilled out to an aghast world" (171). Such Enlightenment versions of lay trauma theory seem eminently reasonable, but they simply do not capture the contingent, sociologically freighted nature of the trauma process. As I try to demonstrate hereafter, complex symbolic processes of coding, weighting, and narrating were decisive in the unpredicted postwar effort to stamp out anti-Semitism in the United States.

13. See the observation by the sociological theorist Gerard Delanty (2001: 43):

"What I am drawing attention to is the need to address basic questions concerning cultural values, since violence is not always an empirical objective reality, but a matter of cultural construction in the context of publicly shaped discourses and is generally defined by reference to an issue."

14. For this notion of the "means of ritual production," see Collins (1992) and, more generally, Pierre Bourdieu, for example, his *Language and Symbolic Power* (1991).

15. To think of what might have been, it is necessary to engage in a counterfactual thought experiment. The most successful effort to do so has occurred in a best-selling piece of middlebrow fiction called *Fatherland,* by Robert Harris, a reporter for the London *Times* (Harris, 1992). The narrative takes place in 1967, in Berlin, during the celebrations of Adolph Hitler's seventieth birthday. The former Soviet Union and the United Kingdom were both conquered in the early 1940s, primarily because Hitler's general staff had overruled his decision to launch the Russian invasion before he had completed his effort to subjugate Great Britain. The story's plot revolves the protagonists' efforts to reveal the hidden events of the Holocaust. Rumors had circulated of the mass killings, but no objective truth had ever been available. As for the other contention of this paragraph, that Soviet control over the camps' discoveries would also have made it impossible for the story to be told, one may merely consult the Soviets' presentation of the Auschwitz death camp outside Krakow, Poland. While Jewish deaths are not denied, the focus is on class warfare, Polish national resistance, and communist and Polish deaths. It is well known, for example, that the East Germans, under the Soviet regime, never took responsibility for their anti-Semitic past and its central role in the mass killing of Jews, focusing instead on the Nazis as nonnational, class-based, reactionary social forces.

16. In her detailed reconstruction of the shifting balance between doubt and belief among Western publics, Zelizer demonstrates that the Soviets' discovery of the Majdanek death camp in 1944 failed to quell disbelief because of broad skepticism about Russian reporters, particularly a dislike for the Russian literary news-writing style and tendency to exaggerate: "Skepticism made the Western press regard the liberation of the eastern camps as a story in need of additional confirmation. Its dismissive attitude was exacerbated by the fact that the U.S. and British forces by and large had been denied access to the camps of the eastern front [which made it] easier to regard the information trickling out as Russian propaganda" (Zelizer, 1998: 51).

17. In contemporary sociology, the great empirical student of typification is Harold Garfinkel, who, drawing up Husserl and Schutz, developed a series of supple operationalizations such as ad-hocing, indexicality, and the "etc. clause" to describe how typification is carried out empirically.

18. See Fussell (1975) for an unparalleled account of the rhetorical deconstruction of Romanticism and melodrama.

19. See Herf (1984) and also Philip Smith's investigations of the coding of Nazism and communism as variations on the modernist discourse of civil society (Smith, 1998b).

20. For how the coding of an adversary as radical evil has compelled the sacrifice of life in modern war, see Alexander (1998).

21. Just so, the earlier failure of such nations as France to vigorously prepare for war against Germans had reflected an internal disagreement about the evility of Nazism, a disagreement fuelled by the longstanding anti-Semitism and anti-Republicanism triggered by the Dreyfus affair. For a discussion of this, see William Shirer's classic, *The Collapse of the Third Republic* (1969).

22. Statements and programs supporting better treatment of Jews were often, in fact, wittingly or unwittingly accompanied by anti-Semitic stereotypes. In the months be-

fore America entered the war against Germany, *Time* reported: "A statesmanlike program to get a better deal for the Jews after the war was launched last week by the American Jewish Congress and the World Jewish Congress, of which the not invariably statesmanlike, emotional, and politics dabbling Rabbi Steven S. Wise is respectively president and chairman" (July 7, 1941:44). Indeed, in his statistical compilation of shifting poll data on the personal attitudes of Americans during this period, Stember shows that the percentage of Americans expressing anti-Semitic attitudes actually increased immediately before and during the early years of the anti-Nazi war, though it remained a minority, (Stember, 1966). For one of the best recent discussions of anti-semitism in the early twentieth century, see Hollinger (1996).

23. Higham shows that how left-leaning intellectuals, artists, academics, and journalists set out to oppose the nativism of the 1920s and viewed the rise of Nazism in this context. While they focused particularly on the Jewish problem, they also discussed issues of race.

24. From the phrase of Clifford Geertz: "anti-anti-relativism" (Geertz, 1984), which he traced to the phrase from the McCarthy era, "anti-anti-communism." Geertz writes that his point was not to embrace relativism but to reject anti-relativism, just as anti-McCarthyites had not wanted to embrace communism but to reject anticommunism. Just so, progressives Americans of that time did not wish to identify with Jews but to reject anti-Semitism, because, I am contending, of its association with Nazism.

25. The premise of the following argument is that "salvation" can continue to be a massive social concern even in a secular age. I have made this theoretical argument in relation to a reconsideration of the routinization thesis in Max Weber's sociology of religion and employed this perspective in several other empirical studies of secular culture.

26. See Turner's irreplaceable analysis of "liminality"—his resconstruction of Van Gennep's ritual process—in *The Ritual Process* (Turner, 1969) and his later works.

27. In regard to the eventual peace treaty that would allow progress, the reference was, of course, to the disastrous Versailles Treaty of 1919, which was viewed in the interwar period as having thwarted the progressive narrative that had motivated the Allied side during World War I. President Woodrow Wilson had presented the progressive narrative of that earlier struggle by promising that this "war to end all wars" would "make the world safe for democracy."

28. I should add by the Jewish *and non-Jewish* victims as well, for millions of persons were victims of Nazi mass murder in addition to the Jews—Poles, gypsies, homosexuals, handicapped persons, and political opponents of all types. (For more discussion of this issue see below.) That virtually all of these non-Jewish victims were filtered out of the emerging collective representation of the Holocaust underlines the "arbitrary" quality of trauma representations. By arbitrary, I mean to refer to Saussure's foundational argument, in his *Course in General Linguistics,* that the relation between signifier and signified is not based on some intrinsically truthful or accurate relationship. The definition of the signifier—what we normally mean by the symbol or representation—comes not from its actual or "real" social referent per se but from its position within the field of other signifiers, which is itself structured by the broader sign system, or language, already in place. This is essentially the same sense of arbitrariness that is invoked by Wittgenstein's argument against Augustine's language theory in the opening pages of *Philosophical Investigations.* This notion of arbitrariness does not mean, of course, that representation is unafected by noncultural developments, as the historically contextual discussion in this chapter demonstrates.

29. In February 1943 the widely read popular magazine *American Mercury* published a lengthy story by Ben Hecht called "The Extermination of the Jews" (February 1943: 194–203) that described in accurate detail the events that had already unfolded and

would occur in the future. The following report also appeared in *Time:* "In a report drawn from German broadcasts and newspapers, Nazi statements, smuggled accounts and the stories of survivors who have reached the free world, the [World Jewish] Congress told what was happening in Poland, slaughterhouse of Europe's Jews. By late 1942, the Congress reported, 2,000,000 had been massacred. *Vernichtungskolonnen* (extermination squads) rounded them up and killed them with machine guns, lethal gas, high-voltage electricity, and hunger. Almost all were stripped before they died; their clothes were needed by the Nazis" ("Total Murder," March 8, 1943: 29). Two months later, *Newsweek* reported the Nazi destruction of the Warsaw ghetto: "When [the] Gestapo men and Elite Guard were through with the job, Warsaw, once the home of 450,000 Jews, was 'judenrein' (free of Jews). By last week all had been killed or deported" (May 24, 1943: 54). In October 1944 the widely popular journalist Edgar Snow published details about the "Nazi murder factory" in the Soviet liberated town of Maidanek, Poland, in the *Saturday Evening Post* (October 28, 1944: 18–9).

Abzug (1985) agrees that "the more sordid facts of mass slaughter, labor and death campus, Nazi policies of enslavement of peoples deemed inferior and extermination of Europe's Jews" were facts that were "known through news sources and widely publicized since 1942" (Abzug, 1985: 17). In the manner of Enlightenment lay trauma theory— which would suggest that knowledge leads to redemptive action—Abzug qualifies his assertion of this popular knowledge by insisting that the American soldiers who opened up the camps and the American audience alike suffered from a failure of "imagination" in regard to the Nazi terror (17). According to the theory of cultural trauma that informs our analysis, however, this was less a failure of imagination that a matter of collective imagination being narrated in a certain way. It points not to an absence of perception but to the power of the contemporary, progressive narrative framework, a framework that was brought into disrepute by later developments, which made it appear insensitive and even inhumane.

30. Another historian, Peter Novick, makes the same point:

For most Gentiles, and a great many Jews as well, [the Holocaust] was seen as simply one among many dimensions of the horrors of Nazism. Looking at World War II retrospectively, we are inclined to stress what was distinctive in the murderous zeal with which European Jewry was destroyed. Things often appeared differently to contemporaries.

. . . Jews did not stand out as the Nazis' prime victims until near the end of the Third Reich. Until 1938 there were hardly any Jews, qua Jews, in concentration camps, which were populated largely by Socialists, Communists, trade unionists, dissident intellectuals, and the like. Even when news of mass killings of Jews during the war reached the West, their murder was framed as one atrocity, albeit the largest, in a long list of crimes, such as the massacre of Czechs at Lidice, the French at Oradour, and American prisoners of war at Malmedy. (Novick, 1994: 160)

31. The term was introduced in 1944 by an American author, Ralph Lemkin in his book *Axis Rule in Occupied Europe* (Lemkin, 1944). As Lemkin, defined it, genocide applied to efforts to destroy the foundations of national and ethnic groups and referred to a wide range of antagonistic activities, including attacks on political and social institutions, culture, language, national feelings, religion, economic existence, and personal security and dignity. It was intended to cover all of the antinational activities carried out by the Nazis against the occupied nations inside Hitler's Reich. In other words, when first coined, the term definitely did not focus on the element of mass murder that after the discovery of the death camps came to be attributed to it.

32. The author, Frank Kingdon, was a former Methodist minister.

33. In an article on the success of *Gentleman's Agreement*, in the *Saturday Review of Literature* (December 13, 1947: 20), the author asserted that "the Jewish people are the

world symbol of [the] evil that is tearing civilization apart" and suggested that the book and movie's success "may mean that the conscience of America is awakening and that something at least will be done about it."

34. Short makes this Jewish exceptionalism clear when he writes that "with war raging in the Pacific, in Europe and in the shipping lanes of the Atlantic, Hollywood made a conscious effort to create a sense of solidarity amongst the nation's racial and ethnic groups (*excepting* the Japanese-Americans and the blacks)" (Short, 1981: 157, italics added).

35. See also Higham (1984) and Silk (1986).

36. It remains an empirical question whether American Jews were themselves traumatized by contemporary revelations about the Nazi concentration camps. Susan Sontag's remembered reactions as a California teenager to the revelatory photographs of the Belsen and Dachau death camps are often pointed to as typical of American Jewish reaction more generally: "I felt irrevocably grieved, wounded, but a part of my feelings started to tighten; something went dead; something still is crying" (quoted in Shapiro, 1992: 3, and in Abzug, 1985: vii). Yet that this and other oft-quoted retrospective reactions were shared by the wider Jewish public in the United States has been more of a working assumption by scholars of this period, particularly but by no means exclusively Jewish ones. Not yet subject to empirical demonstration, the assumption that American Jews were immediately traumatized by the revelations reflects Enlightenment lay trauma theory. It might also represent an effort at post hoc exculpation vis-à-vis possible guilt feelings that many American and British Jews later experienced about their lack of effort or even their inability to block or draw attention to the mass murders.

37. *Symbolic action* is a term developed by Kenneth Burke to indicate that understanding is also a form of human activity, namely an expressive form related to the goal of parsing meaning. The term became popularized and elaborated in the two now classical essays published by Clifford Geertz in the early 1960s, "Religion as a Cultural System" and "Ideology as a Cultural System" (Geertz, 1973 [1964]). My reference to "culture structure" refers to my effort to treat culture as a structure in itself. Only by analytically differentiating culture from social structure—treating it as a structure in its own right—does it move from being a dependent to an independent variable.

38. See Wilhelm Dilthey, "The Construction of the Historical World in the Human Sciences" (Dilthey, 1976). For two related discussions of the idea of "culture structure," see Anne Kane (1998) and Eric Rambo and Elaine Chan (1990).

39. By the early 1990s, knowledge of the Holocaust among American citizens greatly exceeded knowledge about World War II. According to public opinion polls, while 97 percent of Americans knew about the Holocaust, far fewer could identity "Pearl Harbor" or the fact that the United States had unleashed an atomic bomb on Japan. Only 49 percent of those polled realized that the Soviets had fought with Americans during that war. In fact, the detachment of the Jewish mass killings from particular historical events had proceeded to the point that, according to an even more recent survey, more than one-third of Americans either don't know that the Holocaust took place during World War II or insisted that they "knew" it did not (Novick, 1999: 232).

40. Yehuda Bauer, in his editor's introduction to the first issue of *Holocaust and Genocide Studies*, suggested this new, *weltgeschichte* (world-historical) sensibility:

There is not much point in dealing with one aspect of the Holocaust, because that traumatic event encompasses all of our attention; therefore, no concentration on one discipline only would meet the needs . . . We arrived at the conclusion that we would aim at a number of readers' constituencies: students, survivors, high school and college teachers, academics generally, and that *very large number of people who feel that the Holocaust is something that has changed our century, perhaps all centuries*, and needs to be investigated. (9 [1] 1986: 1, italics added)

This journal not only embodied the newly emerging generalization and universalization I am describing here but can also be viewed as an institutional carrier that aimed to promote its continuation. Thus, two years later, in an issue of the journal dedicated to papers from a conference entitled, "Remembering for the Future," held at Oxford in July 1988, Bauer pointedly observed that "one half of the authors of the papers *are not Jewish*, bearing witness to the fact that among academics, at least, there exists a growing realization of the importance of the event to our civilization, *a realization that is becoming more widespread among those whose families and peoples were not affected by the Holocaust*" (3 [3] 1988: 255, italics added).

41. The historian Peter Gay, who coedited the *Columbia History of the World* in 1972, was reportedly embarrassed to find later that the enormous volume contained no mention of Auschwitz nor of the murder of six million Jews, an embarrassment exacerbated by the fact that he himself was a Jewish refugee from Germany (Zelizer, 1998: 164–5).

42.

In 1949, there was no "Holocaust" in the English language in the sense that word is used today. Scholars and writers has used "permanent pogrom" . . . or "recent catastrophe," or "disaster," or "the disaster." Sometimes writers spoke about annihilation and destruction without use of any of these terms. In 1953, the state of Israel formally injected itself into the study of the destruction of European Jewry, and so became involved in the transformation [by] establish[ing] Yad Vashem as a "Martyrs" and "Heroes' Remembrance Authority" . . . Two years later Yad Vashem translated *shoah* into "Disaster". . . . But then the change occurred quickly. When catastrophe had lived side by side with disaster the word holocaust had appeared now and then. . . . Between 1957 and 1959, however, "Holocaust" took on . . . a specific meaning. It was used at the Second World Congress of Jewish Studies held in Jerusalem, and when Yad Vashem published its third yearbook, one of the articles dealt with "Problems Relating to a Questionnaire on the Holocaust." Afterwards Yad Vashem switched from "Disaster" to "Holocaust" . . . Within the Jewish world the word became commonplace, in part because Elie Wiesel and other gifted writers and speakers, in public meetings or in articles . . . made it coin of the realm. (Korman, 1972: 259–61)

43. On "shoah," see Ofer (1996). In telling the story of linguistic transformation inside the Hebrew language, Ofer shows that inside of Israel there was a similar narrative shift from a more progressive to a more tragic narrative frame and that this shift was reflected in the adoption of the word *shoah*, which had strong biblical connotations related to apocalyptic events in Jewish history, such as the flood and Job's sufferings: *shoah* was conspicuously not applied to such "everyday" disasters as pogroms and other repeated forms of anti-Semitic oppression. On the relative newness of the American use of the term "Holocaust"—its emergence only in the postprogressive narrative period—see John Higham's acute observation that "the word does not appear in the index to Richard H. Pells, *The Liberal Mind in a Conservative Age: American Intellectuals in the 1940s and 1950s*—in spite of the attention he gives to European influence and Jewish intellectuals" (Higham, personal communication). According to Garber and Zuckerman (1989: 202), the English term was first introduced in relation to the Jewish mass murder by Elie Wiesel in the *New York Times Book Review* of October 27, 1963, but there is some debate about the originality of Wiesel's usage. Novick, for example, relates that the American journalist Paul Jacobs employed the term in an article on the Eichmann trial, in 1961, that he filed from Jerusalem for the American liberal magazine *New Leader*. Significantly, Jacobs wrote of "the Holocaust, as the Nazi annihilation of European Jewry is called in Israel." Whatever its precise origins—and Wiesel's 1963 usage may well have marked the beginning of a common useage—the symbolically freighted semantic transition,

which first occurred in Israel and then America, had wide ramifications for the universalization of meaning vis-à-vis the Jewish mass killing. Until the late 1970s, for example, Germans still used "bureaucratic euphemisms" to describe the events, such as the "Final Solution." After the German showing of the American television miniseries *Holocaust*, however, "Holocaust" replaced these terms, passing into common German usage. One German scholar, Jean Paul Bier, described "Holocaust" as an "American word" (Bier, 1986: 203); another testified that, after the television series, the term "'Holocaust' became a metaphor for unhumanity" (Zielinski, 1986: 273).

44. For the central role of our time in the tropes of contemporary historical narratives, see chapter 8.

45. This is not to say, however, that christological themes of redemption through suffering played no part in the tragic dramatization. As anti-Semitic agitation increased in the late nineteenth century, Jesus frequently was portrayed by Jewish artists as a Jew and his persecution presented as emblematic not only of Jewish suffering but of the Christian community's hypocrisy in relation to it. During this same period, important Christian artists like Goya and Grosz began to develop "a new approach to Christ, using the Passion scenes outside their usual Biblical context as archetypical of the sufferings of modern man, especially in times of war" (Amishai-Maisels, 1988: 457). As the Nazi persecution intensified before and during World War II, this theme emerged with increasing frequency, for example in the despairing paintings of Marc Chagall. Again, the aim was to provide a mythically powerful icon of Jewish martyrdom and, at the same time, "to reproach the Christian world for their deeds" (464). With the liberation of the camps, there emerged a far more powerful way to establish this icon—through the images of emaciated, tortured bodies of the victims themselves. Immediately after the war, artists such as Corrado Cagli and Hans Grundig stressed the similarity between the camp corpses and Holbein's Dean Christ, and Grundig even set the corpses on a gold background, emphasizing their similarity to medieval representations of martyrs. . . . The most telling similarity between Christ and the corpses was not, however, invented by artists but was found in photographs of those corpses whose arms were spread out in a cruciform pose. One such photograph, published under the title "Ecce Homo-Bergen Belsen," is said to have had an immediate and lasting effect on the artistic representation of the Holocaust (467). It was undoubtedly the case that, for many religious Christians, the transition of Jews from killers of Christ to persecuted victims of evil was facilitated by such iconographic analogies. Nonetheless, even here, in the pictorial equation of Jesus with the Nazi victims, the theme was tragedy but not redemption in the eschatological sense of Christianity. The symbolization held the pathos but not the promise of the crucifixion, and it was employed more as a criticism of the promises of Christianity than as an identification with its theodicy of hope. It should also be mentioned, of course, that the religious rituals surrounding the death of Christ draw heavily from the classical tragic aesthetic form.

46. "Pity involves both distance and proximity. If the sufferer is too close to ourselves, his impending misfortune evokes horror and terror. If he is too distant, his fate does not affect us. . . . The ethical and political questions are: whom should we pity? . . . The tragic hero? Ourselves? Humanity? All three, and three in one" (Rorty, 1992: 12–3). Against Adorno's claim that the Holocaust must not be aestheticized in any way, Hartman insists that "art creates an unreality effect in a way that is not alienating or desensitizing. At best, it also provides something of a sage-house for emotion and empathy. The tears we shed, like those of Aeneas when he sees the destruction of Troy depicted on the walls of Carthage, are an acknowledgment and not an exploitation of the past" (Hartman, 1996: 157).

47. In these psychological terms, a progressive narrative inclines the audience toward projection and scapegoating, defense mechanisms that allow the actor to experience no

responsibility for the crime. This distinction also points to the difference between the genres of melodrama and tragedy, which have much in common. By breaking the world into complete blacks and whites and by providing assurance of the victory of the good, melodrama encourages the same kind of projection and scapegoating as progressive narratives; in fact, melodramatic narratives often drive progressive ones. For the significance of melodramatic narratives in the nineteenth century and their connection to stories, both fictional and realistic, of ethical triumph, see Brooks (1995). In practice, however, dramatizations of the Holocaust trauma, like virtually every other dramatization of tragedy in modern and postmodern society, often overlap with the melodramatic.

48. By the early 1940s, the Polish Ministry of Information, independent journalists, and underground groups released photos of corpses tumbled into graves or stacked onto carts. One such depiction, which appeared in the *Illustrated London News* in March 1941 under the headline "Where Germans Rule: Death Dance before Polish Mass Execution," portrayed victims digging their own graves or facing the death squad. The journal told its readers that "behind these pictures is a story of cold-blooded horror reminiscent of the Middle Ages" (Zelizer, 1998: 43).

49. This is the radical and corrosive theme of Bauman's provocative *Modernity and the Holocaust* (1989). While Bauman himself professes to eschew any broader universalizing aims, the ethical message of such a perspective seems clear all the same. I am convinced that the distrust of abstract normative theories of justice as expressed in such postmodern efforts as Bauman's *Postmodern Ethics* (Bauman, 1993) can be understood as a response to the Holocaust, as well, of course, as a response to Stalinism and elements of the capitalist West. In contrast to some other prominent postmodern positions, Bauman's ethics is just as strongly opposed to communitarian as to modernist positions, an orientation that can be understood by the centrality of the Holocaust in his critical understanding of modernity. Bauman's wife, Janina, is a survivor and author of an immensely moving Holocaust memoir, *Winter in the Morning* (Bauman, 1986). The dedication of *Modernity and the Holocaust* reads: "To Janina, and all the others who survived to tell the truth."

50. "Lachrymose" was the characterization given to the historical perspective on Jewish history developed by Salo Baron. The most important academic chronicler of Jewish history in the United States, Baron held the first Chair of Jewish History at Harvard. Baron was deeply affected by what seemed, at the time, to be the reversal of Jewish assimilation in the fin-de-siècle period. In response to this growth of modern anti-Semitism, he began to suggest that the medieval period of Jewish-Gentile relations— the long period that preceded Jewish "emancipation" in the Enlightenment and nine-teenth century—actually may have been better for the Jewish people, culturally, politically, economically, and even demographically, than the postemancipation period. Postwar Jewish historiography, not only in the United States but also in Israel, often criticized Baron's perspective, but as the progressive narrative of the Holocaust gave way to the tragic frame his lachrymose view became if not widely accepted then at least much more positively evaluated as part of the whole reconsideration of the effects of the Enlightenment on modern history. See Liberles (1995).

51. This has, of course, been the complaint of some intellectuals, from the very beginning of the entrance of the Holocaust into popular culture, from *The Diary of Anne Frank* to Spielberg's most recent dramas. As I will suggest below, the real issue is not dramatization per se but the nature of the dramatic form. If the comic frame replaces the tragic or melodramatic one, then the "lessons" of the Holocaust are, indeed, being trivialized.

52. She adds that "The appeal to pity is . . . also an appeal to fellow feeling."

53.

Tragedy . . . provides us with the appropriate objects towards which to feel pity and fear. Tragedy, one might say, trains us or habituates us in feeling pity and fear in response to events that are worthy of those emotions. Since our emotions are being evoked in the proper circumstances, they are also being educated, refined, or clarified. . . . Since virtue partially consists in having the appropriate emotional responses to circumstances, tragedy can be considered part of an ethical education. (Lear, 1992: 318)

Is it necessary to add the caveat that to be "capable" of exercising such an ethical judgment is not the same thing as actually exercising it? This cultural shift I am referring here is about capability, which, while clearly a prerequisite of action, does not determine it.

54. Such a notion of further universalization is not, of course, consistent with postmodern social theory or philosophy, and the intent here is not to suggest that it is.

55. I hope that my aim in this section will not be misunderstood as an effort to aestheticize and demoralize the inhuman mass murders that the Nazis carried out. I am trying to denaturalize, and therefore sociologize, our contemporary understanding of these awful events. For, despite their heinous quality, they could, in fact, be interpreted in various ways. Their nature did not dictate their interpretation. As Robert Braun suggests: "Historical narratives do not necessarily emplot past events in the form of tragedy and this form of emplotment is not the only node of narration for tragic events" (Braun, 1994: 182).

What I am suggesting here is a transparent and eerie homology between the tragic genre—whose emotional, moral, and aesthetic qualities have been studied since Aristotle—and how we and others have come to understand what the Holocaust "really was." Cultural sociology carries out the same kind of "bracketing" that Husserl suggested for his new science of phenomenology: the ontological reality of perceived objects is temporarily repressed in order to search for those subjective elements in the actor's intentionality that establish the sense of verisimilitude. What the Holocaust "really was" is not the issue for this sociological investigation. My subject is the social processes that allowed the events that are now identified by this name to be seen as different things at different times. For the lay actor, by contrast, the reality of the Holocaust must be taken as an objective and absolute. Moral responsibility and moral action can be established and institutionalized only on this basis.

In historical and literary studies, there has developed over the last two decades an intense controversy over the relevance of the kinds of cultural methods I employ here. Scholars associated with the moral lessons of the Holocaust, for example Saul Friedlander, have lambasted the deconstructive methods of narrativists like Hayden White for eliminating the hard and fast line between "representation" (fiction) and "reality." Friedlander organized the tempestuous scholarly conference that gave birth to the collective volume *Probing the Limits of Representation* (Friedlander, 1992). In the conference and the books he drew an analogy between the cultural historians' questioning of reality with the politically motivated efforts by contemporary Italian fascists, and all the so-called revisionists since then, to deny the mass murder of the Jews. While I would strongly disagree with Friedlander's line of criticism, there is no doubt that it has been stimulated by the way the aestheticizing, debunking quality of deconstructive criticism has, from Nietzsche on, sought to present itself as a replacement for, rather than a qualification of, the traditional political and moral criticism of the rationalist tradition. By contrast, I am trying here to demonstrate that the aesthetic and the critical approach must be combined.

56. Each national case is, of course, different, and the stories of France, the United Kingdom, Italy, and the Scandinavian countries would depart from this account in significant ways. Nonetheless, as Diner remarks, insofar as "the Holocaust has increasingly become a universal moral icon in the realm of political and historical discourse," the

"impact of the catastrophe can be felt in various European cultures, with their disparate legacies [and] even within the realm of collective . . . identities" (Diner, 2000: 218). Nonwestern countries, even the democratic ones, have entirely different traumas to contend with, as I have pointed out in my introduction.

57. In fact, I believe that it is because of the symbolic centrality of Jews in the progressive narrative that so relatively little attention has been paid to the Nazis' equally immoral and unconscionable extermination policies directed against other groups, for example, Poles, homosexuals, gypsies, and handicapped. Some frustrated representatives of these aggrieved groups—sometimes for good reasons, other times for anti-Semitic ones—have attributed this lack of attention to Jewish economic and political power in the United States. This analysis suggests, however, that cultural logic is the immediate and efficient cause for such a focus. This logic is also propelled, of course, by geopolitical and economic forces, but such considerations would apply more to the power and position of the United States in the world system of the postwar world than to the position of Jews in the United States.

As I have shown, it was not the actual power of Jews in the United States but the centrality of "Jews" in the progressive American imagination that defined the crimes of Nazis in a manner that focused on anti-Semitism. In terms of later developments, moreover, it was only because of the imaginative reconfiguring of the Jews that political-economic restrictions were eliminated in a manner that eventually allowed them to gain influence in mainstream American institutions. As I will show below, moreover, as American power declined, so did the exclusive focus on Jews as a unique class of Holocaust victims. This suggests, as I will elaborate later, that the contemporary "omnipresence" of the Holocaust symbol has more to do with "enlarging the circle of victims" than with focusing exclusively on Jewish suffering.

The most recent scholarly example of this tendentious focus on "Jewish power" as the key for explaining the telling of the Holocaust story is Peter Novick's book *The Holocaust in American Life* (Novick, 1999). To employ the categories of classical sociological theory, Novick might be described as offering an instrumentally oriented "status group" explanation à la Weber, in contrast to the more culturally oriented late-Durkheimian approach taken here. Novick suggests that the Holocaust became central to contemporary history because it became central to America, that it became central to America because it became central to America's Jewish community, and that it became central to Jews because it became central to the ambitions of Jewish organizations who were central to the mass media in all its forms (207). Jewish organizations first began to emphasize the Holocaust because they wanted to "shore up Jewish identity, particularly among the assimilating and intermarrying younger generations" (186) and to maintain the Jews' "victim status" in what Novick sees as the identity politics shell game of the 1980s— "Jews were intent on permanent possession of the gold medal in the Victimization Olympics" (185). Despite acknowledging that it is "impossible to disentangle the spontaneous from the controlled" (152), he emphasizes the "strategic calculations" (152) of Jewish organizations, which motivated them to emphasize the Holocaust in responsive to "market forces"(187).

This analysis fundamentally departs from Novick's. Whereas Novick describes a particularization of the Holocaust—its being captured by Jewish identity politics—I will describe a universalization. Where Novick describes a nationalization, I trace an internationalization. Where Novick expresses skepticism about the metaphorical transferability of the "Holocaust," I will describe such metaphorical bridging as essential to the social process of moral engagement. In terms of sociological theory, the point is not to deny that status groups are significant. As Weber clarified in his sociology of religion, such groups must be seen not as creators of interest per se but as "carrier groups." All broad cultural currents are carried by—articulated by, lodged within—particular material and ideal interests. Even ideal interests, in other words, are represented by groups, in this case status groups rather than classes. But, as Weber emphasized, ideal and material interests can be pursued only along the "tracks" that have been laid out by larger cultural ideas.

The sense of the articulation between these elements in the Holocaust construction is much more accurately represented in Edward T. Linenthal's book *Preserving Memory: The Struggle to Create the Holocaust Museum* (1995). Linenthal carefully and powerfully documents the role of status group interests in the fifteen-year process involved in the creation of the Holocaust Museum in Washington, D.C. He demonstrates, at the same time, that the particular parties were deeply affected by the broader cultural context of Holocaust symbolization. President Carter, for example, initially proposed the idea of such a museum partly on political grounds—in order to mollify a key democratic constituency, the Jews, as he was making unprecedented gestures to Palestinians in the diplomatic conflicts of the Middle East (17–28). Yet, when a Carter advisor, Stuart Eizenstat, first made the written proposal to the president, in April 1978, he pointed to the great popularity of the recently broadcast *Holocaust* miniseries on NBC. In terms of the broader context, in which the Holocaust was already being universalized, Eizenstat also warned the president that other American cities, and other nations, were already engaged in constructing what could be competing Holocaust commemorative sites. Even Linenthal, however, sometimes loses sight of the broader context. Describing the contentious struggles over representation of non-Jewish victims, for example, he speaks of "those committed to Jewish ownership of Holocaust memory" (39), a provocative phrasing that invites the kind of reductionist, status-group interpretation of strategic motivation that Novick employs. As I have shown in this essay, the Holocaust as a unversalizing symbol of human suffering was, in a fundamental sense, inextricably related to the Jews, for the symbol was constructed directly in relationship to the Jewish mass murder. This was not a matter of ownership but a matter of narrative construction and intensely experienced social drama, which had been crystallized long before the struggles over representation in the museum took place. As a result of the early, progressive narrative of the Nazis' mass murder, non-Jewish Americans had given to Jews a central pride of place and had greatly altered their attitudes and social relation to them as a result. The conflicts that Linenthal documents came long after this crystallization of Jewish centrality. They were about positioning vis-à-vis an already firmly crystallized symbol, which had by then become renarrated in a tragic manner. Engorged with evil and universalized in its meaning, the "Holocaust" could not possibly be "owned" by any one particular social group or by any particular nation. The Holocaust museum was able to gain consensual support precisely because the symbol of evil had already become highly generalized such that other, non-Jewish groups could, and did, associate and reframe their own subjugation in ways that strengthened the justice of their causes. See my later discussion of metonymy, analogy, and legality, below.

Norman G. Finkelstein's book *The Holocaust Industry: Reflections on the Exploitation of Jewish Suffering* (2000) represents an even more tendentious and decidedly more egregious treatment of Holocaust centrality than Novick's, in a sense representing a long and highly polemical asterisk to that earlier, more scholarly book. Finkelstein bothers not at all with the ambiguity of motives, flatly saying that the Jewish concentration on the Holocaust, beginning in the late 1960s, was "a ploy to delegitimize all criticism of Jews" (37). The growing crystallization of the Holocaust as a metaphor for evil invites from Finkelstein only ridicule and ideology-critique: "The abnormality of the Nazi holocaust springs not from the event itself but from the exploitive industry that has grown up around it . . . 'The Holocaust' is an ideological representation of the Nazi holocaust. Like most ideologies, it bears a connection, if tenuous, with reality . . . Its central dogmas sustain significant political and class interests. Indeed, The Holocaust has proven to be an indispensable ideological weapon" (150–1).

58. Higham (1984) rightly notes that a range of factors involving what might be called the "modernization" of America's Jewish population—increasingly high rates of urbanization and education, growing professionalization—also facilitated the identification with them of non-Jews. Other, more specifically cultural processes, however, were also fundamentally involved.

59. According to a 1990 survey, when Americans were presented with a list of well-known catastrophic events, a clear majority said that the Holocaust "was *the* worst tragedy in history" (quoted in Novick, 1999: 232, italics in original).

60. The tragic and personal qualities of the *Diary*, which set it against the "progressive narrative" structure of the early postwar period, initially had made it difficult to find a publisher.

Queriod, the literary publishing house in Amsterdam, rejected the manuscript of *Het Achterhuis*, giving as its reasons the fact that "in 1947 it was certain that war and everything to do with it was stone dead. . . . Immediately as the terror was over and the anxieties of that pitch-black night were banished, people did not want to venture again into the darkness. They wished to give all their attention to the new day that was dawning" (Strenghold, 1988: 337).

61. Doneson's very helpful historical reconstruction of the dramatization of the *Diary* also emphasizes the personal focus. Like many other commentators (e.g., Rosenfeld, 1995), however, she suggests this focus undermines the tragic message of the Holocaust rather than generalizing it. In this, she joins the increasing ranks of those who decry the "Americanization" of the Holocaust, an interpretation with which, as I have mentioned, my approach strongly disagrees.

62. This clash of genres was demonstrated by the storm of controversy inside Germany that greeted the decision by a new German cable company to broadcast old episodes of *Hogan's Heroes* in 1995.

63. See the extensive social scientific discussion in Zielinski (1986), from which this discussion is derived.

64. It was after this crystallizing event that some of the intellectuals who had been most associated with focusing public discussion the Holocaust began to criticize its transformation into a mass collective representation. Elie Wiesel made his famous declaration (quoted earlier) that the ontological nature of Holocaust evil made it impossible to dramatize. Complaining, in effect, that such dramatization stole the Holocaust from those who had actually suffered from it, Wiesel described the television series as "an insult to those who perished, and those who survived" (quoted in Morrow, 1978). Such criticism only intensified in response to the subsequent flood of movie and television dramatizations. In *One, by One, by One: Facing the Holocaust,* for example, Miller issued a fervent critique of the appropriation of the original event by the mass media culture of the "Holocaust industry" (Miller, 1990: 232). Rather than seeing the widespread distribution of the mass-mediated experience as allowing universalization, he complained about its particularization via "Americanization," presumably because it was in the United States that most of these mass media items were produced: "Europe's most terrible genocide is transformed into an American version of kitsch."

Aside from knee-jerk anti-Americanism, which has continued to inform critiques of the "Holocaust industry" in the years since, such a perspective also reflects the anti–popular culture, hermeneutic tone-deafness of the Frankfurt School's "culture industry" approach to meaning. (See Docker [1994] for a vigorous postmodern criticism in this regard.) Such attacks stand outside the interpretive processes of mass culture. In place of interpretations of meaning, they issue moral condemnations: "This vulgarization is a new form of historical titillation . . . In societies like America's, where the public attention span is measured in seconds and minutes rather than years or decades, where sentimentality replaces insight and empathy, it represents a considerable threat to dignified rememberance" (Miller, 1990: 232). Such complaints fundamentally misapprehend cultural processes in general and cultural trauma in particular. (See my later discussion of the "dilemma of uniqueness.")

While these leftist complaints are well intended, it is revealing that their "anti-commodification" arguments overlap quite neatly with the conservative, sometimes anti-Semitic language that German conservatives employed in their effort to prevent "*Holocaust*" mini-series from being shown in their country. Franz Joseph Strauss, the right-wing, nationalist leader of the Bavarian Christian Democrats, called the series "a fast-buck operation." The German television executives opposed to airing the series condemned it as "a cultural commodity . . . not in keeping with the memory of the victims." *Der Spiegel* railed against "the destruction of the Jews as soap opera . . . a commercial horror show . . . an imported cheap commodity . . . genocide shrunken to the level of *Bonanza* with music appropriate to *Love Story.*" After the series was televised and its great impact revealed, one German journalist ascribed its effect to its personal dramatization: "No other film has ever made the Jews' road of suffering leading to the gas chambers so vivid. . . . Only since and as a result of 'Holocaust' does a majority of the nation know what lay behind the horrible and vacuous formula 'Final Solution of the Jewish Question.' They know it because a U.S. film maker had the courage to break with the paralyzing dogma . . . that mass murder must not be represented in art" (quoted in Herf, 1986: 214, 217).

65. See the Arendt-Jaspers correspondence on these issues and the astute analysis by Richard J. Bernstein in *Hannah Arendt and the Jewish Question* (1996).

66. "The capture and trial of Eichmann and, in the following years, the controversies surrounding Hannah Arendt's *Eichmann in Jerusalem* were something of a curtain raiser to the era of transition. For the mass public this was the first time the Holocaust was framed as a distinct and separate process, separate from Nazi criminality in general" (Novick, 1994: 161). It was only as a result of this separation that the poet A. Alvarez could have made his much-noted remark in the *Atlantic Monthly*, to the effect that "while all miseries of World War II have faded, the image of the concentration camp persists" (quoted in Zelizer, 1998: 155).

67. Novick goes on to observe that "it was in large part as a result of the acceptance of Arendt's portrait of Eichmann (with an assist from Milgram) that 'just following orders' changed, in the Ameircan lexicon, from a plea in extenuation to a damning indictment."

68. See, in more depth, Browning, "Ordinary Germans or Ordinary Men? A Reply to the Critics," in Berenbaum and Peck (1998: 252–65), and Goldhagen, "Ordinary Men or Ordinary Germans?" in Berenbaum and Peck (1998: 301–8).

69. "Spielberg does not show what 'Germans' did but what *individual* Germans did, offering hope that one of them—Schindler—would become one of many. Unlike *Holocaust* . . . Spielberg can tell a 'true tale' that must seem doubly strange. While the events in Schindler's List may contradict the idea of the Nazi state as the perfect machine, the State's and Schindler's deficiencies provide a paradox of choice—'the other Nazi,' the German who did good" (Wiessberg, 1997: 178, italics in original).

70. By "force of arms" I refer to the ability of the North Vietnamese to successfully resist the United States and South Vietnamese on the ground. David Kaiser's *American Tragedy* (Kaiser, 1999) demonstrates that, in purely military terms, the Americans and South Vietnamese forces were never really in the game, and that in fact, the kind of interventionist war the United States benightedly launched could not have been won short of using nuclear arms. If the United States had not intervened militarily in Vietnam,

America might not have lost control over the means of symbolic production, and the Holocaust might not have been universalized in the same way.

71. The power of this symbolic reversal is attested to by the fact that, two decades later, an American psychologist, Herbert C. Kelman, and a sociologist, V. Lee Hamilton, published *Crimes of Obedience: Toward a Social Pyschology of Authority and Responsibility* (1989), which in developing a theory of "sanctioned massacre" drew explicit connections between American military behavior at My Lai and German Nazi behavior during the Holocaust.

72. One recent demonstration of this polluting association was provided by the *New York Times* review of a much-trumpeted televised television show called *Nuremberg*.

Here's the defining problem with "Nuremberg," TNT's ambitious, well-meaning two-part mini-series about the trial of Nazi war criminals: the "best" character in the movie is Hermann Goring. Through Brian Cox's complex performance, Goring (founder of the Gestapo, Hitler's No. 2) becomes his finest self. He is urbane, loyal and courageous—and he gets the best lines. "The victors will always be the judges, the vanquished always the accused," he says with world-weary knowingness. (Julie Salamon, "Humanized, but Not Whitewashed, at Nuremberg," July 14, 2000: B 22)

73. In 1995, the Smithsonian Museum in Washington, D.C., had planned to mount an exhibition commemorating the Allies' defeat of Japan and the successful conclusion of World War II. The plans included highlighting the plane that had dropped the atomic bomb on Hiroshima. The public uproar that greeted these plans eventually had the effect of preventing the exhibition from ever going forward. See Linenthal (1995).

74. These suggestions were made, for example, in both Laqueur (1980) and Dawidowicz (1982). The scholarly arguments along these lines culminated with the publication of David S. Wyman's book *The Abandonment of the Jews: America and the Holocaust, 1941–1945* (Wyman, 1984).

75. Unfortunately, Linenthal's very helpful discussion implies that, in this case as in others, there is a disjunction, perhaps a morally reprehensible one, between the dissensus about empirical facts and the interpretive frame. I would suggest that these are different arenas for the mediation of cultural trauma, and each arena has its own framework of justification.

76. See especially the brilliantly written, highly mythologizing biography of Jean Lacouture, *De Gaulle: The Rebel 1890–1944* (Lacouture, 1990). After the Allied armies, primarily British and American, had allowed the relatively small remnant of the French army under De Gaulle to enter first into Paris, as a symbolic gesture, De Gaulle dramatically announced to an evening rally that Paris "has risen to free itself" and that it had "succeeded in doing so with its own hands."

77. Max Ophuls's film *Le chagrin et la pitie* exercised a profound expressive effect in this regard, as did the American historian Robert O. Paxton book *La France de Vichy*. For an overview of these developments, see Hartman, "The Voice of Vichy" (Hartman, 1996: 72–81).

78. Whether Austrians themselves—or the Swiss, for that matter (see hereafter)— have come to accept this new position in the Holocaust story is not the issue, and it is obviously open to some doubt in light of the recent plurality given in the national elections to the Freedom Party, headed by Joerg Haider, who has famously minimized Nazi atrocities against Jews. There is, nonetheless, a significant group of Austrians who have accepted the symbolic inversion from victim to perpetrator. The *Los Angeles Times* recently reported on Austrian's Gedenkdienst or Commemorative Service Program, a government-sponsored but privately organized program in which young men can perform alternative service by volunteering in a Holocaust-related institution somewhere in the world: "The interns are challenging their country's traditional notion of its wartime

victimization—that Austria simply fell prey to Nazi aggression. In fact, thousands of Austrians acted as Nazi collaboraters and likely committed war crimes against Jews. . . . "I want to tell [people] that I acknowledge it," Zotti [a Gedenkdienst volunteer] says, "It's important for me. It's my country. It's my roots. I want to put it in the light of what it is" (July 30, 2000: E3).

79. The phrase has been evoked innumerable times over the last three decades in both theological and secular contexts, for example, Vigen Guroian's "Post-Holocaust Political Morality" (Guroian, 1988).

80. In a recent poll, between 80 and 90 percent of Americans agreed that the need to protect the rights of minorities, and not "going along with everybody else," were lessons to be drawn from the Holocaust. The same proportion also agreed that "it is important the people keep hearing about the Holocaust so that it will not happen again" (quoted in Novick, 1999: 232).

81. On May 20, 1999, the *San Francisco Chronicle* ran the following story from the *Los Angeles Times* wire service:

> The Justice Department renewed its long legal battle yesterday against alleged Nazi death camp guard John Demjanjuk, seeking to strip the retired Cleveland autoworker of his U.S. citizenship. For Demjanjuk, 79, the action marks the latest in a 22-year-old case with many twists and turns. . . . The Justice Department first accused Demjanjuk of being Ivan the Terrible in 1977, and four years later a federal judge concurred. Demjanjuk was stripped of his U.S. citizenship and extradited in 1986 to Israel, where he was convicted of crimes against humanity by an Israeli trial court and sentenced to death. But Israel's Supreme Court found that reasonable doubt existed on whether Demjanjuk was Ivan the Terrible, a guard [in Treblinka] who hacked and tortured his victims before running the engines that pumped lethal gas into the chambers where more than 800,000 men, women and children were executed. . . . Returning to a quiet existence in Cleveland, Demjanjuk won a second court victory last year when [a] U.S. District Judge— citing criticism of government lawyers by an appellate court panel—declared that government lawyers acted "with reckless disregard for their duty to the court" by withholding evidence in 1981 that could have helped Demjanjuk's attorneys. . . . The Justice Department [will] reinstitute denaturalization proceedings based on other evidence.
> ("U.S. Reopens 22-Year Case against Retiree Accused of Being Nazi Guard": A4)

82. The first issue of the journal *Holocaust and Genocide Studies* carried an article by Seena B. Kohl entitled "Ethnocide and Ethnogenesis: A Case Study of the Mississippi Band of Choctaw, a Genocide Avoided" (1[1] 1986: 91–100). After the publication of his *American Holocaust: The Conquest of the New World* (1991) David E. Stannard wrote:

> Compared with Jews in the Holocaust . . . some groups have suffered greater *numerical* loss of life from genocide. The victims of the Spanish slaughter of the indigenous people of Mesoamerica in the sixteenth century numbered in the tens of millions. . . . Other groups also have suffered greater proportional loss of life from genocide than did the Jews under Hitler. The Nazis killed 60 to 65 per cent of Europe's Jews, compared with the destruction by the Spanish, British, and Americans of 95 per cent or more of numerous ethnically and culturally distinct peoples in North and South American from the sixteenth through the nineteenth centuries. . . . Among other instances of clear genocidal intent, the first governor of the State of California openly urged his legislature in 1851 to wage war against the Indians of the region "until the Indian race becomes extinct."
> (Stannard, 1996: 2, italics in original)

Stannard is ostensibly here denying the uniqueness of the Holocaust, even while he makes of it pivotal reference for moral determinations of evil.

83. Delanty (2001: 43) makes an apposite observation, suggesting that "the discourse of war around the Kosovo episode was one of uncertainty about the cognitive status of

war and how it should be viewed in relation to other historical events of large-scale violence." Delanty also directly links this discursive conflict, which he locates in what he calls the "global public sphere," to the ethical questions of what kind of interventionist action, if any, outsiders were morally obligated to take: "The implications of this debate in fact went beyond the ethical level in highlighting cultural questions concerning the nature of war and legtimate violence . . . about what exactly constitutes violence [and] who was the victim and who was perpetrator [and] the constitution of the 'we' who are responsible." Yet because Delanty views this discursive conflict as primarily cognitive, between more or less similarly valued "cognitive models," he fails sufficiently to appreciate the moral force that the Holocaust's engorged evility lent to the metaphors of ethnic cleansing and genocide. This leads Delanty to make the perplexing observation that "as the war progressed, the nature of the subject of responsibility, the object of politics and whether moral obligations must lead to political obligation became more and more uncertain," with the result that the "obligation to intervene was severely limited." If the analysis just presented is correct, it suggest precisely the opposite: Given the uneven weighting of the polluted symbols of violence, as the Yugoslavian wars progressed, during the decade of the 1990s, the Holocaust symbol gained increasing authority and thus the nature of the immanent obligations increasingly certain and the obligation to intervene increasingly available.

84. The very same day, the *San Francisco Chronicle* reported that Germany's deputy foreign minister for U.S. relations, a social democrat, "suggested why Germany was able to participate in the NATO assault on Yugoslavia: The '68ers,' veterans of the student movement, used to tell their elders, 'We will not stand by, as you did while minority rights are trampled and massacres take place.' Slobodan Milosevic gave them a chance to prove it" (May 14: A1).

85. For a detailed discussion of the fundamental analogizing role played during media construction of the Balkan crisis by recycled Holocaust photos, see Zelizer (1998: 210–30).

86. The date was December 11, 1946.

87. On the fiftieth anniversary of that proclamation, Michael Ignatieff recalled that "the Holocaust made the Declaration possible," that it was composed in "the shadow of the Holocaust," and that "the Declaration may still be a child of the Enlightenment, but it was written when faith in the Enlightenment faced its deepest crisis of confidence" (Ignatieff, 1999: 58).

88.

The World War II trials [should] receive credit for helping to launch an international movement for human rights and for the legal institutions needed to implement such rights. Domestic trials, inspired in part by the Nuremberg trials, include Israel's prosecution of Adolph Eichmann for this conduct during World War II; Argentina's prosecution of 5,000 members of the military junta involved in state terrorism and the murder of 10,000 to 30,000 people; Germany's prosecution of border guards and their supervisors involved in shooting escapees from East Germany; and Poland's trial of General Jaruzelski for his imposition of martial law. . . . Nuremberg launched a remarkable international movement for human rights founded in the rule of law; inspired the development of the United Nations and of nongovernmental organizations around the world; encouraged national trials for human rights violations; and etched a set of ground rules about human entitlement that circulate in local, national, and international settings. Ideas and, notably, ideas about basic human rights spread through formal and informal institutions. Especially when framed in terms of universality, the language of rights and the vision of trials following their violation equip people to call for accountability even where it is not achievable. (Minow, 1998: 27, 47–8)

89. Yehuda Bauer. See note 41.

90. Despite his misleading polemics against what he pejoratively terms the "Holocaust industry," it is revealing that even such a critic of popularization as Finkelstein realizes that the uniqueness of Holocaust evility does not preclude, and should not preclude, the event's generalization and universalization:

For those committed to human betterment, a touchstone of evil does not preclude but rather invites comparisons. Slavery occupied roughly the same place in the moral universe of the late nineteenth century as the Nazi holocaust does today. Accordingly, it was often invoked to illuminate evils not fully appreciated. John Stuart Mill compared the condition of women in that most hallowed Victorian institution, the family, to slavery. He even ventured that in crucial respects it was worse. (Finkelstein, 2000: 148)

Citing a specific example of this wider moral effect, Finkelstein observes that, "seen through the lens of Auschwitz, what previously was taken for granted—for example, bigotry—no longer can be. In fact, it was the Nazi holocaust that discredited the scientific racism that was so pervasive a feature of American intellectual life before World War II" (Finkelstein, 2000: 148).

91. This instrumentalizing, desacralizing, demagicalizing approach to routinization is captured in the quotation with which Max Weber famously concluded *The Protestant Ethic and the Spirit of Capitalism* (Weber, 1958 [1904]: 182). Observing that modernity brought with it the very distinct possibility of "mechanized petrification, embellished with a sort of convulsive self-importance," Weber added this apposite passage: "Specialists without spirit, sensualists without heart; this nullity imagines that it has attained a level of civilization never before achieved." This understanding has been applied to the memorialization process—as kind of inevitable, "developmental" sequence—by a number of commentators, and, most critically, in Ian Buruma, *The Wages of Guilt* (1994), and Peter Novick, *The Holocaust in American Life* (1999).

92. On the relationship between the liquid and crystallized forms of the sacred, see Alexander, "Les Regles secrètes: L'argument souterrain de Durkheim pour la subjectification de la sociologie" (1996b).

93. I am grateful to the author for sharing his findings with me.

94. Internal memo from Alice Greenwald, one of the museum's consultants, and Susan Morgenstein, the former curator and subsequently director of temporary exhibits, February 23, 1989.

95. Interview with Ralph Applebaum, Chief Designer of the Holocaust Museum.

96. Internal memo from Cindy Miller, project director, March 1, 1989.

97. This is Linenthal's own observation.

98. A recent *Los Angeles Times* description of the museum brings together its tragic dramatization, its participatory, experiential emphasis, and its universalizing ambition: "The 7-year-old West Los Angeles museum is internationally acclaimed for its high-tech exhibits, for pushing ideas instead of artifacts. You know right away that this is not the kind of museum where you parade past exhibits on the walls. The place is dark and windowless with a concrete bunker kind of feel, lit by flashes from a 16-screen video wall featuring images of civil rights struggles and blinking list of words: *Retard. Spic. Queen.*" (July 30, 2000: E1, italics in original). The exhibition at the Los Angeles museum begins by asking visitors to pass through one of two doors marked "unprejudiced" and "prejudiced."

*Chapter 3.*

1. This theoretical model is my personal effort to crystallize a collective intellectual effort. In 1998–99, under the auspices of the Center for Advanced Studies in the Behav-

ioral Sciences in Palo Alto, and sponsored in part by the Hewlett Foundation, I had the fortunate opportunity to organize a research project that engaged the collaboration of Ron Eyerman, Bernhard Giesen, Neil Smelser, Piotr Sztompka, and Bjorn Wittrock. The idea of cultural trauma as a sociological topic came about as the result of our initial discussions. Once the idea crystallized, we elaborated it in the course of months of theoretical argument and empirical discussion. This chapter is my introduction to our collective book *Cultural Trauma and Collective Identity* (Alexander, Eyerman, Giesen, Smelser, and Sztompka. Berkeley: University of California Press, forthcoming). See also Eyerman 2001.

2. Whether the lay perception of events as "traumatic" was at some point in historical time confined to the West or whether the language was also intrinsic to the preglobalization cultural discourse of non-Western societies is an issue that merits further investigation. It does not, however, concern me directly here. My premise is that, in the context of modern globalization, members of both Western and non-Western collectivities do employ such a framework. The claim, then, is that the theory of cultural trauma presented here is universal in a postfoundational sense, and throughout this chapter I will illustrate the model with examples from both Western and non-Western societies.

The notion that this theory of cultural trauma is universally applicable does not suggest, however, that different regions of the globe—eastern and western, northern and southern—share the same traumatic memories. This is far from the case, as I remark upon in chapter 6.

3. The ultimate example of such naturalization is the recent effort to locate trauma in a specific part of the brain through Positron Emission Tomography (PET) scanning, the brain color imaging that has become a research tool of neurology. Such images are taken as proof that trauma "really exists" because it has a physical, material dimension. We would not wish to suggest that trauma does not, in fact, have a material component. Every component of social life exists on multifold levels. What we object to is reduction, that trauma is a symptom produced by a physical or natural base. In this sense, trauma theory bears marked resemblance to another naturalistic understanding that has permeated contemporary social life, namely the notion of "stress." According to contemporary lingo, persons are "placed under stress," that is, stress is a matter of their environments, not of the mediation of actors who construct an environment as stressful according to their social position and cultural frame.

4. A more distinctively sociological representation of the psychoanalytic approach to trauma is *Presenting the Past: Psychoanalysis and the Sociology of Misremembering*, Jeffrey Prager's (1998) study of repression and displacement in the case of a patient who claimed sexual harassment by her father. Prager goes beyond lay trauma theory by demonstrating how the individual's memory of trauma was the product not only of her actual experience but also of the contemporary cultural milieu, which by its emphasis on "lost memory syndrome" actually presented the possibility of trauma to her.

5. For a nonpsychoanalytic, emphatically sociological approach to memory, derived from the Durkheimian tradition, see the important statement by Paul Connerton, *How Societies Remember* (1989).

6. For an analysis of Lacan in the psychoanalytically informed humanities, see specifically Caruth's "Traumatic Awakenings: Freud, Lacan, and the Ethics of Memory" (Caruth, 1996: 91–112).

7. For another illuminating and influential work in this tradition, see Dominick La Capra, *Representing the Holocaust: History, Theory, Trauma* (1994).

8. Unpublished manuscript. All quotations are from pp. 5–7.

9. The concept of "claims" is drawn from the sociological literature on moral panics. See Thompson (1998).

10. In relation to issues of cultural change and conflict, Weber's concept has been developed further by S. N. Eisenstadt (1982) and, most recently, Bernhard Giesen in *Intellectuals and the Nation* (1998). Claim-making groups correspond also to the concept of "movement intellectuals" developed, in a different context, by Ron Eyerman and Andrew Jamison in *Social Movements: A Cognitive Approach* (1991). Smelser (1974) illuminated the group basis for claim-making in his reformulation of Tocqueville's notion of "estate."

11. The foundation of speech act theory can be found in the pragmatically inspired interpretation and extension of Wittgenstein carried out by J. L. Austin in *How to Do Things with Words* (1962). In that now classic work, Austin developed the notion that speech is directed not only to symbolic understanding but to achieving what he called "illocutionary force," that is, to having a pragmatic effect on social interaction. The model achieved its most detailed elaboration in John Searle's *Speech Acts* (1969). In contemporary philosophy, it has been Jürgen Habermas who has demonstrated how speech act theory is relevant to social action and social structure, beginning with his *Theory of Communicative Action* (1984). For a culturally oriented application of this Habermasian perspective to social movements, see Maria Pia Lara, *Feminist Narratives in the Public Sphere* (1998).

12. He also speaks of a "representational process." Stuart Hall develops a similar notion, but he means by it something more specific than what I have in mind here, namely the articulation of discourses that have not been linked before the panic began.

13. For the contingency of this process of establishing the nature of the pain, the nature of the victim, and the appropriate response in the aftermath of the "trauma" created by the Vietnam War, see J. William Gibson (1994).

14. Maillot's representation of the difficulties of the Northern Ireland peace process combines these different aspects of the classifying process.

> None of the "agents of violence" would agree on the reasons for the violence and on its
> nature. In fact, only the supporters of the IRA and, to a much less extent, part of the
> nationalist community, would agree that there was an actual "War" going on. For a sub-
> stantial section of the Unionist community, the IRA is entirely to blame. "Our whole
> community, indeed our whole country, has been the victim of the IRA for over 30 years,"
> said Ian Paisley Jr. . . . As all the other issues discussed in the run-up to the signing of
> the Good Friday Agreement, the question of victims proved highly emotional and con-
> troversial . . . one which enabled all participants to vent their frustration and their
> anger, and one that revealed the different approaches each side was to take. Indeed, the
> very term "victims" proved controversial, as participants disagreed on the people who
> constituted this group.

15. The notion of transparency, so necessary for creating a normative, or philosophical, theory of what Habermas has called his "discourse ethics," is debilitating for creating a sociological one.

16. Smelser described how state agencies and other agents of social control make efforts to "handle and channel" what I am calling the trauma process.

17. Insofar as such memorializations are not created, it reflects the fact the traumatic suffering has either not been persuasively narrated or has not been generalized beyond the immediately affected population. This is markedly the case, for example, with the 350-year enslavement of Africans in the United States. Eyerman (2001) demonstrates how this experience came to form the traumatic basis for black identity in the United States. However, despite the fact that white Americans initiated what has been called the "second Reconstruction" in the 1960s and 1970s, and despite the permeation among not only black but white American publics of fictional and factual media representations of slavery and postslavery trauma, white power centers in American society have not

dedicated themselves to creating museums to memorialize the slavery trauma. A recent letter to the editor in the *New York Times* points eloquently to this absence and to the lack of black-white solidarity it implies:

The worthy suggestion that the Tweed Courthouse in Lower Manhattan be used as a museum to memorialize New York City's slave history . . . evokes a broader question: Why is there no *national* museum dedicated to the histoy of slavery? One can only imagine the profound educational and emotional effect a major institution recounting this period of our history would have on *all* Americans. Perhaps President-elect George W. Bush, in striving to be a uniter of people, would consider promoting such a project in our capital? (December 16, 2000: *New York Times,* Section A page 18 Col. 4).

18. There are, in other words, not only empirical but also moral consequences of this theoretical disagreement about the nature of institutionalization. For example, the routinization of recent trauma processes—those concerned with the democratic transitions of the last decade—has produced a body of specialists who, far from being dessicated and instrumental, have worked to spread a new message of moral responsibility and inclusion. As this book goes to press, the *New York Times* has published the following report under the headline "For Nations Traumatized by the Past, New Remedies."

From temporary offices on Wall Street, a new international human rights group has plunged into work with 14 countries, helping them come to terms with the oppressions that mark their recent past. The International Center for Transitional Justice opened its doors on March 1, incubated by the Ford Foundation and led by Alex Boraine, an architect of South Africa's Truth and Reconciliation Commission. The South African commission was the first to hold public hearings where both victims and perpetrators told their stories of human rights abuses in the era of Apartheid. With a growing number of countries turning to truth commissions to heal the wounds of their past, many governments and human rights groups in Asia, South America, Africa and Europe are now asking for advice, information and technical assistance from those have been through the process . . . The foundation . . . asked Mr. Boraine . . . to develop a proposal for a center that would conduct research in the field and help countries emerging from state sponsored terrorism or civil war. . . . "The day we got our funds, we were actually in Peru, and it has been a deluge ever since." (July 29, 2001: A5)

19. For one of the first and still best sociological statements, see Kuper (1981).

20. This insightful work, by one of the most important contemporary French sociologists, develops a strong case for the moral relevance of mediated global images of mass suffering but does not present a complex causal explanation for why and where such images might be compelling, and where not.

*Chapter 4.*

1. "The values which come to be constitutive of the structure of a societal system are, then, the conceptions of the desirable type of society held by the members of the society of reference and applied to the particular society of which they are members. . . . A value-pattern then defines a direction of choice, and consequent commitment to action" (Parsons, 1968: 136).

This approach was elaborated by Robin M. Williams, the most authoritative sociological interpreter of American values in the postwar period: "A value system is an organized set of preferential rules for making selections, resolving conflicts, and coping with needs for social and psychological defenses of the choices made or proposed. Values steer anticipatory and goal-oriented behavior; they also 'justify' or 'explain' past conduct" (Williams, 1971: 123–59, esp. p. 128).

While Parsons and Williams both represent a specific tradition within sociology—the early and middle period of Durkheim and the later, structural-functional school—their equation of culture with the desirable is shared by every other school of sociological thought.

2. See the demonstration of this point in Marshall Sahlins's discussion of polluted food and clothing symbolism: "Le Pensée Bourgeoise," in *Culture and Practical Reason* (1976: 166–204).

3. A clear statement of this Durkheimian position is Caillois (1959 [1939]), in which Caillois criticizes Durkheim for not distinguishing clearly enough between the sacred, the profane, and the routine.

4. Two of the most compelling contemporary, neo-Aristotelian analyses of "evil-versus-good" in cultural narratives are Northrop Frye, *The Anatomy of Criticism* (1971 [1957]), and Vladimir Propp, *Morphology of the Folktale* (1969 [1928]). More recently, see Robin Wagner-Pacifici, *The Moro Morality Play: Terrorism as Social Drama* (1986).

5. In contemporary social science, the most influential analysis of ritual has been Victor Turner, *The Ritual Process* (Chicago: Aldine, 1969).

6. The sacred-profane refers to Durkheim's later "religious sociology," the promise of salvation to Weber's *Sociology of Religion* (1964 [1922]); see the introduction and chapter 1 herein.

7. See Bataille (1957 [1990], 142–5).

8. "It is inherent in our entire philosophic tradition that we cannot conceive of a 'radical evil,' and this is true both for Christian theology, which conceded even the devil himself a celestial origin, as well as for Kant. . . . Therefore we have nothing to fall back on in order to understand a phenomenon that nevertheless confronts us with its overpowering reality" (Arendt, 1951:459).

Richard Bernstein shares this view. "The larger question looming in the background is whether our philosophic tradition—especially the modern philosophic tradition—is rich and deep enough to enable us to comprehend what we are asserting when we judge something to be evil" (Bernstein, "Radical Evil: Kant at War with Himself," 2001: 56). After an exhaustive investigation of Kant's thinking, Bernstein's answer is no. It is a similar perception of this failure in the philosophic tradition that provides the focus for María Pía Lara's edited collection of essays *Rethinking Evil* (2001), as well as Susan Neiman's *Evil in Modern Thought: An Alternative History of Philosophy* (2002).

9. In his reconstruction of the republican theory of virtue, Quentin Skinner emphasizes the role of altruistic cultural commitments within it. See his book *The Foundations of Modern Political Thought* (1978).

10. This communicative-normative logic, which so strikingly adumbrates Habermas's later theory, is perhaps most clearly articulated in Dewey's *Democracy and Education* (1966 [1916]). Because pragmatism has supplied social science with its theoretical resources for conceptualizing agency and selfhood, this enthusiastic equation of valuation—the act of valuing—with goodness has undermined the ability of social scientists to understand how social creativity, agency, often contributes to evil. Cushman emphasizes the role that agency plays in the social creation of evil in his sociological investigation of Serbian genocide, which also contains a cogent theoretical criticism of the way the pragmatist tradition ignored the agentic capacity for evil.

Sociological theorists of agency have, like sociological theorists in general, displaced evil. This displacement has much to do with the unbridled political optimism of the progenitors of the pragmatic theories of action [who] simply ignored the idea that the pragmatic, reflexive self could engage in action that was ferocious, malicious, and cruel in its genesis or outcomes. Action and reflexivity was, for these thinkers and their later followers, always considered as progressive. This development was ironic, and perhaps even naive, since such theories developed in a world historical context in which it was rather evident that agents used the infrastructure of modernity for nefarious rather than progressive ends. This belief in the optimistic and moral ends of agency is very clear [for example] in the work of Anthony Giddens, perhaps the most important contemporary theorist of agency. (Cushman, 1998: 6)

11. This dichotomy informs, for example, the work of the influential sociological critic Robert Bellah. His collaborative book, *Habits of the Heart,* is informed by the republican version of American communitarianism, decrying individualism as evil because it supposedly makes it impossible for Americans to connect to any value outside their selves.

Americans tend to think of the ultimate goals of a good life as matters of personal choice.
. . . Freedom is perhaps the most resonant, deeply held American value. In some ways, it
defines the good in both personal and political life. Yet freedom turns out to mean being
left alone by others. . . . What it is that one might do with that freedom is much more
difficult for Americans to define. . . . It becomes hard to forge bonds of attachment to,
or cooperation with, other people, since such bonds would imply obligations that necessarily impinge on one's freedom. . . . The large hope that [one's] freedom might encompass
an ability to share a vision of a good life or a good society with others, to debate that vision, and come to some sort of consensus, is precluded in part by the very definition of freedom. (Bellah, Madsen, Sullivan, Swidler, & Tipton, 1985: 22–4)

Charles Taylor's reply to Bellah is worth noting in this context. "The deeper moral vision, the genuine moral sources invoked in the aspiration to disengaged reason or epressive fulfillment tend to be overlooked," Taylor (1990: 511) writes, "and the less impressive motives—pride, self-satisfaction, liberation from demanding standards—brought to the fore."

A different version of this communitarian value/no value dichotomy can be found in the more philosophically rigorous position Michael Walzer sets out in *Spheres of Justice* (1984), which equates particular values with the values of a sphere or community, thus solving the issue of moral rightness through a kind of a priori pluralism. Zygmunt Bauman developed a particularly strong sociological critique of this position in *Postmodern Ethics,* calling it a naive response to "the cold and abstract territory of universal moral values" associated with modernity. This "'community first' vision of the world," Bauman writes, once "consigned to oblivion by the dominant thought which proudly described itself as 'marching with time,' scientific and progressive," *is* now so popular in the social sciences that "it comes quite close to being elevated to the canon and uncontested 'good sense' of human sciences" (1993: 42–3).

12. I think this is what Bataille was trying to get at when he called for "the rectification of the common view which inattentively sees Good in opposition to Evil. Though Good and Evil are complementary, there is no equivalence. We are right to distinguish between behavior which has a humane sense and behavior which has an odious sense. But the opposition between these forms of behavior is not that which theoretically opposes Good to Evil" (1990: 144).

13. For a sociological consideration of these standard philosophical divisions and an empirical response to them see Alexander (2000: 271–310).

14. In his *Lectures on the Philosophical Doctrine of Religion,* Kant wrote, "Thus evil in the world can be regarded as incompleteness in the development of the germ toward the good. Evil has no special germ; for it is mere negation and consists only in the limitation of the good. It is nothing beyond this, other than incompleteness in the development of the germ to the good out of uncultivatedness" (quoted in Bernstein, 2001: 84).

It is this Kantian inability to conceptualize what I have called here the *sui generis* autonomy of evil that leads Bernstein ultimately to conclude his investigation of Kant's notion of radical evil by suggesting that, when we analyze what Kant means, the results are quite disappointing. . . . Radical evil seems to be little more than a way of designating the tendency of human beings to disobey the moral law, [that is] not to do what they ought to do. There is a disparity between Kant's rhetoric—his references to "wickedness," "perversity" "corruption"—and the content of what he is saying. . . . Kant's concept of an evil maxim is too limited and undifferentiated. The distinction between a good man and an evil man depends on whether or not he subordinates the "incentives of his sensuous nature" to the moral law as an incentive. (Bernstein, 2001: 84)

The phrase "incentives of his sensuous nature" refers to the egoistic self who is not able to make a connection to values, which themselves are conceived inevitably as representations of the good.

15. For the earlier writings, see, for example, Habermas, "Labor and Interaction: Remarks on Hegel's Jena *Philosophy of Mind*," in *Theory and Practice* (1973: 142–69). For the prototypical later renditions of this dichotomy, see his *Theory of Communicative Action* (1984). I believe that in his most recent writings, those that have tried to articulate the role of culture in the public sphere of "discourse ethics," Habermas has been determined to distance himself from this kind of binary thinking. In my view, he will not be able to do so until he jettisons his narrowly pragmatic approach to discourse as speech acts and incorporates discourse in a broader, more semiotic and hermeneutic sense.

16. For an expansion of this critique, see Alexander and Lara (1996).

17. Quoted in Richard Hecht, unpublished manuscript.

18. Foucault would seem to be the obvious, and in some ways all-important, exception to this argument, as I have indicated earlier. Foucault, and the postmodernist archeologists of modernity who followed him, found the production of evil, in the form of domination and pollution of the other, to be at the heart of modern thought and practice. Despite this understanding, Foucault did not interpretively reconstruct "evil values" in the manner I am calling for here. Instead he considered domination and pollution to be the product of "normal" procedures of scientific rational knowledge and the "normalizing" social control accompanying it. In other words, Foucault followed the mainstream tradition in considering evil to follow, as an unintended consequence, from the (however misguided) normatively inspired effort to institutionalize the good. In this regard, Foucault may have been influenced by the spirit of Bataille, but he did not follow the late-Durkheimian roots of his thinking.

19. This, of course, is the standard criticism of Parsons's "oversocialized conception of man," but it is connected here not with his functionalism but with a much more general inadequacy in understanding the nature of culture—a problem, I am suggesting, that Parsons shared not only with his antifunctionalist critics but with virtually the entire spectrum of social and political thinkers. For an argument that Parsons can be seen within the Republican tradition, see Alexander (2001).

20. See Niklas Luhmann, "Durkheim on Morality and the Division of Labor," in *The Differentiation of Society* (1982: 9–10).

According to Durkheim . . . we are not confronted with factually moral and factually immoral actions. . . . Instead, it has been conceptually decided in advance that, essentially, there is only morality and solidarity, but that under certain regrettable circumstances these can be cut short from their full realization. Durkheim . . . conceives negation as mere deprivation, and to that extent his theory remains Aristotelian. Despite all his understanding for corruption and incompleteness, he expresses an affirmative attitude toward society. (Luhmann, 1982: 9–10)

21. For an earlier historical discussion that also roots Nazism in strongly held "evil" values, see George L. Mosse's closely related and much earlier historical investigation, *The Crisis of German Ideology: Intellectual Origins of the Third Reich* (1964).

22. As this sentence suggests, the sociological perspective on evil presented here does not aim at making distinctions among different qualities of evil, as philosophers do, for example, when they distinguish between the banality of evil and radical evil. From a sociological point of view, the structures and processes, both institutional and symbolic, involved in establishing the range of different qualities of evil are the same. Each involves evoking and maintaining a sharp distinction between the pure and the impure.

23. As Ferrara writes, "the criterion for the radicality of radical evil ought perhaps to be internal to us, the moral community, rather than external, objective. Evil then is perhaps best conceived as a *horizon* that moves with us, rather than as something that stands over against us" (2001: 189).

24. For other empirical studies of such evil-representing events, their sociocultural causes, and their subsequent social impacts, see Jacobs (2000), Smith (1996, 1991), and Alexander (1987). For an overview of the phenomenon of moral panics, see Kenneth Thompson, *Moral Panics* (1998).

25. This is not to say that the attribution of evil to an action, and the subsequent punishment of the agent, is unjustified, either empirically or morally. What is suggested is that such attributions and punishments are arbitrary from the sociological point of view, that is, they do not grow "naturally" from the qualities of the actions themselves. The identification of evil and its punishment are as much determined by social and cultural processes—by context—as by the nature of the actions themselves, though the latter obviously plays an important role.

26. This conception derives from anthropological discussions of taboo, for example, Franz Steiner, *Taboo* (1956). In *Stigma* (1963), Erving Goffman has developed the most general and persuasive treatment of this phenomenon in contemporary social science

27. See Stanley Cohen, *Folk Devils and Moral Panics: The Creation of the Mods and Rockers* (1972), and, more generally, Thompson (1998). For the notion of boundary danger, see Kai Erikson, *Wayward Puritans: A Study in the Sociology of Deviance* (1966).

28. Suggested to me by Steven J. Sherwood, personal communication.

29. The notion of the limit experience is the centerpiece of James Miller's fascinating but one-sided investigation into what he views as the amoral, antihumane life of Foucault, *The Passion of Michel Foucault* (1993: 29, 398 n. 49). Without disputing Miller's moral judgment of Foucault's sexual behavior later in his life, which by several accounts evidenced a lack of concern for spreading HIV, I do question Miller's effort to generalize this accusation to a theoretical and philosophical indictment of Foucault's concentration on evil rather than on the good. Miller takes the notion of the "limit experience" as indicating the moral, even the social endorsement of the antigood morality that transgression allows. This is not the perspective of Bataille, as I indicate in the following, nor should it necessarily be attributed to the theoretical perspective of Foucault, no matter what the nature of his own personal and idiosyncratic fascination with transgression was.

30. For discussions of Bataille's life and work, and the context of his time, see Michael Richardson, *Georges Bataille* (1994), and Carolyn Bailey Gill, ed., *Bataille: Writing the Sacred* (1995). The ambiguity and complexity of Bataille's thinking have made it difficult to incorporate his thinking into streams of thought other than French-inspired postmodernist literary theory. While drawing fruitfully from the "later" religious sociology of Durkheim and Mauss (see Bataille, 1990 [1957]: 208 n. 48), Bataille also tried, much less fruitfully in my view, to develop a kind of totalizing historical and existential philosophy that included not only an ontology and a metaphysics but also a Marxist-inspired political economy. Despite its genuine intellectual interest, the short-lived "College de France," which Bataille initiated with the third-generation Durkheimian Roger Caillois in the late 1930s, had a cultic and antinomian quality that aspired to the

status of the surrealist group of the World War I era. See Michèle Richman, "The Sacred Group: A Durkheimian Perspective on the College de Sociologie," in Gill (1995: 58–76).

31.

To be "bad" is to be mean in a precise sense of the term. Badasses manifest the transcendent superiority of their being, specifically by insisting on the dominance of their will, that "I mean it," when the "it" itself is, in a way obvious to all, immaterial. They engage in violence not necessarily sadistically or "for its own sake" but to back up their meaning without the limiting influence of utilitarian considerations or a concern for self-preservation. To make vivid sense of all the detailed ways of the badass, one must consider the essential project as transcending the modern moral injunction to adjust the public self sensitively to situationally contingent expectations. (Katz, *Seductions of Crime: Moral and Sensual Attractions of Doing Evil* [1988: 81])

See also Richard Stivers, *Evil in Modern Myth and Ritual* (1982).

32. I draw here from "Human Rights Language in Amnesty International" (n.d.), section 4, 24–5. I cannot locate the author of this very interesting manuscript, which, as far as I know, is as yet unpublished.


*Chapter 5.*

1. For the initial statement of this argument, see Alexander (1992). Our argument that subsystems within the social structure possess binary codes will be familiar to readers of Luhmann (e.g., 1989: 36–50). For Luhmann, binary codes are a functional necessity explicable in terms of the need of differentiated subsystems to process information concerning their environment. This theoretical position seemingly results in an overdetermination of the content of codes by social structure. In our theory the question of meaning is central to understanding the nature of codes. We propose that the codes for any given subsystem create a complex discourse because they consist of extended chains of concepts instead of a single binary pair. Moreover, in that our codes are charged with the symbology of the sacred and the profane, they respond to specifically cultural problems of interpretation, as well as the systemic problems of channeling communication, information, and output.

2. Readers familiar with cultural work in the area of gender will be familiar with many of these binary codings, and the application of the negative discourse to women— especially during the nineteenth century—as a means of securing their exclusion and subordination. We see nothing inherently gendered in the discourses, however, insofar as they are also applied to constitute marginal groups in which sexual identity is not an issue. That is to say, the same deep codes are used as a basis for discrimination by race, geographic location, class, religion, and age.

3. Of course the codes we propose are not arbitrary, insofar as each code element and its partner can be described from the point of view of logical philosophy as mutually exclusive opposing qualities. The codes are, however, arbitrary in two ways. First, complex semantic codes enchain these binary pairs into larger structures in an entirely conventional manner—the code is the result of a cultural bricolage (see Lévi-Strauss, 1967). American civil society, then, allocates qualities to sacred and profane codings on a different, but no more or less necessary, basis from communitarian or fascist civil societies. Second, the association between the code element and the extrasymbolic reality of the social world is entirely dependent on contingent processes of association and interpretation undertaken by social actors. The indexical relation between the codes as "signs" and the world of "things" is thus as conventional as the link between Saussure's "acoustic image" and "concept."

4. *Congressional Globe,* 42nd Congress, 2nd session, 1872, 4110.

5. Ibid., 4120.

6. Ibid., 4111.

7. Ibid., 4111.

8. Ibid., 4111.

9. *Congressional Globe,* 42nd Congress, 2nd session, 1872, appendix, 18: 522.

10. Ibid., 523.

11. Ibid., 524.

12. Ibid., 523.

13. Ibid., 527.

14. Ibid., 530.

15. Mr. Mallory, *Congressional Globe,* 40th Congress, 2nd session, 1868, appendix, 18: 227.

16. Mr. Driggs, ibid., 276. Mr. Price, *Congressional Globe,* 40th Congress, 2nd session, 18: 1367. 1868.

17. See Garfinkel, *Studies in Ethnomethodology* (1967).

18. Mr. Humphrey, *Congressional Globe,* 40th Congress, 2nd session, 1868, appendix, 18: 268.

19. Mr. Mungen, ibid., 211.

20. Mr. Humphrey, ibid., 269.

21. Report of speech by Mr. Clayton, *Register of Debates in Congress,* vol. 8 [12]): n.p., n.d.

22. Mr. Mitchell, ibid., 1946.

23. "Report of Minority Committee of Ways and Means," in *Register of Debates in Congress,* vol. 8 [3], appendix: 148. n.d.

24. Mr. Mitchell, *Register of Debates in Congress,* vol. 8 [2]: 1945.

25. President Jackson, "Message to Congress," in *Register of Debates in Congress,* vol. 8 [3]. appendix: 75, n.d. 79. n.d.

26. Mr. McDuffie, *Register of Debates in Congress,* vol. 8 [2]: 1885–86. n.d.

27. Mr. Denney, ibid., 1945. n.d.

28. Mr. McDuffie, ibid., 1882. n.d.

29. Mr. McDuffie, ibid., 1887. n.d.

30. "Report of Committee of Ways and Means," in *Register of Debates in Congress,* vol. 8 [3]: 2120. n.d.

31. Resolution submitted by Clay to the Senate, *Congressional Globe,* 23rd Congress, 1st session, vol. 1: 54. n.d.

32. Clay, ibid., 54.

33. Mr. Stanley, *Congressional Record,* 1924, vol. 65 [2]: 1676.

34. Mr. Heflin, ibid., 1311.

35. Mr. McKellar, ibid., 1682.

36. Mr. Stanley, ibid., 1678.

37. President Coolidge, a speech of February 12, 1924, extracted in *Washington Post* editorial, February 13, 1924.

38. Mr. Heflin in *Congressional Record,* vol. 65 [2]: 1312.

39. "An Ordinance to Nullify Certain Acts of Congress of the United States," in *Register of Debates in Congress,* 1832, vol. 9 [2], appendix 162.

40. "Address to the People of South Carolina by their Delegates in Convention," ibid., 163.

41. "Governor Haynes' Proclamation," ibid., 195.

42. "Message of President of the United States to the Senate and House," ibid., 147, 151, 149–50.

43. Messrs. Brooks et al., "Report on the Impeachment of Richard M. Nixon, President of the United States," in *Congressional Record*, 1974. vol. 120 [22]: 29-293.

44. Mr. Rangel, ibid., 29302.

45. Mr. Conyers, ibid., 29295.

46. Ibid., 292–5.

47. Ms. Holtzman, in *Debate* on *Articles of Impeachment* (Washington, D.C.: U.S. Government Printing Office, 1974): 124.

48. Mr. Eilberg, ibid., 44.

49. Mr. Hutchinson, in *Debate on Articles of Impeachment* (1974): 340.

50. Mr. Dennis, ibid., 43–44.

51. Mr. Latta, ibid., 116.

52. Mr. Sandman, ibid., 19.

53. Mr. Dennis, ibid,, 43.

54. Mr. Latta, ibid., 115.

55. Chairman Hamilton, in *Taking the Stand: The Testimony of Lieutenant-Colonel Oliver C. North* (1987): 742. Daniel Schorr, ed.

56. Chairman Hamilton, in ibid., 743.

57. Representative Stokes, in ibid., 695.

58. Chairman Hamilton, in ibid., 745.

59. Chairman Hamilton, in ibid., 741.

60. North, in ibid., 9,

61. North, in ibid., 504.

62. North, in ibid., 264.

63. North, in ibid., 510.

64. North, in ibid., 262–263.

65. North, in ibid., 266.

66. North, ibid., 264.

67. North, in ibid., 266.

68. North, ibid,, 267.

69. Fred Warner Neal, *Los Angeles Times,* February 12, 1987: n.p.

70. Richard Barnet, *Los Angeles Times,* December 19, 1987: n.p.

71. Stephen Cohen, *Los Angeles Times,* June 7, 1987: n.p.

72. Robert Kaiser, *Washington Post,* December 14, 1987: n.p.

73. Jeane Kirkpatrick, *Washington Post,* December 14, 1987: n.p.

74. David Broder, *Washington Post,* December 12, 1987: n.p.

75. Daniel Pipes and Adam Garfinkle, *Los Angeles Times,* June 3, 1988: n.p.

76. Henry Kissinger, *Los Angeles Times,* December 18, 1988: n.p.

77. See Jane Lewis, ed., *Before the Vote Was Won: Arguments for and Against Women's Suffrage* (1987); George Frederickson, *The Black Image in the White Mind* (1971). See also note 2.


*Chapter 6.*

1. These figures are drawn from the 1972–74 panel survey taken by the American National Election study conducted by the Institute for Social Science Research at the University of Michigan.

2. I am drawing here on an intensive investigation of the televised news reports on Watergate-related issues available in the Vanderbilt University Television Archives in Nashville, Tennessee. I examined every item reported on the CBS Evening News from June 1972 to August 1974.

3. This observation is based on a systematic sampling of national news magazine and televised news reports from 1968 through 1976.

4. For an important general discussion about how the medium of television can transform social occasion into ritual "events," see Dayan and Katz (1988).

5. That Nixon struggled against television in order to prevent ritualization underscores the peculiar qualities of this medium's esthetic form. In his pioneering essay *What Is Cinema?* André Bazin (1958) suggested that the unique ontology of cinema, as compared to written art forms such as novels, is realism. Bazin meant not that artifice is absent from cinema but that the end results of cinema artifice give the unmistakable impression of being real, lifelike, and true. The audience cannot distance itself from talking and speaking images as easily as from static, impersonal, literary forms. This forceful realism is as true for television, particularly documentary and news television, as for the classic cinema, though in this case the medium of contrast is the newspaper rather than the novel. Thus, ever since its appearance after World War II, political leaders have sensed that to command the medium of television, with the hidden artifice of its *mise-en-scène*, means that one's words will possess—in the public's mind—the ontological status of truth.

In this sense, Nixon's struggle against televising the hearings was a struggle to contain information about the Senate hearings within the less convincing aesthetic package of newsprint. He and his supporters sensed that if the televised form were to be achieved, the battle already would be partly lost.

This insight from the philosophy of aesthetics should, however, be modified in two ways. First, because live television coverage of news events is contingent, the realism of the Senate hearings was necessarily uncertain. The "possession" of the Watergate *mise-en-scène*—the play-by-play of the hearings—was far from determined. But Bazin's aesthetic dictum must be modified in another sociological way as well. Television, even "factual" television, is a medium that depends on influence, and the willingness to be influenced—to accept statements of fact at face value—depends on trust in the persuader. The degree to which factual television is believed—how and to what degree it achieves the ontological status to which it is, as it were, aesthetically entitled—depends on the degree to which it is viewed as a differentiated, unbiased medium of information.

Indeed, the analysis of poll data from this period suggests that one of the strongest predictors of support for impeachment was the belief that television news was fair. It follows that one of the primary reasons for the failure to accept Watergate as a serious problem—let alone Nixon's culpability—before the 1972 election was the widespread perception that the media was not independent but part of the "liberal" modernist movement, a linkage that was strongly promoted by vice-president Spiro Agnew. Because of the processes I have described, however, between January and April 1973 the media was gradually rehabilitated. Feelings of political polarization had ebbed, and other key institutions now seemed to support the media's earlier reported "facts." Only because the medium of television now could draw on a fairly wide social consensus, I believe, could its message begin to attain the status of realism and truth. This shifting social context for the aesthetic form is therefore critical for understanding the impact of the Senate hearings.

6. The figures in these last two paragraphs are drawn from the poll data presented in Lang and Lang (1983: 88–93, 114–17). Appropriating the term "serious" from the polls, however, the Langs do not sufficiently differentiate the precise symbolic elements to which the designation referred.

7. Shils (1975; see Eisenstadt, 1968) reads Weber's charisma theory in a different, made less instrumental way, which is much more consistant with the approach I have

taken here. Shils makes routinization the corollary of institutionalization and suggests its continuing sacrality. Shils's overt reliance on Weber and charisma, however, tells us more about what Harold Bloom calls the anxiety of influence than it does about the real theoretical origins of his work, for he clearly draws more on Parsons's and Durkheim's later thought than on Weber himself.

### Chapter 7.

1. As Habermas (1968a: 58) wonderingly puts it, "Marx equates the practical insight of a political public with successful technical control."

2. The data in the following are samples from the thousands of articles written about the computer from its introduction in 1944 up until 1984. I selected for analysis ninety-seven articles drawn from ten popular American mass magazines: *Time* (T), *Newsweek* (N), *Business Week* (BW), *Fortune* (F), *The Saturday Evening Post* (SEP), *Popular Science* (PS), *Reader's Digest* (RD), *U.S. News and World Report* (USN), *McCall's* (Mc), and *Esquire* (E). In quoting or referring to these sources, I cite first the magazine, then the month and year: for example, T8/63 indicates an article in *Time* magazine that appeared in August 1963. These sampled articles were not randomly selected but chosen by their value-relevance to the interpretive themes of this work. I would like to thank David Wooline for his assistance.

3. Many of these anthropomorphic references, which originated in the "charismatic" phase of the computer, have since become routine in the technical literature, for example in terms such as *memory* and *generations*.

4. Technological discourse has always portrayed a transformation that would eliminate human labor and allow human perfection, love, and mutual understanding, as the rhetoric of Marx's descriptions of communism amply demonstrates.

5. While I examined several neutral accounts of technology, I have not, in fact, spent much time on truly benign accounts. Marx qualifies for this category, and his account is double edged. A more contemporary and more pronounced example of the social scientific translation of salvation discourse is Turkle's (1984) discussion, which was widely noted at the time. Her account, presented as objective data gleaned from her informants, is breathless in its sense of imminent possibility.

> Technology catalyzes changes not only in what we do but in how we think. It changes people's awareness of themselves, of one another, of their relationship with the world. The new machine that stands beyond the flashing digital signal, unlike the clock, the telescope, or the train, is a machine that "thinks." It challenges our notions not only of time and distance, but of mind. (13)

> Among a wide range of adults, getting involved with computers opens up long-closed questions. It can stimulate them to reconsider ideas about themselves and can provide a bias for thinking about large and puzzling philosophical issues. (165)

> The effect is subversive. It calls into question our ways of thinking about ourselves. (308)

### Chapter 8.

1. As I remember the event, and it was certainly an event, the entire audience became rather heated up. One leading leftist sociologist of development offered the sarcastic intervention that modernization theory had actually produced worldwide poverty and made the pointed suggestion that Inkeles try selling his tired modernization line somewhere else. At this point shouts arose from various quarters of the audience, and this

distinguished social scientist had to be physically restrained from underscoring his theoretical point in a decidedly nonintellectual manner. The article from which I am quoting, written by Wallerstein and published in a collection in 1979, clearly was drawn from the ASA talk referred to earlier, although my references to the talk are drawn from memory. Tiryakian (1991) places Wallerstein's article in a similar historical perspective and provides an analysis of the fate of modernization theory that bears a marked similarity to the one I undertake here..

2. This impossibility is strikingly expressed in the *cri de coeur* issued by Shoji Ishitsuka, one of Japan's leading Lukács scholars and "critical theorists":

> The whole history of Social Enlightenment, which was so great for its realization of the
> idea of equality, as well as so tragic for its enforcement of dictatorship, has ended. . . .
> The crisis of the human sciences [which has resulted] can be described as a crisis of recog-
> nition. The progress-oriented historical viewpoint has totally disappeared because the his-
> torical movement is now toward capitalism from socialism. The crisis also finds its expres-
> sion in the whole decline of stage-oriented historical theory in general. (Ishitsuka, 1994)

See Hobsbawm (1991: 17): "All this is now over. . . . We are seeing not the crisis of a type of movement, regime, of economy, but its end. Those of us who believed that the October Revolution was the gate to the future of world history have been shown to be wrong." Or Bobbio (1991: 3): "In a seemingly irreversible way, the great political utopia . . . . has been completely upturned into its exact opposite."

3. "We should henceforth conclude that the future of socialism, if it has one, can only lie within capitalism," writes Steven Lukes (1990: 574) in an effort to come to grips with the new transitions. For an intelligent, often anguished, and revealing intraleft debate on the ideological and empirical implications of these events, see the debate of which Lukes's essay forms a part: Goldfarb (1990), Katznelson (1990), Heilbroner (1990), and Campeanu (1990). See also the important and revealing collection *After the Fall* (Blackburn, 1991a).

4. With *scientific* I do not evoke the principles of empiricism. I do mean to refer, however, to the explanatory ambition and propositions of a theory, which must be evaluated in their own terms. These can be interpretive and cultural and can eschew narrative or statistical causality and, indeed, the natural scientific form. By *extrascientific* I mean to refer to a theory's mythical or ideological function.

5. I draw here from a broad range of writings that appeared in the 1950s and early 1960s by such figures as Daniel Lerner, Marion Levy, Alex Inkeles, Talcott Parsons, David Apter, Robert Bellah, S. N. Eisenstadt, Walt Rostow, and Clark Kerr. None of these authors accepted each of these propositions as such, and some of them, as I will show, "sophisticated" them in significant ways. Nonetheless, these propositions can be accepted as forming the common denominator on which the great part of the tradition's explanatory structure was based. For an excellent overview of this tradition that, while more detailed, agrees in fundamental respects with the approach taken here, see Sztompka (1993: 129–36).

6. Probably the most sophisticated formulation of this truth is Smelser's elaboration (e.g., 1968), during the final days of modernization theory, of how modernization produced leads and lags between subsystems, a process that, borrowing from Trotsky, he called uneven and combined development. Like virtually every other important younger theorist of the period, Smelser eventually gave up on the modernization model, in his case for a "process" model (Smelser, 1991) that delineated no particular epochal characteristics and allowed subsystems to interact in a highly open-ended way.

7. I am grateful to Muller (1992: 118) for recalling this passage. Muller notes the acute sense of reality displayed in modernization theory's "amazing hypotheses" (112) about the eventual demise of state socialism. He insists, quite correctly in my view, that

"it was not the [neo-Marxist] critique of capitalism in the 1970s which correctly read the secular trends of the late twentieth century—it was Parsons' theory" (112).

8. "Seen historically, 'modernization' has always been a process propelled by intercultural exchange, military conflicts and economic competition among states and power blocks—as, likewise, Western postwar modernization took place within a newly created world order"(Muller, 1992: 138).

9. This existential or mythical dimension of social scientific theory is generally ignored in interpretations of social scientific thought, except for those occasions when it is glossed as political ideology (e.g., Gouldner, 1970). Simmel acknowledged a genre of speculative work in social science, which he called "philosophical sociology," but he carefully differentiated it from the empirical disciplines or parts thereof. For example, he wrote in his *Philosophy of Money* that a philosophical sociology was necessary because there exist questions "that we have so far been unable either to answer or to discuss" (quoted in Levine, 1991: 99). As I see it, however, questions that are essentially unanswerable lie at the heart of all social scientific theories of change. This means that one cannot neatly separate the empirical from the nonempirical. In terms I employ hereafter, even theorists in the social sciences are intellectuals, even if most intellectuals are not social scientific theorists.

10.

We can comprehend the appeal of historical discourse by recognizing the extent to which it makes the real desirable, makes the real into an object of desire, and does so by its imposition, upon events that are represented as real, of the formal coherency that stories possess. . . . The reality that is represented in the historical narrative, in "speaking itself," speaks to us . . . and displays to us a formal coherency that we ourselves lack. The historical narrative, as against the chronicle, reveals to us a world that is putatively "finished," done with, over, and yet not dissolved, not falling apart. In this world, reality wears the mask of a meaning, the completeness and fullness of which we can only imagine, never experience. Insofar as historical stories can be completed, can be given narrative closure, can be shown to have had a plot all along, they give to reality the odor of the ideal. (White, 1980: 20)

11. As Caillois (1959 [1939]) pointed out, and as Durkheim's original work obscured, there are actually three terms that so classify the world, for there is also the "mundane." Myth disdains the very existence of the mundane, moving between the highly charged poles of negative repulsion and positive attraction. See chapter 3.

12. The retrospective account by Lerner, one of the architects of modernization theory, indicates the pivotal nature of the American reference:

[After] World War II, which witnessed the constriction of European empires and the diffusion of American presence . . . one spoke, often resentfully, of the Americanization of Europe. But when one spoke of the rest of the world, the term was "Westernization." The postwar years soon made clear, however, that even this larger term was too parochial. . . . A global referent [was needed]. In response to this need, the new term "modernization" evolved. (Lerner, 1968: 386)

An interesting topic of investigation would be the contrast between European theorists of modernization and American ones. The most distinguished European and the most original, Raymond Aron, had a decidedly less optimistic view of convergence than his American counterparts, as he demonstrated, for example, in his *Progress and Disillusion* (1968), which forms an extremely interesting counterpart to his convergence argument in *Eighteen Lectures on Industrial Society* (1962). While there seems little doubt that Aron's version of convergence theory also represented a response to the cataclysm of World War II, it was more a fatalistic and resolute reaction than an optimistic and pragmatic one. See the account in his *Memoirs* (Aron, 1990).

13.

The Forties was a decade when the speed with which one's own events occurred seemed as rapid as the history of the battlefields, and for the mass of people in America a forced march into a new jungle of emotion was the result. The surprises, the failures, and the dangers of that life must have terrified some nerve of awareness in the power and the mass, for, as if stricken . . . the retreat to a more conservative existence was disorderly, the fear of communism spread like an irrational hail of boils. To anyone who could see, the excessive hysteria of the Red wave was no preparation to face an enemy, but rather a terror of the national self. (Mailer, 1987 [1960]: 14)

14. In terms of the break induced in American intellectuals by the postwar period, it is revealing to compare this later change theory of Parsons with his earlier one. In the essays on social change he composed in the decade after 1937, Parsons consistently took Germany as his model, emphasizing the destabilizing, polarizing, and antidemocratic implications of social differentiation and rationalization. When he referred to modernization in this period, and he rarely did, he employed the term to refer to a pathological, overrationalizing process, one that produced the symptomatic reaction of "traditionalism." After 1947, Parsons took the United States as the type case for his studies of social change, relegating Nazi Germany to the status of deviant case. Modernization and traditionalism were now viewed as structural processes rather than as ideologies, symptoms, or social actions.

15. It is ironic that one of the best recent explications of, and justifications for, Frye's version of generic history can be found in the Marxist criticism of Jameson, which purports to refute its bourgeois form yet makes heavy use of its substantive content. Jameson (1980: 130) calls Frye's method a "positive hermeneutic" because "his identification of mythic patterns in modern texts aims at reinforcing our sense of the affinity between the cultural present of capitalism and the distant mythical past of tribal societies, and at awakening a sense of the continuity between our psychic life and that of primitive peoples." He offers his "negative hermeneutic" as an alternative, asserting that it uses the "narrative raw material" shared by myth and "historical" literatures to sharpen our sense of historical difference, and to stimulate an increasingly vivid apprehension of what happens when plot falls into history . . . and enters the force fields of the modern societies" (130).

Despite the fact that Jameson is wedded to a reflection theory of ideology, he produces, in fact, an excellent rationale for the use of genre analysis in understanding historical conflicts. He argues that an influential social "text" must be understood as "a socially symbolic act, as the ideological—but formal and immanent—response to a historical dilemma" (1980: 139). Because of the strains in the social environment that call texts forth, "it would seem to follow that, properly used, genre theory must always in one way or another project a model of the coexistence or tension between several generic modes or strands." With this "methodological axiom," Jameson suggests, "the typologizing abuses of traditional genre theory criticism are definitely laid to rest" (141).

For the relevance of generic theory to the analysis of social rather than literary texts, see the historical writings of Slotkin (1973), the sociological studies of Wagner-Pacifici (1986, 1994, 2000), Gibson (1991), Jacobs (2001), Ku (1999), and Somers (1992). For the particularities of my own approach to social genre and its relation to cultural codes, I am indebted to conversations with Philip Smith (1991, 1993) and Steven Sherwood (1994), whose writings are important theoretical statements in their own right.

16. By using the postmodern term "grand narrative" (Lyotard, 1984), I am committing anachronism, but I am doing so in order to demonstrate the lack of historical perspective implied by the postmodernist slogan "the end of the grand narrative." Grand narratives, in fact, are subjected to periodic historical deflation and inflation, and there are

always other, less-inflated generic constructions "waiting" to take their place. I will point out hereafter, indeed, that there are important similarities between the postwar period of narrative deflation and the 1980s, which produced a broadly similar in-turning that postmodernism characterized to such great effect as a historically unprecedented social fact.

17. Romanticism is used here in the technical, genre sense suggested by Frye (1971 [1957]), rather than in the broad historical sense that would refer to postclassical music, art, and literature, which in the terms employed here was more "heroic" in its narrative implications.

18. When I arrived at the University of California, Berkeley, for graduate studies in sociology in 1969, some of the department's ethnographic school sociologists, influenced by Goffman and Sartre, announced an informal faculty-student seminar on "authenticity." This represented an existentialism-inspired response to the alienation emphasis of the sixties. As such it was historically out of phase. Nobody attended the seminar.

19. The present account does not, in other words, assume complete intellectual consensus during the phases described. Countertrends existed, and they should be noted. There is also the very real possibility (see n. 27) that intellectuals and their audiences had access to more than one code/narrative at any given point in historical time, an access that postmodern theory calls discursive hybridity. My account does suggest, however, that each of these phases was marked, indeed was in part constructed by, the hegemony of one intellectual framework over others. Narratives are constructed on binary codes, and it is the polarity of binary oppositions that allows historicizing intellectuals to make sense of their time. "Binarism" is less an esoteric theoretical construct than an existential fact of life.

20. In Jamison and Eyerman's *Seeds of the Sixties* (1994), their insightful account of these fifties critical intellectuals, they argue that these intellectuals failed to exert influence at the time primarily because of the conservatism of the dominant society. It seems important to add that their own ideology was partly responsible, for it was insufficiently historical in the future-oriented, narrative sense. Further, insofar as Jamison and Eyerman accept "mass society" as an actual empirical description of both social structural and cultural modernization in the fifties, they mistake an intellectual account for a social reality. These vestiges of a realist epistemology—in what is otherwise an acutely cultural and constructivist approach—makes it difficult to appreciate the compelling humanism that informed so much of the work of the very fifties intellectuals whom these critics often attacked.

21. A publication that in retrospect takes on the appearance of a representative, and representational, turning point between these historical phases, and between modernization theory and what succeeded it, is David Apter's edited book *Ideology and Discontent* (1964). Among the contributors were leading modernization social scientists, who grappled with the increasingly visible anomalies of this theory, particularly the continuing role of utopian and revolutionary ideology in the third world, which inspired revolutions, and, more generally, with the failure of "progressive" modernizing development. Geertz's "Ideology as a Cultural System" (in Geertz, 1973 [1964]), so central to developments in postmodernization theories, appeared first in this book. Apter himself, incidentally, demonstrated a personal theoretical evolution paralleling the broader shifts documented here, moving from an enthusiastic embrace, and explication, of third world modernization, that concentrated on universal categories of culture and social structure (see, e.g., Apter, 1963) to a postmodern skepticism about "liberating" change and an emphasis on cultural particularity. This latter position is indicated by the self-consciously antimodernist and antirevolutionary themes in the striking deconstruction of Maoism that Apter published in the late 1980s (1987). The intellectual careers of Robert Bellah and Michael Walzer reveal similar though not identical contours.

These examples and others (see n. 8 and 20) raise the intriguing question that Mills described as the relationship between history and biography. How did individual intellectuals deal with the historical succession of code/narrative frames, which pushed them into interstitial positions vis-à-vis the "new world of our time"? Some remained committed to their earlier frameworks and became, as a result, either permanently or temporarily "obsolete." Others changed their frameworks and became contemporary, not necessarily for opportunistic reasons but because of personal encounters with profoundly jarring historical experiences, which sometimes gave them a keen appreciation for "the new."

22. See, for example, the millennial tone of the contemporary articles collected in *Smiling through the Apocalypse: Esquire's History of the Sixties* (*Esquire*, 1987).

23. An illustrative case study of one dimension of this evolution would be the British *New Left Review*. Created initially as a forum for disseminating humanistic Marxism—oriented toward existentialism and consciousness—vis-à-vis the mechanistic perspective of the Old Left, in the late 1960s, it was an important forum for publishing Sartre, Gramsci, Lefebvre, Gorz, and the early Lukács. By 1970 it had turned into a forum for Leninism and Althusserianism. The cover of its fall 1969 issue was emblazoned with the slogan "Militancy."

24. In order to forestall misunderstanding in regard to the kind of argument I am making here, I should emphasize that this and other correlations I am positing between code, narrative, and theory constitute what Weber, drawing on Goethe, called "elective affinities" rather than historically, sociologically, or semiotically causal relations. Commitment to these theories could, in principle, be induced by other kinds of ideological formulations, and have been in earlier times and other national milieux. Nor need these particular versions of code and narrative always be combined. Nonetheless, in the historical periods I consider here, the positions did mesh in complementary ways.

25. This brief reference about the "lag" in generational production is important to emphasize. It is primarily new generations coming to political and cultural self-consciousness that produces new intellectual ideologies and theories, and, as Mannheim first emphasized, generational identities tend to remain constant despite shifts in historical time. The result is that, at any given point, the "intellectual milieu" considered as a totality will contain a number of competing ideological formulations produced by historically generated archeological formations. Insofar as authoritative intellectual figures remain within each generation, furthermore, earlier intellectual ideologies will continue to socialize some members of succeeding generations. Authoritative socialization, in other words, exacerbates the lag effect, which is further increased by the fact that access to the organizational infrastructures of socialization—for example, control of graduate training programs in major universities, editorships of leading journals—may be attained by the authoritative members of generations whose ideology/theory may already be "refuted" by developments that are occurring among younger generations. These considerations produce layering effects that make it difficult to recognize intellectual successions until long after they are crystallized.

These inertial effects of generational formations suggest that new ideologies/theories may have to respond not only to the immediately preceding formation—which is their primary reference point—but in a secondary way to all the formations that remain in the social milieu at the time of their formation. For example, while postmodernism will be portrayed here as a response primarily to antimodernization theories of revolutionary intent, it is also marked by the need to posit the inadequacy of postwar modernism and, indeed, of prewar Marxism. As I indicate hereafter, however, postmodernism's responses to the latter movements are mediated by its primary response to the ideology/theory immediately preceding it. Indeed, it only understands the earlier movements as they have been screened by the sixties generation.

26. This sense of imminent, apocalyptic transformation was exemplified in the 1980s by the post-Marxist and postmodern British magazine *Marxism Today,* which hailed, in millennial language, the arrival of "New Times": "Unless the Left can come to terms with those New Times, it must live on the sidelines. . . . Our world is being remade. . . . In the process our own identities, our sense of self, our own subjectivities are being transformed. We are in transition to a new era" (October 1988, quoted in Thompson, 1992: 238).

27. A compendium of postmodernism's middle-level innovations in social scientific knowledge has been compiled by Crook, Pakulski, and Waters (1992). For a cogent critique of the socio-economic propositions such middle-range theories of the postmodern age either advance or assume, see Herpin (1993), Archer (1987), and Giddens (1991).

28. In December 1986, the *Guardian,* a leading independent British newspaper broadly on the left, ran a three-day-long major series, "Modernism and Post-Modernism." In his introductory article, Richard Gott announced by way of explanation that "the revolutionary impulses that had once galvanized politics and culture had clearly become sclerotic" (quoted in Thompson, 1992: 222). Thompson's own analysis of this event is particularly sensitive to the central role played in it by the historical deflation of the heroic revolutionary myth:

> Clearly this newspaper thought the subject of an alleged cultural shift from modernism
> to post-modernism sufficiently important for it to devote many pages and several issues
> to the subject. The reason it was considered important is indicated by the sub-heading:
> "Why did the revolutionary movement that lit up the early decades of the century fizzle
> out. In a major series, *Guardian* critics analyse late twentieth-century malaise." . . .
> The subsequent articles made it even clearer that the cultural "malaise" represented by
> the shift from modernism was regarded as symptomatic of a deeper social and political
> malaise. (222)

The stretching of revolutionary fervor, and the very term "modernism," to virtually the entirety of the pre-postmodernism twentieth century—sometimes, indeed, to the entire post-Enlightenment era—is a tendency common to postmodernist theory. A natural reflection of its binary and narrative functions, such broad claims play a vital role in situating the "postmodern" age vis-à-vis the future and the past.

29. "La révolution qu'anticipaient les avant-gardes et les partis d'extrême gauche et que dénonçaient les penseurs et les organisations de droit ne s'est pas produite. Mais les sociétés avancés n'en ont pas moins subi one transformation radicale. Tel est le constat commun que font les sociologues . . . qui ont fait de la postmodernité le théme de leurs analyses" (Herpin, 1993: 295).

30. It is these sentiments precisely that characterize C. Wright Mills's early musings about what he called the "Fourth Epoch," in a 1959 radio interview that, to my knowledge, marked the first time that the term "postmodern" in its contemporary sense ever appeared.

> We are at the end of what is called The Modern Age. Just as Antiquity was followed by
> several centuries of Oriental ascendancy which Westerners provincially call The Dark
> Ages, so now The Modern Age is being succeeded by a post-modern period. Perhaps we
> call it: The Fourth Epoch. The ending of one epoch and the beginning of another is, to be
> sure, a matter of definition. But definitions, like everything social, are historically spe-
> cific. And now our basic definitions of society and of self are being overtaken by new
> realities. I do not mean merely that we feel we are in an epochal kind of transition, I
> mean that too many of our explanations are derived from the great historical transition
> from the Medieval to the Modern Age; and that when they are generalized for use today,
> they become unwieldly, irrelevant, not convincing. And I mean also that our major
> orientations—liberalism and socialism—have virtually collapsed as adequate explana-

tions of the world and of ourselves. (Mills, 1963 [1959]: 236, italics added; quoted in Thompson, forthcoming)

As an anticapitalist critical theorist who experienced deep disappointment with the heroic utopianism of class-oriented communism and social movements, Mills's personal situation anticipated the "transition experience" that compelled the postmodernist movement twenty years later. In 1959, however, the time of high modernist hegemony, Mills's efforts at historical sense-making could hardly have had the ring of truth. Liberalism was yet to have its greatest days, and the heroic radicalism of the 1960s was scarcely foreseen. This shows, once again, that while in any historical period there exist contending mythical constructions, those that are out of phase will he ignored; they will be seen as failing to "explain" the "new world of our times."

31. This mood of pessimism should be compared to the distinctly more optimistic tone of Jameson's preface to *The Political Unconscious*, his collection of essays written during the 1970s, in which he seeks to "anticipate. . . . those new forms of collective thinking and collective culture which lie beyond the boundaries of our own world," describing them as the "yet unrealized, collective, and decentered cultural production of the future, beyond realism and modernism alike" (1980: 11). Scarcely a decade later, what Jameson found to be beyond modernism turned out to be quite different from the collective and liberating culture he had sought.

32. Postmodern theorists trace their antimodern roots to Romanticism, to anti-Enlightenment figures like Nietzsche, to Simmel, and to themes articulated by the early Frankfurt School. Yet the earlier, more traditionally Marxist rebellion against modernization theory often traced its lineage in similar ways. As Seidman (1983) demonstrated before his postmodern turn, Romanticism itself had significant universalizing strains, and between Nietzsche and Simmel there exists a fundamental disagreement over the evaluation of modernity itself.

33. It depends on a number of other contingent decisions as well, for example on ignoring postmodernism's own claim that it does not have or advocate a general theory. (See, e.g., my early exchange with Seidman [Alexander, 1991] and his response [Seidman, 1991a].) There is, in addition, the much more general problem of whether postmodernism can even be spoken of as a single point of view. I have taken the position here that it can be so discussed, even while I have acknowledged the diversity of points of view within it. There is no doubt, indeed, that each of the four theories I examine here only exists, as such, via an act of hermeneutical reconstruction. Such an ideal-type methodology is, I would argue, not only philosophically justifiable (e.g., Gadamer, 1975) but intellectually unavoidable, in the sense that the hermeneutics of common sense continually refers to "postmodernism" as such. Nonetheless, these considerations should not obscure the fact that a typification and idealization is being made. In more empirical and concrete terms, each historical period and each social theory under review contained diverse patterns and parts.

34. The link between *glasnost* and *perestroika* and President Ronald Reagan's military buildup—particularly his Star Wars project—has been frequently stressed by former Soviet officials who participated in the transition that began in 1985. For example:

Former top Soviet officials said Friday that the implications of then-President Reagan's "Star Wars" proposal and the Chernobyl accident combined to change Soviet arms policy and help end the Cold War. Speaking at Princeton University during a conference on the end of the Cold War, the officials said . . . Soviet President Mikhail Gorbachev was convinced that any attempt to match Reagan's Strategic Defense Initiative of 1983 . . . could do irreparable harm to the Soviet economy. (Reuters News Service, February 27, 1993)

35. This sense of fundamental, boundary-destroying break is clearly exhibited, for ex-

ample, in the work of Kenneth Jowitt, which searches for biblical imagery to communicate a sense of how widespread and threatening is the contemporary genuine intellectual disorientation:

> For nearly half a century, the boundaries of international politics and the identities of its
> national participants have been directly shaped by the presence of a Leninist regime
> world centered in the Soviet Union. The Leninist extinction of 1989 poses a fundamental
> challenge to these boundaries and identities. . . . Boundaries are an essential compo-
> nent of a recognizable and coherent identity. . . . The attenuation of or dissolution of
> boundaries is more often than not a traumatic event—all the more so when boundaries
> have been organized and understood in highly categorical terms. . . . The Cold War
> was a "Joshua" period, one of dogmatically centralized boundaries and identities. In con-
> trast to the biblical sequence, the Leninist extinction of 1989 has moved the world from
> a Joshua to a Genesis environment: from one centrally organized, rigidly bounded, and
> hysterically concerned with impenetrable boundaries to one in which territorial, ideo-
> logical, and issue boundaries are attenuated, unclear, and confusing. We now inhabit a
> world that, while not "without form and void," is one in which the major imperatives are
> the same as in Genesis, "naming and bounding." (Jowitt, 1992: 306–7)

Jowitt compares the world-reshaping impact of the events of 1989 with those of the Battle of Hastings in 1066.

36. One of the little-noticed battle-grounds of intellectual ideology over the last thirty years has been the "shopping center," a.k.a. "the mall." Making its appearance after World War II in the United States, it came to represent for many conservative liberals the continuing vitality—contrary to the dire predictions of Marxist thought in the 1930s—of "small business" and the "petit bourgeoisie." Later neo-Marxists like Mandel devoted a great deal of space to the shopping centers, suggesting that this new form of organization had staved off capitalism's ultimate economic stagnation, describing it as the organizational equivalent of advertising's "artificial creation" of "false needs." In the 1980s, the same sprawling congeries of mass capitalism, now transformed into upscale but equally plebeian malls, became the object of attack by postmodernists, who saw them not as wily stopgaps to stagnation but as perfect representations of the fragmentation, commercialism, privatism, and retreatism that marked the end of utopian hope (and possibly of history itself). The most famous example of the latter is Jameson (e.g., 1988) on the Los Angeles Hyatt Bonaventure Hotel.

37. For example, in his plea to fellow members of the academic Left—many if not most of whom are now postmodern in their promotion of difference and particularism—Todd Gitlin argues not only that a renewal of the project of universalism is necessary to preserve a viable critical intellectual politics but also that such a movement has already begun:

> If there is to be a Left in more than a sentimental sense, its position ought to be: This
> desire for human unity is indispensable. The ways, means, basis, and costs are a subject
> for disciplined conversation. . . . Now, alongside the indisputable premise that knowl-
> edge of many kinds is specific to time, place, and interpretive community, thoughtful
> critics are placing the equally important premise that there are unities in the human con-
> dition and that, indeed, the existence of common understandings is the basis of all com-
> munication (= making common) across boundaries of language and history and experi-
> ence. Today, some of the most exciting scholarship entails efforts to incorporate new
> and old knowledge together in unified narratives. Otherwise there is no escape from
> solipsism, whose political expression cannot be the base of liberalism or radicalism.
> (Gitlin, 1993: 36–7)

38. Arnaud Sales, who worked earlier in a strongly Marxist tradition, now insists on a

universal relatedness among conflict groups and incorporates the language of "public" and "civil society."

> If, in their multiplicity, associations, unions, corporations, and movements have always defended and represented very diversified opinions, it is probable that, despite the power of economic and statist systems, the proliferation of groups founded on a tradition, a way of life, an opinion or a protest has probably never been so broad and so diversified as it is at the end of the twentieth century. (Sales 1991: 308)

39. This would seem, at first glance, to confirm Said's quasi-Marxist insistence that it was the rise of the West's actual power in the world—imperialism—that allowed the ideology of orientalism to proceed. What Said does not recognize, however, is that there is a more general code of sacred and profane categories of which the "social representations" of orientalism is a historically specific subset. The discourse of civil society is an ideological formation that preceded imperialism and that informed the pollution of diverse categories of historically encountered others—Jews, women, slaves, proletarians, homosexuals, and more generally enemies—in quite similar terms.

40. Exceptions to this amnesia can be found in the current debate, particularly among those French social theorists who remain strongly influenced by the Republican tradition. See, for example, Wieviorka's (1993: 23–70) lucid argument for a contested and double-sided understanding of nationalism and Dominique Schnapper's (1994) powerful—if limited—defense of the national character of the democratic state.

41. In a telling observation on the paradoxical relationship of nationalism to recent events, Wittrock (1991) notes that when West Germany pressed for reunification, it affirmed both the abstract universalism of notions like freedom, law, and markets and, at the same time, the ideology of nationalism in its most particularistic, ethnic, and linguistic sense, the notion that the "German people" could not be divided.

# REFERENCES

Abzug, Robert H. 1985. *Inside the Vicious Heart: Americans and the Liberation of Nazi Concentration Camps*. New York: Oxford University Press.

Adorno, T., E. Frankel-Brunswick, D.J. Levinson, & N. Sanford. 1950. *The Authoritarian Personality*. New York: Harpers.

Alexander, Jeffrey C. 1982. *Theoretical Logic in Sociology*, 4 vols. Berkeley: University of California Press.

Alexander, Jeffrey C. 1986. "The Dialectic of Individualism and Domination: Max Weber's Rationalization Theory and Beyond." In Sam Whimster and Scott Lash, eds. *Max Weber and Rationality*. London: Allen and Unwin.

Alexander, Jeffrey C. 1987. *Twenty Lectures: Sociological Theory since World War II*. New York: Columbia University Press.

Alexander, Jeffrey C. 1987. "Culture and Political Crisis: Watergate and Durkheimian Sociology." In *Durkheimian Sociology: Cultural Studies,* ed. Jeffrey C. Alexander. New York: Cambridge University Press.

Alexander, Jeffrey C. 1988. "Action and Its Environments." In *Action and Its Environments, Toward a New Synthesis*, ed. J. Alexander. New York: Columbia University Press.

Alexander, Jeffrey C. 1990. "Introduction: Understanding the 'Relative Autonomy' of Culture." In *Culture and Society: Contemporary Debates*, ed. Jeffrey C. Alexander & Steven Seidman. Cambridge: Cambridge University Press.

Alexander, Jeffrey C. 1991a. "Sociological Theory and the Claim to Reason: Why the End Is Not in Sight." Reply to Seidman. In *Sociological Theory* 9 (2 ): 147–53.

Alexander, Jeffrey C. 1992. "Citizen and Enemy as Symbolic Classification: On The Polarizating Discourse of Civil Society." In Michèle Lamont and Marcel Fournier, eds. *Cultivating Differences*. Chicago: University of Chicago Press.

Alexander, Jeffrey C. 1995a. *Fin-de-siecle Social Theory.* London: Verso.

Alexander, Jeffrey C. 1996b "Modern, Post, Anti, and Neo: How Intellectuals Have Tried to Understand the 'Crisis of our Time.'" *New Left Review* 210: 63–102.

Alexander, Jeffrey C. 1996a. "Cultural Sociology or Sociology of Culture?" *Culture* 10: 3–4, 1–5.

Alexander, Jeffrey C. 1996b. "Les Regles Secretes: L'argument Souterrain de Durkheim

Pour la Subjectification de la Sociologie." In *Les Règles Après 100 Ans,* ed. Charles-Henri Coin. Paris: PUF.

Alexander, Jeffrey C. 1998, Winter. "Bush, Hussein, and the Cultural Preparation for War: Toward a More Symbolic Theory of Political Legitimation." *Epoche 21* (1): 1–14.

Alexander, Jeffrey C. 2000a. "Theorizing the Good Society: Hermeneutic, Normative, and Empirical Discourses." *Canadian Journal of Sociology* 25 (3): 271–310.

Alexander, Jeffrey C. 2000b. "This-worldly Mysticism." *Journal of Adult Development.* 7(4): 267–272.

Alexander, Jeffrey C. 2001a. "Parsons as a Republican Critic of Industrial Society: A New Understanding of the Early Writings." *Parsons' The Structure of Social Action and Contemporary Debates.* ed. G. Pollini, D. LaValle, & G. Sciortino. Milan: Franco Angeli. pp. 15–24.

Alexander, Jeffrey C. 2001b. "On the Social Construction of Moral Universals: The Holocaust From War Crime to Trauma Drama." *European Journal of Social Theory* 4: 4.

Alexander, Jeffrey C. Forthcoming. "From War Crime to Holocaust Trauma: Progressive and Tragic Narrations of the Nazi's Mass Murder of the Jews." In *Cultural Trauma.* ed. Jeffrey Alexander, Ron Eyerman, Bernhard Giesen, Neil Smelser, & Peter Sztompka. Berkeley: University of California Press.

Alexander, Jeffrey C. Forthcoming. "From the Depths of Despair: Performance, Counter-Performance, and 'September 11.'" *Sociological Theory.*

Alexander, Jeffrey C., & Paul Colomy," eds. 1990. *Differentiation Theory and Social Change.* New York: Columbia University Press.

Alexander, Jeffrey C. 1995. "Traditions and Competition: Preface to a Postpositivist Approach to Knowledge Accumulation." In *Neofunctionalism and Beyond,* ed. Jeffrey Alexander. New York: Blackwell.

Alexander, Jeffrey C., Bernhard Giesen, Richard Munch, & Neil Smelser. 1987. *The Micro-Macro Link.* Berkeley: University of California Press.

Alexander, Jeffrey C., & Maria Pia Lara. 1996. "Honneth's New Critical Theory of Recognition." *New Left Review* 220: 126–52.

Alexander, Jeffrey C., & Steven Sherwood. 1992, February 2. "Why Yeltsin Can't Get No Respect in America." *Los Angeles Times,* M2.

Alexander, Jeffrey C., & Steven Sherwood. 2002. "'Mythic Gestures': Robert N. Bellah and Cultural Sociology." In *Meaning and Modernity: Religion, Polity, and Self,* ed. R. Madsen, W. M. Sullivan, A. Swidler, & S. M. Tipton. Berkeley: University of California Press.

Alexander, Jeffrey, & Philip Smith. 1993. "The Discourse of American Civil Society: A New Proposal for Cultural Studies." *Theory and Society* 22: (2): 151–207.

Alexander, Jeffrey, & Philip Smith. 1998. "Sociologie Culturelle Ou Sociologie de la Cultural." *Sociologie et Sociétés* 30 (1): 107–16.

Alexander, Jeffrey C., Ron Eyerman, Bernhard Giesen, Neil Smelser, and Piotr Sztompka. Forthcoming. *Cultural Trauma and Collective Identity.* Berkeley: University of California Press.

Amishai-Maisels, Ziva. "Christological Symbolism of the Holocaust." 1988. *Holocaust and Genocide Studies* 3 (4): 457–81.

Anderson, Benedict. 1991. *Imagined Communities.* London: Verso.

Anderson, Perry. 1979. *Considerations on Western Marxism.* London: Verso.

Apter, David. 1963. *Ghana in Transition.* New York: Atheneum.

Apter, David. 1987. "Mao's Republic." *Social Research* 54(4): 691–729.

Apter, David, ed. 1964. *Ideology and Discontent.* London: Free Press.

Archer, Margaret. 1987. "Revisiting the Revival of Relativism." *International Sociology* 2 (3): 235–50.

Arendt, Hannah. 1951. *The Origins of Totalitarianism*. New York: Harcourt Brace Jovanowich.

Aristotle. *Poetics I.* 1987. (Richard Janko, trans.) Indianapolis: Hackett.

Aron, Raymond. 1962. *Eighteen Lectures on Industrial Society.* New York: Free Press.

Aron, Raymond. 1968. *Progress and Disillusion: The Dialectics of Modern Society*. New York: Praeger.

Aron, Raymond. 1990. *Memoirs: Fifty Years of Political Reflection.* New York: Holmes and Meier.

Austin, J. L. 1962. *How to Do Things with Words.* Oxford: Clarendon Press.

Baer, Alejandro. "Visual Testimonies and High-Tech Museums: The Changing Embodiment of Holocaust History and Memorialization." Unpublished manuscript. Department of Sociology 4, University of Madrid.

Bailyn, Bernard. 1967. *The Ideological Origins of the American Revolution.* Cambridge, MA: Harvard University Press.

Banfield, E.C., ed. 1991. *Civility and Citizenship.* New York: Paragon.

Baran, P.A., & P. M. Sweezy. 1966. *Monopoly Capital.* New York: Monthly Review Press.

Barber, Bernard. 1983. *The Logic and Limits of Trust.* New Brunswick, NJ: Rutgers University Press.

Barbour, I. 1974. *Myths, Models, and Paradigms: The Nature of Scientific and Religious Language.* London: SCM Press.

Barthes, Roland. 1977. "Introduction to the Structural Analysis of Narratives." In *Image-Music-Text.* London: Fontana.

Bataille, Georges. *Eroticism.* 1986 [1957]. London: Boyars.

Bataille, Georges. 1990 [1957]. *Literature and Evil.* London: Boyars.

Baudrillard, J. 1983. *In the Shadow of the Silent Majorities—Or the End of the Social and other essays.* New York: Semiotext(e).

Bauer, Yehuda. 1986. Editor's introduction to *Holocaust and Genocide Studies* 1 (1): pp. 1–2.

Bauman, Janina. 1986. *Winter in the Morning.* London: Virago.

Bauman, Zygmunt. 1989. *Modernity and the Holocaust.* Cambridge: Polity Press.

Bauman, Zygmunt. 1993. *Postmodern Ethics.* Oxford: Blackwell.

Bazin, Andre. 1958. *Qu' est-ce que le cinema?* Vol. 1. Paris: Editions du Cerf.

Beck, U. 1994. "The Reinvention of Politics: Towards a Theory of Reflexive Modernization." In *Reflexive Modernization: Politics, Tradition and Aesthetics in the Modern Social Order,* ed. U. Beck, A. Giddens, & S. Lash. Cambridge: Polity Press.

Beisel, N. 1993. "Morals versus Art." *American Sociological Review* 38: 145–62.

Bell, Daniel. 1962. *The End of Ideology: On the Exhaustion of Political Ideas in the Fifties.* New York: Free Press.

Bell, Daniel. 1973. *The Coming of Post-Industrial Society.* New York: Basic Books.

Bell, Daniel. 1976. *The Cultural Contradictions of Capitalism.* New York: Basic Books.

Bell, Daniel. 1977. "The Return of the Sacred?" *British Journal of Sociology* 27(4): 419–49.

Bell, Daniel. 1978. "The Disjuncture of Realms." Unpublished manuscript.

Bellah, Robert, ed. 1970. *Beyond Belief.* New York: Harper and Row.

Bellah, Robert, Richard Madsen, William M. Sullivan, Ann Swidler, & Steven M. Tipton, eds. 1985. *Habits of the Heart.* New York: Harper and Row.

Bellah, Robert. 1957. *Tokugawa Religion.* Boston: Beacon Press.

Bellah, Robert, & C. Glock, eds. 1976. *The New Religious Consciousness.* Berkeley: University of California Press.

Bendix, Reinhard. 1964. *Nation-Building and Citizenship.* New York: Doubleday.

Bendix, Reinhard, ed. 1968. *State and Society.* Berkeley: University of California Press.

Benn, David Wedgewood. "Perceptions of the Holocaust: Then and Now." *World Today* June 51 pp. 102–3.

Bercovitch, Sacvan. 1978. *The American Jeremiad*. Madison: University of Wisconsin Press.

Berenbaum, Michael. 1998. Preface to *The Holocaust and History: The Known, the Unknown, the Disputed, and the Reexamined*. ed. Berenbaum & Abraham J. Peck. Bloomington: Indiana University Press.

Berenbaum, Michael, & Abraham J. Peck, eds. 1998. *The Holocaust and History: The Known, the Unknown, the Disputed, and the Reexamined*. Bloomington: Indiana University Press.

Bernstein, Basil. 1971. *Class, Codes and Control*. London: Routledge.

Bernstein, Richard J. 1996. *Hannah Arendt and the Jewish Question*. Cambridge: Polity Press.

Bernstein, Richard J. 2001 "Radical Evil: Kant at War with Himself." In *Rethinking Evil*, ed. Maria Pia Lara. Berkeley: University of California Press.

Bier, Jean-Paul. 1986. "The Holocaust, West Germany, and Strategies of Oblivion, 1947–1979." In *Germans and Jews since the Holocaust: The Changing Situation in West Germany*, ed. Anson Rabinbach & Jack Zipes. New York: Holmes and Meier.

Blackburn, R. 1991a. *After the Fall: The Failure of Communism and the Future of Socialism*. London: Verso.

Blackburn, R. 1991b. "Fin-de-Siécle: Socialism after the Crash." In *After the Fall: The Failure of Communism and the Future of Socialism*, ed. Blackburn. London: Verso.

Blau, Judith. 1989. *The Shape of Culture*. Cambridge: Cambridge University Press.

Bloor, David. 1976. *Knowledge and Social Imagery*. London: Routledge.

Bobbio, N. 1991. "The Upturned Utopia." In *After the Fall: The Failure of Communism and the Future of Socialism*, ed. R. Blackburn. London: Verso.

Boltanski, Luc. 1999. *Distant Suffering: Morality, Media and Politics*. New York: Cambridge University Press.

Boltanski, Luc, and Laurent Thevenot. 1991. *De la Justification*. Paris: Gallirard.

Bonacich, E. 1972. "A Theory of Ethnic Antagonism: The Split Labor Market." *American Sociological Review* 37: 547–59.

Boudon, Raymond. 1992. *L'Idéologie, ou L'origine des idées reçus*. Paris: Fayard.

Bourdieu, Pierre. 1962. "Les Relations Entre Les Sexes Dans la Société Paysanne." *Les Temps Modernes* 195: 7–331.

Bourdieu, Pierre. 1977. *Outline of a Theory of Practice*. Cambridge: Cambridge University Press.

Bourdieu, Pierre. 1984. *Distinction: A Social Critique of The Judgement of Taste*. Cambridge, MA: Harvard University Press.

Bourdieu, Pierre. 1991. *Language and Symbolic Power*. (Gino Raymond & Matthew Anderson, trans.) Cambridge, MA: Harvard University Press.

Bourricaud, François. 1987. "'Universal Reference' and the Process of Modernization." In *Patterns of Modernity*, vol. 1, ed. S. N. Eisenstadt. London: Pinter.

Braun, R. 1994. "The Holocaust and Problems of Historical Representation." *History and Theory* 33 (2): 172–97.

Brenner, Neil. 1994. "Foucault's New Functionalism." *Theory and Society* 23: 679–709.

Brooks, Peter. 1995. *The Melodramatic Imagination*. New York: Columbia University Press.

Brown, N. O. 1959. *Life against Death*. Middletown, CT: Wesleyan University Press.

Brown, N. O. 1966. *Love's Body*. New York: Vintage Books.

Browning, C. 1992. *Ordinary Men: Reserve Police Battalion 101 and the Final Solution in Poland*. New York: Harper Collins.

Browning, Christopher. 1996. "Human Nature, Culture, and The Holocaust." *The Chronicle of Higher Education*. October 18: A72.

Brubaker, Rogers. 1992. *Citizenship and Nationhood in France and Germany*. Cambridge, MA: Harvard University Press.

Brubaker, Rogers. 1994. "Nationhood and the National Question in the Soviet Union and Post Soviet Euvasia: An Institutional Account." *Theory and Society*. 23(1): 47–78.

Buck, Pearl S. 1947, February. "Do You Want Your Children to Be Tolerant?" *Better Homes and Gardens*, 33.

Buckley, W. 1951 *God and Man at Yale*. Chicago: Regnery.

Burn, W. L. 1974. *The Age of Equipoise*. London: George Allen and Unwin.

Buruma, Ian. 1994. *The Wages of Guilt: Memories of War in Germany and Japan*. New York: Farrar Straus Giroux.

Caillois, Roger. 1959 [1939]. *Man and the Sacred*. New York: Free Press.

Calhoun, C. 1993. "Nationalism and Civil Society: Democracy, Identity and Self-Determination." *International Sociology* 8 (4): 387–411.

Campeanu, P. 1990. "Transition in Europe." *Social Research* 57 (3): 587–90 .

Carter, Hodding. 1947, November. "How to Stop the Hate Mongers in Your Home Town." *Better Homes and Gardens,* 45.

Caruth, Cathy. 1996. *Unclaimed Experience: Trauma, Narrative, and History*. Baltimore: Johns Hopkins University Press.

Caruth, Cathy, ed. 1995. *Trauma: Explorations in Memory*. Baltimore: Johns Hopkins University Press.

Chan, Elaine. 1994. Tian-Anmen and The Crisis of Chinese Philosophy: A Cultural Analysis of Ritual Process. Unpublished Ph. D. Thesis, UCLA, Los Angeles, California.

Chang, Iris. 1997. *The Rape of Nanking: The Forgotten Holocaust of World War II*. New York: Basic Books.

Chirot, Daniel. 1990. "After Socialism, What? Ideological Implications of the Events of 1989 in Eastern Europe for the Rest of the World." Manuscript.

Clendinnen, Inga. 1999. *Reading the Holocaust*. Cambridge: Cambridge University Press.

Clifford, James. 1988. *The Predicament of Culture*. Cambridge, MA: Harvard University Press.

Cohen, J., & A. Arato. 1992. *Civil Society and Political Theory*. Cambridge, MA: MIT Press.

Cohen, Roger. 1999, June 26. "Berlin Holocaust Memorial Approved." *New York Times,* A 3.

Cohen, Stanley. 1972. *Folk Devils and Moral Panics: The Creation of the Mods and Rockers*. London: MacGibbon and Kee.

Cole, R. E. 1979. *Work, Mobility, and Participation: A Comparative Study of the American and Japanese Automobile Industry*. Berkeley: University of California Press.

Coleman, J. 1990. *Foundations of Social Theory*. Cambridge, MA: Harvard University Press.

Collins, Randall. 1976. *Conflict Sociology*. New York: Academic Press.

Collins, Randall. 1992. "The Durkheimian Tradition in Conflict Sociology." In Jeffrey C. Alexander (ed.) *Durkheimian Sociology: Cultural Studies*, pp. 107–128. New York: Cambridge University Press.

Comaroff, J. L., & P. C. Stern. 1994. "New Perspectives on Nationalism and War." *Theory and Society* 23 (1): 35–46.

Connerton, Paul. 1989. *How Societies Remember*. Cambridge: Cambridge University Press.

Coser, Lewis. 1956. *The Functions of Social Conflict*. New York: Free Press.

Crane, Diana. 1992. *The Production of Culture*. Newbury Park, CA: Sage.

Crespi, F. 1992. *Power and Action*. Oxford: Blackwell.

Crook, S., J. Pakulski, & M. Waters. 1992. *Postmodernization: Change in Advanced Society.* London: Sage.

Crossman, R., ed. 1950. *The God That Failed.* New York: Harper and Row.

Cushman, Thomas. 1998, April 9. *The Reflexivity of Evil.* Paper presented at the colloquium "The Question of Evil," University of Virginia, Charlottesville, VA.

Dahrendorf, R. 1959. *Class and Class Conflict in Industrial Society.* Stanford, CA: Stanford University Press.

Davis, Mike. 1992. *City of Quartz.* New York: Vintage Books.

Dawidowicz, Lucy. 1982. *On Equal Terms: Jews in America, 1881–1981.* New York: Holt, Rinehart, and Winston.

Dayan, Daniel, & Elihu Katz. 1988. "Articulating Consensus: The Ritual and Rhetoric of Media Events." In *Durkheimian Sociology: Cultural Studies,* ed. Jeffrey Alexander. New York: Cambridge University Press.

Delanty, Gerard. 2001. "Cosmopolitanism and Violence." *European Journal of Social Theory* 4 (1): 41–52.

Deutscher, Isaac. 1968. "The Jewish Tragedy and the Historian." In *The Non-Jewish Jew and Other Essays,* ed. Tamara Deutscher. London: Oxford University Press.

Dewey, John. 1966 [1916]. *Democracy and Education.* New York: Free Press.

Diamond, Sander A. 1969. "The Kristallnacht and the Reaction in America." *Yivo Annual of Jewish Social Science* 14: 196–208.

Dilthey, Wilhelm. 1976. "The Construction of the Historical World in the Human Sciences." In *Dilthey: Selected Writings.* Cambridge: Cambridge University.

Dilthey, Wilhelm. 1962. *Pattern and Meaning in History.* New York: Harper and Row.

DiMaggio, Paul, and Walter Powell, eds. 1991. *The New Institutionalism in Organizational Analysis.* Chicago: University of Chicago Press.

Diner, Dan. 2000. *Beyond the Conceivable: Studies on Germany, Nazism, and the Holocaust.* Berkeley: University of California Press.

Dinnerstein, Leonard. 1981–82, September–June. "Anti-Semitism Exposed and Attacked, 1945–1950." *American Jewish History* 71: 134–49.

Docker, John. 1994. *Postmodernism and Popular Culture: A Cultural History.* Cambridge: Cambridge University Press.

Dodson, Dan W. 1946, July. "College Quotas and American Democracy." *American Scholar* 15 (3): 267–76.

Doneson, Judith E. 1987. "The American History of Anne Frank's Diary." *Holocaust and Genocide Studies* 2 (1): 149–60.

Douglas, Mary. 1966. *Purity and Danger.* London: Routledge and Kegan Paul.

Drinan, Robert F. 1987. "Review of Ann Tusa and John Tusa, *The Nuremberg Trial,*" *Holocaust and Genocide Studies* 3 (2): 333–4.

Durkheim, Emile. 1933. *Division of Labor in Society.* New York: Free Press.

Durkheim, Emile. 1937 [1897]. *Suicide.* New York: Free Press.

Durkheim, Emile. 1968 [1951]. *The Elementary Forms of Religious Life.* London: Allen and Unwin.

Ebihara, May and Judy Ledgerwood. 2002. "Aftermaths of Genocide: Cambodian Villagers." In Alexander Laban Hinton, ed. *Annihilating Difference: The Anthropology of Genocide.* 272–91. University of California Press.

Edles, Laura. 1998. *Symbol and Ritual in the New Spain.* Cambridge: Cambridge University Press.

Eisenstadt, S. N. 1963. *The Political System of Empires.* New York: Free Press.

Eisenstadt, S. N. 1964. "Social Change, Differentiation, and Evolution." *American Sociological Review* 29: 235–47.

Eisenstadt, S. N., ed. 1968. *The Protestant Ethic and Modernization: A Comparative View.* New York: Basic Books.

Eisenstadt, S. N., ed. 1971. *Political Sociology.* New York: Basic Books.

Eisenstadt, S. N. 1982. "The Axial Age: the Emergence of Transcendental Visions and the Rise of Clerics." *European Journal of Sociology* 23(2): 294–314.

Eisenstadt, S. N. 1986. *The Origins and Diversity of Axial Age Civilizations.* Albany: SUNY Press.

Eisenstadt, S. N. 1987. Preface to *Patterns of Modernity, vol. I, The West,* ed. Eisenstadt. London: Pinter.

Elder, Glen H. 1974. *Children of the Great Depression: Social Change in Life Experience.* Chicago: University of Chicago Press.

Eliade, M. 1954. *The Myth of the Eternal Return.* Princeton: Princeton University Press.

Elias, Norbert. 1978. *The Civilizing Process.* New York: Unizen Books.

Ellul, Jacques. 1964. *The Technological Society.* New York: Vintage Books.

Elster, J. 1989. *The Cement of Society: A Study of Social Order.* New York: Cambridge University Press.

Emirbayer, Mustafa and Ane Mische. 1998. "What is Agency?" *American Journal of Sociology* 103(4): 962–1023.

Emirbayer, Mustafa and Jeff Goodwin. 1996. "Symbols, Positions, Objects: Toward a New Theory of Revolutions and Collective Action." *History and Theory* 35(3): 358–74.

Empson, W. 1935. *Seven Types of Ambiguity.* London: Chatto and Windus.

Entrikin, Nicholas. 1991. *The Betweenness of Place.* Baltimore: Johns Hopkins University Press.

Erikson, Kai. 1966 *Wayward Puritans: A Study in the Sociology of Deviance.* Wiley.

Erikson, Kai. 1976. *Everything in Its Path.* New York: Simon and Schuster.

Erlanger, Steven. 2001, April 2. "After the Arrest: Wider Debate about the Role of Milosevic, and of Serbia." *New York Times* A 8.

*Esquire.* 1987. *Smiling through the Apocalypse: Esquire's History of the Sixties.* New York: Esquire.

Etzioni, A. 1968. *The Active Society.* New York: Free Press.

Evans, P., D. Rueschemeyer, & T. Skocpol, eds. 1985. *Bringing the State Back In.* New York: Cambridge University Press.

Eyerman, Ron. 1992. "Intellectuals: A Framework for Analysis, with Special Reference to the United States and Sweden." *Acta Sociologica* 35: 33–46.

Eyerman, Ron. 2001. *Cultural Trauma: Slavery and the Formation of African American Identity.* New York: Cambridge University Press.

Eyerman, Ron, & Andrew Jamison. 1991. *Social Movements: A Cognitive Approach.* Cambridge: Polity Press.

Ferrara, Alessandro. 2001. "The Evil That Men Do." In *Rethinking Evil,* ed. Maria Pia Lara. Berkeley: University of California Press.

Fiedler, L. 1955. *An End to Innocence.* Boston: Beacon Press.

Fine, Gary Alan. 1987. *With the Boys.* Chicago: University of Chicago Press.

Finkelstein, Norman G. 2000. *The Holocaust Industry: Reflections on the Exploitation of Jewish Suffering.* London: Verso.

Fiske, John. 1987. *Television Culture.* New York: Routledge.

Foucault, Michel. 1970. *The Order of Things.* London: Tavistock.

Foucault, Michel. 1972. *The Archaeology of Knowledge.* London: Tavistock.

Foucault, Michel. 1977. *Discipline and Punish: The Birth of the Prison.* New York: Pantheon.

Foucault, Michel. 1993. *The Passion of Michel Foucault.* New York: Simon and Schuster.

Frank, A. G. 1966. "The Development of Underdevelopment." *Monthly Review* 18 (4): 17–31.

Freud, Sigmund. 1961 [1930]. *Civilization and Its Discontents*. New York: Norton.

Friedman, Lawrence. 1985. *Total Justice*. New York: Russell Sage Foundation.

Friedland, Roger, & Robert Alford. 1991. "Bringing Society Back In: Symbols, Practices and Institutional Contradictions." In *The New Institutionalism in Organizational Analysis*, ed. Walter. W. Powell & Paul DiMaggio. Chicago: University of Chicago Press.

Friedland, Roger, & John Mohr, eds. Forthcoming. *The Cultural Turn*. Cambridge: Cambridge University Press.

Friedland, Roger, & A. F. Robertson, eds. 1990. *Beyond the Marketplace: Rethinking Economy and Society*. New York: de Gruyter.

Friedlander, Saul. 1978. *History and Psychoanalysis*. New York: Holmes & Meier.

Friedlander, Saul. 1992a. *Probing the Limits of Representation*. Berkeley: University of California Press.

Friedlander, Saul. 1992b, Spring/Summer. "Trauma, Transference and 'Working Through' in Writing the History of the Shoah." *History and Memory* 4(1): 39–59.

Fromm, E. 1955. *The Sane Society*. New York: Reinhard.

Fromm, E. 1956. *The Art of Loving*. New York: Harper and Row.

Frye, Northrop. *Anatomy of Criticism*. 1971 [1957]. Princeton: Princeton University Press.

Fussell, P. 1975. *The Great War and Modern Memory*. Oxford: Oxford University Press.

Gadamer, H. G. 1975. *Truth and Method*. New York: Seabury.

Garber, Zev, & Bruce Zuckerman. 1989. "Why Do We Call the Holocaust 'The Holocaust'? An Inquiry into the Psychology of Labels." *Modern Judaism* (9) 2: 197–211.

Garfinkel, Harold. 1967. *Studies in Ethnomethodology*. Englewood Cliffs, NJ: Prentice Hall.

Geertz, Clifford. 1971. "After the Revolution: The Fate of Nationalism in the New States." In *Stability and Social Change*, ed. Bernard Barber & Alex Inkeles. Boston: Little Brown.

Geertz, Clifford. 1973 [1964]. *The Interpretation of Cultures*. New York: Basic Books.

Geertz, Clifford. 1983. "Common Sense as a Cultural System." In *Local Knowledge*. New York: Basic Books.

Geertz, Clifford. 1984. "Distinguished Lecture: Anti Anti-Relativism." *American Anthropologist* 86: 263–78.

Geertz, Clifford. 1988. *Works and Lives*. Stanford, CA: Stanford University Press.

Gibson, J. W. 1991. "The Return of Rambo: War and Culture in the Post-Vietnam Era." In *America at Century's End*, ed. Alan Wolfe. Berkeley: University of California Press.

Gibson, J. W. 1994. *Warrior Dreams: Paramilitary Culture in Post-Vietnam America*. New York: Hill and Wang.

Giddens, A. 1990. *The Consequences of Modernity*. Cambridge: Polity Press.

Giddens, A. 1991. *Modernity and Self Identity: Self and Identity in the Late Modern Age*. Cambridge: Polity Press.

Giddens, A. 1992. *The Transformation of Intimacy*. Cambridge: Polity Press.

Giddens, A. 1994a. "Living in Post-Traditional Society." In *Reflexive Modernization: Politics, Tradition and Aesthetics in the Modern Social Order*, ed. U. Beck, Giddens, & S. Lash, Cambridge: Polity Press.

Giddens, A. 1994b. *Beyond Left and Right*. Cambridge: Polity Press.

Giesen, Bernhard. 1998. *Intellectuals and the German Nation: Collective Identity in an Axial Age*. New York: Cambridge University Press.

Gill, Carolyn B., ed. 1995. *Bataille: Writing the Sacred*. New York: Routledge.

Gitlin, T. 1987. *The Sixties.* New York: Bantam.

Gitlin, T. 1993. "From Universality to Difference: Notes on the Fragmentation of the Idea of the Left." *Contention* 2 (2): 15–40.

Gleason, Philip. 1981. "Americans All: World War II and the Shaping of American Identity." *Review of Politics* 43 (4): 483–518.

Goffman, Erving. 1956. *The Presentation of Self in Everyday Life.* New York: Anchor Doubleday.

Goffman, Erving. 1963. *Stigma.* Englewood Cliffs, NJ: Prentice Hall.

Goldfarb, J. C. 1990. "Post-Totalitarian Politics: Ideology Ends Again." *Social Research* 57 (3): 533–56.

Goldhagen, Daniel. 1996. *Hitler's Willing Executioners: Ordinary Germans and the Holocaust.* New York: Knopf.

Goldthorpe, J., D. Lockwood, F. Beckhofer, & J. Platt, eds. 1969. *The Affluent Worker and the Class Structure.* Cambridge: Cambridge University Press.

Gorz, A. 1982. *Farewell to the Working Class.* London: Pluto.

Gottdiener, Mark. 1995. *Postmodern Semiotics.* Blackwell: Oxford.

Gouldner, Alvin. 1970. *The Coming Crisis of Western Sociology.* New York: Equinox.

Gouldner, Alvin. 1929. *The Future of Intellectuals and the Rise of The New Class.* New York: Seabury.

Gramsci, Antonio. 1971. *Selections from the Prison Notebooks.* New York: International.

Granovetter, M. 1974. *Getting a Job: A Study of Contracts and Careers.* Cambridge, MA: Harvard University Press.

Granovetter, M. 1985. "Economic Action and Social Structure: A Theory of Embeddedness." *American Journal of Sociology* 91 (3): 481–510.

Granovetter, M., & R. Swedberg, eds. 1992. *The Sociology of Economic Life.* Boulder, CO: Westview Press.

Greene, Joshua M., & Shiva Kumar. 2000. Editors' introduction to *Witness: Voices from the Holocaust,* ed. Joshua M. Greene & Shiva Kumar. New York: Free Press.

Greenfeld, Liah. 1992, September 21. "Kitchen Debate: Russia's Nationalist Intelligentsia." *New Republic,* 22–5.

Greenfeld, Liah, & Daniel Chirot. 1994. "Nationalism and Aggression." *Theory and Society* 23 (1): 79–130.

Griswold, Wendy. 1983. "The Devil's Techniques: Cultural Legitimation and Social Change." *American Sociological Review* 48: 668–80.

Grossberg, Lawrence, Cary Nelson, & Paula Treichler. 1991. *Cultural Studies.* New York: Routledge.

Guroian, Vigen. 1988. "Post-Holocaust Political Morality: The Litmus of Bitburg and the Armenian Genocide Resolution." *Holocaust and Genocide Studies* 3 (3): 305–22.

Gusfield, J. 1966. "Tradition and Modernity: Misplaced Polarities in the Study of Social Change." *American Journal of Sociology* 72: 351–62.

Habermas, Jürgen. 1968. "Technical Progress and the Social Life-World." In *Toward a Rational Society.* Boston: Beacon Press.

Habermas, Jürgen. 1968b. "Technology and Science as 'Ideology.'" In *Toward a Rational Society.* Boston: Beacon Press.

Habermas, Jürgen. 1973. "Labor and Interaction: Remarks on Hegel's Jena *Philosophy of Mind.*" In *Theory and Practice.* Boston: Beacon Press.

Habermas, Jürgen. 1981. "Modernity versus Postmodernity." *New German Critique* 22: 3–14.

Habermas, Jürgen. 1984. *Theory of Communicative Action.* Boston: Beacon Press.

Habermas, Jürgen. 1989 [1962]. *The Structural Transformation of the Public Sphere.* Boston: Beacon Press.

Habermas, Jürgen. 1990. "What Does Socialism Mean Today? The Rectifying Revolution and the Need for New Thinking on the Left." *New Left Review* 183: 3–21.

Hall, J. 1985. *Powers and Liberties: Causes and Consequences of the Rise of the West*. Oxford: Oxford University Press.

Hall, J. 1993. "Nationalism Classified and Explained." *Daedalus* 122 (3): 1–28.

Hall, Stuart, C. Critcher, T. Jefferson, J. Clarke, & B. Roberts. 1978. *Policing the Crisis*. London: Macmillan.

Halpern, D. 1990. *One Hundred Years of Homosexuality and Other Essays on Greek Love*. New York: Routledge.

Hannerz, Ulf. 1987. "The World in Creolization." *Africa* 57(4): 546–59.

Hannerz, Ulf. 1989. "Notes on The Globel Ecumene." *Public Culture* 1(2): 66–75.

Harrington, M. 1962. *The Other America*. New York: Macmillan.

Harris, Robert. 1992. *Fatherland*. London: Hutchinson.

Hart, Walter R. 1947. July. "Anti-Semitism in N.Y. Medical Schools." *American Mercury* 65: 53–63.

Hartman, Geoffrey H. 1996. *The Longest Shadow: In the Aftermath of the Holocaust*. Bloomington: Indiana University Press.

Hartman, Geoffrey H. 2000. "Memory.com: Tel-Suffering and Testimony in the Dot Com Era." *Raritan* 19: 1–18.

Hartz, Louis. 1955. *The Liberal Tradition in America*. New York: Harcourt, Brace.

Harvey, D. 1989. *The Conditions of Post-Modernity*. Oxford: Blackwell.

Hawthorn, G. *Plausible Worlds: Possibility and Understanding in History and the Social Sciences*. 1991. Cambridge: Cambridge University Press.

Hayes, Peter, ed. 1999. *Memory, Memorialization, and Denial*, vol. 3 of *Lessons and Legacies*. Evanston, IL: Northwestern University Press.

Heilbroner, R. 1990. "Rethinking the Past, Rehoping [sic] the Future." *Social Research* 57 (3): 579–86.

Heilbroner, R., ed. 1986. *The Essential Adam Smith*. New York: Norton.

Held, David. 1987. *Models of Democracy*. Stanford, CA: Stanford University Press.

Held, David and Daniele Archibugi, eds. 1995. *Cosmopolitan Democracy*. Cambridge, MA: Blackwell.

Herf, Jeffrey. 1984. *Reactionary Modernism*. New York: Cambridge University Press.

Herf, Jeffrey. 1986. "The 'Holocaust' Reception in West Germany." In *Germans and Jews since the Holocaust: The Changing Situation in Western Germany*, ed. Anson Rabinbach & Jack Zipes. New York: Holmes and Meier.

Herpin, N. 1993. "Au-delà de la consummation de mass? Une discussion critique des sociologues de la post-modernité." *L'anneé Sociologique* 43: 294–315.

Higham, John. 1984. *Send These to Me*. Baltimore: Johns Hopkins University Press.

Hinton, Alexander Laban. 2002. *Annihilating Difference: The Anthropology of Genocide*. Berkeley: University of California Press.

Hobsbawm, E. 1991. "Goodbye to All That." In *After the Fall: The Failure of Communism and the Future of Socialism*, ed. R. Blackburn. London: Verso.

Hollinger, David. 1996. *Science, Jews, and Secular Culture: Studies in Mid-Twentieth-Century American Intellectual History*. Princeton, NJ: Princeton University Press.

Holton, R. 1992. *Economy and Society*. London: Routledge.

Holton, R., & B. Turner. 1986. *Talcott Parsons on Economy and Society*. London: Routledge and Kegan Paul.

Honneth, Axel. 1986. "The Fragmented World of Symbolic Forms." *Theory, Culture and Society* 3: 55–66.

Honneth, Axel. 1995. *The Struggle for Recognition*. London: Verso.

Horkheimer, Max, & Theodor Adorno. *Dialectic of Enlightenment.* 1972 [1947]. London: Verso.

Horowitz, D., & P. Collier. 1989. *Destructive Generation: Second Thoughts about the Sixties.* New York: Summit.

Huntington, Samuel P. 1968. *Political Order in Changing Societies.* New Haven: Yale University Press.

Huntington, Samuel P. 1981. *American Politics: The Promise of Disharmony.* Cambridge, MA: Harvard University Press.

Huntington, Samuel P. 1996. *The Clash of Civilizations and the Remaking of World Order.* New York: Simon & Schuster.

Huyssen, A. 1986. "Mapping the Postmodern." In *After the Great Divide.* Bloomington: Indiana University Press.

Ignatieff, Michael. 1999, May. "Human Rights: The Midlife Crisis." *New York Review of Books* 20: 58–62.

Inkeles, A. 1991. "Transitions to Democracy." *Society* 28 (4): 67–72.

Inkeles, A., & D. H. Smith. 1974. *Becoming Modern: Industrial Change in Six Developing Countries.* Cambridge, MA: Harvard University Press.

Ishitsuka, S. 1994. "The Fall of Real Socialism and the Crisis in Human Sciences." *Social Justice* 27 (3): 25–33.

Jacobs, Ronald. 1996. "Civil Society and Crisis: Culture, Discourse and the Rodney King Beating." *American Journal of Sociology* 101 (5): 1238–72.

Jacobs, Ronald. 2000. *Race, Media and the Crisis of Civil Society.* Cambridge: Cambridge University Press.

Jacobs, Ronald. 2001. "The Problem with Tragic Narratives: Lessons from the Los Angeles Uprising." *Qualitative Sociology.* 24(2): 221–43.

Jacobs, Ronald, & Philip Smith. 1997. "Romance, Irony and Solidarity." *Sociological Theory* 15 (1): 60–80.

Jameson, Fredric. 1980. *The Political Unconscious: Narrative as a Socially Symbolic Act.* Ithaca, NY: Cornell University Press.

Jameson, Fredric. 1988. "Postmodernism and Consumer Society." In *Postmodernism and Its Discontents,* ed. E. A. Kaplan. London: Verso.

Jamison, A., & Ron Eyerman. 1994. *Seeds of the Sixties.* Berkeley: University of California Press.

Jay, M. 1973. *The Dialectical Imagination.* Boston: Beacon Press.

Jelin, Elizabeth & Susana Kaufman. "Layers of Memories: Twenty Years After in Argentina." Unpublished Manuscript. n.d.

Johnson, P. 1983. *Modern Times: The World from the Twenties to the Eighties.* New York: Harper and Row.

Jowitt, K. 1992. *New World Disorder: The Leninist Extinction.* Berkeley: University of California Press.

Kaiser, David. 1999. *American Tragedy.* Cambridge, MA: Harvard University Press.

Kampe, Norbert. 1987. "Normalizing the Holocaust? The Recent Historians' Debate in the Federal Republic of Germany." *Holocaust and Genocide Studies* 2 (1): 61–80.

Kane, Anne. 1992, Spring. "Cultural Analysis in Historical Sociology: The Analytic and Concrete Forms of the Autonomy of Culture." *Sociological Theory* 9 (1): 53–69.

Kane, Anne. 1998. "Analytic and Concrete Forms of the Autonomy of Culture." In *The New American Cultural Sociology,* ed. Philip Smith. New York: Cambridge University Press.

Kant, Immanuel. 1960. *Religion Within the Limits of Reason Alone* (Theodore M. Greene & Hoyt H. Hudson, trans.). New York: Harper.

Katz, Jack. 1988. *Seductions of Crime: Moral and Sensual Attractions of Doing Evil*. New York: Basic Books.

Katznelson, I. 1990. "Does the End of Totalitarianism Signify the End of Ideology?" *Social Research* 57 (3): 557–70.

Keane, John, ed. 1988a. *Civil Society and the State*. London: Verso.

Keane, John, ed. 1988b. *Democracy and Civil Society*. London: Verso.

Keller, Suzanne. 1963. *Beyond the Ruling Class*. New York: Random House.

Kelman, Herbert C., & V. Lee Hamilton. 1989. *Crimes of Obedience: Toward a Social Psychology of Authority and Responsibility*. New Haven: Yale University Press.

Kennedy, P. 1987. *The Rise and Fall of Great Powers: Economic Change and Military Conflict 1500–2000*. New York: VintageBooks.

Kennedy, P. 1993. *Preparing for the Twenty-First Century*. New York: Random House.

Khosrokhavar, F. 1993. *L'Utopie sacrifiée: Sociologic de la revolution iranienne*. Paris: Presses de la Fondation Nationale des Sciences Politiques.

Kleinman, Arthur, Veena Das, & Margaret Lock, eds. 1997. *Social Suffering*. Berkeley: University of California Press.

Kohl, Seena B. 1986. "Ethnocide and Ethnogenesis: A Case Study of the Mississippi Band of Choctaw, a Genocide Avoided." *Holocaust and Genocide Studies* 1 (1): 91–100.

Kolko, G. 1962. *Wealth and Power in America*. London: Thames and Hudson.

Kolko, G. 1967. *Triumph of Conservativism: Reinterpreting American History 1900–1916*. NewYork: Free Press.

Konrad, George, & I. Szelenyi. 1979. *The Intellectuals on the Road to Class Power*. New York: Harcourt Brace.

Korman, Gerd. 1972. "The Holocaust in American Historical Writing," *Societies: A Reviewing of Social History* vol 2: 251–70.

Kornai, J. 1990. *The Road to a Free Economy. Shifting from a Socialist System: The Example of Hungary*. New York: Norton.

Ku, A. 1999. *Narrative, Politics and the Public Sphere*. Aldershot, UK: Ashgate.

Kumar, K. 1992. "The Revolutions of 1989: Socialism, Capitalism, and Democracy." *Theory and Society* 21: 309–56.

Kuper, Leo. 1981. *Genocide: Its Political Use in the Twentieth Century*. New Haven: Yale University Press.

La Capra, Dominick. 1994. *Representing the Holocaust: History, Theory, Trauma*. Ithaca: Cornell University Press.

Lacouture, Jean. 1990. *De Gaulle: The Rebel, 1890–1944*. (Patrick O'Brien, trans.). New York: HarperCollins.

Laing, R. D. 1967. *The Politics of Experience*. New York: Ballantine Books.

Lamont, Michele. 1988. "The Power-Culture Link in a Comparative Perspective." Paper prepared for the Third German-American Theory Conference in Bremen, West Germany.

Lamont, Michele. 1992. *Money, Morals and Manners*. Chicago: University of Chicago Press.

Lamont, Michele, & Marcel Fournier, eds. 1993. *Cultivating Differences*. Chicago: University of Chicago Press.

Lang, Gladys, & Kurt Lang. 1983. *The Battle for Public Opinion*. New York: Columbia University Press.

Langer, Lawrence L. 2000. "Foreword." In *Witness: Voices from the Holocaust*, (eds). Joshua M. Greene & Shiva Kumar. New York: Free Press.

Laqueur, Walter. 1980. *The Terrible Secret: Suppression of the Truth about Hitler's "Final Solution."* Boston: Little, Brown.

Lara, Maria Pia. 1998. *Moral Textures: Feminist Narratives in the Public Sphere*. Cambridge: Polity Press.

Lara, Maria Pia, ed. 2001. *Rethinking Evil: Contemporary Perspectives*. Berkeley: University of California Press.

Lasch, Christopher. 1978. *The Culture of Narcissism*. New York: Norton.

Lash, S. 1985. "Postmodernity and Desire."*Theory and Society* 14 (7): 1–31.

Lash, S. 1990. *Sociology of Postmodernism*. London: Routledge.

Lash, S. 1994. "Reflexivity and Its Doubles: Structure, Aesthetics, Community." In *Reflexive Modernization: Politics, Tradition and Aesthetics in the Modern Social Order*, ed. U. Beck, A. Giddens, & S. Lash. Cambridge: Polity Press.

Latour, Bruno, & S. Woolgar. 1986. *Laboratory Life*. Princeton, NJ: Princeton University Press.

Lear, Jonathan. 1992. "Katharsis." In *Essays on Aristotle's Poetics*, ed. Amelie Oksenberg Rorty. Princeton, NJ: Princeton University Press.

Leijonhufvud, A. 1993. *The Nature of the Depression in the Former Soviet Union*. Unpublished manuscript. Department of Economics, UCLA Los Angeles.

Lemkin, Ralph. 1994. *Axis Rule in Occupied Europe*. Washington DC: Carnegie Endowment for International Peace.

Lerner, D. 1968. "Modernization: Social Aspects." *International Encyclopedia of Social Science* 10: 386–95.

Levine, D.N. 1991. "Simmel as Educator: On Individuality and Modern Culture." *Theory, Culture and Society* 8: 99–117.

Lévi-Strauss, Claude. 1963. *Structural Anthropology*. New York: Basic Books.

Lévi-Strauss, Claude. 1967. *The Savage Mind*. Chicago: University of Chicago Press.

Lévi-Strauss, Claude. 1974. *Tristes Tropiques*. New York: Atheneum.

Levy, Bernard H. 1977. *Barbarism with a Human Face*. New York: Harper and Row.

Levy, Marion. 1949. *Family Revolution in Modern China*. Cambridge: Harvard University Press.

Lewis, Jane. 1983. *The Pursuit of Happiness: Family and Values in Jefferson's Virginia*. New York: Cambridge University Press.

Lewis, Jane. ed. 1987. *Before the Vote Was Won: Arguments For and Against Women's Suffrage*. New York: Routledge and Kegan Paul.

Liberles, Robert. 1995. *Salo Wittmayer Baron: Architect of Jewish History*. New York: New York University Press.

Linenthal, Edward T. 1995. *Preserving Memory: The Struggle to Create the Holocaust Museum*. New York: Viking Books.

Lipset, Seymour Martin. 1990, Summer. "The Death of the Third Way." *National Interest* 20: 25–37.

Lipset, Seymour Martin, & Renhard Bendix. 1960. *Social Mobility in Industrial Society*. Berkeley: University of California Press.

Lipset, Seymour Martin and William Schneider. 1983. *The Confidence Gap*. New York: Free Press

Lipstadt, Deborah E. 1996. "America and the Memory of the Holocaust, 1950–1965." *Modern Judaism* 16: 195–214.

Locke, John. 1960. *Two Treatises of Civil Government*. Cambridge: Cambridge University Press.

Lockwood, David. 1992. *Solidarity and Schism*. Oxford: Oxford University Press.

Lowi, T. 1969. *The Land of Liberalism.* New York: Norton.

Lukes, S. 1990. "Socialism and Capitalism, Left and Right." *Social Research* 57 (3): 571–7.

Luhmann, Niklas. 1982. *The Differentiation of Society.* New York: Columbia University Press.

Luhmann, Niklas. 1989. *Ecological Communication.* Chicago: University of Chicago Press.

Lukács, Georg. 1971. "Reification and the Consciousness of the Proletariat." In *History and Class Consciousness.* Cambridge, MA: MIT Press.

I.yotard, Jean-Francois. 1984. *The Postmodern Condition: A Report on Knowledge.* Minneapolis: University of Minnesota Press.

Ma, Sheng Mei. "Contrasting Two Survival Literatures: On the Jewish Holocaust and the Chinese Cultural Revolution." *Holocaust and Genocide Studies* 2 (1): 81–93.

McClelland, D. 1953. *The Achievement Motive.* New York: Appleton-Century-Crofts.

Maccoby, Hyam. 1992. *Judas Iscariot and the Myth of Jewish Evil.* New York: Free Press.

Magnuson, E. 1997. "Ideological Conflict in American Political Culture." *International Journal of Sociology and Social Policy* 17 (6): 84–130.

Mailer, N. 1987. "Superman Comes to the Supermarket: Jack Kennedy as a Presidential Candidate." In *Smiling through the Apocalypse: Esquire's History of the Sixties,* ed. *Esquire.* New York: Esquire.

Mandel, E. 1968. *Marxist Economic Theory.* 2 vols. New York: Monthly Review.

Mann, Michael. 1973. *Workers on the Move.* Cambridge: Cambridge University Press.

Mann, Michael. 1985. *The Origins of Social Power.* Vol. 1. New York: Cambridge University Press.

Mann, Michael. 1986. *The Sources of Social Power.* Vol. 1. New York: Cambridge University Press.

Manz, Beatriz. 2002. "Terror, Grief and Recovery: Genocidal Trauma in a Mayan Village in Guatemala." In *Annihilating Difference*, Alexander Hinton, ed. University of California Press.

Marcuse, Herbert. 1963. *One-Dimensional Man.* Boston: Beacon.

Marx, Karl. 1963a [1867]. *Capital,* Vol. 1. Moscow: Foreign Languages Publishing House.

Marx, Karl. 1963b. "Economic and Philosophical Manuscripts." In *Karl Marx: Early Writings.* New York: McGraw-Hill.

Mayhew, L. 1990. "The Differentiation of the Solidary Public." In *Differentiation Theory and Social Change*, ed. J. C. Alexander & P. Colomy. New York: Columbia University Press.

Merton, Robert K. 1970. *Science, Technology and Society in Seventeenth-Century England.* New York: Harper and Row.

Meyer, J., & B. Rowan. 1977. "Institutionalized Organizations: Formal Structure as Myth and Ceremony." *American Journal of Sociology* 83: 340–63.

Miller, Judith. 1990. *One, by One, by One: Facing the Holocaust.* New York: Simon and Schuster.

Miller, P., & N. Rose. 1990. "Governing Economic Life." *Economy and Society* 19 (2): 1–31.

Mills, C. W. 1948. *The New Men of Power: America's Labor Leaders.* New York: Harcourt Brace.

Mills, C. W. 1963. "Culture and Politics: The Fourth Epoch." *Listener.* Reprinted in Mills, *Power, Politics, People.* New York: Ballantine.

Minow, Martha. 1998. *Between Vengeance and Forgiveness: Facing History after Genocide and Mass Violence.* Boston: Beacon Press.

Moene, K. O., & M. Wallerstein. 1992. *The Decline of Social Democracy.* Working Paper Series: 225. Institute of Industrial Relations, UCLA, Los Angeles, California.

Moore, B. 1966. *The Social Origins of Dictatorship and Democracy.* Boston: Beacon Press.

Morgan, Edmund. 1958. *The Puritan Dilemma.* Boston: Little, Brown.

Morrow, Lance. 1978, May. "Television and the Holocaust." *Time*, 1, 53.

Moscovici, S. 1984. "The Phenomenon of Social Representations." In *Social Representations*, ed. R. M. Farr & S. Moscovici. Cambridge: Cambridge University Press.

Mosse, George L. 1964. *The Crisis of German Ideology: Intellectual Origins of the Third Reich* New York: Universal Library.

Muller, K. 1992. "'Modernizing' Eastern Europe: Theoretical Problems and Political Dilemmas." *European Journal of Sociology* 33: 109–50.

Muller, K. 1994. "From Post-Communism to Post-Modernity? Economy and Society in the Eastern European Transformations." In *Social Change and Modernization: Lessons from Eastern Europe*, ed. B. Grancelli. New York: de Gruyter.

Myrdal, Gunnar. 1944. *An America Dilemma.* New York: Harper.

Naimark, Norman. 2001. *Fires of Hatred: Ethnic Cleansing in Twentieth-Century Europe.* Cambridge, MA: Harvard University Press.

Neal, Arthur. 1998. *National Trauma and Collective Memory.* Armonk, NY: Sharpe.

Nee, Victor. 1989. "A Theory of Market Transition: From Redistribution to Markets in State Socialism." *American Sociological Review* 54: 663–81.

Neiman, Susan. 2002. *Evil in Modern Thought: An Alternative History of Philosophy.* Princeton, NJ: Princeton University Press.

Nettl, J. P., & R. Robertson. 1968. *International Systems and the Modernization of Societies.* New York: Basic Books.

Niebuhr, R. 1952. *The Irony of American History.* New York: Scribners.

Norich, Anita. 1998–99, fall-winter. "*Harbe sugyes*/Puzzling Questions: Yiddish and English Culture in America during the Holocaust." *Jewish Social Studies* 1 and 2: 91–110.

Novick, Peter. 1994. "Holocaust and Memory in America." In *The Art of Memory: Holocaust Memorials in History*, ed. James E. Young. Munich: Prestel-Verlag.

Novick, Peter. 1999. *The Holocaust in American Life.* New York: Houghton Mifflin.

Nussbaum, Martha. 1992. "Tragedy and Self-sufficiency: Plato and Aristotle on Fear and Pity." In *Essays on Aristotle's Poetics*, ed. Amelie Oksenberg Rorty. Princeton, NJ: Princeton University Press.

Ofer, Dalia. 1996. "Linguistic Conceptualization of the Holocaust in Palestine and Israel, 1942–53." *Journal of Contemporary History* 31(3): 567–95.

Ollman, B. 1971. *Alienation: Marx's Concept of Man in Modern Society.* Cambridge: Cambridge University Press.

Parsons, Talcott. 1951. *The Social System.* New York: Free Press.

Parsons, Talcott. 1960. "Some Principal Characteristics of Industrial Societies." In *Structure and Process in Modern Societies*, ed. Parsons. New York: Free Press.

Parsons, Talcott. 1964. "Evolutionary Universals in Society." *American Sociological Review* 29 (3): 339–57.

Parsons, Talcott. 1966. *Societies: Evolutionary and Comparative Perspectives.* Englewood Cliffs, NJ: Prentice Hall.

Parsons, Talcott. 1967. "Some Comments on the Sociology of Karl Marx." In *Sociological Theory and Modern Society*, ed. Parsons. New York: Free Press.

Parsons, Talcott. 1968. "On the Concept of Value-Commitments," *Sociological Inquiry* 38: 136.

Parsons, Talcott. 1971. *The System of Modern Societies*. Englewood Cliffs, NJ: Prentice Hall.

Parsons, Talcott, & Robert F. Bales, et.al. 1955. *Family, Socialization and Interaction Process*. Glencoe, Ill: Free Press.

Parsons, Talcott, & Edward Shils, eds. 1951. *Towards a General Theory of Action*. New York: Harper and Row.

Parsons, Talcott & Gerald M. Platt. 1973. *The American University*. Cambridge: Harvard University Press.

Parsons, Talcott, & Neil Smelser. 1956. *Economy and Society*. New York: Free Press.

Peirce, Charles. 1985. "Logic as Semiotic: The Theory of Signs." In *Semiotics*, ed. Robert E. Innis. Bloomington: Indiana University Press.

Perlez, Jane. 2001, April 2. "Milosevic Should Face Trial by Hague Tribunal, Bush Says." *New York Times*, A 6.

Perry, George Sessions. 1948, November 13. "Your Neighbors: The Golombs." *Saturday Evening Post*, 36.

Peterson, R. 1985. "Six Constraints on the Production of Literary Works." *Poetics* 14: 45–67.

Pevsner, N. 1949. *Pioneers of Modern Design from William Morris to Walter Gropius*. New York: Museum of Modern Art.

Pocock, J. G. A. 1975. *The Machiavellian Moment*. Princeton: Princeton University Press.

Pocock, J. G. A. 1987. "Modernity and Anti-modernity in the Anglophone Political Traditions." In *Patterns of Modernity*, Vol. 1, *The West*, ed. S. N. Eisenstadt. London: Pinter.

Polanyi, K. 1957. *The Great Transformation: The Political and Economic Origins of Our Time*. Boston: Beacon Press.

Pool, Ithiel de Sola. 1983. *Technologies of Freedom*. Cambridge: Belknap.

Powell, W. N. 1991. "Neither Market nor Hierarchy: Network Forms of Organization." In *Research in Organizational Behavior*, Vol. 12, ed. B. M. Shaw & L. L. Cummings. New York: JAI Press.

Prager, Jeffrey. 1998. *Presenting the Past: Psychoanalysis and the Sociology of Misremembering*. Cambridge, MA: Harvard University Press.

Propp, Vladimir. *Morphology of the Folktale*. 1969 [1928]. Austin: University of Texas Press.

Przeworski, A. 1985. *Capitalism and Social Democracy*. New York: Cambridge University Press.

Przeworski, A. 1991. *Democracy and the Market: Political and Economic Reforms in Eastern Europe and Latin America*. New York: Cambridge University Press.

Pynchon, Thomas. 1984, 28 October. "Is It O.K. to Be a Luddite?" *New York Times Book Review*, 1.

Rambo, Eric, & Elaine Chan. 1990. "Text, Structure, and Action in Cultural Sociology: A Commentary on 'Positive Objectivity' in Wuthnow and Archer." *Theory and Society* 19: 635–48.

Rand, A. 1957. *Atlas Shrugged*. New York: Random House.

Reisman, D., N. Glazer, & P. Denny. 1950. *The Lonely Crowd*. New Haven: Yale University Press.

Rex, J. 1961. *Key Problems in Sociological Theory*. London: Routledge and Kegan Paul.

Richardson, M., ed. 1994. *Georges Bataille*. New York: Routledge.

Rieff, P. 1959. *Freud: Mind of the Moralist*. New York: Anchor Doubleday.

Rhoades, Richard. 1987. *The Making of the Atomic Bomb*. New York: Simon and Schuster.

Ricoeur, Paul. 1971. "The Model of the Text: Meaningful Action Considered as a Text." *Social Research* 38: 529–62.

Ricoeur, Paul. 1977. *The Rule of Metaphor.* Toronto: Toronto University Press.

Ricoeur, Paul. 1984. *Time and Narrative.* Vol. 1. Chicago: University of Chicago Press.

Robertson, R. 1992. *Globalization: Social Theory and Global Culture.* London: Sage.

Rochberg-Halton, E. 1986. *Meaning and Modernity.* Chicago: University of Chicago Press.

Rohde, David. 1999, June 2. "The Visitor: Wiesel, a Man of Peace, Cites Need to Act." *New York Times,* A 1.

Rorty, Amelie Oksenberg. 1992. "The Psychology of Aristotelian Tragedy." In *Essays on Aristotle's Poetics,* ed. Rorty. Princeton, NJ: Princeton University Press.

Rorty, Richard. 1979. *Philosophy and the Mirror of Nature.* Princeton, NJ: Princeton University Press.

Rorty, Richard. 1985. "Postmodern Bourgeois Liberalism." In *Hermeneutics and Praxis,* ed. R. Hollinger. Notre Dame, IN: Notre Dame University Press.

Rorty, Richard. 1989. *Contingency, Irony, and Solidarity.* New York: Cambridge University Press.

Rose, N. 1993. "Government, Authority and Expertise in Advanced Liberalism." *Economy and Society* 22 (3): 283–99.

Rosenau, P .M. 1992. *Postmodernism and the Social Sciences.* Princeton: Princeton University Press.

Rosenfeld, Alvin H. 1995. "The Americanization of the Holocaust." *Commentary* 90 (6): 35–40.

Roszak, T. 1969. *The Making of a Counter-Culture: Reflections on the Technocratic Society and Its Youthful Opposition.* New York: Doubleday.

Rousseau, Jean Jacques. *On the Social Contract.* 1983. Indianapolis: Hackett.

Rueschemeyer, Dietrich. 1986. *Power and the Division of Labor.* Stanford, CA: Stanford University Press.

Rueschemeyer, Dietrich. 1993. "The Development of Civil Society after Authoritarian Rule." Unpublished manuscript. Department of Sociology, Brown University, Providence, RI.

Sahlins, Marshall. 1976. *Culture and Practical Reason.* Chicago: University of Chicago Press.

Sahlins, Marshall. 1981. *Historical Metaphors and Mythical Realities: Structure in the Early History of the Sandwich Islands Kingdom.* Ann Arbor: University of Michigan Press.

Said, E. 1978. *Orientalism.* New York: Pantheon.

Said, E. 1991, January 11. "A Tragic Convergence." *New York Times,* 1, p. 29.

Sales, A. 1991. "The Private, the Public, and Civil Society: Social Realms and Power Structures." *International Political Science Review* 12 (4): 295–312.

Schluchter, Wolfgang. 1979. "The Paradoxes of Rationalization." In *Max Weber's Vision of History,* ed. Guenther Roth & W. Schluchter. Berkeley: University of California Press.

Schluchter, Wolfgang, & G. Roth, eds. 1979. *Max Weber's Vision of History.* Berkeley: University of California Press.

Schnapper, D. 1994. *La Communauté des citoyens: Sur l'idee moderne de nation.* Paris: Gallimard.

Schorr, Daniel, ed. 1987. *Taking The Stand: The Testimony of Lieutenant-Colonel Oliver C. North.* New York: Simon and Schuster.

Schudson, Michael. 1992. *Watergate and American Memory.* New York: Basic Books.

Sciulli, D. 1990. "Differentiation and Collegial Formations: Implications of Societal Constitutionalism." In *Differentiation Theory and Social Change,* ed. J. C. Alexander & P. Colomy. New York: Columbia University Press.

Searle, John. 1969. *Speech Acts: An Essay in the Philosophy of Language.* London: Cambridge University Press.

Seidman, Steven. 1983. *Liberalism and the Origins of European Social Theory*. Berkeley: University of California Press.

Seidman, Steven. 1988. "Transfiguring Sexual Identity." *Social Text* 9: 20, 187–206.

Seidman, Steven. 1991a. "The End of Sociological Theory: The Postmodern Hope." *Sociological Theory* 9 (2): 131–46.

Seidman, Steven. 1991b *Romantic Longings: Love in America, 1830-1980*. New York: Routledge.

Seidman, Steven. 1992. "Postmodern Social Theory as Narrative with a Moral Intent." In *Postmodernism and Social Theory*, ed. S. Seidman & D. G. Wagner. New York: Blackwell.

Seligman, Adam. 1987. *Human Agency, the Millenium, and Social Change*. Ph.D. diss., Hebrew University, Jerusalem.

Sewell, William H., Jr. "A Theory of Structure: Duality, Agency, and Transformation." *American Journal of Sociology* 98(1): 1–29.

Shapiro, Edward S. 1992. *A Time for Healing: American Jewry since World War II*. Baltimore: Johns Hopkins University Press.

Sherwood, Steve. 1993. "The British Are Coming." *Contemporary Sociology* 22 (2): 370–75.

Sherwood, Steve, Philip Smith, & Jeffrey C. Alexander. 1994. "Narrating the Social: Postmodernism and the Drama of Democracy." *Journal of Narrative and Life History* 4 (1/2): 69–88.

Shils, Edward. 1951. "Values, Motives, and Systems of Action." In *Towards a General Theory of Action*, ed. T. Parsons & E. Shils. Cambridge, MA: Harvard University Press.

Shils, Edward. 1972. *Intellectuals and the Powers*. Chicago: Chicago University Press.

Shils, Edward. 1975. *Center and Periphery: Essays in Macrosociology*. Chicago: University of Chicago Press.

Shils, Edward. 1991a. "Civility and Civil Society." In *Civility and Citizenship*, ed. E. C. Banfield. NewYork: Paragon.

Shils, Edward. 1991b. "The Virtue of Civil Society." *Government and Opposition* 26: 3–20.

Shirer, William L. 1969. *The Collapse of the Third Republic: An Inquiry into the Fall of France in 1940*. New York: Simon and Schuster.

Short, K. R. M. 1981. "Hollywood Fights Anti-Semitism, 1945–47." In *Feature Films as History*, ed. K. R. M. Short. Knoxville: University of Tennessee.

Silk, Mark. 1984. "Notes on the Judeo-Christian Tradition in America." *American Quarterly* 36: 65.

Skinner, Quentin. 1978. *The Foundations of Modern Political Thought*. Cambridge. Cambridge University Press.

Skocpol, Theda. 1979. *States and Social Revolutions*. New York: Cambridge University Press.

Slotkin, R. 1973. *Regeneration through Violence: The Mythology of the American Frontier, 1600–1860*. Middletown, CT: Wesleyan University Press.

Smelser, Neil. 1959. *Social Change in the Industrial Revolution*. Chicago: University of Chicago Press.

Smelser, Neil. 1963. *Theory of Collective Behavior*. New York: Free Press.

Smelser, Neil. 1968. "Toward a Theory of Modernization." In *Essays in Sociological Explanation*. Englewood Cliffs, NJ: Prentice Hall.

Smelser, Neil. 1974. "Growth, Structural Change, and Conflict in California Public Education, 1950–1970." In Smelser & Gabriel Amond, *Public Higher Education in California*. Berkeley: University of California Press.

Smelser, Neil. 1991. *Social Paralysis and Social Change: British Working-Class Education in the Nineteenth Century.* Berkeley: University of California Press.

Smith, Henry Nash. 1970 [1950]. *Virgin Land.* New York: Vintage Books.

Smith, Philip. 1991. "Codes and Conflict." *Theory and Society* 20: 103–38.

Smith, Philip. 1998a. "The New American Cultural Sociology." In *The New American Cultural Sociology,* ed. Smith. Cambridge: Cambridge University Press.

Smith, Philip, ed. 1998b. *The New American Cultural Sociology.* Cambridge: Cambridge University Press.

Smith, Philip. 1998. "Barbarism and Civility in the Discourses of Fascism, Communism, and Democracy." In J. Alexander (ed.) *Real Civil Societies.* pp. 115–37. Condon-Sage.

Smith, Philip, & Jeffrey C. Alexander. 1996. "Durkheim's Religious Revival." *American Journal of Sociology* 102 (2): 585–92.

Snyder, Jack. 2000. *From Voting to Violence: Democratization and Nationalist Conflict.* New York: Norton.

Somers, Margaret R. 1992. "Narrativity, Narrative Identity, and Social Action: Rethinking English Workng-Class Formation." *Social Science History* 16 (4): 591–630.

Somers, Margaret R. 1995. "Narrating and Naturalizing Civil Society and Citizenship Theory." *Sociological Theory* 13 (3): 229–74.

Stannard, David E. 1991. *American Holocaust: The Conquest of the New World.* Oxford: Oxford University Press.

Stannard, David E. 1996, August 2. 'The Dangers of Calling the Holocaust Unique." *Chronicle of Higher Education,* B1–2.

Stember, Charles Herbert. 1966. *Jews in the Mind of America.* New York: Basic Books.

Stepan, A. 1985. "State Power and the Strength of Civil Society in The Southern Cone of Latin America." pp. 317–43. In P. Evans, D. Rueschemeyer, and T. Skocpol eds. *Bringing the State Back In.* New York: Cambridge University Press.

Steiner, Frank. 1956. *Taboo.* London: Cohen and West.

Stivers, Richard. 1982. *Evil in Modern Myth and Ritual.* Atlanta: University of Georgia Press.

Strenghold, Leendert. 1988. "Review of *Back to the Source.*" *Holocaust and Genocide Studies* 3 (3): 337–42.

Swidler, Ann. 1986. "Culture in Action: Symbols and Strategies." *American Sociological Review* 51(3): 273–86.

Sztompka, Piotr. 1991a. "The Intangibles and Imponderables of the Transition to Democracy." *Studies in Comparative Communism* 34: 295–311.

Sztompka, Piotr. 1991b. *Society in Action: The Theory of Social Becoming.* Cambridge: Polity Press.

Sztompka, P. 1993. *The Sociology of Social Change.* Oxford: Blackwell.

Szelenyi, Ivan. 1988. *Socialist Embourgeoisement in Rural Hungary.* Madison: University of Wisconsin Press.

Szelenyi, Ivan, & Bill Martin. 1987. "Theories of Cultural Capital and Beyond." In *Intellectuals, Universities, and the State in Western Modern Societies,* ed. Ron Eyerman, L. G. Svensson, & T. Soderquist. Berkeley: University of California Press.

Taylor, Charles. 1990. *Sources of the Self.* New York: Cambridge University Press.

Thomas, G. M., & P. Lauderdale. 1988. "State Authority and National Welfare Programs in World System Context." *Sociological Forum* 3 (3): 383–99.

Thompson, Edward P. 1963. *The Making of the English Working Class.* New York: Pantheon.

Thompson, Edward P. 1978. *The Poverty of Theory.* London: Merlin.

Thompson, Edward P. 1992. "Social Pluralism and Post-Modernity." In *Modernity and Its Futures,* ed. Thompson. Oxford: Blackwell.

Thompson, Kenneth. 1997. *Moral Panics.* London: Routledge.

Thompson, Kenneth. Forthcoming. *Essential Quotations in Sociology.* London: Routledge.

Tiryakian, E. 1988. "From Durkheim to Managua: Revolutions as Religious Revivals." In *Durkheimian Sociology: Cultural Studies,* ed., J. C. Alexander. New York: Cambridge University Press.

Tiryakian, E. 1991. "Modernization: *Exhumetur in pace.*" *International Sociology* 6 (2): 165–80.

Touraine, Alain. 1994. *Qu'est-ce que la démocratie?* Paris: Fayard.

Trilling, Lionel. 1950. *The Liberal Imagination.* New York: Harcourt Brace Jovanovich.

Trilling, Lionel. 1955. *The Opposing Self. Nine Essays in Criticism.* London: Secker and Warburg.

Turkle, Sherry. 1984. *The Second Self: Computers and the Human Spirit.* New York: Simon and Schuster.

Turner, Bryon S. 1986. *Citizenship and Capitalism.* London: Allen and Unwin.

Turner, Victor. 1969. *The Ritual Process.* Chicago: Aldine.

Turner, Victor. 1974. *Dramas, Fields and Metaphors.* Ithaca, NY: Cornell University Press.

van den Berg, A. 1980. "Critical Theory: Is There Still Hope?" *American Journal of Sociology* 86 (3): 449–79.

van Gelder, Lawrence. 1999, May 5. "After the Holocaust, If There Can Indeed Be an After." *New York Times,* D1.

Veeser, H. A., ed. 1989. *The New Historicism.* New York: Routledge.

Wagner-Pacifici, Robin. 1986. *The Moro Morality Play.* Chicago: University of Chicago Press.

Wagner-Pacifici, Robin. 1994. *Discourse and Destruction.* Chicago: University of Chicago Press.

Wagner-Pacifici, Robin. 2000. *Theorizing the Standoff.* Cambridge: Cambridge University Press.

Wagner-Pacifici, Robin, & Schwartz, Barry. 1991. "The Vietnam Veterans Memorial." *American Journal of Sociology* 97 (2): 376–420.

Wallerstein, Immanuel. 1979. "Modernization: *Requiescat in Pace.*" In *The Capitalist World-Economy.* New York: Cambridge University Press.

Walzer, Michael. 1965. *Revolution of the Saints.* Cambridge, MA: Harvard University Press.

Walzer, Michael. 1970. *Obligations: Essays on Disobedience, War, and Citizenship.* Cambridge, MA: Harvard University Press.

Walzer, Michael. 1984. *Spheres of Justice.* New York: Basic Books.

Walzer, Michael. 1992a. "The Civil Society Argument." In *Dimensions of Radical Democracy: Pluralism, Citizenship, Community,* ed. C. Mouffe. London: Verso.

Walzer, Michael. 1992b. "Constitutional Rights and the Shape of Civil Society." In *The Constitution of the People: Reflections on Citizens and Civil Society,* ed. R. E. Calvert. Lawrence: University Press of Kansas.

Weber, Max. 1946A. "The Meaning of Discipline." In *From Max Weber,* ed. H. Gerth & C. W. Mills. New York: Oxford University Press.

Weber, Max. 1946b. "Religious Rejections of the World and Their Directions." In *From Max Weber,* ed. H. Gerth & C. W. Mills. New York: Oxford University Press.

Weber, Max. 1958 [1904]. *The Protestant Ethic and the Spirit of Capitalism.* New York: Scribners.

Weber, Max. 1964 [1922]. *The Sociology of Religion.* Boston: Beacon Press.

Weber, Max. 1968. *Economy and Society*. Berkeley: University of California Press.

Weiner, J. 1984. *Come Together: John Lennon in His Times*. New York: Random House.

Weinstein, J. 1968. *Corporate Ideology in the Liberal State, 1900–1918*. Westport, CT: Greenwood Press.

Welles, Sumner. 1945, May 5. "New Hope for the Jewish People." *Nation* 160: 511–3.

White, Hayden. 1980. "The Value of Narrativity in the Representation of Reality." In *On Narrative*, ed. W. J. T. Mitchell. Chicago: University of Chicago Press.

White, Hayden. 1987. *The Content of Form: Narrative Discourse and Historical Representation*. Baltimore: Johns Hopkins University Press.

Whitman, Howard. 1949, January 8. "The College Fraternity Crisis." *Collier's*, 34–5.

Wiesel, Elie. 1978, April 16. "Trivializing the Holocaust." *New York Times*, 2: 1.

Weissberg, Liliane. 1997. "The Tale of a Good German: Reflections on the German Reception of *Schindler's List*." In *Spielberg's Holocaust: Critical Perspectives on "Schindler's List*," ed. Yosefa Loshitzky. Bloomington: University of Indiana Press.

Wieviorka, Michel. 1993. *La Démocratie a l'épreuve: Nationalisme, populisme, ethnicité*. Paris: Editions La Découverte.

Williams, Robin. 1971. "Change and Stability in Values and Value Systems." In *Stability and Social Change*, ed. Bernard Barber & Alex Inkeles. Boston: Little Brown.

Willis, Paul. 1977. *Learning to Labour*. Farnborough, UK: Saxon House.

Wilson, J. Q. 1991. "Incivility and Crime." In *Civility and Citizenship*, ed., E. C. Banfield. New York: Paragon.

Wines, Michael. 1999, June 13. "Two Views of Inhumanity Split the World, Even in Victory." *New York Times*, 4: 1.

Wittrock, B. 1991. "Cultural Identity and Nationhood: The Reconstitution of Germany—Or the Open Answer to an Almost Closed Question." In *University and Society: Essays on the Social Role of Research and Higher Education*, ed. M. Trow & T. Nybom. London: Kingsley.

Wolff, R. P., H. Marcuse, & B. Moore, Jr. 1965. *A Critique of Pure Tolerance*. Boston: Beacon Press.

Wright, E. O. 1985. *Classes*. London: Verso.

Wuthnow, Robert. 1987. *Meaning and Moral Order*. Berkeley: University of California Press.

Wuthnow, Robert. 1988. "Religious Discourse as Public Rhetoric." *Communication Research* 15 (3): 318–38.

Wuthnow, Robert. 1989. *Communities of Discourse*. Cambridge, MA: Harvard University Press.

Wyman, David S. 1984. *The Abandonment of the Jews: Americans and the Holocaust, 1941–1945*. New York: Pantheon Books.

Young, James E. 1993. *The Texture of Memory: Holocaust Memorials and Meaning*. New Haven: Yale University Press.

Zelizer, Barbie. 1998. *Remembering to Forget: Holocaust Memory through the Camera's Eye*. Chicago: University of Chicago.

Zielinski, Siegfried. 1986. "History as Entertainment and Provocation: The TV Series 'Holocaust' in West Germany." In *Germans and Jews since the Holocaust: The Changing Situation in West Germany*, ed. Anson Rabinbach & Jack Zipes. New York: Holmes and Meier.

# INDEX

genre theory of, 263 n.15
and "negative hermeneutics," 201
and postmodernism, 209, 211

Kant, Immanuel
and culture-as-the-good, 112, 253 n.14
on radical evil, 30, 231 n.10, 252 n.8
*Kristallnacht*, 35–37

lay trauma theory
enlightenment version of, 31, 86–88
psychoanalytic version of, 31, 88–91
Lévi-Strauss, Claude, 11, 14
and cultural codes, 124, 189, 256 n.3
and structuralism, 16

macrosociology, 16, 193–208
Marx, Karl
antimodernist interpretation of, 207
early writings of, 15
on role of intellectuals, 193–194
and technology, 179–180, 260 n.5
and values, 114–115
Marxism, 261 n.2
and Bataille, 255 n.30
Birmingham School of, 17
Frankfurt school of, 114, 211, 243
n.64
and the history of the Holocaust, 50
and neomodernism, 215, 225, 268
n.38, 269 n.29
and the *New Left Review*, 265 n.23
and postmodernism, 209, 265 n.25,
266 n.26, 267 n.32, 268 n.36
on technology, 180, 184
and theories of ideology, 199
Merton, Robert, 181
Milgram experiments, 61–62
Modernity, 8, 15, 179, 196, 206
*Modernity and the Holocaust*, 114, 239 n.49
modernization theory, 197, 207, 210, 224
Monicagate, 174
narratives
and cultural theory, 25
of Holocaust, progressive, 37–48, 238
n.47
of Holocaust, tragic, 48–66
of modernization, 197
in postmodern societies, 5
of trauma, 31, 90, 94

nationalism, 221–223
Nazism, 33–35, 37–43, 96, 254 n.21
neomodernism, 213–228
Nietzsche, Friedrich, 110, 267 n.32
Nuremburg trials, 41, 73–74, 97

objectivity, 170, 184

Parsons, Talcott
and culture-as-the-good, 251 n.1, 254
n.19
and functionalism, 15–17, 113
and generalized communication, 126,
170–172
and modernization theory, 198, 202,
205, 213–216, 225, 261 n.5, 263
n.14
on objectivity in modernity, 184
on technology, 181

Plato, 111
*Pioneers of Modern Design*, 203
postmodernism societies, 5, 119
postmodernism, 208–211, 263 n.16, 267
n.32, 267 n.33
*Pride of the Marines*, 46
psychoanalysis, 4, 6, 31, 88–91, 249 n.4
psychological identification, 30, 55
punishment, 116–117

Ricoeur, Paul, 22, 196
Romanticism, 202, 264 n.17, 267 n.32
Rorty, Richard, 211

Sahlins, Marshall, 23, 25, 187, 252 n.2
Saussure, Ferdinand de, 6, 16, 21, 234
n.26
scandals, 117, 177
*Schindler's List*, 81
science and technology, 179–192
shoah, 51, 237 n.42, 237 n.43
Simmel, Georg, 262 n.9, 267 n.32
Smelser, Neil
and cultural sociology, ix
and cultural trauma, 232 n.11,
249 n.1
and generalized communication, 126,
170–172
and modernization theory, 261 n.6
socialism, 193–194, 204–208